The Seventh Star of the Confederacy:
Texas during the Civil War

Edited by
Kenneth W. Howell

Number 10 in the War and the Southwest Series

University of North Texas Press
Denton, Texas

©2009 University of North Texas Press

Printed in the United States of America.

10 9 8 7 6 5 4 3 2 1

Permissions:
University of North Texas Press
1155 Union Circle #311336
Denton, Texas 76203-5017

The paper used in this book meets the minimum requirements of the American National Standard for Permanence of Paper for Printed Library Materials, z39.48.1984. Binding materials have been chosen for durability.

Library of Congress Cataloging-in-Publication Data

The seventh star of the Confederacy : Texas during the Civil War / edited by Kenneth W. Howell. -- 1st ed.
      p. cm. -- (War and the Southwest series ; no. 10)
   Includes bibliographical references and index.
   ISBN 978-1-57441-259-8 (cloth : alk. paper)
   1. Texas--History--Civil War, 1861-1865. 2. Texas--Politics and government--1861-1865. 3. Texas--Social conditions--19th century.
I. Howell, Kenneth Wayne, 1967- II. Series: War and the Southwest series ; no. 10.
   E580.S43 2009
   973.7'464--dc22
                              200805313

The Seventh Star of the Confederacy: Texas during the Civil War is Number 10 in the War and the Southwest Series

To Erin Buenger,
who is an inspiration to those who know her,
and in memory of Bill Stein, who was the
Prince of Colorado County history and
a true Renaissance man.

Contents

Part IV Political, Social, and Cultural Life during the War

Illustrations

Maps

Preface

I first became fascinated with the Civil War as a young boy after viewing the movie *Horse Soldiers*, starring John Wayne. I have vivid memories of watching this film with my father and afterwards going outside to reenact various scenes from the movie in my backyard. As I grew older, I read numerous books on the Civil War, especially those written by Bruce Catton. In college, I took a class on the Civil War with Dr. James Smallwood at the University of Texas at Tyler. As part of the course requirements, I wrote a paper on Terry's Texas Rangers. Having recently found a copy of the paper tucked away in one of my file cabinets, I realize now that it was a pitiful scholarly effort, but it did further my academic interest in the subject of Texas's involvement in the war.

Shortly after graduating from UT-Tyler, I viewed Ken Burns's PBS special *The Civil War*. I still remember being mesmerized by Burns's documentary, especially the stories related to the social and cultural aspects of the war. Just as Burns attempted to do in his documentary, I have tried to provide a balance of military, social, and cultural history to explain Texas's involvement in one of the most pivotal moments in American history. However, I must confess that before I decided to edit this volume, I was actually in the early stages of working on a proposal for an edited volume covering Reconstruction Texas. One night as I discussed various ideas and topics for this project with my close friend James Smallwood, he suggested that I might first consider editing a similar book on the Civil War. Our conversation became the genesis of this volume. During the weeks that followed, I came to the conclusion that Smallwood was right, especially since the sesquicentennial of the war was quickly approaching. As a result, I began work on this volume.

Early in this study, readers are introduced to the causes of the Civil War and the motivations behind Texas's decision to leave the Union. Overwhelmingly, the people of Texas supported the actions of the delegates at the secession convention in a statewide referendum, paving the way for the state to secede from the Union and to officially become the seventh state to join the Confederacy. Quickly after secession, Texans found themselves engaged in a bloody and prolonged civil war against their Northern brethren. During the course of this war, the lives of thousands of Texans, both young and old, were changed forever. This study will examine how Texans experienced the conflict. The contributors to this anthology will take us from the battlefront to the home front; from inside the walls of a Confederate prison to inside the walls of the homes of women and children who were left to fend for themselves while their husbands and fathers were away on distant battlefields; and from the halls of the state capitol to the halls of the county commissioner's court in Colorado County.

Some scholars might question the need for another study of the Civil War, especially considering the large volume of works already in print. I would answer their question by saying that it is indeed time to revisit the role that Texas played in the war. Currently, the most comprehensive anthology of the Civil War experience of Texans is Ralph Wooster's *Lone Star Blue and Gray: Essays on Texas in the Civil War.* I have used Dr. Wooster's book many times in preparing classroom lectures and find it a treasure trove of information. Having said this, I also recognize that it is now time for a new volume on Texas in the Civil War. While Dr. Wooster did a masterful job of editing his anthology of previously published articles, one cannot help but notice that the most recent article included in his work was published in 1991. A breakdown of the articles reveals that the majority of the articles were published prior to 1980. As such, I believed that a new volume was needed—one that benefited from the wealth of scholarly research that has been compiled on the subject over the last two and half decades.

This study provides new facts and interpretations about well-known battles that took place in or near Texas, such as the Battle of Galveston, the Battle of Nueces, the Battle of Sabine Pass, and the Red River Campaign. At the same time, the anthology includes new research on the social and cultural aspects of the war, including the experiences of women, African Americans, Union prisoners of war, and frontier troops.

In the early process of organizing this volume, I became aware that my friend and colleague Dr. Charles Grear of Prairie View A&M University was in the process of editing a similar book on Texans and the Civil War. After lengthy conversations with Dr. Grear regarding the themes and subjects that he planned to cover in his volume, I was able to develop a book very different from that of my colleagues. It is my hope that most readers will view our work as complementary, covering different aspects of similar topics. In fact, it would be a great surprise if both our volumes did not find their places on the shelves of serious scholars of Civil War Texas.

While it is impossible for an editor to put together an anthology which represents a perfect balance between topics, *The Seventh Star of the Confederacy: Texas during the Civil War* comes as close as one can in a single volume. Aside from the scholarly overviews, there are seven chapters that have social and cultural themes and eight chapters that deal with traditional military topics. The chapters of this study are separated into four parts.

Part One, "A Historical Overview of Texas and the Civil War," provides a scholarly treatment of the subject. While Alwyn Barr examines the recent scholarship on Civil War Texas, Archie McDonald provides a basic overview of the war, setting the stage for the articles that follow.

Part Two, "The Time for Compromise Has Passed," examines Texas's role in the coming of the Civil War. In this section, Dr. Smallwood explores how Texas became engulfed in the secession movement of the 1850s and eventually broke its ties with the Union, while Linda S. Hudson provides a detailed quantitative analysis of Texas membership in the Knights of the Golden Circle and highlights the role that the Military Degree Knights played in the early phase of the war.

Part Three, "In Sight of My Enemy," focuses on Texas battlefronts. The contributors in this section provide coverage of specific events involving the Lone Star State and Texans during the years between 1861 and 1865. John Gorman's quantitative analysis of the frontier regiments offers insights into the types of men serving on the Texas frontier. His study furthers our understanding of the frontier regiment, a group that has often been neglected in Civil War Texas historiography. Mary Jo O'Rear examines in detail the Battle of Nueces, reminding readers of the consequences that pro-Unionist Germans in Central Texas suffered at the hands of Texas Confederates. Don Willett provides a social account of the Battle of Galveston. His study brings to light new questions about potential pro-Union spies in Galveston and highlights the inept leadership of Confederate commanders at the beginning of the battle. Additionally, his study details the experiences of residents living on Galveston Island during the period of Union occupation. Edward Cotham, Charles Spurlin, and Gary Joiner provide vivid accounts of the few battles that directly impacted Texas society. The authors' coverage of the battles at Sabine Pass, in the Coastal Bend region, and in the areas affected by General Banks's Red River Campaign adds to our understanding of the war's military impact on Texas. Charles Grear and James Smallwood offer valuable insights into two areas that historians have neglected. Grear studies the intricate relationship between white Confederate soldiers and their Indian allies during the war and reveals how their hatred for black troops moved them beyond their traditional contempt for one another. Smallwood's coverage of Camp Ford provides new insights into daily life inside the camp from the perspective of Union POWs.

Part Four, "Political, Social, and Cultural Life during the Civil War," examines topics of the war that too often have been overlooked by Civil War historians. Here readers are introduced to how the state's chief executives experienced the war; to the impact of the war on women and African Americans throughout the state; and to how the war shaped the lives of Texans at the local level in Central Texas (Colorado County). Ken Hendrickson explains the hardships that the Civil War governors of Texas faced in protecting the interests of their constituents and at the same time supporting the newly formed Confederacy. Vickie Betts examines the financial difficulties and other burdens that the war placed on women who struggled to survive while their men were away fighting on distant fronts. Ron Goodwin and Bruce Glasrud's study provides fresh insights into how black Texans experienced the war. Carol Taylor examines the difficulties that Texas cattle ranchers experienced during their efforts to feed distant Confederate armies, while Bill Stein reveals how the war disrupted the lives of those living in Colorado County.

★Acknowledgments

Throughout this project I have had the opportunity to work with an exceptional group of scholars. Some of them have had to overcome extraordinary obstacles to complete their chapters. Charles Spurlin became gravely ill while working on his chapter, spending more than three weeks in the hospital. Amazingly, he was the first author to send his completed chapter to me. Gary Joiner suffered a near-debilitating problem with his vision, but he also finished his chapter on time. Where other contributors might have withdrawn from such a project, these men never wavered in their commitment to completing their assigned chapters. They remain my heroes, and I am happy to report that both are recovering from their ailments. My other contributors have also amazed me. Not one of the original contributors withdrew from this project, a rarity when it comes to publishing edited volumes. I express my deepest gratitude to all the contributors for their professionalism and their untiring efforts in making this a meaningful book. I will forever be indebted to each of them. Unfortunately, while this work was in the final stages of production, I learned of the death of Bill Stein, a dear friend and a contributor to this volume. As is the case with many exceptional people, Bill died too young. He will be missed by all who knew him, and I will cherish the friendship that we shared for the rest of my life. This book is dedicated in part to his memory.

Also, I greatly appreciate the staff and editors at University of North Texas Press, especially Ron Chrisman. He patiently listened to my idea at the fall 2006 meeting of the East Texas Historical Association and offered many valuable suggestions for making this volume a better book. Chrisman's belief in this project and professionalism was very comforting during the publication process. Additionally, I want to thank my copy editors, Bonnie Lovell and Karen DeVinney, for improving the readability of the original manuscript.

In addition, I want to thank Erin Buenger for being a source of inspiration. As many already know, Erin is the daughter of my former graduate advisor at Texas A&M University, Walter Buenger, and his lovely wife, Vickie. While I was a Ph.D. candidate at TAMU, Dr. Buenger taught me how to be a professional historian, but it was Erin who taught me that life is a precious gift from God. In the summer of 2002, Erin was diagnosed with neuroblastoma, an aggressive form of cancer that affects thousands of children across the nation. Since her diagnosis, Erin has fought a determined battle to overcome her disease. During the last few years, I have read the updates that her parents have diligently posted to Erin's web page. These reports discuss Erin's progress and reveal important milestones in her life. Through her web page, I have come to the conclusion that Erin is the bravest person that I have ever had the pleasure to know. She not only has continued to successfully battle her disease, but she also has become a crusader for other children suffering from the same ailment. She made trips to Washington, D.C., to talk to members of Congress, helping to convince them to pass the Conquer Childhood Cancer Act. In addition, Erin is a model student; she plays soccer; she rides horses; and she is something of an outdoor adventurer. Erin is nothing short of a superhero. Because Erin has provided inspiration to all those who know her, this book is also dedicated to her.

Finally, I want to express my deepest gratitude to my family for all their prayers, advice, encouragement, and moral support, and especially to Felesha, my wife, and Zachary and Tyler, my children. They have contributed to this project in their own special way. Despite all the professional assistance that I have received, as the editor, I accept full responsibility for all errors of fact, faulty interpretations, and mistaken conclusions.

Part I

A Historical Overview of Texas and the Civil War

Chapter 1

The Impact of New Studies about Texas and Texans on Civil War Historiography

by Alwyn Barr

The Civil War in Texas and Texans in the war have continued to attract both professional and non-professional historians. Especially notable in recent years are the first modern general history of those topics by Ralph Wooster and the first volume providing a visual sense of the people involved in the conflict across the Lone Star State by Carl Moneyhon and Bobby Roberts.[1] Thoughtful summaries of historical writings also have appeared in important essays by Randolph B. Campbell and Walter F. Bell. Campbell discussed a broader era from 1846 to 1876 with a focus on non-military topics including "population, the frontier, the economy . . . , social life and social structure, and politics." He also raised the key questions of how much change occurred and how much continuity remained.[2] Bell began after secession and concentrated primarily on writings about military campaigns and leadership, political and economic activities including Confederate-state tensions, and Confederate efforts to control or eliminate Union sentiment.[3]

Rather than overlap with those works of historiography, this essay will focus on what writings about Texans since 1990 contribute to some of the newer debates and questions raised by Civil War historians. Have other studies clarified our understanding of the reasons for the secession movement that led to war? Social historians have influenced military history by calling for a better sense of the enlisted men, their places in society, and their attitudes about the conflict. Social historians also have encouraged a broader understanding of how the war impacted society, including the roles of women and the status of minorities—African Americans, Mexican Americans, and Native Americans. Ultimately all of these questions may be related to the ongoing discussions of how the Union won the war and why the Confederacy lost.

Two books clarify specific events of 1860 and 1861 leading to secession. Donald E. Reynolds presents a careful analysis of fires in Texas towns during 1860 that quickly came to be blamed on slaves and abolitionists. Although an unusually hot summer and faulty new matches provided a better explanation, fears by many Texans who remembered John Brown's raid into Virginia in 1859 led to paranoia and a wave of vigilante violence against slaves and Northerners in the Lone Star State. Anti-Republican newspaper editors who favored secession used the fires to promote their cause in Texas and across the South.[4] Dale Baum, using statistical analysis, has reviewed the presidential election of 1860 and the secession referendum in 1861. He concludes that Brown's raid and the fires, often called the "Texas Troubles," led to the collapse of the Unionist coalition that had elected Sam Houston governor in 1859. Baum also notes economic and religious influences, with wheat farmers, who were often Disciples of Christ, in North Texas counties settled from the Upper South and German Lutherans in Central Texas as the strongest opponents of secession. Kenneth W. Howell offers the most detailed account of the anti-secession efforts by James W. Throckmorton during this period.[5]

Most writing on the Civil War in Texas has continued to focus on military affairs. Military campaigns and commanders have received further attention that is reviewed appropriately by Walter Bell. Three additional studies that have appeared since his essay deserve comment. Stephen A. Townsend considers the Rio Grande expedition by the Union army and navy that occupied the lower valley and the Texas coast up to Matagorda from November 1863 to March 1864. He concludes that it became the most successful Federal advance into the state by reducing the flow of cotton through Mexico and forcing a more expensive route to Laredo and Eagle Pass. Furthermore, Union forces showed United States' concern about the French role in the Mexican civil war. Finally, the expedition allowed Unionist A. J. Hamilton to return to Texas at least briefly as its appointed governor. Different views in the Federal high command led to withdrawal of most soldiers in favor of the unsuccessful Red River Campaign in the spring of 1864.[6]

Historians of the Federal advance up the Red River have presented several accounts that debate the quality of leadership on both sides and whether Confederates could have achieved more with a different strategy. Jeffery S. Prushankin offers a fresh analysis by suggesting that Edmund Kirby Smith employed a Fabian retreat in the style of Joseph E. Johnston that resulted from his need to defend the entire Trans-Mississippi Department. Richard Taylor followed the more aggressive style of Stonewall Jackson as a means of defending his smaller District of Louisiana. Prushankin concludes that their efforts led to Confederate success, while their differences generated a major "crisis in command." In a broader study, Stephen A. Dupree concludes that Gen. Nathaniel P. Banks attained most goals given him by the Union War Department, but failed as a field commander, especially in efforts to invade Texas.[7] Federal focus on more important war goals and questionable decisions about how to invade Texas combined with successful Confederate defense efforts to limit the impact of the conflict on the state.

Two biographies further understanding of command by a Texan and by the longest-serving leader of the District of Texas. Thomas W. Cutrer presents Ben McCulloch as an able general based on experience in frontier conflicts, whose opportunity for higher rank in the Confederate army ran afoul of preference by President Jefferson Davis for United States Military Academy graduates. The complexities of commanding the Military District of Texas are explored by Paul D. Casdorph as he discusses the career of John B. Magruder.[8]

The enlisted men from Texas who fought in the Civil War have received increased attention in the growing number of regimental, brigade, and division histories. Like older accounts of such units, the new studies discuss movements and engagements. Unlike most early unit histories, some of the new volumes explore the group images that emerge from quantitative analysis of the soldiers. By comparing the profiles of units recruited in different areas at varied times a more complex picture begins to appear.

Two of the best unit histories provide useful examples and contrasting results. Douglas Hale describes Confederate soldiers recruited in 1861 for the Third Texas Cavalry regiment. They came from families in East Texas counties that averaged almost $13,000 in property, double the level for all families in the state. Slightly over half of the men's families owned slaves, a direct commitment to the institution and again twice the percentage for families across Texas. With a median age of about 23, only about 20 percent of the men were married with families, which allowed most to pursue more easily a combination of adventure and commitment to a cause. A little over 50 percent of the men had been engaged in aspects of agriculture, compared to about 75 percent of those in the state. Sixty percent had been born in the Lower South, which seemed to generate a stronger commitment to the Confederacy. About 30 percent came from Upper South backgrounds, while less than 10 percent came from the North or another country.[9]

Almost a year later Confederate leaders raised eleven regiments and a battalion of infantry in East Texas. Richard Lowe describes the men of those units that formed Walker's Texas Division. Much like the Third Texas Cavalry and other units from the region, over three-fifths came from the Lower South, while about half as many came from the Upper South. Only one in twenty had Northern or immigrant backgrounds. These soldiers differed from the volunteers of 1861 in various ways. They averaged about four years older, with roughly half already heads of families, twice as many as in the Third Texas. They more clearly fit the general pattern of Texans with three-fourths involved in agriculture, but they held only half the amount of wealth as the average family heads across the state. One in five owned slaves, compared to one of four Texans. Thus they proved to be a more middle-class group than the elite young men of the Third Texas. Their motivations appear to have been related to concern with Union advances and maintaining a stable way of life "including white control of the black underclass." Randolph B. Campbell, using statistics to analyze soldiers from Harrison County, offers support for most of these conclusions by Lowe and Hale. Campbell adds that a higher percentage of prosperous Texans served the Confederacy than among those of more modest means, which runs counter to the image of a rich man's war but a poor man's fight.[10]

Even greater ethnic and occupational diversity existed among Texas soldiers. Stanley S. McGowen discusses the presence of a company of German immigrants from the Hill Country in the First Texas Cavalry of the Confederate army. Charles D. Spurlin, in his introduction and conclusion to a Confederate soldier's diary, discusses the German immigrants in some companies of the Sixth Texas Infantry from the Coastal Bend region.[11] Jerry D. Thompson, in two new books, reviews and clarifies the roles and attitudes of Mexican Americans in South Texas and Mexicans in Northern Mexico who served in both the Union and Confederate armies during the American Civil War as well as in the Mexican civil war of the same period.[12] These volumes offer fewer details about the backgrounds of the soldiers, however, which limits comparisons.

Regional differences also appear in units from North Texas. In his introduction to the diary and letters of a Confederate officer from Texas, Richard Lowe describes the men of Company H, Ninth Texas Cavalry, as recruited in 1861 from a North Texas county that voted against secession. Most of these young men came from Upper South backgrounds. Their families usually owned small farms with less wealth than the average Texas household. Slaveholders formed just one-sixth of the unit, less than the average for Texas families. Yet their early enlistment probably reflected greater commitment to Confederate views and set them apart from many neighbors who preferred to remain in the Union.[13]

Many of the same studies contribute to an understanding of the factors that led to a decline in the size of military units and the armies in which they served. Douglas Hale again points to key problems. In the fall of 1861 while still west of the Mississippi River the Third Texas Cavalry faced a wave of illness, primarily measles and typhoid, which left eighteen men dead and 145 discharged. Following reorganization in early 1862, the regiment had been reduced by one-third. Illness killed 9 percent of the cavalrymen during the war. Another 7 percent died on the battlefield, while 16 percent suffered wounds. Fourteen percent became prisoners at some point, with 7 percent listed as deserters. The collective impact can be seen when the regiment entered the Atlanta Campaign in the spring of 1864 with 46 percent of its remaining soldiers listed as absent.[14] Lowe in his discussion of the Ninth Texas Cavalry, another regiment in Ross's Texas Cavalry Brigade, adds that as a result of "disease, death, desertion, and wounds" the brigade had fallen from its initial strength of 4,000 men to 686 present for duty, or less than 20 percent, by November 1864.[15]

Lowe describes similar problems as well as some differences in his history of the infantrymen in Walker's Division that served in the Trans-Mississippi region. His quantitative analysis suggests that during 1862, the first year of service for those men, disease and illness caused the death or discharge of about 2,300 out of 12,000 soldiers. Perhaps 700 more received discharges because of age. Transfers, resignations of officers, injuries from accidents, and desertions probably removed another 1,000 men from the ranks. The division had been reduced to about 8,000 soldiers by the end of the summer. Similar problems brought the division strength down to 6,000 men, half its original size, by the spring of 1863 before seeing serious combat. Thereafter the men fought in several skirmishes and battles in which over 1,400 men met death or suffered wounds, while more than 700 became prisoners or missing. Periods of desertions resulted from lack of furloughs, supplies, and pay, combined with declining morale after Confederate defeats such as Vicksburg in 1863. Opposition to possible transfer east of the Mississippi River in 1864 caused about 450 men to head home, although officers brought back many and some others later returned. Walker's Division had been reduced to a little more than one-fourth of it initial size by the end of the Red River Campaign.[16] Lowe does not offer a figure for total desertions from the division. M. Jane Johansson, in her history of the Twenty-eighth Texas Cavalry, which had been dismounted to serve in Walker's command, lists total losses that were below average for the division. The 44 desertions included in her figures, when projected as an average for all twelve regiments, suggest over 500 men absent without leave at some point, which may be a low estimate. Available service records for Confederate units usually do not include figures for the final months of 1864 and early 1865 when desertions increased in many military organizations. Charles Grear suggests that even some soldiers who volunteered early in the war and served east of the Mississippi River left units to protect their families in Texas, especially in those final months. Campbell in his quantitative study of Confederate soldiers from Harrison County adds further complexity to the picture by estimating that about half of the draft-age males in Texas served in some military unit. That falls below earlier projections of 60 to 75 percent, although it is still slightly higher than the average for Union states. About 20 percent of those who joined the military died of disease, illness, or combat. Yet if almost half of military age Anglo Texans did not serve in the army, then approximately 90 percent of them survived the conflict and most could help revive the state's economy and society after the conflict.[17]

Because the Third Texas Cavalry faced some combat from 1861 until the end of the war, while Walker's infantry engaged Union troops from 1863 to 1865, it is difficult to compare their casualty levels. Hale does offer a comparison, however, using the losses of Hood's Texas Brigade of infantry in the East to conclude that foot soldiers suffered heavier losses than cavalry.[18] Another infantry unit, the Sixth Texas Infantry that served first in the Trans-Mississippi and later east of the Mississippi River, provides support for that pattern of losses, while adding further complexity. Spurlin shows that 157 men in the regiment died of disease or illness, 83 of them in Union prison camps, with 90 more discharged—about one-fourth of the regiment. Only 19 men deserted, but after Union forces captured the regiment at Arkansas Post, 152 men agreed to declare allegiance to the United States. Furthermore, 116 men obtained reassignment to other duty. Together these groups composed over a quarter of the regiment. Those killed in combat numbered 60, while 157 suffered wounds and 75 became prisoners of war separately after Arkansas Post—almost a third of the regiment. The combined losses totaled 826 men, over 80 percent of the original enlistments.[19]

Histories of units from areas outside of East Texas reveal more varied patterns. Richard McCaslin describes the Eleventh Texas Cavalry, raised in North Texas, as composed in part of prewar Unionists who shifted their support to the Texas state government in 1861, primarily to defend the frontier against possible Indian raids. Other members of the regiment had favored secession after the 1860 fires and fears of an abolitionist-inspired slave revolt. When the governor transferred the unit to the Confederate commander in Texas, who ordered the men to Arkansas, more than 20 percent refused to extend their service although many paid for substitutes to fill their places. Temporary conversion of the regiment to infantry in early 1862, followed by orders to cross the Mississippi River, led to numerous desertions, discharges for health reasons, and resignations by officers. The regimental strength fell from almost 800 to about 250 in three months. New recruits did allow the unit to survive and continue service east of the Mississippi.[20]

National background also played a role in shaping commitment. German immigrants formed companies that served in Confederate regiments with results that varied according to circumstances. McGowen explains that a company of Germans from the Hill Country served on the nearby frontier and in South Texas except for a few weeks in Louisiana during the Red River Campaign as part of the First Texas Cavalry. Probably they felt more comfortable because a German immigrant colonel, Augustus Buchel, led the regiment for a year.[21] Terry Jordan edited letters from an Austin County German immigrant company that participated in the service of the Fourth Texas Cavalry from New Mexico to Texas and Louisiana.[22]

Walter Kamphoefner explains that German immigrants formed three companies for Waul's Legion, with most from Austin County. When Union troops captured one company, however, several of the men signed the oath of allegiance to the United States. In similar fashion German immigrants from DeWitt and Victoria counties provided one company and half of another in the Sixth Texas Infantry. When the men of that regiment became prisoners of war at Arkansas

Post in 1862, most of the German soldiers also signed oaths of support for the Union.[23] Two new studies by Jerry Thompson consider the divided and sometimes shifting allegiance of Mexican Americans in South Texas.[24] More German immigrants and Mexican Americans served in Confederate units than for the Union, in part because of social pressure, conscription, and practical decisions about what action would create the least disruption in their lives. Some had assimilated to Anglo Texas society, while others changed sides when faced with new circumstances such as capture and prison camps. Others made the more difficult effort to leave the state and join the Union army.

Some Civil War historians, such as Richard E. Beringer, Herman Hattaway, Archer Jones, and William N. Still, Jr., have argued that declining levels of men present for duty in Confederate armies reflect desertion and contributed to final defeat. Other historians, especially Gary Gallagher, have focused on low desertion statistics for some units to counter that view.[25] Valuable studies of Texas units reveal a more complex picture. Desertions remained under 10 percent in units raised early in the war, especially from East Texas when slavery and Southern culture dominated. Greater levels of desertion and shifting allegiance appeared in units recruited in Texas counties near the state borders and frontiers, particularly after passage of the conscription law and in areas settled from the Upper South and by German immigrants and Hispanics with less commitment to Southern institutions and society. Civil War historians have been aware that more soldiers died of disease and illness than were killed on battlefields or died of their wounds. The figures for Texas units confirm that impact, but also clarify the significance of numerous discharges based on illness, disability, and age for men who could not sustain active duty. Other men gained transfers or temporary assignments to different units or duty. Together these losses reduced the size of units to one-third or one-fourth of their initial numbers by 1864, levels that clearly undercut the chances of final success. While Union regiments in general suffered similar losses, they still could be replaced because of a larger manpower pool.

Richard Beringer and his coauthors, who emphasize the impact of internal issues within the Confederacy as causes for defeat, focus less on states' rights and more on the incomplete formation of Confederate nationalism. They also suggest that defeats in the later stages of the war raised doubts among Confederates about slavery and their religious belief that God was on their side. Wooster and Bell devote attention to the tensions between Texas Governor Pendleton Murrah and Confederate military commanders in Texas and the Trans-Mississippi Department during the latter stages of the war. They clashed over transfer of state troops to the Confederate army and which level of government would regulate the cotton trade through Mexico. These issues created distractions for all involved.

Dale Baum applies quantitative analysis to wartime elections that often revolved around support for or opposition to the Confederate government as it expanded its powers. Other issues helped produce mixed results, although supporters of the Davis administration proved more successful. Even Governor Murrah defeated a candidate who was more critical of the Confederacy.[26] John Anthony Moretta, in his biography of William Pitt Ballinger, adds to the sense of political complexity. Ballinger, a prewar lawyer and Unionist, served the Confederacy as a receiver of the property of alien enemies. Yet he experienced growing efforts by Texans who for economic reasons hid property owned by, or debts owed to, Northerners. At other times the attorney wrote editorials defending the Confederate conscription acts and martial law, while criticizing Murrah's efforts to control state troops and the cotton trade. In the debates with state leaders, Confederate nationalism had a firm defender in Ballinger.[27] Texas nationalism is offered by Clayton E. Jewett as an explanation for Murrah's actions in conflict with the Confederate authorities. State efforts to stimulate industry and provide for some societal needs also are cited as aspects of Lone Star nationalism. Yet some of the state activities may be seen as complementary to those of the Confederacy, rather than as acts of separate nationalism. Jewett has posed a new interpretation, but the varied strength of his evidence and arguments leaves room for lively debate. Jewett follows his theme further by editing a complete edition of the memoir by Confederate Senator Williamson S. Oldham of Texas, a strong critic of many activities by the Confederate central government.[28] Governor Murrah should be ranked with his counterparts in Georgia and North Carolina as one of the most outspoken defenders of state authority during the war. Despite the Confederate-state tensions, it appears the two sides found at least temporary compromises that kept their differences from reaching the level of major disruption or a full-scale political challenge to Confederate nationalism.

Historians of Confederate women, such as Drew Gilpin Faust, have pointed to diverse situations and reactions as some wives and mothers sought to maintain traditional gender roles while others faced new conditions that forced varied degrees of change in roles and attitudes.[29] Two published collections of letters from the wives of East Texas slaveholders reveal their concerns and views. In a volume edited by Erika Murr, the role of planter's wife appeared to create frustrations for Lizzie Neblett even before the war. The conflict increased the tension she experienced with her absent spouse, Will, their children, and her own failings. A sense of isolation as well as difficulties in directing slaves and finding an acceptable overseer became topics for letters that at times urged her husband to come back to his family.[30] M. Jane Johansson has edited letters written by Harriet Perry, who worried about similar problems as well as childbirth and fears that her husband might be killed in the war. Moving in with relatives helped her morale, however, as did her decision to hire out slaves. The illness of her children and deaths in the family added distress as did inflation and short-ages. Yet she did become increasingly involved in family economic decisions with advice from her husband and father.[31] Richard Lowe provides additional insights into women's attitudes in his chapter on the exchange of letters between husbands in Walker's Division and their wives. He notes Neblett's views, but also those of other wives who offered reassurances, encouragement, and affection to sustain the soldiers' morale.[32]

Joleene Maddux Snider describes the less common case of Sarah Devereux, a planter's wife who had assumed direction of the plantation when her husband, Julien, died before the war. Previously she had borne and raised children, served as a plantation mistress, whose duties including supervising house servants, and participated in a local church. When her husband had to travel out of town, she had shared direction of the field workers with an overseer and also had paid bills. While she functioned within the family concept of gender roles while he lived, her wider range of experiences allowed her to operate a profitable plantation after his death. The Civil War brought new concerns including higher taxes, impressments of some slaves to labor for the government, and worry about sons who were nearing military age. Yet she survived the conflict and, according to Snider, "expanded her concept of the boundaries of southern femininity."[33]

Angela Boswell offers the most analytical account of Texas women during the war in her study of their lives in Colorado County. Family problems ranged from men absent in the army, including some who died, to inflation and short-ages. As a result, widows, single women, and some wives of soldiers had to make economic decisions even though that overlapped the realm of men's gender roles. With acceptance by most men, women created debts, leased and sold slaves and land, and directed slave labor. Some worked to operate farms. Others requested and received local government aid in feeding their families. Although divorce did not become extensive, it did increase in the immediate postwar years. Boswell concludes that the women accepted the Southern ideal in gender roles, but expanded their right to act, with the goal of sustaining the family, when husbands could not or did not fulfill their roles.[34] These new studies focus on the East Texas region where Southern ideas about gender roles would be strongest and consider primarily upper- and middle-class women whose attitudes would be more fully shaped by those roles. East Texas also avoided Federal invasion, which created greater disruption and change in several regions of the Confederacy. In other areas of Texas greater conflict as well as social, economic, and ethnic differences probably created a greater range of conditions and attitudes for women.

Texas towns remained small in the 1860s compared to southern river and seaports such as New Orleans and Mobile. Yet their significant place in trade and government activities gave them a potential influence beyond their size. Alwyn Barr has explored the impact of war on Galveston, the state's leading port and second-largest town, which faced a Union blockade throughout the war and a brief occupation in late 1862. Many civilians became refugees to Houston and other inland towns, while Confederate soldiers garrisoned the island community. Blockade runners came and went sporadically, although trade and employment declined. Churches and schools closed at times and then reopened. Soldiers and their wives protested the quality of supplies and food provided by the army, with wives being temporarily ordered off the island as a result. Yellow fever added further disruption. Some slaves escaped to Union ships or joined whites in robbery gangs. The activities of women became more diverse including the operation of some new businesses. Postwar Galveston adjusted to the end of slavery and revived with renewed trade, however, at a faster pace than many rural areas.[35]

Houston citizens increased their economic activities during the war, explains Paul A. Levengood, as a result of Galveston's problems and new trade through Mexico. Consumer goods remained available despite some shortages and inflation. White refugees, often with slaves, increased the population. New businesses opened and established ones expanded. Cultural and charitable activities continued, as did schools and both white and black churches. Mary M. Cronin discusses R. R. Gilbert who wrote humorous articles for Texas newspapers that helped relieve some of the wartime tensions.[36]

Some Austin businessmen also conducted trade through Mexico, including business with Northern cities, as noted by Peyton O. Abbott, who edited the diary of an Austin merchant. David C. Humphrey shows that Austin suffered problems in acquiring accurate information about wartime events—especially battles. The Union blockade and a lack of rail and telegraph connections led to frequent confusion and misinformation. Confederate editors censored some news favorable to the Federal cause, probably because of the large number of Unionists in the community. Austin Confederates often celebrated early reports of victories that sometimes proved to be defeats. Thus civilian morale fluctuated wildly at times. Both Confederates and Unionists became doubtful of all news stories. After Federal forces gained control of the Mississippi River, Texas newspapers had to rely more and more on information in the Northern press about events east of that river, despite doubts about accuracy. Better reporting of Confederate victories on the Texas coast could boost morale, while fears of Union invasion in South Texas produced alarm. Humphrey suggests that perhaps the dominant themes became isolation, grasping at rumors, and doubt.[37] Depending on location and local conditions, urban experiences in Texas ranged from disruption to prosperity to isolation and confusion.

Randolph B. Campbell and other historians have described the impact of the Civil War on slavery in Texas as limited because Union armies did not penetrate East Texas where most slaves labored. Campbell also points to the growth of the institution since white refugees brought slaves into the state to avoid their emancipation by advancing Federal forces in Arkansas and Louisiana. The Confederate army did impress slaves to construct earthworks for defense of coastal towns. As a result some planters expressed concern for the loss of labor, while slaves might face disease and dangers in new locations. Late in the war some owners sold slaves fearing their loss if the Union won, although others continued to buy bondsmen in the spring of 1865. Some slaves did continue to escape to Mexico, into towns, or to the Union navy, while others resisted slavery in individual acts.[38] As Alwyn Barr has noted, some slaves facing less supervision during the conflict did in subtle ways assume more control over punishment, work pace, and their daily lives. Milton Holland, the free black son of a Texas planter and a slave mother, had been sent north for an education. He later volunteered for the Union army and as a sergeant in Virginia during 1864 received the Congressional Medal of Honor for leadership in battle.[39]

Historians in recent years have begun to explore more fully the instances in which Confederate soldiers shot down African Americans in the Union army who tried to surrender like other men when surrounded by the opposing army. Some Texas Confederates participated along with other troops in such actions at Poison Spring in Arkansas as well as others in the Indian Territory and Louisiana. Racial ideas and prewar fears of slave revolts apparently produced the strong emotions that led to these tragic excesses. After Poison Spring, black troops retaliated during the battle at Jenkins's Ferry in Arkansas.[40]

In 1864 and 1865 Confederate military and government leaders debated the possibility of trying to recruit slaves for their army by promising some individual freedom for those who served. Philip D. Dillard offers a comparison of attitudes in Lynchburg, Virginia, and Galveston, Texas, on the proposal. In Lynchburg, close to heavy fighting in the final months of conflict, support emerged for the proposal, even though it might undercut the original reason for secession. By contrast, most Confederates in Galveston, facing no immediate threat at that time and less aware of precarious Confederate fortunes elsewhere, opposed the action as unnecessary and disruptive of society. Neither the few Galveston supporters of using black soldiers nor their numerous critics suggested that any guilt about the mistreatment of slaves influenced their views. Dillard concludes that greater war pressures had created stronger Confederate nationalism in Virginia than in Texas.[41] Without a Union invasion, slavery in Texas appeared less disrupted as an institution than in most Confederate states, despite the hopes of slaves and the fears of some slaveholders. No sense of guilt about the treatment of slaves appears in the newly published collections of letters by women and their husbands in the Confederate army.

The only mentions of religious concerns appear in descriptions of revivals among soldiers in 1863 and 1864. Thomas W. Cutrer has edited the letters written to newspapers in Texas by Robert F. Bunting, the chaplain of the Eighth Texas Cavalry, known as Terry's Rangers. Bunting preached to the soldiers, buried the dead as crusading martyrs, and tried through his letters to sustain civilian morale.[42] It does not appear that concerns about slavery or religion played an important role in undermining Confederate morale among Texans.

Gary Gallagher has argued that Robert E. Lee and his Army of Northern Virginia through their early successes in 1862 and 1863 became the most important symbols of Confederate nationalism. Gallagher believes that view outweighed economic, social, and political concerns and helped maintain the morale of Confederates into the spring of 1865.[43] His evidence comes primarily from the eastern Confederacy, therefore it seems useful to consider whether the new studies of Texans in the West support that concept. Humphrey suggests that the mood of Austinites rose and fell with victories and defeats wherever they might occur, with frequent confusion as the result of false rumors. Events along or near the Mississippi River, such as the Union capture of Vicksburg, or attacks along the Texas coast seemed to stir the strongest responses. Texas soldiers in the West seemed to share those views. In their letters, Lizzie and Will Neblett and Theophilus and Harriet Perry reflected a variety of views about Lee that ranged from hopeful to worried in 1863 and 1864. The only clear exception to these patterns was Gideon Lincecum, the author of letters edited by Jerry Bryan Lincecum, Edward Hake Phillips, and Peggy A. Redshaw. Lincecum, an ardent Confederate, criticized Unionists, speculation, Confederate impressment, and wealthy families helping sons avoid conscription, while recognizing public discontent with government leaders. Yet he retained confidence in Lee as late as March 1865 and, perhaps wishfully, thought others shared his view. Among Texans in the Trans-Mississippi Department, Lee's image appeared positive but less reassuring than in the East because it was overshadowed by events closer to home.[44]

If trade through Mexico and the absence of a Federal invasion allowed East Texas to live with fewer problems and frustrations than many other regions of the Confederacy, the same cannot be said of most border regions in Texas. Political differences in the state led to fears and violent suppression of dissent that reveal some limits of Confederate nationalism. Some Texas Unionists accepted the judgment of secession, while others left the state, served in frontier defense units, or avoided participation in the war until passage of the first Confederate conscription act in early 1862. Richard McCaslin has written a thorough and analytical account of the most striking event that followed. In North Texas counties that opposed secession, desertions and opposition to the draft led to talk of organizing a Peace Party. A pro-Confederate vigilante committee in the fall of 1862 seized about 150 men, formed an extralegal court and under mob pressure hanged 22 men in Cooke County north of Dallas. The killing of a

Confederate officer brought a new wave of retaliation including 24 more deaths by lynch law. Government leaders at last reestablished a degree of order. Some military officers continued to harass and kill dissenters over the following year. Confederate and state policy later shifted from hunting Unionists to accepting them for frontier defense units. McCaslin suggests that seeking order through vigilante tactics only led to more disorder.[45] Another volume, by David Pickering and Judy Falls, extends the study of Union dissent and pro-Confederate violent opposition to Hunt and Hopkins counties east of Dallas. There too vigilantes rounded up dissenters who then faced a sham trial and hanging. Other Unionists hid in thickets to avoid similar treatment. Postwar efforts to bring vigilantes to justice failed as sympathizers helped them escape jail or manipulate the judicial system.[46]

Walter Kamphoefner extends the story of Unionist opposition to conscription into the central and southeastern Texas counties with large German immigrant populations, noting the Confederate use of martial law in both areas. The memoir of a Hill Country German American, edited by David R. Hoffman, lends support to that view. Stanley S. McGowen clarifies the confrontation on the Nueces River in 1862 as an attack by Confederate troops on armed Unionists headed for Mexico who initially defended themselves. Later, however, some Confederates did execute at least nine wounded Unionists. In a new general account of desertion in the Confederacy, Mark A. Weitz confirms the presence of men avoiding the draft or deserting into Mexico from Central and South Texas.[47]

When the United States Army withdrew from forts in West Texas after secession in 1861, the state government sought to replace them with Texas troops who would help recent settlers control areas still claimed by American Indians. A retreat by settlers of up to 100 miles resulted from Indian raids during the war according to the standard view of earlier histories about the Texas frontier. David Paul Smith in a thoughtful study clarifies three stages of Confederate and state efforts, which involved no more than a thousand men at any time. Debate over control of troops on the frontier did add to the tension between Confederate military commanders and Governor Murrah, resulting in a short-term compromise. The tasks of the soldiers in West Texas became more complex as growing numbers of Confederate deserters, Unionists avoiding conscription, and outlaws appeared in some parts of the region. While the defense units withdrew to a second line of forts, Smith argues that the farms and ranches of most settlers lay behind that line and did not have to be abandoned. He concludes that frontier defense during the war proved comparable to that of the prewar period. Glen Sample Ely adds further complexity by arguing that Unionists, including some frontier defense rangers, left for California amid growing chaos in 1864–1865, a time in which frontier ranchers also sold cattle to the Union army in New Mexico.[48]

Gary Clayton Anderson presents a different perspective on West Texas during the Civil War period in his volume on Anglo-American efforts to drive Native Americans out of Texas in the nineteenth century. He describes harsh winters and summer droughts that caused the deaths of many Plains Indians as well as their horses and left them too weakened to push back the advance of Anglo settlement. Instead he offers evidence of organized white outlaws stealing horses and trying to throw the blame on Native Americans. Men associated with political and military leader John R. Baylor seem to have played active roles in these schemes. Both Confederate and Union efforts in the Indian Territory to provide food for Indians also reduced their need to raid. Anderson agrees with Smith in focusing more attention on the struggle between loyal Unionists and Confederate troops and vigilantes, as well as on some Indian raids conducted for the purpose of taking cattle and other foodstuffs that were needed to feed starving tribes in the Indian territory.[49] A synthesis of the conclusions in these studies may lead to a better-balanced understanding of wartime events on the frontier. A comparison of the Confederate-Indian relations with the Union-Indian relations across the West, as described by Alvin M. Josephy, suggests that the larger numbers of Union volunteers made greater inroads on Indian lands than the Confederates in Texas.[50]

Historians of Anglo-Indian relations in postwar Texas usually have described a time of increasing conflict. Additional studies of Reconstruction have added a sense of widespread racial violence directed at the newly freed African Americans and white Unionists as a means of reasserting Confederate dominance. Other volumes extend the study of violence by exploring the use by outlaws of Confederate imagery to gain public support. One book by Barry Crouch, Larry Peacock, and James M. Smallwood and another by Crouch and Donaly E. Brice focus on Northeast Texas, while a third volume, by Smallwood, considers the South Central region of the state. In a more sweeping analysis William D. Carrigan suggests that repeated spasms of violence and vigilantism over time, including the prewar fire scare, the extralegal wartime hangings, frontier fighting, and Reconstruction murders created a culture in which lynching would continue to be acceptable into the early twentieth century.[51] This may provide a partial answer to the question by Randolph Campbell about patterns of continuity in a period of change.

Several additional studies of the Civil War in Texas and Texans in the war provide a variety of fresh insights into the attitudes and actions of soldiers and civilians during the period. Relating those views and activities to larger questions about secession, soldiers' commitments, and the impact of war on women, ethnic minorities, Confederate nationalism, and factors in victory or defeat seems more daunting and open to debate. Books related to secession in Texas suggest that fears of slave revolt and abolitionists clearly strengthened the

separatist movement. Significant reductions in soldiers present for duty probably did weaken Confederate armies late in the war. Yet health and fitness problems joined battle losses as apparently having greater impacts than desertion in
East Texas units with the strongest Deep South background and commitment
to slavery and the Confederate cause. Higher levels of desertion or shifts of allegiance existed in units from border areas of the state that were less involved with
Southern culture and institutions. Unionist-Confederate tensions contributed
to greater disruption and conflict in those areas.

Additional studies suggest that responses of Texas women to the war ranged
from frustrations to subtly expanded roles for meeting new problems and man-
aging family economic affairs. With no Federal advance into most of Texas and
continued trade through Mexico, women and other civilians in East Texas seem
to have faced fewer disruptions than their counterparts in many Confederate
states. Under those circumstances, concerns about the treatment of slaves and a
loss of God's support in the war seem to have had little impact on the attitudes
of Confederate Texans. With fewer military and economic pressures, perhaps
Texans and their leaders felt less need for stronger Confederate nationalism in
the form of controls over state troops or the possible recruiting of slaves as soldiers. The desire of Texas soldiers in the Trans-Mississippi Department to protect their families is understandable, even when it led to temporary desertions
during 1863 and 1864 in response to the possibility their units might be sent
across the Mississippi River. Since Confederate defeat ultimately occurred east
of the Mississippi, however, their reluctance to serve farther from home could
be interpreted as a form of regionalism and a further limitation on Confederate
nationalism.

To the questions of continuity or change in this era there are at least two
additional answers. The reoccurring instances of violence and vigilante activity
across the state from the secession period throughout the war and into Reconstruction suggest a tragic example of continuity in an era of change. On a more
positive note, more men seem to have survived the war than was once thought,
which contributed to a more rapid revival of the postwar Texas economy and
society. Discussions of change and continuity in the Civil War period can be
enlivened by also considering some of the thoughtful studies about the interac-
tion of popular myth and history. One volume on that topic offers two essays
related to what appear to be contrasting popular myths, one supporting continuity and one favoring change. Kelly McMichael describes the campaign in the
early twentieth century by the United Daughters of the Confederacy to build
monuments honoring Confederate soldiers. Yet she sees that effort as also aimed
at recognizing women's contributions to the Lost Cause and developing their
own cultural influence, albeit with mixed results. Elizabeth Hayes Turner discusses Juneteenth, the annual African American celebrations of emancipation,

that kept alive hope of equality through years of discrimination.[52] Each essay, one clearly and the other with subtlety, reflect changes that for Texans began primarily in the Civil War era.

Notes

1   Ralph A. Wooster, *Texas and Texans in the Civil War* (Austin: Eakin Press, 1995); Carl Moneyhon and Bobby Roberts, *Portraits of Conflict: A Photographic History of Texas in the Civil War* (Fayetteville: University of Arkansas Press, 1998).

2   Randolph B. Campbell, "Statehood, Civil War, and Reconstruction," in Walter L. Buenger and Robert A. Calvert, eds., *Texas through Time: Evolving Interpretations* (College Station: Texas A&M University Press, 1990), 166.

3   Walter F. Bell, "Civil War Texas: A Review of the Historical Literature," *Southwestern Historical Quarterly* (hereafter cited as *SHQ*) 109 (October 2005): 205–232.

4   Donald E. Reynolds, *Texas Terror: The Slave Insurrection Panic of 1860 and the Secession of the Lower South* (Baton Rouge: Louisiana State University Press, 2007).

5   Dale Baum, *The Shattering of Texas Unionism: Politics in the Lone Star State During the Civil War Era* (Baton Rouge: Louisiana State University Press, 1998); Kenneth Wayne Howell, "'When the Rabble Hiss, Well May Patriots Tremble': James Webb Throckmorton and the Secession Movement in Texas, 1854–1861," *SHQ* 109 (April 2006): 465–93.

6   Stephen A. Townsend, *The Yankee Invasion of Texas* (College Station: Texas A&M University Press, 2006).

7   Jeffery S. Prushankin, *A Crisis in Confederate Command: Edmund Kirby Smith, Richard Taylor, and the Army of the Trans-Mississippi* (Baton Rouge: Louisiana State University Press, 2005); Stephen A. Dupree, *Planting the Union Flag in Texas: The Campaigns of Major General Nathaniel P. Banks in the West* (College Station: Texas A&M University Press, 2008).

8   Thomas W. Cutrer, *Ben McCulloch and the Frontier Military Tradition* (Chapel Hill: University of North Carolina Press, 1993); Paul D. Casdorph, *Prince John Magruder: His Life and Campaigns* (New York: John Wiley, 1996).

9   Douglas Hale, *The Third Texas Cavalry in the Civil War* (Norman: University of Oklahoma Press, 1993), chap. 3.

10 Richard Lowe, *Walker's Texas Division C.S.A.: Greyhounds of the Trans-Mississippi* (Baton Rouge: Louisiana State University Press, 2004), chap. 2:19; Randolph B. Campbell, "Fighting for the Confederacy: The White Male Population of Harrison County in the Civil War," *SHQ* 104 (July 2000): 23–39.

11 Stanley S. McGowen, *Horse Sweat and Powder Smoke: The First Texas Cavalry in the Civil War* (College Station: Texas A&M University Press, 1999), chap. 6; Charles D. Spurlin, ed., *The Civil War Diary of Charles A. Leuschner* (Austin: Eakin Press, 1992).

12 Jerry Thompson and Lawrence T. Jones III, *Civil War and Revolution on the Rio Grande Frontier: A Narrative and Photographic History* (Austin: Texas State Historical Association, 2004), chaps. 1–2; Jerry Thompson, *Cortina: Defending*

the Mexican Name in Texas (College Station: Texas A&M University Press, 2007), chaps. 4–5.

13   Richard Lowe, ed., introduction to *A Texas Cavalry Officer's Civil War: The Diary and Letters of James C. Bates* (Baton Rouge: Louisiana State University Press, 1999).

14   Hale, *Third Texas Cavalry*, 71–73, 280–83.

15   Lowe, *A Texas Cavalry Officer's Civil War*, 327.

16   Lowe, *Walker's Texas Division*, 27–28, 38–39, 115–17, 235–40, 263–65.

17   M. Jane Johansson, *Peculiar Honor: A History of the 28th Texas Cavalry 1862–1865* (Fayetteville: University of Arkansas Press, 1998), 137; Charles Grear, "Texans to the Home Front: Why Lone Star Soldiers Returned to Texas during the War," *East Texas Historical Journal* 45 (Fall 2007): 14–25; Campbell, "Fighting for the Confederacy," 38.

18   Hale, *Third Texas Cavalry*, 281.

19   Spurlin, *Civil War Diary of Charles A. Leuschner*, 13–14, 59–60, 61–99.

20   Richard B. McCaslin, "Conditional Confederates: The Eleventh Texas Cavalry West of the Mississippi River," *Military History of the Southwest* 21 (Spring 1991): 87–99.

21   McGowen, *Horse Sweat and Powder Smoke*, chaps. 7–8.

22   Terry G. Jordan-Bychkov, Allen R. Branum, and Paula K. Hood, eds., "The Boesel Letters: Two Texas Germans in Sibley's Brigade," trans. Irma Ohlendorf Schwarz, *SHQ* 102 (April 1999): 456–84.

23   Walter D. Kamphoefner, "New Perspectives on Texas Germans and the Confederacy," *SHQ* 102 (April 1999): 440–55; Spurlin, *Civil War Diary of Charles A. Leuschner*, 13–14, 59–60.

24   Thompson and Jones, *Civil War and Revolution on the Rio Grande*, chaps. 1–3.; Thompson, *Cortina*, chaps. 4–5.

25   Richard E. Beringer, Herman Hattaway, Archer Jones, and William N. Still, Jr., *Why the South Lost the Civil War* (Athens: University of Georgia Press, 1986), 327, 334, 435, 439; Gary Gallagher, *The Confederate War* (Cambridge: Harvard University Press, 1997), 31–32.

26   Beringer, Hattaway, Jones, and Still, *Why the South Lost the Civil War*, chaps. 4 and 10.

27   Baum, *The Shattering of Texas Unionism*, chap. 3; John Anthony Moretta, *William Pitt Ballinger: Texas Lawyer, Southern Statesman, 1825–1888* (Austin: Texas State Historical Association, 2000), chap. 7.

28   Clayton E. Jewett, *Texas in the Confederacy: An Experiment in Nation Building* (Columbia: University of Missouri Press, 2002); Clayton E. Jewett, ed., *Rise and Fall of the Confederacy: The Memoir of Senator Williamson S. Oldham, C.S.A.* (Columbia: University of Missouri Press, 2006).

29   Drew Gilpin Faust, *Mothers of Invention: Women of the Slaveholding South in the American Civil War* (Chapel Hill: University of North Carolina Press, 1996).

30   Erika L. Murr, ed., *A Rebel Wife in Texas: The Diary and Letters of Elizabeth Scott Neblett, 1852–1864* (Baton Rouge: Louisiana State University Press, 2001).

31   M. Jane Johansson, ed., *Widows by the Thousand: The Civil War Letters of Theophilus and Harriet Perry, 1862–1864* (Fayetteville: University of Arkansas Press, 2000).

32   Lowe, *Walker's Texas Division*, chap. 4.

33   Joleene Maddox Snider, "Sarah Devereux: A Study in Southern Femininity," *SHQ* 97 (January 1994): 479–508.

34   Angela Boswell, *Her Act and Deed: Women's Lives in a Rural Southern County, 1837–1873* (College Station: Texas A&M University Press, 2001).

35   Alwyn Barr, "The 'Queen City of the Gulf' Held Hostage: The Impact of War on Confederate Galveston," *Military History of the West* 27 (Fall 1997): 119–38.

36   Paul A. Levengood, "In the Absence of Scarcity: The Civil War Prosperity of Houston, Texas," *SHQ* 101 (April 1998): 401–26; Charles A. Israel, "From Biracial to Segregated Churches: Black and White Protestants in Houston, Texas, 1840–1870," *SHQ* 101 (April 1998): 428–58; Mary M. Cronin, "'Confounding the Wise, If Not the Devil Himself': Rediscovering Forgotten Civil War Humorist R. R. Gilbert," *SHQ* 106 (April 2008): 389–416.

37   Peyton O. Abbott, "Business Travel Out of Texas during the Civil War: The Travel Diary of S. B. Brush, Pioneer Austin Merchant," *SHQ* 96 (October 1992): 259–71; David C. Humphrey, "'A Very Muddy and Conflicting' View: The Civil War as Seen from Austin, Texas," *SHQ* 94 (January 1991): 369–414; James Marten, ed., "The Diary of Thomas H. DuVal: The Civil War in Austin, Texas, February 26 to October 9, 1863," *SHQ* 94 (January 1991): 434–57.

38   Randolph B. Campbell, *An Empire for Slavery: The Peculiar Institution in Texas, 1821–1865* (Baton Rouge: Louisiana State University Press, 1989), chap. 12.

39   Alwyn Barr, "Black Texans during the Civil War," in Donald Willett and Stephen Curley, eds., *Invisible Texans: Women and Minorities in Texas History* (Boston: McGraw-Hill, 2005), 86–93.

40   Gregory J. W. Irwin, ed., *Black Flag Over Dixie: Racial Atrocities and Reprisals in the Civil War* (Carbondale: Southern Illinois University Press, 2004).

41   Philip D. Dillard, "'What Price Must We Pay for Victory?' Views on Arming Slaves from Lynchburg, Virginia, to Galveston, Texas," in Lesley J. Gordon and John C. Inscoe, eds., *Inside the Confederate Nation: Essays in Honor of Emory M. Thomas* (Baton Rouge: Louisiana State University Press, 2005), 316–31.

42   Thomas W. Cutrer, ed., *Our Trust Is in the God of Battles: The Civil War Letters of Robert Franklin Bunting, Chaplain, Terry's Texas Rangers, C.S.A.* (Knoxville: University of Tennessee Press, 2006).

43   Gallagher, *The Confederate War*, 85–89, 139–40.

44   Humphrey, "A 'Very Muddy and Conflicting' View," 369–414; Murr, *A Rebel Wife in Texas*, 138, 418, 428, 448; Johansson, *Widows by the Thousand*, 144–46, 152, 185, 237; Jerry Bryan Lincecum, Edward Hake Philips, and Peggy A. Redshaw, eds., *Gideon Lincecum's Sword: Civil War Letters from the Texas Home Front* (Denton: University of North Texas Press, 2001), 7–8, 293–94, 316–17.

45   Richard B. McCaslin, *Tainted Breeze: The Great Hanging at Gainesville, Texas, 1862* (Baton Rouge: Louisiana State University Press, 1994).

46   David Pickering and Judy Falls, *Brush Men and Vigilantes: Civil War Dissent in Texas* (College Station: Texas A&M University Press, 2000).

47   Kamphoefner, "New Perspectives on German Texans and the Confederacy," 440–55; David R. Hoffman, "A German-American Pioneer Remembers: August Hoffman's Memoir," *SHQ* 102 (April 1999): 486–509; Stanley S. McGowen, "Battle or Massacre?: The Incident on the Nueces, August 10, 1862," *SHQ* 104 (July 2000): 65–86; Mark A. Weitz, *More Damning Than Slaughter: Desertion in the Confederate Army* (Lincoln: University of Nebraska Press, 2005), 175, 231.

48   David Paul Smith, *Frontier Defense in the Civil War: Texas Rangers and Rebels* (College Station: Texas A&M University Press, 1992); Glen Sample Ely, "Gone from Texas and Trading with the Enemy: New Perspectives on Civil War West Texas," *SHQ* 110 (April 2007): 439–63.

49   Gary Clayton Anderson, *The Conquest of Texas: Ethnic Cleansing in the Promised Land, 1820–1875* (Norman: University of Oklahoma Press, 2005), chap. 21.

50   Alvin M. Josephy, Jr., *The Civil War in the American West* (New York: Knopf, 1991).

51   Barry A. Crouch, Larry Peacock, and James M. Smallwood, *Murder and Mayhem: The War of Reconstruction in Texas* (College Station: Texas A&M University Press, 2003); Barry A. Crouch and Donaly E. Brice, *Cullen Montgomery Baker: Reconstruction Desperado* (Baton Rouge: Louisiana State University Press, 1997); James M. Smallwood, *The Feud That Wasn't: The Taylor Gang, John Wesley Hardin, and Reconstruction Violence in Texas* (College Station: Texas A&M University Press, 2008); William D. Carrigan, *The Making of a Lynching Culture: Violence and Vigilantism in Central Texas, 1836–1916* (Urbana: University of Illinois Press, 2004).

52   Gregg Cantrell and Elizabeth Hayes Turner, eds., *Lone Star Pasts: Memory and History in Texas* (College Station: Texas A&M University Press, 2007), chaps. 4 and 6.

Chapter 2

The Civil War and the Lone Star State: A Brief Overview

by Archie P. McDonald

Union with the United States lost its luster for many Texans during the decade of the 1850s. Against the backdrop of such separating wedges as disagreement with the enforcement of the Compromise of 1850 and resulting disenchantment over their loss of so much western land, the strident activity of abolitionists, and especially the violence in Kansas, many Texans reflected their Southern heritage by affirming their belief in states' rights, especially as that related to slavery, and their acceptance of the principle of secession as the ultimate expression of that right.

Hardin R. Runnels's victory over Sam Houston in the governor's race in 1857 can be traced to this feeling, but Houston's victory in 1859 over Runnels came despite it. The legislature's selection of Louis T. Wigfall, an ardent fire-eater and secession advocate, to Houston's seat in the Senate signifies the mood of the majority more than does the election of "Old Sam Jacinto" to the governorship. He won that office with hard campaigning, which invoked memories of his past leadership, but he never masked his true feelings—he was first and last a Union man.

The presidential election of 1860 crystallized Texans into a secession posture. Texas delegates to the Democratic convention in Charleston, South Carolina, including Runnels, Francis R. Lubbock, Guy M. Bryan, R. B. Hubbard, and Tom Ochiltree, joined other Southerners in a demand for a party platform embracing slavery and opposing Stephen A. Douglas's majority position on popular sovereignty.

Since the *Dred Scott* decision confirmed the right of slave owners to take their property into the territories, Southerners assumed that slavery should be secured forever. But the election of 1860 alarmed them; the prospect of a victory by the new and radical Republican Party, a single-issue group demanding an end to slavery in the territories and eventually an end to it in the states, seemed real. Douglas was nominated by the mainstream Democrats at a second convention in Baltimore, and John Cabell Breckinridge of Kentucky won the nomination of still another group of Democrats meeting at Richmond, Virginia. Most

Illustration 1 Gov. Sam Houston.   *Courtesy Library of Congress.*

Texans supported Breckinridge and joined other Southerners in the threat to leave the Union in the event of a victory by the Republican Party and its nominee, Abraham Lincoln.

The Constitutional Union Party entered the contest, hoping to block an electoral majority and force the election into the House of Representatives where a compromise candidate might be selected. Sam Houston tried for the nomination of this party and outdrew John Bell of Tennessee on the first ballot, 57 to 68.5 votes, but when Bell was nominated, Houston thought of running as an independent candidate before finally deciding against such a move. In November, Texans voted for Breckinridge by a margin of three to one, emphasizing the secessionists' threat to leave the Union in the event of a Lincoln victory. Breckinridge received 47,548 votes to Bell's 15,463; Douglas received only 410 votes. Lincoln's name was not on the Texas ballot.

In response to the election, on December 20, 1860, South Carolina made good its threat to secede from the American Union. Georgia, Florida, Alabama, Mississippi, and Louisiana followed by the end of January, and Texas was expected to become the seventh state to secede. It did so over the political corpse of Sam Houston.

Houston attempted to ignore the popular clamor for a secession convention that began as soon as news of South Carolina's action reached the state. When secessionist leaders became convinced that Houston would not call the legislature to consider withdrawal from the Union, they usurped his powers by calling for elections within each judicial district on January 8, 1861, to select delegates for an ad hoc secession convention. Houston then summoned the legislature into session, hoping to steal the thunder of the secessionists. His legislature would meet on January 21, a week before the convention's delegates met on January 28. Houston hoped the legislature would prevent the convention from gathering, but many legislators were also members of the convention, and a majority of the remainder endorsed it.

The convention met in Austin on January 28. That afternoon, delegates elected Oran M. Roberts as their presiding officer and passed a preliminary motion to secede from the Union by a vote of 152 to 6. During the next two days, members of the convention worked out the details of a formal ordinance of secession. A final vote on the ordinance was taken in convention on February 1. The vote was conducted in a tense session, and when James Webb Throckmorton cast a negative vote, hisses and boos rained from the gallery. Throckmorton's courageous response, "Mr. President, when the rabble hiss, well may patriots tremble," gave testimony that Houston did not stand completely alone. Unlike the other states of the Lower South, the delegates decided to place their ordinance before the citizens of Texas for final approval. The popular vote took place on February 23.

The convention's declaration of causes for its action for the people's consideration included criticism of the government's administration of commonly held territories to the exclusion of Southerners, provocative activity in Kansas, failure to protect Texans from the Indians adequately, Northern hostility to the South and its systems (slavery), the South's minority status within the Union, and the election of a president committed to the elimination of slavery. With these considerations, the convention adjourned until March 2 to await the result of the election.

The argument between secessionists and unionists was bitter. The *Galveston News* and the *Texas Republican* backed the secessionists, while the *Southerner Intelligencer* and the *Bastrop Advertiser* attacked them, but the outcome was inevitable: 46,129 in support of secession, with only 14,697 opposed. Ten Central Texas counties, a few in North Texas along the Red River, and Angelina County in East Texas, an island in a sea of secessionism, voted no. Every other county voted affirmatively.

The convention met again in Austin on March 2, Texas Independence Day, and within three days confirmed separation from the Union and also Texas's affiliation with the Confederate States of America, newly organized in

Montgomery, Alabama. The Texas convention had sent unofficial delegates to the Montgomery meeting, and when official word of the secession vote arrived from Texas, the Confederate group voted their acceptance even before a formal request for admission was received.

The Texas convention's work continued. They summoned all elected officials to take an oath of loyalty to the new government on March 16. Houston agonized the entire night of March 15, and the next day, although present in the capitol, sat silently and heard his name called three times to take the oath, then heard his office vacated and his lieutenant governor, Edward Clark, sworn in to complete his term. Lincoln had offered Houston the use of 2,700 Federal troops in Texas under the command of Gen. David Twiggs, but Houston refused. He had fought for Texas, he reasoned, and even when Texas was wrong, he would not fight against her. This romantic pledge paralleled a more practical reason—Houston's desire to avoid bloodshed.

The presence of Twiggs's command bothered many Texans, and they made an immediate demand for the Union commander to surrender his troops and all Federal property. Twiggs sympathized with the secessionists, and he tried to avoid betraying his oath to the United States by resignation. Before Twiggs was relieved, Ben McCulloch led an armed group to army headquarters in San Antonio and demanded surrender. Twiggs complied to avoid a fight, and his entire command, representing more than 10 percent of all Union forces at the time, in effect became prisoners of war, although war did not then technically exist. Most were exchanged before the fighting began in earnest.

The convention also prepared for elections under Confederate statehood. Party activity, present but weak in the 1850s, ceased; the secessionists controlled the state's affairs completely. Francis R. Lubbock defeated Edward Clark by only 124 votes to become Texas's first Confederate governor, and John M. Crockett, mayor of Dallas, won the lieutenant governor's post.

Lubbock's administration supported the Confederate government enthusiastically, but he left after only one term to serve President Jefferson Davis in other capacities. His successor was Pendleton Murrah of Harrison County, who defeated T. J. Chambers by 17,501 to 12,455 votes in 1863. John H. Reagan became Texas's highest ranking Confederate civilian official when he received appointment as postmaster general in Davis's cabinet. Louis T. Wigfall and W. S. Oldham represented Texas in the Confederate Senate.

Lubbock's job became largely the work of continuing domestic policies of the Houston-Clark administrations where war conditions permitted, and grappling with new difficulties posed by the conflict. He supported the war effort and the Confederate administration without reservation, organized home guards to fight against Indians on the frontier, mustered soldiers for fighting outside the state, and mobilized the legislature to provide for the state's needs. Through a

Military Board, consisting of the governor, comptroller, and treasurer, Lubbock tried to establish a proper priority: win the war without undue domestic suffering. The board attempted to dispose of bonds of the United States held in Texas to purchase needed military supplies; it also suspended the debtor laws because so many of the state's workers served in the military, raised local revenue for the support of the military units in the field, and expended Confederate treasury warrants on state needs.

Murrah inherited a working state government, but one that suffered the same decline as did its parent government. Lubbock's administration had doubled state taxes, a heavy blow since so many taxes had been remanded during the 1850s, but still the war demanded more revenue, and needy families of soldiers also increased their demand on the government. Cotton cards were purchased by the state as a relief measure for homemakers to card, spin, and weave their own cotton. A portion of local tax revenues was designated for the relief of the destitute. Murrah remained a thorough Confederate until the end of the war and he presided over the steady decline of the economic productivity of his state while the public debt increased. War's end coincided with a near collapse of the state's economy.

Texas performed much better in fielding men for military service. Lubbock organized military districts and organized the militia for action under the state's initial commander, Gen. Earl Van Dorn. Gen. Paul Octave Hébert soon succeeded Van Dorn and was himself replaced in November 1862, following a dispute over the conscription laws, by Gen. John Bankhead Magruder.

Texas had no need for conscription in 1861. The census of 1860 revealed over 90,000 men between the ages of eighteen and forty-five, and of these an estimated 60,000 to 70,000 served in the military. Over 20,000 volunteered in the first year of the war. Usually a person of wealth organized a unit, financed its first operation, and, for obvious reasons, often was elected as its initial commander. Later, conscription added increased numbers of Texans to the army. The first draft selected men between the ages of 18 and 35, but later drafts expanded to include youths of 17 and older men of 45 and 50. Texas's most prominent soldier, Albert Sidney Johnston, commanded the Western Theater of the Confederate army until his death at the Battle of Shiloh in April 1862. Other general officers from Texas included Felix Huston Robertson, the only native-born Texan to achieve such rank.

Most Texans served outside the state. Lubbock raised thirty-two companies in 1862, calling them the Texas Brigade. They were joined by their first commander, John Bell Hood of Kentucky, later supplemented with units from Arkansas and North Carolina, and fought principally in the Eastern Theater under the command of Robert E. Lee. "My Texans," as Lee called them, learned that his affection often placed them at the center of his battles. Over 4,000 men served in the unit, but fewer than 700 survived the war. Another notable unit, Terry's Texas Rangers, commanded by Gen. B. F. Terry, fought primarily in the Western Theater. Lawrence Sullivan Ross's Brigade, organized later in the war, fought in the Western Theater and in the Trans-Mississippi Department. This department was created in 1863 to provide a separate military organization for the area after the Union regained control of the Mississippi River, thus separating the far west of the Confederacy from its political and economic control center. Gen. Edmund Kirby Smith commanded the Trans-Mississippi Department, including Texas, until the end of the war.

No major battles occurred within Texas, but many significant actions were fought along its borders. As early as May 1861, W. C. Young led volunteers from the Red River country into Indian Territory to attack Forts Arbuckle, Cobb, and Washita. In August, John R. Baylor led a group into southern New Mexico and proclaimed the territory as far west as Tucson as the Confederate territory of Arizona with himself as governor. And Gen. H. H. Sibley, fortunately with Gen. Tom Green along, successfully attacked Valverde with a force of 2,600 men on February 2, 1862. In March, he met Union forces under Edward R. Canby at Glorieta and was repulsed. This effectively saved New Mexico and Arizona from further Confederate encroachment.

The Federal blockade became effective on the Texas coast in July 1861, and Union forces occupied Galveston in October 1862. Magruder attacked them on January 1, 1863, from a troop concentration at Virginia Point, with men on two flat-bottomed riverboats with cotton bales lining the decks for protection. He succeeded in retaking the island, and the Confederate Texans held it until 1865.

Texas's most memorable Civil War battle occurred at Sabine Pass, a narrow inlet from the Gulf of Mexico to Sabine Lake, a saltwater impoundment that received the waters of the Sabine and Neches rivers. Both rivers were navigable to rail lines. In September 1862, Federal naval personnel forced the Confederates to abandon Sabine Pass, but it was soon reoccupied by an artillery battery commanded by Lt. Dick Dowling, a Houston saloonkeeper. When Gen. Nathaniel Banks attempted to send seventeen naval vessels and a force of over 1,500 soldiers through the pass to attack the interior in September 1863, Dowling's guns disabled two vessels in the main channel, blocking the way for the remainder of the ships, and preventing the disembarking of the Union soldiers. The Battle of Sabine Pass was hailed by Jefferson Davis as the most significant action of the war at a time when he hungered for good news after defeats at Vicksburg and Gettysburg. The battle did have a temporary negative effect on American credit in England. Banks was more successful elsewhere. His forces succeeded in capturing or controlling every port from the Rio Grande to just below Galveston, including Corpus Christi, Aransas Pass, and Indianola.

Banks's last attempt to invade Texas occurred in 1864. He ascended the Red River, intending to rendezvous with forces under Gen. Frederick Steele from Little Rock to capture North Texas. Steele was repulsed by Confederates under Van Dorn, and Gen. Richard Taylor stopped Banks at Mansfield, Louisiana. Some East Texans fought in this action as civilians, often with pikes and clubs, to prevent the invasion of their state.

In a final action, John S. Ford led forces against black Union soldiers at Palmito Ranch near Brownsville in May 1865, nearly a month after all other forces had surrendered. During what would be the last battle of the Civil War, the Texans outmaneuvered Union forces under the command of Col. Theodore H. Barrett. Though the battle ended in a Confederate victory, it proved insignificant in changing the outcome of the war.

Serious fighting took place between the Texans and Indians during the Civil War. Texans expected the Confederate army to police Indians as the American army had before the war, but the high command in far-off Virginia had too many Union soldiers on their hands to worry about Texas Indians, so Governor Lubbock organized state troops under James M. Norris for this service. Norris attempted regular patrols in the Indian country, but these proved easy for the Indians to evade, so his successor, J. E. McCord, substituted irregular scouting expeditions. As men organized for Indian service, they were repeatedly transferred to the regular army and service outside the state. Finally, J. W. Throckmorton organized a force that included many like himself who would fight Indians but not Union soldiers.

The most significant Indian action was at Adobe Walls, where Union and Confederate soldiers combined to fight Comanches, and the most unsuccessful occurred at Dove Creek in January 1864, when 370 state troops attacked 1,400 Kickapoos en route to Mexico from Indian Territory. The Texans' heavy losses made them regret the attack.

Texans who remained at home did not suffer the ravages of war as did their fellow Confederates in Virginia and Tennessee; still, they had problems. Some Texans did not like the Confederate affiliation. Some, such as Houston, remained relatively quiet; others, including financier S. M. Swenson, left the state, depriving Texas of needed leadership both during and after the war; and some, such as E. J. Davis, organized Union forces to fight in Texas. Some Texas Germans disliked the Confederacy because they favored Union nationalism and disliked slavery; often they refused to volunteer or to be conscripted, and some tried to escape to Mexico. One such group was apprehended and massacred. Other Germans did serve in the Confederate army. In 1862 the Peace Party, a secret society, was organized in North Texas. It aroused fear in loyal Confederates who hanged over forty Peace Party members in Gainesville and other places. In 1864 the North Texas area also became a gathering place for army deserters and ne'er-do-wells and posed a police problem for the state.

In 1863 a conference of western state representatives in Marshall produced a plan to exchange Confederate cotton in Mexico for needed war materiel. The plan called for the Confederate government to take over the trade by purchasing half of each planter's cotton and exempting the rest from impressment, to make sure the Confederacy's major economic resource would contribute to the war effort. Murrah's government devised an alternate "state plan," which called for the Texas government to transport cotton to the border, return half to the owner, and secure the remainder with state bonds. The Confederate Congress preempted the state's power in this area with a specific act, irritating some Texans.

Cotton production declined steadily during the war years as more and more men entered the military services. Women, minors, men who were exempt from the draft, and some objectors continued to work and produce as best they could. But as state revenue dwindled and Confederate currency inflated, their lot was often difficult. Such necessities as salt became scarce, and people had to return to their pioneer ways to survive. They used corncob ashes as a substitute for soda; parched rye, okra, or acorns for coffee; and they made their own cloth. Murrah was inaugurated in a homespun suit partially to indicate its acceptability and partially because of its availability. Paper also grew scarce, forcing some newspapers to cease operations. Texas had little industry before the war but developed some from necessity. Arms works were established in Austin and Tyler; Marshall supported new factories; iron works functioned in East Texas; and the state penitentiary became a leading producer of cloth.

Texas became a haven for refugees from other Southern states and a shipping point for slaves whose owners sought to move them from threatened territory. Both migrations provided additional problems for Texans, and many immigrants were not happy with their new home. Kate Stone, of Brokenburn Plantation in Louisiana, fled to Smith County during the Vicksburg Campaign and called her haven "the dark corner of the Confederacy." This assessment is perhaps too harsh; Texas functioned well enough, considering its many difficulties, and its war problems were only preliminaries for greater difficulties during Reconstruction.

The war ended for Texans at different times. For the survivors of Hood's Brigade and other Texans in the Army of Northern Virginia, the end came with Lee's surrender to Gen. U. S. Grant at Appomattox on April 9, 1865; for others with the Army of Tennessee, it concluded with Gen. J. E. Johnston's surrender to Gen. W. T. Sherman at Bentonville, North Carolina, on April 19; and Gen. Edmund Kirby Smith surrendered the Department of the Trans-Mississippi, including Texas, on June 2. But for most Texans, the day to remember was June

19. On that day Gen. Gordon Granger arrived in Galveston with 1,800 Federal troops to declare the war at an end and all war proclamations, including the end of African slavery, in effect. White and black Texans would one day view this as a day of liberation. But for decades most whites seethed with resentment and most blacks did not understand fully what it meant or have an opportunity to exercise their freedom.

[Note: The story of Texas during secession and the Civil War has been told many times and well in general works I have read by Rupert Richardson, Ralph W. Steen, T. R. Fehrenbach, Seymour Conner, Robert Calvert and Arnoldo De León, Alwyn Barr, and more recently by James Haley, and many, many others. I have written about these years in fourth- and seventh-grade texts and in such general works as *Texas: All Hail the Mighty State* and *Texas: A Compact History.* I learned the story from these and other excellent historians, especially Ralph Wooster, Frank E. Vandiver, and T. Harry Williams, and herewith acknowledge my considerable debt to each of these, plus scores of other fine historians unmentioned here who have taught me all I know about Texas history.]

Part II

The Time for
Compromise
Has Passed

Chapter 3

The Impending Crisis: A Texas Perspective on the Causes of the Civil War

by James M. Smallwood

Although various economic, political, and social factors help explain the coming of the Civil War, it had only one predominant cause: slavery. Like their Southern brethren, Texans certainly understood the importance slavery played in stirring wartime sentiments. No single event stressed this point more clearly than the Secession Convention of Texas, where elected delegates spelled out in detail their reasons for leaving the Union on February 1, 1861. One need only consider their "Declaration of Causes" to understand that slavery and its extension was the basic cause of the war.[1]

Illustration 2 The Southern Confederacy a fact!!! Acknowledged by a mighty prince and faithful ally. *Courtesy Library of Congress*

32

In their declaration of causes why the state was leaving the Union, Texas secessionists asserted that when their state joined the Union, "she was received as a commonwealth holding, maintaining and protecting the institution known as negro slavery—[and that] the servitude of the African to the white race within her limits . . . should exist in all future time. Her institutions and geographical position established the strongest ties between her and other slave-holding States of the confederacy [the Union]. . . . But what has been the course of the government of the United States, and of the people and authorities of the non-slave-holding States, since our connection with them? The controlling majority of the Federal Government, under various pretenses and disguises has so administered the same as to exclude the citizens of the Southern States, unless under odious and unconstitutional restrictions, from all the immense territory owned in common by all the States on the Pacific Ocean, for the avowed purpose of acquiring sufficient power . . . as a means of destroying the institutions of Texas and her sister slave-holding states."

Continuing, the secessionists said that "by the disloyalty of the Northern States and their citizens and the imbecility of the Federal Government, infamous combinations of incendiaries [arsonists] and outlaws [abolitionists] have been permitted in those States and the common territory of Kansas to trample on federal laws, to war upon the lives and property of Southern citizens in that territory, and finally by violence and mob law to usurp the possession for the same as exclusively the property of the Northern States." The secessionists then alleged that the Federal government had not done enough to protect Texans from "the Indian savages on our border, and more recently against the murderous forays of banditti from the neighboring territory of Mexico."

After briefly mentioning conditions on the state's southern and western borders, the secessionists turned back to the topic of slavery: "The states of Maine, Vermont, New Hampshire, Connecticut, Rhode Island, Massachusetts, New York, Pennsylvania, Ohio, Wisconsin, Michigan, and Iowa . . . have deliberately violated . . . the 3rd clause of the 2d section of the 4th article of the federal constitution [guaranteeing that runaway slaves must be returned to their masters]." Continuing, the Texans alleged that the new Republican Party was hostile to the South's "beneficent and patriarchal system of African slavery, proclaiming [instead] the debasing doctrine of the equality of all men, irrespective of race or color—a doctrine at war with nature, in opposition to the experience of mankind, and in violation of the plainest revelations of the Divine Law. They demand the abolition of negro slavery throughout the confederacy [the United States], the recognition of political equality between the white and negro races, and avowed their determination to press on their crusade against us, so long as a negro slave remains in these States. . . . [T]his abolition organization has been actively sowing the seeds of discord throughout the Union . . . By consolidating their strength, they have placed the slave-holding States in a hopeless minority in the federal congress."

Texas secessionists next accused Northerners of encouraging and sustaining "lawless organizations to steal our slaves and prevent their recapture, and have repeatedly murdered Southern citizens while lawfully seeking their rendition. . . . They have through the mails and hired emissaries, sent seditious pamphlets and papers among us to stir up servile insurrections and bring blood and carnage to our firesides. They have sent hired emissaries among us to burn our towns and distribute arms and poison to our slaves for the same purpose." Summing up, the secessionists argued that the United States was established "exclusively by the white race, for themselves and their posterity; that the African race had no agency in their establishment; that they were rightfully held and regarded as an inferior and dependent race, and in that condition only could their existence in this country be rendered beneficial or tolerable."

The Texas Declaration of Causes is 2,287 words long. Approximately eighty-five of those words pertain to border and frontier problems caused by Indians and Mexican raiders. The other 2,202 words deal with slavery. The six states that left the Union before Texas wrote documents that expressed similar sentiments of support for secession. Since the Texas declaration was comparable to that of other Southern states, it is folly to argue that slavery did not cause the Civil War although some people still engage in that folly.

Texas secessionists were typical of those in other Southern states, and all other potential causes of the Civil War revolved around Dixie's "Peculiar Institution." Slavery was at the root of all the crises that tore the country apart between 1846 and 1861. Some historians have argued that economic differences between the North and South led to the war because capitalists in the North received special consideration by the Federal government while Dixie's planters and yeoman farmers did not. That argument goes back to the administration of George Washington and the financial programs offered by Secretary of the Treasury Alexander Hamilton. But what caused the major economic differences? Slavery. Others argue that in toto the North and South evolved into two distinct "civilizations" that ultimately could not live under the same governing roof. But what was the factor that led to the evolution of two distinctively different regions? Slavery. Yet others argue that Southerners were true to the ideal of an American republic while the North became a hotbed of democracy. But why did Dixie fail to become a democracy? Once again, the answer was slavery (in addition to an aristocracy that would not surrender power to commoners).

Other attempts to explain secession include: Northern democrats pitted against the Southern aristocracy; Northern abolitionists versus Southern "fire-eaters"; a blundering generation of politicians in the 1850s who had not the civility, nor the intelligence, nor the wisdom of older generations of leaders such as Washington, Jefferson, Madison, Monroe et al.; the North's evolution into an industrial society while the South remained committed to agriculture (and the differences between an urban region as opposed to a rural region). Others stress aspects of social history, such as the North's progress in education of its citizens as opposed to the educational backwardness of Dixie. Or, bluntly put, the ignorance of the unschooled, illiterate South where many commoners had to depend on what their "betters" were saying regarding most of the political issues of the day. Another view holds that both the North and South were led by unrealistic men who did not consider what the human costs of a civil war would be, especially fire-eating Southern partisans who clamored for a war against the more powerful Northern states. Treason even adds to the equation. White Southern Confederates voluntarily (that leaves out conscripts) committed treason by trying to overthrow the United States Constitution by force. Why? To save slavery. When the smoke clears, it is obvious that if one digs underneath every other potential cause, whether couched in economic, political, or social terms, slavery rears its ugly head.[2]

Historian Chandra Manning's *What This Cruel War Was Over: Soldiers, Slavery, and the Civil War* investigates the letters of 657 Union and 477 Confederate soldiers and attempts to ascertain the soldiers' perspectives on the war. Manning ask the rhetorical question, "Why did they fight?" She concludes that the vast majority of the soldiers thought they were fighting because of slavery, the blue wanting to banish Dixie's Peculiar Institution, the gray wanting to save it. In this approach, Manning furthers the work of Professor James McPherson's *For Cause and Comrades: Why Men Fought in the Civil War*. There is a message here. The majority of the fighting men said they were fighting for or against slavery, and, maybe, just maybe, we should take their word for it.[3]

One need only examine the immediate causes of the Civil War circa 1846 to 1861 to understand that slavery underlay all other issues that led up to the war. From the opening of the Mexican War in 1846 to the election of Lincoln in 1860, a series of crises beset the land, each acting to drive a wedge between North and South. By 1860, the wedge had created a chasm that could not be bridged. What were the crises: the Mexican Cession, wherein the United States took the present American Southwest from Mexico, a development that opened anew the controversial question of slavery in the territories; the weaknesses of the Compromise of 1850 that tried, but failed, to settle that question; the passage of a new, stronger, and unjust Fugitive Slave Law in 1850; the publication of Harriet Beecher Stowe's *Uncle Tom's Cabin* in 1851–1852; the rise of the Knights of the Golden Circle from 1853 to 1861; the Kansas-Nebraska Act of 1854; the Ostend Manifesto of 1854; civil war in Kansas Territory from 1855 to 1861; the Sumner-Brooks incident of 1856; the Supreme Court's *Dred Scot* decision of 1857; John Brown's raid of 1859; and, finally, the election of Abraham Lincoln in 1860.[4]

If one takes a hard look at the above list of crises that rocked the nation, one cannot deny that slavery was at the root of every major disagreement that pitted Northerners and Southerners against each other.[5] Many professional historians know all this, but students and laymen, especially in today's South, have not grasped the magnitude of the overwhelming problem that slavery caused the United States. Instead we continue to hear about states' rights, a canard if there ever was one. The bludgeon of "states' rights" has always been used by out-groups who press the fight to the in-groups, all this as if human slavery were not even important, much less an abomination. And we still see Confederate flags wave throughout Dixie, the one of choice usually being Robert E. Lee's battle flag of the Army of Northern Virginia. The flags fly, they are painted on the grilles of semitrailer trucks, and they are stuck on the back windshields of pickup trucks. Until recently, a Confederate flag even flew atop the statehouse in South Carolina. The display of the Confederate flag suggests that some Southerners fail to recognize that those flags represent slavery and that slavery is an abomination to be justly condemned.

Lincoln, like many Northerners, opposed the extension of slavery but the Mexican War (1846–1848) brought the issue up in a most dramatic way and ushered in the era of crises that would change America forever. When the United States went to war, many Northern congressmen knew that the administration of James K. Polk, a slaveholder from Tennessee, intended to take territory from the enemy and that most likely the area would be carved into several new slave states. To fight such a development, Pennsylvania Congressman David Wilmot introduced an amendment to the appropriations bill stating neither slavery nor involuntary servitude could exist in any territory taken from Mexico. Thus Wilmot's proposed bill renewed the controversy over slavery, dividing the country over the issue for the first time since the passage of the Missouri Compromise in 1820. The Wilmot Proviso, as the amendment was termed, passed the Northern-dominated House but failed in the Senate where the South had parity. Yet, it was a clear message to the South. The proviso showed the determination of many Northerners to confine slavery to pre-existing areas.

To counter this anti-slavery position, in 1847 U.S. Senator John C. Calhoun of South Carolina, the best-known defender of Dixie and its Peculiar Institution, introduced a series of resolutions into the Senate which came to be known as the "Platform of the South." Calhoun argued that Congress could not constitutionally bar slavery from any territory. Because territories belonged jointly to all states, all should have equal rights in those territories. Southerners could take their property (including slaves) to any territory and could demand protection of that property in those regions. Moreover, Congress should guarantee the rights of slaveholders to establish slave codes in the territories to protect their property. Thus were the lines drawn between the Wilmot Proviso and the Platform of the South. Both sides had thrown down the gauntlet.

With the end of the war in 1848, with the Mexican Cession, and with the discovery of gold in California and the rapid peopling of that region, a policy regarding the new territories had to be hammered out by congressmen, most of whom had the interests of their sections in mind. Compromisers Henry Clay and Stephen Douglas of Illinois stepped forward with the Compromise of 1850. Included were a number of agreements. California entered the Union as a free state, since slavery had not taken hold there. The rest of the new Southwest was organized into New Mexico and Utah territories without mention of slavery, which allowed Southern slaveholders to take their slaves there. It was further stipulated that "popular sovereignty" would decide the slavery issue in the two territories as each would later be admitted to the Union when qualified "with or without slavery as its constitution may prescribe." Other aspects of the compromise included banning the slave trade (but not slavery itself) in the nation's capital; Congress promised the South a stronger fugitive slave law to protect slaveholders' property rights; and, last, Texas ceded her western borderlands claim to New Mexico Territory in return for the Federal government pre-annexation debts. Many Texans opposed giving away so much land to New Mexico Territory, and at one point, it appeared that Texas might clash militarily with the United States, or, perhaps, even withdraw from the Union. In the end, sober heads prevailed, Texas took $10 million for the land lost, half of which retired state debts going back to the days of the Republic. Also, some of the money was put into a permanent endowment for education.[6]

Even with the Texas-New Mexico boundary settlement, the Compromise of 1850 did not satisfy everyone. In some Southern states, such as South Carolina, Georgia, Alabama, Mississippi, and Texas, politicos talked of secession. Reluctantly, those states remained in the Union but fire-eaters emerged and worked constantly through the decade to strengthen the secessionist movement in Dixie. As well, the South demanded strict adherence to the compromise, especially the new Fugitive Slave Law that Congress passed—but it was precisely that act which galled not only diehard abolitionists but Northerners in general. Under the compromise, the Fugitive Slave Act of 1793 was amended thus: Federal commissioners were appointed with authority to issue warrants, summon posses, and force people under pain of fine or imprisonment to help capture runaways. Once caught, the fugitives had no jury trial nor could they testify in their own behalf. Rather, it was necessary only for an owner or his agent to submit an affidavit of ownership.[7]

The undemocratic, anti–civil liberties features of the fugitive law caused immediate crises that would continue until the Civil War. For instance, just after Congress passed the new law, slave catchers came to New York City and seized James Hamlet. Quickly convicted in the special fugitive court, Hamlet was dragged to Maryland before he even had time to say goodbye to his wife and children. Outraged New Yorkers who had known Hamlet for years did not believe the man was a runaway; they established a fund to buy back his freedom. Such travesties became legion. Euphermia Williams had lived free in Pennsylvania for years, but in 1851 slave catchers seized her, and her supposed owner also claimed her six children, all Pennsylvania born. A judge ultimately released Williams who, with her children, continued to live free, but the case further alarmed Northerners who were concerned about civil liberties. During the same year, a Southerner seized Jerry McHenry, who was a substantial citizen of Syracuse, New York, but abolitionists, not believing that he was a runaway, rescued him and facilitated his escape from the area. Also, in 1851 a black abolitionist flung himself into a Boston courtroom to rescue a supposed fugitive. History is replete with many other examples of injustices that occurred because of the new fugitive act. Finally, many Northern politicians had enough. Many states passed "personal liberty" laws to protect the rights of victims falsely accused of being runaways. Oddly, many Southern fire-eaters demanded that the various Northern states—in which people resisted enforcement of the fugitive act—be forced to obey the Federal government—at gunpoint if necessary.

If the new fugitive slave law caused problems between the sections, so did Harriet Beecher Stowe's *Uncle Tom's Cabin*, published first as a series of magazine articles in 1851 and collected into a book in 1852. Mrs. Stowe was the daughter of Ward Lyman Beecher, president of Lane Seminary and an ardent abolitionist who believed that if slaves rebelled in organized fashion, they could win their own freedom. He became famous in part because of his opposition to slavery, which he believed could be done away with if Southern slaves were given "Beecher Bibles." What was a Beecher Bible? A loaded rifle. Not herself an abolitionist, Stowe was roused by the Fugitive Slave Act, which she called an abomination. The outline of *Uncle Tom's Cabin* was simple. It recounted the tale of Tom, a patient, faithful slave; the little white child, Eva; and the scheming callousness of Simon Legree, a hated overseer whom Stowe made a transplanted Yankee. Avoiding the vindictiveness of many abolitionist tracts, Stowe nevertheless told of cruelty and of the suffering of the slaves. She painted scenes of heroism, of pain, of self-sacrifice; of the slave Eliza on the frozen Ohio River heading north toward freedom; of Tom and Eva ascending to heaven. Such a story left many readers in tears.

Uncle Tom's Cabin became a runaway success. Printed in many editions, in several languages, the story was suited for the stage, where it was most effective. Producers and actors began touring with the play, taking its message throughout the North. Even illiterates could understand the point of the play even though they could never read the book. The story had a tremendous impact on public opinion in the North and brought many people to the side of the abolitionists. Even people who were not militant would pause to ask: "Is slavery just?" The story affected the South, too. Calling Stowe a fraud, many Southerners pointed out that her picture of plantation life might be distorted. Others accused her of stirring hatred between the sections. In any case, *Uncle Tom's Cabin* drove another wedge between the North and the South. Many Northerners believed Stowe's version of slavery, while the South closed ranks again in the defense of the Peculiar Institution.[8]

Richard Hubbard, a future governor of Texas (1876–1879) was forced, like many Texans—or soon-to-be migrants to the Lone Star State—to grapple with Stowe's message in 1852 as a student at the prestigious University of Virginia. He found the student body divided, the majority favoring immediate secession; he considered himself a Unionist and was most uncomfortable. Nevertheless, he attended nightly study sessions at Bachelor's Hall. Talk there often turned to *Uncle Tom's Cabin*, and the students were entirely predictable in the political positions that they chose. Southerners damned the novel while Northerners defended it. More nights than not, Southern boys complained about the Northern assault on slavery while Yankee boys condemned the Peculiar Institution as immoral.[9] Hubbard had a similar experience at Harvard Law School after he graduated from the University of Virginia. Stowe's work circulated widely. Her book tore Harvard apart, just as it did the University of Virginia. Classmates turned against classmates and defended their home section.[10]

Two years after publication of *Uncle Tom's Cabin*, another sectional controversy engulfed the nation in a political hurricane, and, again, slavery and its expansion inflamed passions. In 1854 Stephen Douglas guided the Kansas-Nebraska Act through Congress but not without accompanying furor. A real estate and railroad developer from Illinois, Douglas wished to see a transcontinental railroad pass from Chicago to California. But to accomplish that, the Nebraska region needed to be cleared of Indians and given organized government. Led by Jefferson Davis of Mississippi, Southerners—who wanted a southern transcontinental route through New Orleans or Memphis—pointed out that their route passed through organized territory.

Douglas quickly realized that he would have to compromise with Southerners to reach his goal. And they were difficult to deal with because all of Nebraska lay north of latitude 36° 30' where slavery was excluded by the old Missouri Compromise of 1820. Southerners, indeed, were hesitant to create a new free territory that would one day benefit only the North. To win the South, Douglas proposed to divide the region into two territories—Kansas and Nebraska. Then, in what amounted to a repeal of the Missouri line, he argued that the people in the territories could vote slavery up or down in accord with "popular sovereignty" at the time that the territories were created, assuming that Nebraska would go free and Kansas would become a slave state.[11]

Blind both to Northern opinion of his plan and to the moral implications of his compromise, Douglas shepherded the Kansas-Nebraska Act through Congress with almost universal support of Southern congressmen, Sam Houston of Texas being one of the few exceptions. In so doing, Douglas delivered a major victory for slavery, for, according to his plan, the Peculiar Institution could go north of the old Missouri Compromise line. Many Northerners were stunned by the information that slavery could now spread. Abolitionists denounced the act as "a gross violation of a sacred pledge." The unanimity of people in the free states was solidified. Because of the Kansas-Nebraska Act, the Democratic Party lost heavily in the North, as did the Whig Party. Two new parties appeared. One, the American or Know-Nothing Party, appeared to be ultranationalistic, its members simply hoping that the country would forget the slavery issue. Far more important, however, was the formation of the Republican Party. At indignation meetings throughout the Northwest, it sprang up spontaneously. Purely a sectional party, it took a foursquare stance against the extension of slavery, its members supporting the old Wilmot Proviso. The party experienced immediate success. It took more than one hundred seats in the United States House of Representatives and also won control of several state governments.[12]

In Texas, Senator Houston faced a political firestorm for his vote against Kansas-Nebraska. He knew that it would lead to an immediate bloodbath in Kansas and that a national civil war might result, and he said so, but rabid secessionists, or fire-eaters, would not listen. George Chilton of Smith County, who was campaigning to reopen the international slave trade, organized a local protest against Houston's vote, and others around the state took up the cry. In 1855, the Texas legislature officially condemned his vote. Later, at the state Democratic Party meeting of January 1856, Chilton co-sponsored a resolution praising Senator Thomas Rusk for his yea vote on Kansas-Nebraska and damning Houston for his no vote.[13] Such opposition effectively ended Houston's career in the Senate even though his predictions proved all too true.

The Kansas-Nebraska Act led to open conflict in Kansas. From the beginning, it was accepted that Nebraska would be a free territory, but the North and the South fought over Kansas. At first, Southerners, primarily Missourians, went into Kansas and took their slaves with them, but soon Free-Soilers and abolitionists formed the New England Emigrant Aid Society to help pay transportation costs of Northern antislaveryites who were willing to migrate to Kansas. A cold war began as the two sides created dual governments for the territory. Then, the story of Bleeding Kansas began as civil war gripped the region. By the end of 1856, some 200 people had been killed in guerrilla-style warfare and property damage had reached millions of dollars. Although pro-slavery forces finally dominated, the Kansas issue remained unsettled until the coming of the national civil war.[14]

Meanwhile, other events occurred that further weakened the Union. Congress was torn by the troubles in Kansas, and men rushed to defend their sections. One was Senator Charles Sumner of Massachusetts, an abolitionist who was a brilliant orator. In the spring of 1856, he delivered an address titled "The Crime Against Kansas," wherein he used his oratorical skills to lambaste the South. Then, he singled out Douglas of Illinois and U.S. Senator Andrew P. Butler of South Carolina for personal attacks while Butler was not present to defend himself. Later, U.S. Representative Preston S. Brooks of South Carolina, Butler's nephew, rose to his uncle's defense by attacking Sumner with a cane and beating him until he fell unconscious on the floor of the Senate chamber. Both sections made much of the Sumner-Brooks incident, with both men being presented as heroes, Sumner by the North, Butler by the South.[15] The affair amounted to another wedge driven between the North and South. The chasm would become wider because of the activity of a new quasi-secret organization that was dedicated to championing the interests of the South in expanding slavery.

By 1856, the Knights of the Golden Circle (KGC) was flourishing in the South. Founded by George W. L. Bickley, a Virginia-born physician and an adventurer then living in Cincinnati, the organization proposed to created a new "Empire for Slavery." The golden circle would begin in Washington, D.C., swing west-southwest to encompass all of the South, would continue and would encompass Mexico and Central America, and from thence would continue to include several Caribbean islands, including Cuba, before the circle closed in Washington, D. C. Bickley founded the first "castle," or chapter, of the KGC in Cincinnati in 1854 and soon took the organization into the South where he found many people most enthusiastic about the possibility of creating a slave empire that would not only make the North appear to be a dwarf but also completely overwhelm that section politically.[16]

Bickley was particularly popular in Texas because his KGC called for the annexation of Mexico and favored reopening the African slave trade. He founded thirty-three chapters in twenty-eight counties of the Lone Star State. Locations included such towns as Dallas, McKinney, Sulphur Springs, Houston, Galveston, Austin, San Antonio, Jefferson, Marshall, Rusk, Tyler, Huntsville, and Waxahachie. Texans and other Southerners who joined the KGC believed that Dixie *must* establish a vast slave empire to offset the growing political and economic power of the North. In 1860, the Texas KGC made two efforts to mass men at the Rio Grande for the obvious purpose of filibustering into Mexico but the operations failed for lack of sufficient manpower. However, by 1860, the KGC was successful in other ways. First, in Texas and throughout the South, men associated with the organization joined the leadership of the secessionist movement. Also, when the Southern states broke away from the Union, men in the KGC provided the first military leadership and manpower. Again using Texas as the example, the KGC provided at least 150 of the 550 men who joined Texas Ranger Ben McCulloch in February of 1861 in the march to San Antonio to seize the Federal arsenal there.[17]

KGC members were not alone in desiring an empire for slavery. Earlier, in 1854, American diplomats pushed the sections further apart. Secretary of State William L. Marcy directed three American diplomats to pursue a plan to acquire Cuba, which could be carved into at least two slave territories or states. Involved were James Buchanan, the American minister to England; John Y. Mason, minister to France; and Pierre Soulé, minister to Spain. They met in Ostend, Belgium, where they produced an amazing secret document that revealed a plan to buy Cuba from Spain for up to $120 million if necessary. If Spain refused to sell, the document argued that America would be justified in making war on Spain to achieve the objective. When Buchanan, Mason, and Soulé sent the document to the State Department, it was apparently supposed to remain in-house, but news soon leaked out. Many Northerners, including abolitionists and Free-Soilers, were horrified by the advocacy of aggression and by Soulé's vigorous defense of slavery and its extension.[18]

In 1857, the United States Supreme Court momentously intervened in the North-South political struggle over slavery, an intervention that continued to tear the nation asunder. The justices rendered a decision in *Scott v. Sanford* (best known historically as the *Dred Scott* decision). Scott (1795–1858) was a slave from Missouri who in 1834 had accompanied his master, a career military officer, to the free state of Illinois and later to the free territory of Wisconsin. After Scott's first master died, his new master and a friendly attorney allowed the slave to sue for his freedom in 1846, arguing that his stay in a free state and free territory made him a free man.[19]

The Supreme Court ultimately heard the case and settled Scott's status quickly in a seven-to-two ruling that he was not a United States citizen, had no property, and could not sue in federal court. However, Chief Justice Roger Taney, a Virginian, went much further when he declared that the old Missouri Compromise was unconstitutional because it deprived Southerners of due process and security of property (slaves). The case was highly criticized on legal grounds. For example, Northerners against slavery feared that a person could buy a slave in a state where the institution was legal and then bring that slave into a free state and, in effect, make that free state a slave state. For good or ill, the case seemed to settle the question about the extension of slavery: Southern slave owners could go into any territory and take their slaves with them. Essentially, Chief Justice Taney had validated John C. Calhoun's argument delivered in the Platform of the South in 1847. Certainly Taney delivered another victory for slaveholding Dixie, even more of a victory than the Kansas-Nebraska Act. Most Northerners viewed the decision with horror, with abolitionists particularly upset, many vowing to fight the decision. Most Southern slaveholders, including those in Texas, celebrated.

While the *Dred Scott* decision may have caused some abolitionists to give up their crusade against slavery, it strengthened the resolve of others, including the infamous John Brown. An abolitionist from Connecticut, Brown (1800–1859) had earlier been involved in the Kansas civil war. He helped create Bleeding Kansas before being driven out of the region by pro-slavery forces and forced to go into hiding in Canada in 1856. Before the year was out, he returned to the United States and slipped into Massachusetts where he talked to several rich abolitionists who agreed to fund his continued campaign against slavery. Now having backers, Brown developed an amazing scheme to end slavery. He intended to take a small force south and attack Harpers Ferry, Virginia (now West Virginia), the site of a Federal arsenal. Once he had secured the arsenal, Brown planned to seize arms and munitions, free area slaves, arm them, and let them win their own freedom, the result being a black republic in western Virginia, a region of the state not fully committed to slavery. Next, an ever-growing slave army would sweep Dixie, freeing slaves and killing any whites who resisted. Brown even tried to recruit the noted black abolitionist Frederick Douglass, who declined to participate, calling Brown's scheme "ill-advised."

Nevertheless, Brown and a small band of twenty-one men, mostly relatives and close friends, five of whom were black, marched on Harpers Ferry, arriving there on June 3, 1859. Taking an alias until he completed all his plans, he stormed the arsenal on October 16. The Brown forces took the arsenal and a local rifle factory, but townsmen sent a runner to warn the Federal government in Washington, D.C., while farmers, merchants, and white artisans penned Brown and his men inside the arsenal. Colonel Robert E. Lee led marines who rode to Harpers Ferry and attacked the enemy. The soldiers killed ten of Brown's men and captured Brown himself. Virginia authorities tried Brown for treason, conspiracy, and murder, convicting and later hanging him. Knowing that he would soon die, the fiery abolitionist used his trial as a last venue in which he could criticize and damn slavery.[20]

Brown's attack and his later trial polarized the nation. Generally, there was great alarm in the South where people came to think that most Northerners were "devils" who thought as Brown did and who would kill all white Southerners if they could. On the other hand, many Northerners, particularly abolitionists, quickly made Brown a martyr. A transcendentalist poet compared him to Jesus, another to Moses. Brown's conduct at his trial impressed many. Near the end Brown, who had devoted much of his life to freeing the nation's slaves, said that he was ready to forfeit his life in the interest of justice. Thousands of people, who might have earlier been indifferent, now believed that slavery must end.[21] The chasm between North and South grew wider.

Quickly following Brown's raid, the South was gripped with fear in the summer of 1860 when fires—supposedly set by abolitionists working in conjunction with rebellious slaves—appeared to ravage Texas and Tennessee, the former hit the hardest. Southerners became terrified of arson and rumored slave uprisings. On July 8, in Dallas, Denton, and Pilot Point, Texas, apparent acts of arson erupted almost simultaneously. The next day, a Tyler slave patrol killed a man who was supposedly trying to set fire to the downtown district. Among other places, incidents occurred in Black Jack Grove, Cherokee County; Milford, Ellis County; and Honey Grove, Fannin County. To make matters worse, in July eastern Texas experienced an oppressive heat wave. On July 8, the day of the first fires, Marshall recorded a temperature of 115 degrees.[22]

More bad news (and rumors) came fast. False reports soon had Bastrop, Jefferson, Belknap, Gainesville, Waxahachie, and most of Navarro and Kaufman counties in imaginary ashes. One story had it that folks in Waxahachie escaped carnage by hanging more than twenty guilty slaves and two white men, said to be Northern abolitionists. In other locales, whites beat an untold number of blacks after accusing them of being insurrectionists. Almost immediately more rumors were added to a few facts, and fear gripped all of eastern Texas. More horrifying reports—all of them false—were published by area newspapers depicting conspiracy and arson in Marshall, Quitman, Daingerfield, Mount Vernon, Sulphur Springs, Rusk, and Paris. But, on August 5, just before state elections, Henderson was greatly damaged by a conflagration that swept through the downtown business district—and that was fact. Authorities estimated that the fire had consumed $220,000 in property, and they hanged one white man and one black woman, who were supposedly the arsonists ,without a trial. Newspapers reported that across the region, some eighty slaves and thirty-seven whites were executed for arson and/or insurrection and that many others were subjected to the lash.[23]

As the hot summer wore on, whites became even more concerned. New rumors held that abolitionists were urging slaves to poison their masters. In many locales, vigilante groups organized to supervise slaves and to seek out abolitionists. In Tyler more than one hundred men, including the editor and staff of the *Tyler Reporter,* joined local patrols. The woebegone editor exclaimed: "We are completely worn out, and if this excitement continues to exist, we must stop our regular issues, and furnish the news in the form of extras, for it is impossible to watch all night and work all day."[24] Then, surprisingly, near the end of the summer the panic subsided almost as fast as it had begun. Sober investigations finally established that many reported burnings had been rumors only and that new unstable phosphorus matches, which in intense heat were subject to spontaneous combustion, were likely the cause of the few fires that actually occurred. And in most cases where fires started, rumor magnified damages beyond reason. As for the reports that some slaves had poisoned their masters, later investigators examined certain "poisons," which proved to be harmless home medical remedies like paregoric, whiskey, and snakeroot.[25]

Despite the eventual scientific explanation for the summer's fires, many political leaders, especially fire-eating secessionists, and many common people remained unconvinced. Many fearful people still associated fires, destruction, and terror with abolitionists and the new Northern political party, the party of Abraham Lincoln. Secessionists in Texas used that fear and terror to continue efforts to pull the Lone Star State out of the Union. Louis Wigfall, a native of South Carolina who later moved to Marshall, Texas, and became a major secessionist leader in Texas, toured and did all he could to create political discord. In his September 3 speech in Tyler, he thundered: "An enemy is in our midst not with bayonet and broad sword, but with torch and poison."[26]

Knowing that Lincoln was the Republican's presidential nominee, Wigfall added that if the rail-splitter won, he would try to finish the work that John Brown had started at Harpers Ferry. The crazed South Carolinian swore that the Texas fires represented work that was "carried on by [Lincoln's] Texas friends."[27] Wigfall was not alone in politically exploiting the imagined fires and slave plots. All over the South, hysterical newspaper editors and secessionist politicians seized on the "Texas Troubles" to win converts to the secessionist cause. An editor in Montgomery, Alabama, bemoaned the troubles and said that they were the result of *"Practical Lincolnism"*; he warned that if Lincoln won the 1860 election, "Let the people see by the light of the Texas flames, that we shall be forced . . . to go out."[28]

Just as Southern secessionists had warned, the election of 1860 became the final wedge between the Northern and Southern states. The Democrats met in April at Charleston, South Carolina, a hotbed of sedition and secession. Many Northerners believed that Douglas of Illinois was the best hope to avoid a rupture between the sections, but Southerners, led by such fire-eaters as William L. Yancey of Alabama and Wigfall of Texas, now demanded protection of slavery in the territories and statements in support of slavery itself. Douglas could not accept the Southern positions; therefore, his supporters voted the Southern proposals down, whereupon, Yancey and his fellows from Dixie bolted the convention, which then adjourned without naming a candidate.[29]

After the Democrats split, Republicans met in Chicago in mid-May. Knowing that a sectional party standing on a one-issue anti-slavery platform could not win, they drafted a document to appeal to as many people and classes as possible. On slavery, the party did not equivocate: The territories would be free, a position that drew the Free-Soilers deeper into the Republican Party. On other issues, the party promised a protective tariff for Northern industry; a homestead law for all agrarians; federal spending for internal improvements, and federal support for agricultural and mechanical schools. After agreeing on their platform, Republicans turned to the question of a candidate. New York Senator William Seward, an abolitionist, was a front-runner who led on the first ballot, but many delegates did not believe an abolitionist could poll enough votes to win. A drive for a compromise candidate began, and Abraham Lincoln of Illinois took the nomination. Born in a log cabin, a rail-splitter, "Honest Abe" was a self-educated common man who had achieved a name for himself in law. He had gained national attention when he fought Democrat Stephen Douglas for a Senate seat in 1858. Douglas won, but Lincoln emerged as a capable politician who opposed the extension of slavery and, thereby, embraced the Wilmot Proviso. Yet, he was not an extremist; he could appeal to moderates in the North.[30]

In June the Democrats met again but failed to agree. Two wings then formed. Northerners took Douglas while Southerners nominated John C. Breckinridge of Kentucky. A fourth party, the Constitutional Union Party, made up of Southern moderates, chose John Bell of Tennessee to carry its standard.[31]

With four candidates running, some analysts predicted that no one would poll a popular majority; their view was correct. Nevertheless, Lincoln—whom Southerners mislabeled a "Black Republican"—carried the North and the West and swept to a majority in the electoral college.[32] The question remained: Would Southerners, led by fire-eaters, accept him? The now well-known answer was a resounding no, but would Texas follow the secessionists or remain with the Union? Many Texans were torn by having to choose. As Walter Buenger has demonstrated, many people were ambivalent. In 1857, Sam Houston had lost his first important political race, one that apparently ended his political career, his nemesis being the rabid fire-eater Hardin Runnels. The majority of voters appeared to have been influenced by Houston's negative vote on the Kansas-Nebraska Act; they appeared ready to follow the fire-eaters. But in the 1859 state elections, Houston saved his political career by defeating Runnels in the rematch of 1857, and every voter knew that Houston was the Unionist and Runnels the secessionist. Had voters changed their minds? Were they now for the Union? They stayed with Houston even though the state elections occurred after John Brown's raid. But then came Lincoln.[33]

By 1860, secessionists in Texas were well-organized and all the KGC castles in the state were active. The fire-eaters seized on Lincoln's victory as ample cause for breaking the Union, especially after South Carolina seceded in December. They wanted the legislature to convene and consider the question of following South Carolina's lead. But Texas's secessionist leaders faced a major obstacle: Unionist Governor Sam Houston. The legislature was out of session, and, by law, only the governor could reconvene it for a special session. This, Houston refused to do, while denouncing all secessionists as traitors. The governor thus temporarily thwarted the plans of the fire-eaters.[34]

However, mass demonstrations orchestrated by secessionists had already been held in Texas, and more followed once Houston refused to take action. Again, the KGC organized many of them. Many newspaper editor-owners began whipping up the public. Said the *Corsicana Navarro Express* on November 16, 1860: "The North has gone overwhelmingly for NEGRO EQUALITY and SOUTHERN VASSALAGE! Southern men will you SUBMIT to this DEGRADATION?[35] Later, the editor added: "The doctrine of Negro Equality is about to be inaugurated [by the Federal] Government."[36] Clearly, white racism in all of Dixie was on the march. On December 22, the *Marshall Texas Republican* reported that pro-secessionist rallies had been held in fifty-three Texas counties.[37]

Emboldened by the mass demonstrations that were really staged by operatives of the fire-eaters, the state's leading secessionists knew that they needed either a state meeting or some other political vehicle to consider secession. On that question, John F. Overton of Smith County suggested that the Texas Supreme Court summon a gathering, or perhaps the people themselves could call for a conclave in another series of mass demonstrations. Overton's second idea prevailed. Soon, powerful men asserted themselves, the men including Oran Roberts, Chief Justice of the Texas Supreme Court and future governor; John S. "Rip" Ford, already a Texas institution; two other future governors, Richard Hubbard and Francis Lubbock; noted politicians and opinion molders such as William Ochiltree; and the fire-eaters Wigfall, George Chilton, Hardin Runnels, Elkanah Greer (state leader of the KGC), George M. Flournoy, W. P. Rogers, John Marshall, John C. Robertson. Roberts assumed leadership. Along with about sixty other men—some mentioned above and most members of the KGC—Roberts called for a convention to meet in Austin on January 28, 1861.[38]

In dubious elections to pick delegates to the meeting (dubious due to threats against Unionists and voice votes in many cases, where the ones who could shout the loudest won), the "people" chose 177 stalwarts who were ready to go to Austin, but Houston tried to intervene one last time. Seeing that he could not stop the convention, he finally called the legislature into session, hoping that sober heads would stop the breakaway secessionists. The legislature did just the opposite. Its members validated the coming meeting and adjourned. Convening on January 28, 1861, the delegates left no doubt that they were leading Texas out of the Union. After doing their work rapidly, the delegates voted 166 to 8 to that effect on February 1, but submitted the convention's wisdom to the people.[39] By referendum, voters would make the ultimate choice on the question of the Confederacy or the Union. There was little hope for the Union.

According to historian Randolph Campbell, the ambivalence among the people that historian Walter Buenger noted gave way to the "southern consensus."[40] The majority of white men in the consensus now believed that slavery was worth fighting and dying for even if that meant the ruin of old Dixie, ruin that white Southern men visited not only on themselves but also upon their children and grandchildren. But, of course, they could not see the future. Rather, they could only wait for Sam Houston's prophesy to come true: He said that the Union Navy would blockade the southern coasts and starve Dixie's people. The Union would take New Orleans and then split the Confederacy in a related move by taking complete control of the Mississippi River. Cotton would not be king, he said, because the masses in Europe remained most prejudiced against slavery. Finally, he averred that the North was so powerful in relation to the South, its armies eventually would win on the field and that what the Southerners were trying to protect, human slavery, would be no more.[41]

But secessionists would not listen to such sober analysis. Instead, on the day of the referendum, February 23, 1861, an overwhelming majority of 46,153 voters favored secession while only 13,020 opposed. Texas and the rest of the South did not begin to truly recover from the Civil War—the holocaust that Dixie inflicted on itself—until the New Deal and World War II eras.[42]

Notes

1   The entire text of Texas's "Declaration of Causes" is in Ernest William Winkler, ed., *Journal of the Secession Convention of Texas, 1861* (Austin, Texas: Austin Printing Company, 1912). The original is in the archives of the Texas State Library: Texas Department of State, Record Group 307. For varying older views on slavery and the war, see Edwin C. Rozwenc, ed., *Causes of the Civil War* (New York: Heath, 1963).

2   For a two-volume work that reviews the North-South struggle over several decades, see William W. Freehling, *The Road to Disunion: Secession at Bay, 1776–1854*, vol. 1 (New York: Oxford University Press, 1990), and *The Road to Disunion: Secessionists Triumphant, 1854–1861*, vol. 2 (New York: Oxford University Press, 2007). For more on slavery and the war, see Freehling, *The Reintegration of American History: Slavery and the Civil War* (New York: Oxford University Press, 1994) and James L. Huston, *Calculating the Value of the Union: Slavery, Property Rights, and the Economic Origins of the Civil War* (Chapel Hill: University of North Carolina Press, 2003). Another view on economics and slavery is found in Roger L. Ransom's *The Political Economy of Slavery, Emancipation and the American Civil War* (New York: Cambridge University Press, 1989).

3   Chandra Manning, *What This Cruel War Was Over: Soldiers, Slavery, and the Civil War* (New York: Knopf, 2007); also see James M. McPherson, *For Cause and Comrades: Why Men Fought in the Civil War* (New York: Oxford University Press, 1997).

4   A classic account of the sectional crises between 1848 and 1861 and their relation
    to slavery is David Potter's *The Impending Crisis, 1848–1861*, completed and
    edited by Donald E. Fehrenbacher (New York: Harper & Row, 1976). This essay
    follows Potter's approach.

5   For a view stressing slavery and its extension, see Michael F. Holt, *The Fate of Their
    Country: Politicians, Slavery Extension and the Coming of the Civil War* (New York:
    Hill & Wang, 2004).

6   A classic on the Compromise of 1850 is Holman Hamilton's *Prologue to Conflict:
    The Crisis and Compromise of 1850* (Lexington: University of Kentucky Press,
    1964). For brief coverage of the Texas boundary dispute and settlement, see
    Robert A. Calvert, Arnoldo De León, and Gregg Cantrell, *The History of Texas*
    (Wheeling, Illinois: Harlan Davidson, 2002), 114–15. For another brief account,
    see "The Compromise of 1850" (by Roger A. Griffin), *New Handbook of Texas*
    (Austin: Texas State Historical Association, 1996), 2:253.

7   For more on the crisis caused by the new Fugitive Slave Act, see Stanley W.
    Campbell, *The Slave Catchers: Enforcement of the Fugitive Slave Law* (Chapel Hill:
    University of North Carolina Press, 1968).

8   For the impact of Harriet Beecher Stowe and *Uncle Tom's Cabin*, see Wilma King,
    *Toward the Promised Land from 1851 to 1861: From "Uncle Tom's Cabin" to the
    Onset of Civil War* (New York: Chelsea House, 1995).

9   James Smallwood, *Born in Dixie: The History of Smith County, Texas*, 2 vols.
    (Austin, Texas: Eakin Press, 1999), 1:135–36; F. Lee Lawrence, "Richard
    Hubbard: Noble Aristocrat," *Chronicles of Smith County, Texas* 8 (Fall 1969): 1–2.
    For a brief article on Hubbard, see "Richard Bennett Hubbard, Jr." (by Jean S.
    Duncan), *New Handbook of Texas*, 3:757.

10 Smallwood, *Born in Dixie*, 1:136.

11 For the Kansas-Nebraska Act, see Gerald W. Wolff, *The Kansas-Nebraska Bill:
    Party, Section, and the Coming of Civil War* (New York: Revisionist Press, 1977).
    For a solid older work, see James C. Malin, *The Nebraska Question, 1852–1854*
    (Lawrence: University of Kansas Press, 1953).

12 For the ideology of the early Republican Party, see Eric Foner, *Free Soil, Free
    Labor, Free Men: The Ideology of the Republican Party before the Civil War*, rev. ed.
    (New York: Oxford University Press, 1995).

13 Smallwood, *Born in Dixie*, 1:137–38; Francis Richard Lubbock, *Six Decades in
    Texas; or, Memoirs of Francis Richard Lubbock, Governor of Texas in War Time,
    1861–63*, ed. C. W. Raines (Austin, Texas: Ben C. Jones & Company, 1900), 202;
    "Samuel Houston" (by Thomas H. Kreneck), *New Handbook of Texas*, 3:717–20.

14 One book on the civil war in Kansas is Nicole Etcheson's *Bleeding Kansas: Contested
    Liberty in the Civil War Era* (Lawrence: University of Kansas Press, 2004). Also see
    Thomas Goodrich, *War to the Knife: Bleeding Kansas, 1854–1861* (Mechanicsburg,
    Pennsylvania: Stackpole Books, 1998). An older work is James Rawley's *Bleeding
    Kansas and the Coming of the Civil War* (New York: Lippincott, 1969).

15 For the Brooks assault, see T. Lloyd Benson, *The Caning of Senator Sumner*
    (Belmont, California: Wadsworth, 2004). For more on Sumner, see Frederick J.

Blue, *Charles Sumner and the Conscience of the North* (Arlington Heights, Illinois: Harlan Davidson, 1994) and David Herbert Donald, *Charles Sumner and the Coming of the Civil War* (Chicago: University of Chicago Press, 1981).

16   For the Knights of the Golden Circle in the South, see Robert E. May, *The Southern Dream of a Caribbean Empire, 1854–1861* (Baton Rouge: Louisiana State University Press, 1973).

17   For the Knights of the Golden Circle in Texas, see Roy Sylvan Dunn, "The Knights of the Golden Circle in Texas," *Southwestern Historical Quarterly* (hereafter cited as *SHQ*) 70 (April 1978): 248–57 and James Smallwood, *Born in Dixie*, 1:137, 140–41, 145–49, 158, 161, 163–64, 166. For a brief account, see "Knights of the Golden Circle" (by Christopher Long), *New Handbook of Texas*, 3:1145–46.

18   For more on the Ostend Manifesto, see Thomas A. Bailey, *A Diplomatic History of the American People* (New York: Appleton-Century-Croft, 1964). Bailey's work is now dated, but it is excellent and stands the test of time.

19   For issues surrounding Dred Scott's case, see Donald Fehrenbacher, *Slavery, Law, and Politics: The Dred Scott Case* (New York: Oxford University Press, 1981). For more studies, see Jennifer Fleischer, *The Dred Scott Case: Testing the Right to Live Free* (Brookfield, Connecticut: Millbrook Press, 1997) and Earl M. Maltz, *Dred Scott and the Politics of Slavery* (Lawrence: University of Kansas Press, 2007).

20   For an overview of John Brown's raid, see Jonathan Earle's *John Brown's Raid on Harpers Ferry: A Brief History with Documents* (New York: Bedford / St. Martins, 2007).

21   Responses to John Brown's raid were varied. See Paul Finkelman, ed., *His Soul Goes Marching On: Responses to John Brown and the Harpers Ferry Raid* (Charlottesville: University of Virginia Press, 1995). Stephen B. Oates has written the classic biography of John Brown, *To Purge this Land with Blood: A Biography of John Brown* (New York: Harper & Row, 1970).

22   Vicki Betts, *Smith County, Texas in the Civil War* (Tyler, Texas: Smith County Historical Society), 28–30; *Texas State Gazette*, July 14, 1860; *Clarksville (Texas) Northern Standard*, July 14, 1860; *Bonham (Texas) Era*, July 17, 1860; *Marshall Texas Republican*, August 4, 1860; Donald Reynolds, "Smith County and Its Neighbors During the Slave Insurrection Panic of 1860," *Chronicles of Smith County, Texas* 10 (Fall 1971): 1–8; Wesley Norton, "The Methodist Episcopal Church and the Civil Disturbances in North Texas in 1859 and 1860," *SHQ* 73 (January 1965): 317–41. For a brief account of the panic, see James M. Smallwood, "Slave Insurrections," *New Handbook of Texas*, 5:1080–89; Smallwood, *Born in Dixie*, 1:151–52.

23   *Texas State Gazette*, July 28, August 11, 18, 25, September 1, 1860; *Corsicana Navarro Express*, July 28, August 11, 25, September 14, 1860; *Marshall Texas Republican*, August 11, 1860; *San Antonio Ledger and Texan*, August 4, 1860; Smallwood, *Born in Dixie*, 1:152–53.

24   *Tyler (Texas) Reporter*, quoted in Smallwood, *Born in Dixie*, 1:153.

25   *Tyler (Texas) States' Rights Sentinel*, August 18, 1860; *Marshall Texas Republican*, August 25, 1860; Reynolds, "The Slave Panic," 6–7.

26   Wigfall, quoted in Reynolds, "The Slave Panic," 8; and see *Marshall Texas Republican*, September 8, 1860. For a brief account of Wigfall's nefarious career, see "Louis T. Wigfall" (by Alvy L. King), *New Handbook of Texas*, 6:962–63.

27   Wigfall, quoted in Smallwood, *Born in Dixie*, 1:154; and see *Texas State Gazette*, September 15, 1860.

28   *Montgomery (Alabama) Weekly Mail*, August 3, 1860, and see Donald E. Reynolds, *Editors Make War: Southern Newspapers in the Secession Crisis* (Nashville: Vanderbilt University Press, 1970).

29   For brief coverage of the Democratic split, see Robert A. Calvert, Arnoldo De León, and Gregg Cantrell, *The History of Texas* (Arlington Heights, Illinois: Harlan Davidson), 117–18.

30   The best biography of Lincoln is Stephen B. Oates's *Abraham Lincoln: The Man behind the Myths* (New York: HarperCollins, 1994). Also see Oates's *With Malice toward None: A Life of Abraham Lincoln* (New York: HarperCollins, 1994).

31   Calvert, De León, Cantrell, *History of Texas*, 117–18.

32   For brief, standard coverage of Lincoln's election and Southern secession, see Jeanne Boydston et al., *Making a Nation: The United States and Its People* (Upper Saddle River, New Jersey: Prentice Hall, 2002), 412–13.

33   For the voters' uncertainties, see Walter Buenger, *Secession and the Union in Texas* (Austin: University of Texas Press, 1984).

34   Ibid., 119–40.

35   *Corsicana (Texas) Navarro Express*, November 16, 1860.

36   Ibid., November 23, 1860.

37   *Marshall Texas Republican*, December 22, 1860.

38   John W. Overton to Oran Roberts, November 5, 1860; Benjamin A. Long to John B. Long, December 8, 1860, Oran Roberts Papers, Archives, University of Texas at Austin; Dunn, "KGC in Texas," 559–60; Smallwood, *Born in Dixie*, 1:156–67.

39   For more on secession, see Buenger, *Secession and the Union in Texas*. For brief mention, see "Secession" (by Buenger), *New Handbook of Texas*, 5:957–58 and his "Secession Convention," *New Handbook of Texas*, 5:958–59.

40   Randolph B. Campbell, *A Southern Community in Crisis: Harrison County, Texas, 1850–1880* (Austin: Texas State Historical Association, 1983), 197; Smallwood, *Born in Dixie*, 1:134–35.

41   For Houston's predictions, see Edward R. Maher, "Sam Houston and Secession," *SHQ* 55 (April 1952), 452–53; Smallwood, *Born in Dixie*, 1:162.

42   See Buenger, *Secession and the Union in Texas*; "Secession" (by Buenger), *New Handbook of Texas*, 5:957–58 and his "Secession Convention," *New Handbook of Texas*, 5:958–59.

Chapter 4

The Knights of the Golden Circle in Texas, 1858–1861: An Analysis of the First (Military) Degree Knights

by Linda S. Hudson

According to Gen. George W. L. Bickley, national president of the Knights of the Golden Circle (KGC), the organization was begun by prominent Kentuckians on July 4, 1854, to aid the spread of slavery. The association was created as a reaction to the Republican Party that organized to limit the spread of slave labor into Kansas after the United States Congress passed the Kansas-Nebraska Act (1854). Republican Party propagandists during the American Civil War claimed the KGC, as it was most often called, was formed for the purpose of bringing about secession and creating a slave empire reaching from the slave states to the equator. In Texas, KGC members were pro-slavery territorial expansionists and they helped bring about secession. However, rather than being part of a larger conspiracy, these men were moved by a series of events toward secession. After Abraham Lincoln's presidential victory in November 1860, Texas Military Knights helped bring about secession to protect their expansionist goals and slave property from the abolitionist threat they thought lay ahead. Although seldom identified as KGC, Texas members played a significant role in secession. Men who were Knights led the call for a state convention, dominated the secession convention, brought about the surrender of Federal forces, and then commanded the first military units in state service.[1]

The KGC had three levels of membership: the First (Military) Degree, the Second (Financial) Degree, and the Third (Political) Degree. The Military Degree was the lowest rank; its holders took orders from higher-ranked Knights. One was invited to become a Military Knight based on one's absolute commitment to slavery. The Military Knights would receive land from any newly acquired slave territory as payment for their services. Primarily, Knights believed that northern Mexico would be their first prize of conquest. The expansionists would operate like the East India Company and control prices and production of agricultural commodities in their area. The more secret Financial Degree had editors and stockholders who invested in and promoted Knight-owned railroads, steam lines, and real estate. The highest rank and most secret degree was the Political Degree, which was made up of elected officials who would determine policies in and govern newly acquired slave territory. The least secret Military Knights can be identified because their names and activities were reported in local newspapers.[2]

In 1858, the first Military Degree Knights appeared in Texas. These Knights were expansionists and formed to aid Liberals in northern Mexico. Each family that migrated to Mexico would receive a section of land confiscated from the Catholic Church. That year Texas Military Knight Elkanah Greer of Harrison County organized local castles (branches) in Louisiana and East Texas, including one in Jefferson County where his brother-in-law John T. Holcombe lived. The wives of Smith County Military Knight Captains George Chilton, George Bates, and John C. Robertson made a flag with the KGC seal and presented it to the Tyler Guards. The flag at the Smith County Historical Museum has nineteen stripes (ten red stripes and nine white stripes) that represented existing slave states and areas that the KGC wanted to acquire for their empire of slavery. Additionally, the flag bears in the left quadrant the seal of the KGC, consisting of a golden circle surrounding a Maltese cross with a star in the center. United States Vice President John C. Breckinridge of Kentucky wore a lapel pin with the seal of the American Legion Knights of the Golden Circle, as did the editor of the *Whiteman,* John R. Baylor of Weatherford, Texas.[3]

U.S. Senator Sam Houston encouraged the expansionists in February 1858 when he submitted a resolution to the U.S. Senate for the "United States to declare and maintain an efficient protectorate over the States of Mexico, Nicaragua, Costa Rica, Guatemala, Honduras, and San Salvador." In June, Houston's Senate resolution was defeated by a vote of thirty-three to sixteen. The Texas Unionists experienced another defeat in the August state elections when an avowed secessionist, Hardin Runnels of Bowie County, defeated Houston in his bid for governor.[4]

In August 1859 General Bickley called a national convention of the KGC at the Greenbrier Hotel in White Sulfur Springs, Virginia. A Little Rock, Arkansas, reporter estimated that from eighty to one hundred individuals attended the meeting, including the leading political and military men of the day. The reporter was allowed to remain as long as discussion was about steamship and railroad companies and Mexico, but when the discussion turned to disunion he was asked to leave. Looking to further his ambitions, former Texas Ranger and U.S. Marshal Ben McCulloch attended this Knight convention as did Governor Runnels. Back in Texas, Houston, as a Unionist candidate, unseated the incumbent Runnels and became the next governor of Texas.[5]

After October 1859, the number of Texas Knight castles grew when the abolitionist-financed John Brown raided the Harpers Ferry Arsenal in Virginia to arm slaves for an uprising that was to spread across the slave states. By spring 1860 twenty-one Texas cities had castles that drew members from across county lines. Knights still promoted their plans for Mexico, but also they would defend their local communities against the enemies of slavery.[6]

In spring 1860, Elkanah Greer was general and grand commander of the Texas division of 4,000 Military Knights as part of the KGC that would support President James Buchanan's Mexican intervention policy of protecting U.S. transit routes across Mexico. Houston and others believed cooperation with the Knights and the success of the Mexico venture would make him president of the United States. The Knights thought they would soon enter Mexico and absorb these areas. They drilled on county squares and had suppers provided by local ladies with gala sendoffs and patriotic speeches reported in local newspapers. Knights were feted and promoted by local editors along their route toward the Rio Grande. At least twenty Texas Knight groups traveled toward South Texas where they were to join other Knights gathering from across the nation.[7]

The most common characteristic of Texas Military Knights was that they had served in the Mexican War. The end of the war in 1848 did not end the desire of the veterans to have the land they once conquered. In 1851 future Knight and Texas Ranger John S. "Rip" Ford led Texans in northern Mexico with José María de Jesús Carvajal when he attempted to break the northern states away from central Mexico. In 1852 Texans held a fair in Corpus Christi to raise money for Carvajal's cause. Evidence suggests that in 1860 Mexican governors Santiago Vidaurri and Manuel Doblado and the Cuban José A. Quintero cooperated with Knights.[8]

In early 1860 Ben McCulloch was Houston's liaison with United States Secretary of War John B. Floyd to coordinate the efforts of the U.S. military and Greer's Knights for a spring expedition into Mexico. By mid-March it was evident that the worst drought in decades had dried up waterholes and withered grass along the proposed route. After conferring with Greer and others, Houston postponed the venture and ordered Knights camped along the Mexican border to disband. The Knights from other states gathered at New Orleans wanted to continue to Mexico. They published a notice stating that Bickley was a fraud and they wanted him removed as president of the organization.[9]

Bickley called a national KGC convention in early May 1860 in Raleigh, North Carolina. Texas KGC General Greer and Maj. Sam J. Richardson of Van Zandt County attended this meeting along with representatives from twelve other Southern states. At this convention the goals of the Knights became more sectional. In the *Address to the Citizens of the Southern States* published in May 1860, Bickley stated that the Knights' purpose was to aid their "section of the country, in or out of the Union." This was a change in policy from the KGC bylaws published in 1859. *Rules, Regulations, and Principles of the K. G. C.* advocated that peonage would spread back into the states from Mexico, and thereby end slavery and the sectional issue.[10]

The expansionist Knights suffered yet another defeat in May 1860. After debate from January to May, the United States Senate failed to confirm a "treaty of transit and commerce" with the Republic of Mexico made by the Buchanan administration. The agreement would have given the United States three possible transit routes through Mexico protected by United States troops. It would have opened the door for United States legal migration into Mexico. Thus, the United States would have been able to intervene without consent of the Benito Juárez government or local authorities. Additionally, the treaty would have paid Mexico $4 million as compensation, with one half of the amount paid to Mexico and the other half paid to American citizens with claims against Mexico. The Republicans saw the agreements as another plot to extend slavery and increase the power of the slave states in Congress and pro-secessionists in Congress saw it as a way of maintaining the Union.[11]

The Texas KGC gained membership after the summer of 1860 when a series of unexplained fires broke out in nine North Texas cities. Radical editors blamed abolitionists. Slaves were beaten and confessed to crimes of arson and poisoning. In the panic that followed, fifty-six black and white men were executed by vigilance committees. Houston believed that the slave plots sensationalized in the press were for the political purpose of electing radical Democrats to state office in the upcoming statewide elections, speculating that many voters would stay home to protect their property. The fires caused fear, increased acceptance of secession as a way to maintain safety, and resulted in the formation of more castles throughout Texas. In October Bickley and his son Charles came to Texas along with KGC national secretary Virginius D. Groner of Virginia. In November, following the election of Abraham Lincoln as president, Knights formed additional castles, believing that Lincoln's position on slavery would lead to armed conflict between the Northern and Southern states. Twenty Texas newspaper editors promoted Knight membership and published the names of local recruiters and state officers.[12]

It would seem that Texas KGC leaders promoted secession to protect their slaveholding interests since the most active phase of recruitment followed the election of Lincoln. While at least twenty Knight castles existed before his election, an additional twenty-nine groups formed or reorganized afterward. Yet 52 percent of original Military Knight officers owned slaves compared to 38 percent of Military Knight officers who organized groups after the election. As a whole, a higher percentage of Knights owned slaves in comparison to the 28 percent of the Texas population that owned slaves according to the 1860 U.S. Census.[13]

The Texas Knights were involved in every aspect of secession. Cameron County Knight John S. "Rip" Ford helped draft the "Call for Secession" in which 100 percent of the draftees came from counties with Knight castles. One hundred percent of the signers of the "Call for a Convention of the People" came from counties with Knight castles or with castles in adjoining counties. Although ninety-three, or 53 percent, of the secession convention delegates came from counties with Knight castles, sixty-seven, or 37 percent, had castles in counties contiguous to their home county. Convention delegates were elected by state representative districts, and seventy-five (96 percent) of the seventy-eight districts had Knight castles. One hundred percent of the convention officers came from counties with Knight groups. The president of the secession convention, Texas Supreme Court Chief Justice Oran M. Roberts of Smith County, appointed Smith County Knight Capt. John C. Robertson as chair of the Committee of Public Safety in charge of disarming and removing Federal troops from Texas.[14]

The Harvard University-educated Robertson was authorized by the legislature, the governor, and the convention to carry out the physical aspects of secession. Robertson divided Texas into three military districts headed by Military Knight Colonels Henry E. McCulloch of the Northwest District, Ben McCulloch of the Middle Division, and John S. "Rip" Ford of the Rio Grande District. Robertson directed Ben McCulloch to call an armed force of volun-

Illustration 3   The surrender of ex-General Twiggs, late of the United States Army, to the Texan troops in the Gran Plaza, San Antonio, Texas. February 16, 1861. *Originally published in* Harper's Weekly, *March 23, 1861.*

teers to meet at his brother Henry McCulloch's home in Seguin. When U.S. Army Gen. David E. Twiggs refused to turn over the Federal forts to the Committee of Public Safety, commissioners of that body, including Sam Maverick, Thomas J. Devine, and Philip N. Luckett sent for Ben McCulloch and his men. On February 16, well-disciplined volunteers, led by Knight castle officers from Gonzales, Guadalupe, Caldwell, Atascosa, Comal, Medina, DeWitt, and Fayette counties, joined 150 Knights from three Bexar County castles and surrounded the U.S. Army headquarters and 160 Federal troops. The *Austin State Gazette* listed the participating castles and their captains and the *San Antonio Ledger and Texan* stated that four-fifths of the 1,100 volunteers that ultimately gathered in San Antonio were Knights. After two days of tense negotiations with military authorities, McCulloch, Maverick, Devine, and Luckett, all from Knight counties, concluded the surrender by General Twiggs to the State of Texas of twenty-one Federal forts; 2,680 men; and Federal property in Texas valued at $3 million, spread over 1,200 miles of terrain. KGC Middle Division castle officers took temporary control of the San Antonio headquarters and Forts Davis, Lancaster, Mason, Inge, Duncan, and Clark, and Camps Stockton, Hudson, Verde, and Wood. Ben McCulloch reported to Robertson and to former U.S. Representative John H. Reagan and U.S. Senator Louis T. Wigfall, both from counties with KGC, and both attending meetings at the CSA provisional capital in Montgomery, Alabama.[15]

While Ben McCulloch led KGC volunteers from Central Texas, Colonel Ford traveled from Austin to Houston to Galveston assisted by Knight Majors Hugh McLeod and Thomas S. Lubbock. On February 19, Knights from Harris, Galveston, Fort Bend, and Brazoria counties were transported from Galveston to the mouth of the Rio Grande by steamer. U.S. Army Capt. Bennett H. Hill at Fort Brown resisted surrender and Ford sent for additional volunteers. Knights arrived by steamer and by land on March 2 from Jefferson, Liberty, Harris, Nueces, Galveston, and San Patricio counties. Ford had 1,500 men under his command when Commissioner Ebenezar B. Nichols negotiated state control of Forts Brown, Duncan, McIntosh, Ringgold Barracks, Brazos Santiago, and Camp Rio Grande. Ford's men who remained on the Rio Grande came from Knight counties and formed the Second Regiment, Texas Mounted Riflemen. Ford warned his superiors that it was not the time to become embroiled with Mexico as Lincoln would check the expansion of the South in that direction.[16]

While Knights traveled to San Antonio and to the Rio Grande to take control of Federal property, Col. Henry McCulloch rode from Austin on February 11 toward the northwest and Indian Territory. He sent word to Captains Thomas C. Frost, Robert B. Halley, James B. Barry, Harris A. Hamner, and Davie C. Cowan to raise 100 men each and meet him in Brown County. In the sparsely settled frontier, instead of 500 men, only 200, from Bell, Coryell, Comanche,

Bosque, San Saba, and Brown counties, gathered under Lieutenant James Cunningham. At Camp Colorado, Col. Edmund Kirby Smith surrendered Federal property under his authority. Unlike his brother, Henry McCulloch had poorly disciplined volunteers. Instead of waiting for orders, Hamner and Knights from Parker, Tarrant, Dallas, and other counties drove troops from Camp Cooper and did not secure the fort or Federal property for the state. Lt. Cryll Miller of the Lancaster KGC took the U.S. flag from Camp Cooper to *Dallas Herald* secessionist editor Charles Pryor as a memento of the first U.S. flag surrendered to the State of Texas. Knight Baylor returned from a buffalo hunt with his men exhausted and their horses broken down. Because of Indian raids, few men in the area had horses other than the two companies of Rangers under Captains William C. Dalrymple and Aaron B. Burleson sent out earlier by Governor Houston to protect settlers from Indians. The Rangers tendered their service to the new authority and McCulloch enlisted four companies of volunteers to protect Federal property and issued a call for more men. Additional volunteers from the Knight counties of Bexar, Travis, Gonzales, Rusk, and Lamar came to the frontier settlements and served in the First Regiment, Texas Mounted Riflemen.[17]

Governor Houston was confident that Texans would maintain their independence after secession and he communicated with Twiggs and authorized an orderly transition of power from federal to state authority. While Knights, Rangers, and local militias took over the defense of Texas, KGC Maj. John A. Wilcox moved that the secession convention authorize seven members to represent Texas in the Provisional Congress of Slave States meeting at Montgomery, Alabama. These representatives all came from counties with Military Knights or castles in adjoining counties. Knight Samuel A. Lockridge was the official courier between Montgomery and Austin. After the convention voted for Texas to join the Confederate States of America, it was Smith County Knight Chilton who took the message to Governor Houston requiring his allegiance to the Confederate States of America.[18]

The KGC enforced secession in Texas and any open criticism brought negative consequences. The Galveston German newspaper *Die Union* was shut down in January and in May *San Antonio Alamo Express* editor James P. Newcomb found his print shop burned and his press thrown into the San Antonio River. Other Unionists left the state or kept quiet. Public Safety Commissioner to Indian Territory James Bourland counted 120 wagons of families headed north to Kansas. Old-time Texas Ranger Noah Smithwick wrote of intimidation and of seeing hundreds of wagons on the trail as he fled westward to California. Mrs. Houston feared for the life of her husband who was watched by Knights Thomas S. Cook and William W. Montgomery. Texas voters seemed to accept the actions of the convention, but historian Roy Sylvan Dunn studied voting patterns and found that counties with castles had larger percentages of votes for secession and fewer eligible voters casting ballots.[19]

Bickley once stated that Texas had an army of 8,000 Knights ready to enter Mexico. Professor Henry A. Tatum of Eagle Lake, who served as state secretary of the February 1861 KGC state convention at the Alamo, confirmed the same number of Knights in Texas. After the convention new castles reported to George Chilton, who had been promoted to the rank of major, in the Eastern District and to Major Wilcox in the Western District. With the firing on Fort Sumter and Lincoln's call for volunteers to suppress the rebellion, Chilton ordered the captains of each Texas castle to meet in Galveston on May 1, 1861, with complete muster rolls and to hold themselves in readiness for immediate orders. Bickley was in Kentucky organizing castles, but alerted KGC leaders in Southern states to await orders. Additional Texas castles formed and on May 1, 1861, General Bickley wrote from Kentucky that Texas Knights were to respond fully and promptly to their KGC commanders, Chilton , Ford, Wilcox, and Tom Green. At this point, many of the Military Knights received official commissions in the Confederate army, which often did not correspond with their ranks in the KGC. In March, Ben McCulloch became a Confederate general and Henry McCulloch and Ford became Confederate colonels, charged with guarding the frontier and Mexican border. In May, Greer was commissioned a colonel in the Confederate army to raise the Third Texas Cavalry, with Chilton major of the regiment. In June, Knights from North and East Texas counties were mustered into Greer's command at Dallas. In Richmond, former national secretary of the KGC Virginius Groner assigned numerical designations to all Confederate units.[20]

John R. Baylor became lieutenant colonel of the Second Texas Cavalry to patrol the upper Rio Grande. In July 1861 Baylor took his men from El Paso into New Mexico and declared all territory south of the 34th parallel as Confederate Arizona. With himself as governor, Baylor planned to capture the Southwest all the way to the Pacific for the Confederacy. Across Texas, armed and equipped Knights joined cavalry, infantry, and artillery regiments according to pre-arranged plans to Americanize northern Mexico. The last known Texas castle was formed in August 1861 by Capt. Frederick G. Weiselberg in Castroville, Medina County. Instead of fulfilling the Knights' plan for Mexican territory, Confederate leaders asked Governor Ed Clark for 8,000 Texas volunteers to help defend the Confederate States of America. Local castles became the basis for the first military units around which 24,448 Texans volunteered in 1861 for military service.[21]

The KGC in Texas reached its apex in public opinion during summer 1861. Hugh McLeod and Jeremiah Y. Dashiell as editors of the *San Antonio Daily Ledger and Texan* praised the Knights for tendering a tremendous service to the state of Texas. By disarming and removing U.S troops they prevented the war from being fought in Texas. As support for the war faded and martial law, shortages, and the reality of war set in, Knights ceased to be heroes and instead were held responsible for secession, for local retributions against loyal citizens, and for the hardships of the war.[22]

Quantitative evidence suggest that state officers and captains of the lowest-ranking First Degree, or Military, Texas Knights remained lifelong residents of Texas. They were well-educated, middle-class, urban professionals who held elected and appointed local, state, and national leadership positions before, during, and after the Civil War. Although believed to be a secret organization, the Texas Military Knights were as open about their membership as they were about their plans for Mexico. San Antonio, the largest Texas city, had a population of 8,000 with three marching and drilling KGC units. Only fifteen Texas cities had populations of more than 1,000 in 1860, and with Knights from sixty counties drilling and published notices of meetings in local newspapers, a better description of the membership and its goals in 1860 would be exclusive rather than secret.[23]

The age of the average Texas Military Knight leader was 35.5 years old, slightly younger than the Texas male average of 39 years. They represented twenty-three different occupational groups. On average, Knight leaders had lived in Texas a minimum of five years by 1860, but sixteen had lived in Texas for more than fifteen years. When compared to the general Texas population, the Military Knight leader was twice as likely to be urban, and thirteen times more likely to hold political office in his lifetime. In 1860, he was five times more likely to have a profession and two times more likely to be engaged in commerce than the general Texas population.[24]

The Texas Military Knight leaders were not crude frontiersmen. Sixty-eight percent of the leaders graduated from an institute when 37.5 percent of white male Texans could not read or write. An additional 28.5 percent of the leaders had college and university degrees from the universities of Paris and Edinburgh, Transylvania, Pennsylvania, Harvard, William and Mary, and Princeton. Three-fourths of the Knight military leaders were Mexican War veterans, married (72 percent), and Southern-born (75 percent) with slightly less than half born in the Upper and slightly more than half born in the Lower South. Ten were natives of Tennessee, seven migrated directly from Tennessee, while at least ten others migrated to Texas via Mississippi. Foreign-born were a highly visible group and made up 19 percent of the leaders, with the remaining (5.8 percent) Knights born in Pennsylvania, New York, Indiana, and Illinois.[25]

Military Knight leaders tended to be wealthier than the average Texan. Yet, half (twenty-six) fell solidly into the middle class, eleven were poor, and the thirteen wealthiest Knights held 75 percent of all Knight wealth. The average Knight owned $5,000 in real estate, compared to $2,700 statewide. He had $8,400 in personal property, compared to $2,700 average statewide, and held 8.2 slaves per slaveholding household, slightly less than the 8.3 average per slaveholding household statewide. On the other hand, he owned half as much land, on average 34 improved acres, or about half the 66.5 acres statewide average, and had a total worth of $12,000 when the general population averaged about half that amount at $6,393. Wealth can be better understood when grouped according to middle-, upper-, and lower-class wealth. Half, or twenty-six leaders, fell solidly into the Texas middle class with a worth ranging from $500 to $19,999. The thirteen richest leaders, worth more than $20,000, held a 77.7 percent share of all wealth. Age, ranging from twenty to sixty-eight years, was more of a determining factor of wealth than rank. Eleven Knight leaders were in the lower-class category of less than $500 in taxable wealth. Greer had no declared wealth in 1860, but declared $10,470 on county tax rolls in 1861. According to the 1860 population census, Greer, his wife, and children lived with Frances Van Zandt, the nearest neighbor to Greer's father-in-law, Beverley L. Holcolmbe of Wylucing Plantation.[26]

Ninety-four percent of the Military Knight leaders had their names published in relation to some type of secession activity. After secession, but prior to Texas joining the Confederacy, 92 percent of the leaders joined the First or Second Texas Mounted Rifles for three-, six-, and twelve-month periods, after which 81 percent joined Confederate regiments where 65 percent served in the Trans-Mississippi Department.[27]

Knight castles did not automatically become Confederate companies, but three leaders and their companies joined Terry's Eighth Texas Cavalry; two leaders and their companies joined Hood's Eighth Texas Infantry; William Edgar's Alamo Knights became the First Texas Light Artillery; and Trevanion Teel's Knights became Teel's Battery, Second Regiment Texas Mounted Rifles. Nineteen percent of the Knights served in military staff positions, 52 percent served in the cavalry, 25 percent in the infantry, 6 percent in the artillery, and almost 10 percent served in Confederate state or national government. The most Knight leaders associated with any one regiment were the eight who served at one time or another, but not concurrently, under Ford along the Mexican border.[28]

Knight leaders did not retain their rank in Confederate service. Out of the fifty-five Military Degree captains, forty-five enlisted in Confederate military service. A little more than 40 percent (40.5 percent) served as privates and 42 percent served as captains or higher throughout the war. The remaining former Knights, 17 percent, would earn a higher rank. The McCullochs, Greer, and Green became Confederate generals; James Duff, Thomas Lubbock, William Redwood, and John S. Ford were CSA colonels; Chilton, Alfred Hobby, John B. Jones, Sam Lockridge, and Trevanion Teel were majors. Although Confederate service records were hardly kept after 1864, at least sixteen former Knight captains served until Federal troops arrived in Texas in 1865 and they received honorable paroles from the Federal officers.[29]

Some Knights lost their lives in battle, some were traumatized by the war, and some fled to Mexico at war's end. Ben McCulloch, Tom Green, Aaron D. Harris, and Sam Lockridge died in battle; Thomas Lubbock died of typhoid fever; and John A. Wilcox died of apoplexy in the Confederate Congress. San Antonio merchant James Vance went insane and Decimus U. Barziza died of cirrhosis at forty-four years of age. Greer and Bates were said to sit and say little while their wives operated their homes as boardinghouses. Alexander W. Terrell, John Henry Brown, Philip N. Luckett, Ed Clark, Pendleton Murrah, and William P. Hardeman fled to Mexico for a few years, while Luckett and Thomas J. Devine were indicted for treason, held in prison awaiting trial, and eventually pardoned.[30]

The majority of Military Knights put the past and the KGC behind them. They redeemed the state from Republicans in 1873 and led their local communities and the state into the New South era where a few expansionist Knight ideas prevailed. For example, racial segregation was enforced, most former field slaves served in peonage as sharecroppers, but a vocational and trade school taught skills to ambitious black men and women, and railroad lines connected the Texas coast to the Pacific through northern Mexico.[31]

In time former Knights resumed leadership roles. William Edgar became a consulate officer in Mexico, William Baker served as mayor of Houston, Charles Bickley wrote for newspapers in Austin and Houston, George Cupples was the first physician to use anesthetics in Texas, and John B. Jones as adjunct general of the Rangers formed the Frontier Battalion of Texas Rangers. Dr. Weiselberg modernized the state insane asylum, John Lubbock was the first fish commissioner for the forerunner of the Parks and Wildlife Department, Ford turned the Texas Deaf and Dumb Asylum into a trade school, and he and Oran Roberts helped found the Texas State Historical Association. Though much is known about the secret organization, many questions about the true ambitions of the KGC remain unanswered because Knights took their secrets to the grave. Before his death in 1895, Dr. Cupples, former statewide Knight officer, surgeon in the Seventh Texas Mounted Volunteers, and one of the longest-living Knights refused to discuss the KGC with an interviewer, simply stating that was a story that would never be told.[32]

Notes

1   Ollinger Crenshaw, "The Knights of the Golden Circle: The Career of George Bickley," *American Historical Review* 47 (October 1941): 34–38 (hereafter cited as Crenshaw, "Bickley," *AHR*); *An Authentic Exposition of the K. G. C., or a His-*

tory of Secession by a Member of the Order (Philadelphia: T. B. Peterson & Bro., 1861); Edmund Wright [pseud.], *Narrative of Edmund Wright; His Adventure in, and Escape from The Knights of the Golden Circle, "Truth is Stranger than Fiction"* (Cincinnati: J. R. Hawley, 1864); R. H. Williams, *With the Border Ruffians: Memories of the Far West 1852–1868*, ed. E. W. Williams, historical notes by Arthur J. Mayer and Joseph W. Snell (London: Murray, 1907; repr., Lincoln: University of Nebraska Press, 1982), 298; Walter L. Buenger, "Texas and the Riddle of Texas Secession," *Southwestern Historical Quarterly* (hereafter cited as *SHQ*) 87, (October 1983): 152, 174; Roy Sylvan Dunn, "The Knights of the Golden Circle in Texas 1860–1861," *SHQ* 70, (April 1967): 543, 570–71; Robert May, *The Southern Dream of a Caribbean Empire, 1854–1861* (Baton Rouge: Louisiana State University Press, 1973), 11, 136, 149–161, 179; E. W. Winkler, ed., *Journal of the Secession Convention of Texas 1861* (Austin: State Library, 1912), 277n3.

2   Crenshaw, "Bickley," *AHR*, 34–35; George W. L. Bickley, *Address to the Citizens of the Southern States by order of the Convention of the KGC held at Raleigh, North Carolina, May 7–11, 1860*, pamphlet attached to back cover of *K. G. C.: An Authentic Exposition of the Origins, Objects, and Secret Work of the Organization Known as the Knights of the Golden Circle* (n.p.: U.S. National U. C., 1862), 19, 28.

3   The Harrison County Courthouse monument states: "Elkanah Greer was Grand Commander of the Knights of the Golden Circle in Texas organized 1854. This secret order meant to extend slaveholding territories. The Golden Circle centered in Havana and had a 1200 miles radius. Member Knights lived, however, in such remote places as New York and California. Tobacco, sugar, cotton, and possibly rice and coffee were to be the world trade monopoly of the Golden Circle. In first expansion attempt in 1860, failed to take Mexico. 1861–1865 in Texas Golden Circle Knights formed military units, guarded captured forts, and helped expel subversives. The Civil War swallowed up the activities of the Knights of the Golden Circle. Memorial to Texans who served the Confederacy. Erected by the State of Texas, 1964." William H. Bell, in "Knights of the Golden Circle: Its Organization and Activities in Texas prior to the Civil War" (master's thesis, Texas College of Arts and Industries, August 1965) lists castles; Linda S. Hudson, in "Military Knights of the Golden Circle in Texas, 1854–1861" (master's thesis, Stephen F. Austin State University, 1990) lists individuals; Elizabeth Wittenmyer Lewis, *Queen of the Confederacy: The Innocent Deceits of Lucy Holcombe Pickens,* (Denton: University of North Texas Press, 2002), 60–61; KGC flag, Smith County Carnegie Historical Museum (also known as the Carnegie History Center), Tyler, Texas; Wright, *Narrative,* 55; Jerry Thompson, *Colonel John R. Baylor: Texas Indian Fighter and Confederate Soldier* (Hillsboro: Hill Junior College Press, 1971), 5–6, 8–11, 24–34.

4   U.S. Senate, *Journal of the Senate of the United States of America*, 35th Congress, 1st sess., February 16, 1858, 189; U.S. Senate, *Journal of the Executive Proceedings of the Senate of the United States of America*, 36th Congress, 1st sess., May 31, 1860, 199.

5   C. A. Bridges, "The Knights of the Golden Circle: A Filibustering Fantasy," *SHQ* 44 (January 1941): 291; Thomas W. Cutrer, *Ben McCulloch and the Frontier Military Tradition* (Chapel Hill: University of North Carolina Press, 1993), 164; "K. G. C.," *Arkansas True Democrat,* September 7, 1859.

6   Bell, "KGC," 72–86; Hudson, "Military Knights," 124–25. In the spring of 1860 Knights were located in Bexar, Bowie, Cherokee, Collin, Colorado, Dallas, Galveston, Guadalupe, Harris, Harrison, Hopkins, Hunt, Jefferson, Marion, Nueces, Rusk, Smith, Travis, Walker, and Washington counties.

7   Sam Houston, *The Writings of Sam Houston, 1813–1863* (Austin: University of Texas Press, 1938–1943), 7:473, 475, 495; Jack W. Gunn, "Ben McCulloch: A Big Captain," *SHQ* 58 (July 1954): 15; Walter Prescott Webb, *The Texas Rangers* (Austin: University of Texas Press, 1935), 197; "K. G. C.," *Dallas Herald,* March 28, 1860; "Americanizing Mexico," reprinted from *Sulphur Springs Monitor, New York Times,* March 23, 1860; "Some of Uncle Sam's Boys Want Another Slice of Mexico," *Harrison (County) Flag,* October 1, 1858; "God Speed the KGC," *Lexington (Kentucky) Statesman,* March 6, 1860; "Heed the Destiny in Palm of Hand," *Norfolk (Virginia) Daybook,* March 9, 1860; "KGC in Texas, California and Mexico," *New Orleans Crescent,* May 8, 1860; H. L. Wilson, "President Buchanan's Proposed Intervention in Mexico," *American Historical Review* 5 (1900): 687–701; "To Support Mexican Leaders," *Little Rock Arkansas True Democrat,* March 21, 1860; "KGC in Brownsville," *New Orleans Daily Picayune,* April 11, 1860; "K. G. C," *San Antonio Daily Ledger and Texan,* April 17, 1860. Texas KGC from Cass, Hopkins, Hunt, Smith, Harrison, Marion, Bowie, Upshur, Cherokee, Rusk, Van Zandt, and Dallas counties joined Knights from Travis, Bexar, Harris, Galveston, Nueces, Bastrop, Colorado, Fayette, Karnes, Walker, Guadalupe, and Gonzales counties and camped in Gonzales, Nueces, and Cameron counties.

8   Charles D. Spurlin, comp., *Texas Veterans in the Mexican War* (Nacogdoches, Texas: Ericson Books, n.d.); John D. P. Fuller, *The Movement for the Acquisition of All Mexico* (Baltimore: Johns Hopkins Press, 1936; repr., New York: Da Capo Press, 1969), 58, 82, 93, 99; Frederick Merk, *Manifest Destiny and Mission in American History: A Reinterpretation* (New York: Vintage Books, 1963), 125, 131, 137, 181; John Salmon Ford, *Rip Ford's Texas,* ed., Stephen B. Oates (Austin: University of Texas Press, 1963; repr., 1987), 196–97, 204, 215; Robert E. May, *Manifest Destiny's Underworld: Filibustering in Antebellum America* (Chapel Hill: University of North Carolina Press, 2002), 45; Bridges, "Filibustering Fantasy," *SHQ,* 291, 294.

9   Houston, *Writings,* 7:473, 475, 495; Gunn, "Ben McCulloch," *SHQ,* 15; Crenshaw, "Bickley," *AHR,* 27, 39, 43.

10   In attendance: Maj. Charles Bickley, Kentucky; Gen. George Bickley, president of the American Legion; Maj. H. C. Castellanos, civil commandant of the Second Louisiana Regiment; Col. John J. Cook, Montgomery, Alabama; Col. James E. Cureton, Lancaster Court House, South Carolina; Col. F. W. Dillard, Columbus, Georgia; John R. W. Dunbar, surgeon general, Virginia; Colonel Greenborough, commander of Alabama and Louisiana KGC.; Gen. Elkanah Greer, Maj. Sam

Richardson, Texas KGC; Col. V. D. Groner, secretary, KGC, Norfolk, Virginia; Col. Ben M. Harney, Louisville, Kentucky; Maj. J. Ross Howard, secretary of May 1860 convention; William H. Judah, Florida; Captain Lindsay, Virginia; A. J. McAlpin, Raleigh, North Carolina; A. McGibbony, police general, KGC; Mr. Phillips, Baltimore, Maryland; Gen. N. J. Scott, treasurer and paymaster general, Auburn, Alabama; Gen. Paul Semmes, Georgia; the Rev. Dr. Isaac Spangler, chaplain general, Virginia; Col. James H. R. Taylor, Holly Springs, Mississippi; William H. Tolar, Little Rock, Arkansas; Col. R. C. Tyler, chair of May 1860 convention and quartermaster general, Baltimore, Maryland; Col. John L. Walker, Charles City Court House, Virginia; J. Morris Wampler, engineer general, Maryland; Philip D. Woodhouse, Norfolk, Virginia; Maj. William G. Yeager, Baltimore, Maryland. *Military Department Laws, Rules, Regulations, and Principles of the KGC* (Washington, D.C.: 1859), Bickley Papers, George W. L. Bickley, National Archives and Records Service, Washington: General Services Admin., microfilm, Southwest Collection, Texas Tech University.

11   William S. Holt, *Treaties Defeated by the Senate: A Study of the Struggle between the President and Senate over the Conduct of Foreign Relations* (Baltimore: Johns Hopkins Press, 1933), 91–97; Wilson, "Buchanan's Intervention," *AHR*: 698–99; Agustín Cué Cánovas, *El Tratado McLane-Ocampo: Juarez, los Estados Unidos y Europa* (México: Editorial América Nueva, 1956), 113, 121, 151, 156.

12   David Stroud, *Flames and Vengeance: The East Texas Fires and the Presidential Election of 1860* (Kilgore, Texas: Pinecrest, 1992), 108; Donald E. Reynolds, *Editors Make War: Southern Newspapers in the Secession Crisis* (Nashville: University of Tennessee Press, 1966), 4–9; 97–113, 137, 175; *Handbook of Texas Online*, s.v. "Texas Troubles" (by Donald E. Reynolds), http://www.tshaonline.org/handbook/online/articles/TT/vetbr.html; Randy Sparks, "John P. Osterhout: Yankee, Rebel, Republican," *SHQ* 90 (October 1986): 111–38; Marilyn Sibley, *Lone Stars and State Gazettes: Texas Newspapers before the Civil War* (College Station: Texas A&M University Press, 1983), 267, 270; Jimmie Hicks, "Some Letters Concerning the Knights of the Golden Circle in Texas, 1860–1861," *SHQ* 65 (July 1961): 80–86. Newspapers affiliated with KGC were located in Austin, Bastrop, Bellville, Belton, Brenham, Clarksville, Columbus, Corpus Christi, Galveston, Houston, Indianola, Jefferson, McKinney, Marshall, Palestine, San Antonio, Seguin, Tyler, and Weatherford. Crenshaw, "Bickley," *AHR*, 38; "K. G. C.," Richmond *Daily Whig*, July 18, 1860.

13   U.S. Bureau of the Census, *Eighth Census, 1860; Schedule I, Population; Schedule II Agriculture Census; and Schedule IV, Slave Census* (hereafter cited as *U.S. Census, 1860*); Randolph B. Campbell and Richard G. Lowe, *Wealth and Power in Antebellum Texas* (College Station: Texas A & M University Press, 1977), 30, 39, 45, 59. There were 182,566 slaves in Texas with 21,878 slaveholders averaging 8.3 slaves for each household. Some researchers divide total white population by the number of slaveholders, showing that only 5 percent of the population owned slaves, but a more accurate calculation is to divide the 76,781 heads of household by the number of slaveholders, revealing that 28 percent of Texas families held slaves.

14 Winkler, ed., *Journal of the Secession Convention*, 9–13, 21–22, 88–90.

15 Ibid., 277; *Handbook of Texas Online*, s. v. "John C. Robertson" (by Thomas W. Cutrer), http://www.tsha.utexas.edu/handbook/online/articles/RR/fro29.html; "Knights Wielded Great Power," San Antonio *Daily Ledger and Texan*, May 27, 1861; "The Texas Surrender: A Summary of Events and Correspondence of Union and State Officials," February 19, 1861–May 10, 1861, U.S War Dept., *The War of the Rebellion: A Compilation of the Official Records of the Union and Confederate Armies* (hereafter cited as *OR*), comp. Robert N. Scott (Washington, D.C.: U.S. Government Printing Office, 1880–1901), 2, 1:1–104; "Reports, Correspondence, etc., between Headquarters of the Army and General Twiggs," January 2, 1861–May 14, 1861, *OR*, 1, 1:547–636,

16 Winkler, ed., *Journal of the Secession Convention*, 320–34, 394–98; Ford, *Rip Ford's Texas*, 313–28, 393; B. H. Hill, captain, February 19, 24, 1861, *OR*, 1, 1:591–93.

17 Winkler, ed., *Journal of the Secession Convention*, 366–84; "Camp Cooper," *Dallas Herald*, March 13, 1861; A. B. Burleson, February 24, 1861, *OR*, 1, 1: 591–93.

18 Sam Houston, January 7, 1861, *OR*, 4, 1:72–76; D. E. Twiggs, January 15, 1861, *OR*, 1, 1:581–83; E. W. Cave, March 13, 1861, *OR*, 1, 1:611–13; Winkler, ed., *Journal of the Secession Convention*, 74, 178–79, 209, 305.

19 Dale A. Somers, "James P. Newcomb: The Making of a Radical," *SHQ* (April 1969): 459–60; C. Alwyn Barr, "The Making of a Secessionist: The Antebellum Career of Roger Q. Mills," *SHQ* (October 1975): 141; James Bourland, April 23, 1861, *OR*, 4, 1:324–25; Noah Smithwick, *The Evolution of a State or Recollection of Old Texas Days* (Austin: University of Texas Press, 1983), 250–63; Madge Thornall Roberts, *Star of Destiny: The Private Life of Sam and Margaret Houston* (Denton: University of North Texas Press, 1993), 293; Buenger, "Riddle of Secession," *SHQ*, 174–75; Dunn, "KGC in Texas," *SHQ*, 566.

20 Crenshaw, "Bickley," *AHR*, 43; Stephen B. Oates, "Recruiting Confederate Cavalry in Texas," *SHQ* 64 (April 1961), 462, 465; Dunn, "KGC in Texas," *SHQ*, 553; "Headquarters, Army of K. G. C." *Memphis Daily Appeal*, May 7, 1861; "Knights of the Golden Circle," *Little Rock Arkansas True Democrat* May 9, 1861: 1; V. D. Groner, September 30, 1861, December 13, 1861, *OR*, 4, 1:630, 790. On September 30, 1861, eight Texas regiments mustered under Colonels L. T. Wigfall, J. C. Moore, P. N. Luckett, R. T. P. Allen, H. E. McCulloch, John S. Ford, E. Greer, James Reily, Thomas Green, and on December 13, 1861, eight Texas regiments mustered under Colonels Hugh McLeod, John B. Hood, J. J. Archer, John Gregg, James Reily, Thomas Green, William Steele, and B. F. Terry.

21 Ford, *Rip Ford's Texas*, 320–24; Dunn, "KGC in Texas," *SHQ*, 571; "John Robert Baylor" (by Bill Walraven), http://www.tsha.utexas.edu/handbook/online/articles/BB/fbaat.html (accessed July 3, 2007); By-Laws, Castroville Castle, KGC, Center for American History, University of Texas, Austin.

22 "Knights Wielded Power," *San Antonio Daily Ledger and Texan*, May 27, 1861; Llerena B. Friend, "The Texas of 1860," *SHQ* 62 (July 1958): 16; Anna Irene Sandbo, "The First Session of the Secession Convention of Texas," *SHQ* 18 (July

1914), 173–76; Earl W. Fornell, "Texas and Filibusters in the 1850's," *SHQ* 59 (April 1956): 427.

23   Hudson, "Military Knights," in Appendix A ("Biographies"); Linda S. Hudson, "Texas Military K. G. C., 1860–1865: A Quantitative Approach" (unpublished seminar paper, University of North Texas, Denton, Texas, Fall 1992); Campbell and Lowe, *Wealth and Power*, 30, 39, 45, 59; *U.S. Census, 1860*; Texas KGC Data Matrix in author's possession.

24   Campbell and Lowe, *Wealth and Power*, 30, 39, 45, 59; *U.S. Census, 1860*; KGC Data Matrix in author's possession.

25   Hudson, "Military Knights," Appendix A ("Biographies"); Campbell and Lowe, *Wealth and Power*, 30, 39, 45, 59; *U.S. Census, 1860*; KGC Data Matrix in author's possession.

26   *County Tax Rolls*, Bastrop, Bexar, Burleson, Cass, Cherokee, Colorado, Comal, DeWitt, Ellis, Fannin, Fayette, Gonzales, Guadalupe, Harris, Hayes, Karnes, McLennan, Medina, Refugio, Robertson, Rusk, Smith, Travis, Upshur, Van Zandt, Walker, Washington, and Williamson counties; *U.S. Census, 1860, Agriculture Census, and Slave Census*; Campbell and Lowe, *Wealth and Power*, 27, 55, 61, 89, 106; *U. S. Census, 1860*, Harrison County; *Tax Rolls*, Harrison County, 1859, 1860, 1861.

27   Hudson, "Military Knights," Appendix A ("Biographies"); *U.S. Census, 1860*, Texas; Winkler, ed, *Journal of Secession Convention*, Index; *Service Records*, rolls 8–15, 49–52, 231, 249–54, 283, 288, 299–307, 324. Forty-two Knight leaders served in twenty-eight different CSA units; Texas KGC Matrix.

28   Hudson, "Military Knights," Appendix A ("Biographies"); *Service Records*, rolls 8–15, 49–52, 231, 249–54, 283, 288, 299–307, 324.

29   *Service Records*, rolls 8–15, 49–52, 231, 249–54, 283, 288, 299–307, 324.

30   Ibid.; "Paying Guest Home," classified advertisement, *Marshall Texas Republican*, July 21, 1865.

31   Vicki Betts, "'Private and Amateur Hangings': The Lynching of W. W. Montgomery, March 15, 1863,'" *SHQ* 88 (October 1984): 145; Bridges, "Filibustering Fantasy," *SHQ*, 301–2; T. R. Havins, "Administration of the Sequestration Act in the Confederate District Court for the Western District of Texas, 1862–1865," *SHQ* 52 (April 1949): 315.

32   Linda S. Hudson, "Former Texas Military Knights of the Golden Circle In the Dawning Years of the New South" (unpublished seminar paper, University of North Texas, Spring 1992, George Cupples File, Center for American Studies, University of Texas, Austin).

Part III

In Sight of My Enemy

Chapter 5

Frontier Defense: Enlistment Patterns for the Texas Frontier Regiments in the Civil War

by John W. Gorman

The American Civil War is one of the defining moments in American history. It completely altered American society, settled the issue of slavery once and for all, and, in a very real sense, shaped the future development of the United States. Almost immediately in its aftermath, the United States began an unprecedented period of growth that would, within thirty years, see it emerge as an industrial power and a major player in the international arena. But the Civil War was also the most destructive war in American history, lasting over four years, with over 618,000 killed in action, and with almost every person and family deeply affected by the tragic realities of war. For these reasons the Civil War has received a significant amount of attention from historians, who primarily have focused on the military and political aspects of the war.[1] But, with the advent of social history in the 1960s, historians began to explore the effects of the war on individual communities and to delve into the lives of the individuals who served and the communities that supported them.[2]

By the end of the Civil War, more than two million men had served in the Union army and over 800,000 men had served in the Confederate army.[3] Historically, scholars have argued that the Civil War was a poor man's war as the more affluent individuals avoided service by paying commutation fees or hiring a substitute. Recently, historians studying specific local communities in both the North and the South have found a significant degree of variation in enlistment patterns, but overall, evidence suggests that there was an overrepresentation of the lower wealth class, while the more affluent wealth groups were underrepresented throughout the war and this study does tend to support this trend.[4]

Texas possessed the fastest-growing population in the South, as its population increased 184 percent between 1850 and 1860, or from 212,592 in 1850 to 604,215 in 1860. The majority of these people came from the South, especially Tennessee, Missouri, Mississippi, and Georgia. However, almost 10 percent of its total population in 1860 was foreign born, and nearly half of that was German, but, a distinct Irish and Mexican presence can be observed as well. Accessible wealth increased over 500 percent, as the number of improved acres devoted to farming increased from 11 million in 1850 to 23 million in 1860, and cotton production increased from fewer than 60,000 bales in 1850 to over 430,000 bales in 1860. Corn and wheat production experienced a similar expansion. Between 1850 and 1860 corn production increased from 6 million to over 16 million bushels and wheat went from 41,000 to nearly 1.5 million bushels during the same time period.[5]

Texas was not immune to the sectional issues of the period. During the late 1840s and 1850s, the issues of slavery and Southern expansion that shaped events associated with war with Mexico, the Compromise of 1850, and the New Mexico boundary dispute, began to draw Texas closer to the other Southern states. However, as a frontier state, Texans also dealt with unique issues, especially the protection of western settlements from Indian raids, which occupied a considerable amount of the public's attention prior to 1860.

The people of Texas, like those in other Southern states, experienced an initial wave of enthusiasm for the outbreak of war, and over the course of the war, Texas contributed over 88,000 troops to the war effort, which represented around 70 percent of her eligible male population.[6] However, while Texans enthusiastically supported the Confederacy with her sons, and were willing to make sacrifices in its behalf, Texas also possessed a vast frontier that was largely undefended due to the evacuation of Federal troops from the forts along the Texas frontier. The result was that many of the men who lived in frontier communities were reluctant to enlist for service in the Confederate military because of the fear of leaving their homes and families unprotected. In order to meet this challenge, the Committee on Public Safety ordered Henry McCulloch to raise a volunteer regiment to defend the northwestern frontier. Designated the First Regiment of Texas Mounted Rifles, this unit, by the spring of 1861, patrolled an area between the Colorado and the Red rivers providing needed protection to the settlers in the region. Over the course of the war, state and local officials continued to organize units and charge them with the duty of guarding the frontier settlements. At various times, these units were known as minutemen, state troops, Texas Mounted Rifles, Frontier Regiments, and Border Regiments.[7]

The task of frontier defense was immense in scope; entirely one-fourth of the U.S. Army had been charged with frontier defense prior to the outbreak of the Civil War. Among the states of the Confederacy, Texas was the only state that had to contend, not only with dissatisfaction, desertion, and draft evasion, but also with constant pressure from hostile Indians, whose attacks increased in scope and frequency in the absence of a sustained military presence on the frontier.[8]

Frontier defense emerged as a significant issue in Texas during the 1840s due to the rapid economic and population explosion that followed Texas independence. Settlers moved out of East Texas and pushed the boundaries of the frontier farther west, and in the process, threatened and occupied the traditional lands of the Comanches, Kiowas, and other Plains Indians. To meet this threat, the Indians fought back in the only manner they knew how, by attempting to drive the foreign invaders from their lands and, similarly, the Texans living on the frontier sought to protect their families and homes from the attacking Indians. The resultant clash of cultures would be one of the most fearsome and destructive struggles in American history that would continue long after the Civil War.[9]

The onset of the Civil War brought a new urgency to the issue of frontier defense. At the request of Governor Lubbock the state legislature on December 21, 1861, passed an "Act to provide for the protection of the Frontier of the State of Texas." The law called for the creation of a "Frontier Regiment" that was to consist of nine companies raised from counties along the frontier and a tenth company to be raised by the governor from any section of the state.[10] The act further stipulated that the regiment be subject to state control and the legislature requested that the regiment be accepted into the Confederate States Army. While the Confederate Congress passed a law authorizing the state's request, President Davis vetoed the law because of Texas's insistence on maintaining control over the regiment.[11]

Over the next two years frontier defense continued to be a serious problem and finally the Texas legislature created the Frontier Organization in December 1863. Its objectives were threefold: protection of the white settlers and friendly Indians from marauding Plains Indians; defending the Southern cause; and arresting deserters of the Confederate States of America.[12] The units that served along the Texas frontier from the outset were organized and funded by the State of Texas. Texas continually tried to transfer the frontier defense units to Confederate control, but Jefferson Davis wanted Texas to give up control of the units to the Confederacy as well. The result was that nothing was done on the issue until March 4, 1864, when the State of Texas finally reorganized its frontier units from thirty-three military brigades into six new military brigades. However, the new Third Military Brigade that was tasked with protection of the frontier continued to be state troops supported by state funds.[13]

This study will attempt to shed light on who these people were that protected the Texas frontier during the Civil War. In constructing the data set, it was first necessary to consult the Integrated Public Use Microdata Series (IPUMS-98), created at the University of Minnesota in October 1997.[14] A one-to-one-hundred sample was extracted from the IPUMS database, which resulted in an initial sample size of 4,299 individuals. To date, most studies on enlistment patterns define the at-risk population as between the ages of 18 and 45.[15]

However, the at-risk population is somewhat more difficult to define in this case because these men were recruited from areas that had already made significant contributions of their youth to fight in the Civil War. Moreover, patriotism and a willingness to fight for their state and country appear not to have been factors motivating men to enlist in the frontier regiments.

In fact, some of the strongest opposition to secession came from the frontier counties in Central and North Texas. Secession was rejected in ten counties in Central Texas and the North Texas counties of Collin, Jack, Montague, Cooke, Grayson, Fannin, and Lamar and nearly defeated in the counties of Red River, Titus, Hunt, Wise, Denton, and Van Zandt, and these were counties from which recruitment to the frontier regiments was high.[16] These counties contained 6 percent of the eligible male population for the state, but they contributed 10 percent of the total number of enlistees and possessed an index of representation of 156.[17] The result was that an individual's motivation for joining a frontier regiment was more about protecting his family and home and less about a strong desire to support the Confederacy. This tendency is validated by the fact that 7.5 percent of those who served in the frontier regiments were between the ages of 49 and 55, and 45 percent of the enlistees were heads of households. Therefore, all men between the ages of 13 and 55 were extracted from the 1860 federal census and listed by name, age, occupation, position within the household, location within county, net worth, and place of birth. This created a pool of 1,292 men eligible for service. *The Compiled Service Records of Texas Confederate Soldiers* was consulted to produce a list of 2,398 men who could be positively identified as serving in one of the frontier regiments.[18] Additionally, Patricia Adkins-Rochette's multi-volume *Bourland in North Texas and Indian Territory during the Civil War* was also referenced, which resulted in forty-six individuals who could be positively matched to the federal census.[19]

This data set is not without its limitations. There is a statistical bias inherent in the data set because of the enlistees who could not be positively matched to the federal census and many records for Confederate forces and their rosters have been lost.[20] Second, relying on census records tends to favor the native affluent population and discriminate against immigrants, the poor, and those without any property. And, in a few instances, there were too many of a given name in the federal census to determine which one was the enlistee.[21] Furthermore, the relatively small size of the eligible population restricted the possible enlistee matches to between thirty and sixty, which makes linear comparisons over the course of the war impossible. However, these limitations should not diminish the importance of this study. Based on the available sources, the Texas Frontier Regiment data set is relatively complete.

In order to observe general trends concerning the frontier regiments and to make some general conclusions with other community and national studies, it was necessary to break down the eligible male population into two different categories: the entire eligible male population and the men who served. Tables 1 to 3 summarize the general differences and similarities among the subsets of eligible males.

All of the scholarship to date indicates that age is the best predictor for determining enlistment patterns, finding that the average age of enlistees to the Confederate and Union armies to be significantly lower than that of the eligible population.[22] Larry M. Logue found in his study on Mississippi that the average age of the eligible population was 28 and the average age of enlistees to the Confederate army was 25.6. Logue also found that 73 percent of young men between the ages of 18 and 24 enlisted in the Confederate army.[23] Without any comparable study for the state of Texas it is impossible to say with any certainty, but based on trends from other state and national studies it is likely that Texas exhibited similar characteristics. With estimates of between 70 and 90 percent of the eligible population in the South serving in the Civil War, it is not surprising to discover that with most of the youth of Texas serving in the Confederate army, the average age of the enlistees for the frontier regiments in Texas would be slightly higher than that of the eligible population and significantly higher than the average of enlistees to the Confederate army (see table 1).

This trend becomes even more obvious when participation in the frontier regiments is examined in relationship to age group. The 13-to-19 age group constituted only 15 percent of the total enlistments and possessed an index of representation of 62. The 20-to-29 age group and the 30-to-39 age groups were both overrepresented with an index of 118 and 113 respectively, and even the 40-to-55 age group possessed a perfect representation with an index value of 100 (see table 2). As mentioned earlier, the low index value for the 13-to-19 age group is likely explained by their overrepresentation in enlistments for the Confederate army, and the higher participation rates for the remaining age groups could be explained by their desire to stay closer to home and protect their families. However, with more of the youth off serving in the Confederate army, the older age groups were more likely to be called upon to defend the frontier in the first place, and this trend will be reinforced when total wealth is examined.

Historians have often used wealth as a determinant for enlistment patterns, and while there have been some local deviations, it is becoming apparent that age played an important role in the accumulation of wealth, and in the propensity to serve in the Civil War. Specifically, as total wealth increases with each successive age group, a shift occurs as men leave the non-occupational category and move into one of the occupational groups, and, in the process, begin to acquire wealth (see table 9). This pattern suggests a possible reason for the significantly higher proportion of young men who participated in the Civil War. Without any real wealth or property of their own, and with fewer ties to prevent them

from enlisting, the youth of both the North and the South were more susceptible to mustering into the army.[24] The result was that the remaining population
in Texas would have to be tasked with the defense of the frontier.

Total wealth was classified into three categories: a lower wealth class with a
total wealth equal to or less than $99, a middle wealth class with a total wealth
between $100 and $4,999, and an upper wealth class with a total wealth equal
to or greater than $5,000. Fifty percent of the total eligible population was from
the lower wealth group, and they were slightly underrepresented in the frontier
regiments possessing an index value of 91. The middle and upper wealth groups
were slightly overrepresented with an index value of 108 and 112 respectively
(see tables 4 and 5).[25] Specifically, with an average enlistment age of 29.63, it is
clear that frontier defense fell to the older and more affluent individuals.

It has been suggested that ownership of real property was a more accurate
indicator of enlistment patterns than total wealth, and numerous studies have
found a large proportion of enlistees to the Union army were young men who
possessed no real property.[26] In Texas, farm or day laborers and those listed with
no occupation on the 1860 federal census constituted 23 percent of the total
eligible population, but constituted only 9 percent of the frontier enlistments
(see tables 9 and 10). However, when real wealth is examined, those who possessed no real property constituted 67 percent of the eligible population and
71 percent of those who served. This high rate of enlistment for those possessing
no real property does not differ significantly from findings of previous studies
(see table 6).[27] However, the difference in average age and its relationship to
wealth class should be kept in mind as the average age for those possessing no
real property was 24.52, while for those possessing real property it was 37.06.
This trend is even more striking when head-of-household figures are examined.
Twenty-one of the 46 total enlistees were listed as heads of households in the
1860 federal census with an average age of 36.86 and possessing an index value
of 97. The non-head of household group constituted 54 percent of the total eligible male population and 52 percent of the total enlistees with an index of 103
(see tables 7 and 8). Significantly, these index figures indicate that in the frontier
regiments there was no significant fall-off in representation as age increased and
wealth accumulation occurred.

One of the more interesting aspects of the Frontier Regiment data set is in
the way that occupation reinforces both wealth and age as determining factors
of enlistment probabilities. Farmers constituted only 2 percent of the age group
13 to 19, but that figure rises through each successive age group, peaking at
12 percent in the 40-to-55 age group. The other noticeable trend was the sharp
decline in the farm or day laborers and those with no occupation as they moved
into each successive new age group. Not surprisingly, the two groups that dominated the enlistments for the frontier regiments were farmers with 41 percent

of the total enlistments and those listed in the unskilled/day laborer or other category with 30 percent of the total enlistments (see table 10).

Historians have focused a considerable amount of their scholarship on the participation of the immigrant population in the Civil War and recent work suggests that the foreign-born population enlisted at rates that were equal to or less than that of the native-born population.[28] In Texas, of the total eligible male population, 84 percent were native-born Americans while 16 percent were foreign born. Of the men who served on the frontier, 93.5 percent were native born and 6.5 percent were foreign born. The 6.5 percent of Texas's enlistees who were immigrants breaks down as follows: 2.2 percent German, 2.2 percent Mexican, and 2.1 percent other European (see table 11). However, the low number of foreign born within the enlistee population makes comparisons among the various groups impossible. Nonetheless, the foreign-born population in Texas, with an index of value of 41, displayed a strong tendency toward avoiding service in the frontier regiments.[29]

However, Germans were fairly well represented within the state, making up nearly half of the entire foreign-born population and 7.4 percent of the eligible male population, and yet they were severely underrepresented in the frontier regiments with an index value of 30. This might partially be explained by the fact that many Germans had supported the Union and were not enthusiastic supporters of slavery. However by the time of secession, Germans who lived in older, more established communities that were steeped in Southern traditions tended to endorse secession, while those who lived on the frontier tended to retain their strong support for the Union.[30] To highlight this point, German immigrants around Fredericksburg and New Braunfels formed a Union Loyalty League (ULL) in late 1860 or early 1861 and took an oath "never to betray the United States of America." Texas considered the ULL a threat to its sovereignty and over the next year two leaders of the ULL were executed, another German settler was beaten to death, and there were several armed confrontations between German militia and Texas state troops. Ironically, it was Texas's harsh treatment of the ULL and German settlers in the area that convinced many Germans along the frontier to support the Union, and it is this strong anti-Confederacy sentiment among Germans of the frontier communities that might help to explain their low participation rates in the frontier regiments.[31]

Defense of the frontier during the Civil War was an intricate part of the lives of the people who lived there. They faced innumerable challenges and hardships as they attempted to carve out lives for themselves and their families. This study does highlight the problems that frontier communities faced as a result of the Civil War. Specifically, these frontier communities were tasked with the dual burden of supporting the Confederacy and ensuring that their families and homes remained safe from hostile Indian raids.

The most significant aspect of this data set is the underrepresentation of the lower age and wealth groups. This suggests that these individuals were overrepresented in enlistments for the Confederate army and, thus, frontier defense fell to the older age and wealth groups who were likely to have been underrepresented in enlistment rates into the Confederate army. Moreover, the overrepresentation for the higher age and wealth groups also demonstrates that they had to have been highly motivated to have enlisted in such numbers in the frontier regiments. In some cases, individuals enlisted in a frontier regiment to avoid service in the Confederate army. Nevertheless, most of these men appear to have been motivated by a strong desire to remain close to home and to protect their families from marauding hostiles. While the relative size of the data set does place restrictions upon these conclusions, overall, the trends cited here do provide an important first step in understanding the characteristics of the men who served in the Texas frontier regiments.

Statistical Tables for Texas Frontier Regiments in the Civil War

Table 1   Personal Statistics of Eligible Males in Texas

Category	Number Eligible	Number Served	Avg. Age Eligible	Avg. Age Enlistees	Avg. Net Worth Eligible	Avg. Net Worth Enlistees	Head of HH Avg. Net Worth	Non–head of HH Avg. Net Worth
Total	1,292	46	28.68	29.63	$2,746.88	$2,433.27	$5,441.72	$313.96

Table 2   Number of Eligible Males in Texas by Age

Category	13–19	20–29	30–39	40+
Total Eligible	320 (24%)	423 (33%)	293 (23%)	256 (20%)
Total Served	7 (15%)	18 (39%)	12 (26%)	9 (20%)
Index	62	118	113	100

Table 3   Personal Statistics of Those Who Served in Texas

Year Entered Service	Total Number	Avg. Age	Avg. Net Worth	Non–HH Worth	HH Net Worth
All Served	46	29.63	$2,433.26	$898.00	$4,260.95

Table 4   Wealth Distribution of Eligible Males in Texas

Category	HH Wealth $0.00–$99.00	HH Wealth $100–$4,999	HH Wealth >$5,000
Total Eligible	647	494	151
Avg. Age	22.12	34.26	38.52
% of Total	50.07	38.23	11.68

Table 5   Wealth Distribution of Enlistees in Texas

Category	$0.0–$99.00	$100–$4,999	>$5,000	Total
Total # of Enlistees	21	19	6	46
Avg. Age	21.67	34.63	41.67	
% of Total	45.65	41.30	13.04	
Index	91	108	112	

Table 6   Real Wealth Statistics for Texas

Category	Number Eligible	Total Served	Avg. Age Eligible	Ave. Age Served	Index	Enlistment Rate
No Real Property	863	33	24.52	26.06	107	3.8%
% of Total	66.80%	71.74%				
Having Real Property	428	13	37.06	38.69	85	3.0%
% of Total	33.13%	28.26%				

Table 7   Head of Household Personal Statistics

Category	Number Eligible	Total Served	Avg. Net Worth	Avg. Age Eligble	Ave. Age Served
Head of Household	613	21	$5,441.76	36.19	36.86
% of Total	47.5%	1.6%			
Index		97			

Table 8   Non–Head of Household Personal Statistics

Category	Number Eligible	Total Served	Avg. Net Worth	Avg. Age Eligble	Avg. Age Served
Non–Head of Household	679	25	$313.96	21.9	23.56
% of Total	52.5%	54			
Index		103			

Table 9   Eligible Males for Texas by Occupation

Occupation	13–19	20–29	30–39	40–45	Total
Farmer	26	135	143	155	459
% of Total Eligible	2%	10.5%	11.1%	12%	35.5%
High White Collar/Professional	——	21	16	17	54
% of Total Eligible		1.6%	1.2%	1.3%	4.2%
Low White Collar	5	53	28	17	103
% of Total Eligible	0.4%	4.1%	2.2%	1.3%	8.0%
Blue Collar/Skilled Trades	5	32	23	24	84
% of Total Eligible	0.4%	2.5%	1.8%	1.9%	6.5%
Blue Collar/Semiskilled	2	20	19	13	54
% of Total Eligible	0.2%	1.6%	1.5%	1.0%	4.2%
Unskilled/Day Laborer	55	117	44	21	237
% of Total Eligible	4.3%	9.1%	3.4%	1.6%	18.3%
None/Other	227	45	20	9	301
% of Total Eligible	17.6%	3.5%	1.6%	0.7%	23.3%
Total	320	423	293	256	1,292
% Total Eligible	24.8%	32.7%	22.7%	19.8%	

*High White Collar: Professionals, Major Proprietors, Managers, and Officials
*Low White Collar: Clerks and Salesmen, Semiprofessionals, Petty Proprietors, Managers, and Officials.
*Blue Collar Skilled: Skilled Trades
*Blue Collar/Semiskilled: Apprentices to Trades, Service Workers, Factory Operatives.
*Unskilled/Day Laborer: Agricultural or Unskilled Laborers and Menial Service Workers.
*For a more detailed explanation on the socioeconomic breakdown of occupations see:
Stephan Thernstrom, The Other Bostonians: Poverty and Progress in the American Metropolis, 1880–1970, Appendix B, "On the Socio-economic Ranking of Occupations" (Cambridge: Harvard University Press, 1973), 289–302.

Table 10: Enlistment Patterns for Texas by Occupation

Occupation	13–19	20–29	30–39	40–45	Total
Farmer	1	7	3	8	19
% of Total Eligible	0.08%	0.5%	0.2%	0.6%	1.5%
Index	4	4.8	1.8	5	4.2
High White Collar/Professional	——	——	2	——	2
% of Total Eligible			0.2%		\0.2%
Index			16		4.8
Low White Collar	——	2	3	——	5
% of Total Eligible		0.2%	0.2%		0.4%
Index		4.9	9.1		5
Blue Collar/Skilled Trades	——	2	2	1	5
% Total Eligible		0.2%	0.2%	0.08%	0.4%
Index		8	11	4	6
Blue Collar/Semiskilled	——	——	1	——	1
% of Total Eligible			0.08%		0.08%
Index			5		2
Unskilled/Day Laborer	4	5	1	——	10
% of Total Eligible	0.3%	0.4%	0.08%		0.8%
Index	7	4	2		4
None/Other	2	2	——	——	4
% of Total Eligible	0.2%	0.2%			0.3%
Index	1	6\			1.2
Total	7	18	12	9	46
Percent of Total Eligible	0.5%	1.4%	0.9%	0.7%	
Index	2	4	4	4	

Table 11   Eligible Males of Texas Divided by Place of Birth

Place of Birth	Total Eligible	% of Total Eligible	Total Enlistees	Avg. Age Eligible	Avg. Age Enlistees	% of Total Served	Index
United States	1,088	84%	43	28.34	29.86	93.5%	111
Northern States	42	3.3%	2	35.43	32.50	4.3%	130
Southern States	879	68%	29	28.05	30.79	63%	93
Midwest/ Western States	51	4%	3	27.88	22.33	6.5%	163
Border States	116	9%	9	28.22	28.78	13%	144
Total Foreign Born	204	15.8%	3	30.48	26.33	6.5%	41
Ireland	24	1.9%	——	30.88	——		0
Germany	95	7.4%	1	31.08	22.00	2.2%	30
Other European	4	0.3%	——	27.50	——		——
European Catholic	6	0.5%	——	35.50	——		——
European Protestant	24	1.9%	1	30.33	31.00	2.1%	116
Non-European	51	4%	1	——	——	2.2%	55
Canada	2	0.2%	——	29.00	——		——
Mexico	49	4%	1	28.86	26.00	2.2%	55
Total	1,292		46				

*Northern States: Connecticut, Maine, New Hampshire, New Jersey, New York, Pennsylvania, Rhode Island, and Vermont.
*Southern States: Georgia, Virginia, North Carolina, South Carolina, Tennessee, Texas[, Louisiana, Mississippi, and Alabama
*Midwest/Western States: Indiana, Illinois, Iowa, Ohio, Michigan, and Wisconsin
*Border States: Kentucky, Maryland, Missouri, and Delaware.
*Other European Protestants: England, Norway, Scotland, Sweden, and Switzerland
*Other European Catholics: France, Italy

Notes

1   Maris A. Vinovskis, *Have Social Historians Lost the Civil War?* (New York: Cambridge University Press, 1990), 6.

2   Gerald N. Grob and George A. Billias, *Interpretations of American History: Patterns and Perspectives*, 6th ed. (New York: Free Press, 1992), 1:388.

3   In 1860 the Confederacy had a military population of 1,064,193, of which she
    provided no less than 90 percent to the military population while the North deliv-
    ered only around 45 percent. See William F. Fox, *Regimental Losses in the Ameri-
    can Civil War* (Albany, New York: Albany Publishing,1889), 552. While there is
    some disagreement over the actual number of men who served, it is safe to say
    that a clear majority of the Southern population served and more than a quarter-
    million were killed, or one in five of the South's entire military-age population.
    See Larry Logue, "Who Joined the Confederate Army? Soldiers, Civilians, and
    Communities in Mississippi," *Journal of Social History* 26 (Spring 1993): 611.

4   Studies by Kurt Hackemer in Kenosha County, Wisconsin, and Maris Vinovskis
    in Newburyport, Massachusetts, found enlistment rates of the middle wealth class
    were equal to or exceeded that of the lower wealth class. See Hackemer, "Response
    to War: Civil War Enlistment Patterns in Kenosha County, Wisconsin," *Military
    History of the West* 29 (Spring 1999): 45; Vinovskis, *Have Social Historians Lost the
    Civil War*, 16. In Ashe County, North Carolina, Martin Crawford found a similar
    relationship among the middle and lower wealth groups. See Martin Crawford,
    "Confederate Volunteering and Enlistment in Ashe County, North Carolina,
    1861–1862," *Civil War History* 37 (1991): 29–50. However, a study by William
    J. Harris of three Georgia counties found an underrepresentation of the upper
    wealth groups. See William J. Harris, *Plain Folk and Gentry in a Slave Society:
    White Liberty and Black Slavery in Georgia's Hinterlands* (Middletown, Connecti-
    cut, Wesleyan University Press, 1985), 152–53. The trend is also confirmed in two
    studies by John Gorman, which found that in Hancock County, Indiana, and in
    Massachusetts the lower wealth group was overrepresented throughout the war.
    Gorman, "Hoosiers in the Civil War: Enlistment Patterns in Hancock County,
    Indiana" and "New Englanders in the Civil War: Enlistment Patterns in New
    England," unpublished mss. in the author's possession.

5   Ralph A. Wooster, *Texas and Texans in the Civil War* (Austin, Texas: Eakin Press,
    1995), 32.

6   Ibid. Stephen B. Oates's Texas enrollment figures have the breakdown of Texas
    soldiers as follows: 58,000 cavalry and 30,000 joined the infantry and artillery.

7   Stanley S. McGowen, *Horse Sweat and Powder Smoke: The First Texas Cavalry in
    the Civil War* (Texas: Texas A&M University Press, 1999), 3.

8   David Paul Smith, *Frontier Defense in the Civil War: Texas Rangers and Rebels*
    (College Station: Texas A&M University Press, 1992), xii.

9   Ibid., xiii.

10 Ibid., 42. One regiment was to be formed from each of the following groups of
    counties: Group 1: Clay, Montague, Cooke and Wise; Group 2: Young, Jack,
    Palo Pinto, and Parker; Group 3: Stephens, Eastland, Erath, and Bosque; Group
    4: Coryell, Hamilton, Lampasas, Comanche, and Brown; Group 5: San Saba,
    Mason, Llano, and Burnet; Group 6: Gillespie, Hays, and Kerr; Group 7: Blanco,
    Bandera, Medina, and Uvalde; group 8: Frio, Atascosa, Live Oak, Karnes, and
    Bee; Group 9: El Paso and Presidio.

11 Ibid., 43.

12   Patricia Adkins-Rochette, *Bourland in North Texas and Indian Territory during the Civil War* (Duncan, Oklahoma: privately published, 2004), vii.

13   Adkins-Rochette, *Bourland*, vii. CSA President Jefferson Davis, who had served as Franklin Pierce's Secretary of War from 1853 to 1857, knew of the tremendous costs of maintaining cavalry posts along the Texas frontier and with the Confederacy constantly strapped for cash, this was an extra expense he could not afford to take on.

14   The IPUMS database consists of twenty-seven high-precision samples of the American population drawn from fourteen federal censuses and comprises our richest source of quantitative information on long-term changes in the American population.

15   For determining the range of the at-risk population Kurt Hackemer in his study on Kenosha County, Wisconsin, and Larry M. Logue in his study on Mississippi relied on E. B. Long's *The Civil War Day by Day: An Almanac, 1861–1865*, 707. In his study of Concord, Massachusetts, W. J. Rorabaugh used a different age range of 16 to 49. See W. J. Rorabaugh, "Who Fought for the North in the Civil War? Concord, Massachusetts, Enlistments," *The Journal of American History* 73 (December 1986): 696–701.

16   Wooster, *Texas and Texans in the Civil War*, 19. It appears that these counties' opposition to secession was based, at least in part, on the fact that most of their residents were non-slaveholding farmers who had migrated from the Upper South or Midwest.

17   To highlight the level of participation of enlistees, the use of an index of representation is useful in allowing for comparisons between the various groups. The index of representation was arrived at by dividing the percent served of the subgroup with the percent eligible for that particular group and then multiplying that number by 100 to arrive at an index value. A value of 100 represents a perfect relationship between the percent of a particular group within the eligible population and its rate of enlistment. Index values over 100 represent overrepresentation while values less than 100 represent underrepresentation.

18   United States War Department, *Index to Compiled Service Records of Confederate Soldiers Who Served in Organizations from the State of Texas* (National Archives: Washington, D.C., 1955), microfilm.

19   This work contains an appendix with about 130 pages of unit rosters and is an excellent place to start when researching frontier defense in North Texas.

20   A further drawback to working with Confederate military records is that at the time of enlistment a soldier usually filled out an index card with his name and regiment on it, but in many instances these index cards possessed only a first initial and last name, thus making positive identification impossible.

21   When it was impossible to identify a soldier on the federal census because there were too many individuals with a particular name, all of the names were removed from the data set.

22   In Concord: 35 percent of those aged 16–20 enlisted, 22 percent of those aged 21–29, 13 percent of those aged 30–39, and 8 percent of those aged 40–49. See

Rorabaugh, "Who Fought for the North?," 696. In Kenosha County: 21.6 percent of those aged 13–19 in 1860 enlisted, 16 percent of those 20–29, 7 percent of those aged 30–39, and 5 percent aged 40–45. See Hackemer, "Response to War," 45. In Newburyport: 50 percent of those aged 16–17 in 1860 enlisted, 40 percent of those 18–24, 17 percent of those 30–39, and 5 percent aged 40–49. See Vinovskis, *Have Social Historians Lost the Civil War?* 16.

23 Logue, "Who Joined the Confederate Army?" 613.

24 See the author's own two previous studies for a more detailed explanation of this relationship between age, wealth, and occupation. Gorman, "Hoosiers in the Civil War," and "New Englanders in the Civil War." Rorabaugh has found similar trends concerning the youth of Concord, Massachusetts, during the Civil War. See Rorabaugh, "Who Fought for the North in the Civil War?" 699–700.

25 The sum of $4,999 was used as the cutoff for the middle class because the 151 men with a household wealth greater than that amount represented the top 10 percent of the eligible male population. The wealth range for the lower wealth class is pretty well established with a range of $0 to $100. However, due to local variations in economic conditions there is significant deviation in the defined range of the middle and upper wealth groups.

26 Rorabaugh, "Who Fought for the North in the Civil War?" 699–700. Hackemer found similar trends in his study of Kenosha County with only 23.4 percent of the eligible population being heads of households and owners or real property. See Hackemer, "Response to War," 46.

27 In Kenosha County, Hackemer found 76.6 percent of the total enlistments came from those without any real wealth. See Hackemer, "Response to War," 46. And in Hancock County, Indiana, Gorman found that 70 percent of the total enlistments came from those without any real property.

28 Vinovskis found that the foreign born were far less likely to enlist than the native-born population. See Vinovskis, *Have Social Historians Lost the Civil War?* 16. These rates are confirmed by Hackemer's study which finds a significant under-represention for foreign-born enlistment rates for the Union Army. See Hackemer, "Response to War," 48.

29 Hackemer found in Kenosha County an Irish index of representation of 57 and an index of 63 for Germans with an undeterminable religious affiliation. See Hackemer, "Response to War," 50. Likewise, Vinovskis states that ethnicity was the second-best predictor of participation in the Civil War next to age. He found in Newburyport a similar trend in regard to the immigrant population. See Vinovskis, *Have Social Historians Lost the Civil War?* 16.

30 Wooster, *Texas and Texans in the Civil War*, 21.

31 McGowen, *Horse Sweat and Powder Smoke*, 66–72.

Chapter 6

Reckoning at the River: Unionists and Secessionists on the Nueces, August 10, 1862

by Mary Jo O'Rear

The sun beat heavily on the shoulders of the Confederate cavalrymen, causing fresh sweat to soak their already sodden shirts as they rode down grassy hills and crossed rock-encrusted streambeds in the German Hill Country of Texas. In early August 1862, Confederate military leaders had dispatched Lt. Colin D. McRae to command this unit, which included among its members James Duff's Partisan Rangers.

Prior to this mission, Duff's men had been camped on the Pedernales River, resting in the shade of live oak trees along its banks and harvesting fish from its slow-moving current. Outside of a few scouting patrols into the hills and the occasional remand of prisoners to Fredericksburg or San Antonio, the men had been enjoying a well-earned break from their normal duties.[1]

Following the secession of Texas and the removal of Federal troops from the state in February 1861, the borderlands had become vulnerable. Comanche warriors had attacked ranches along the Frio River, slaughtered cattle by the Medina River, and killed homesteaders living along the entire frontier region. The government responded by hastily ordering out ranging companies, but these small forces proved ineffective against such adversaries. It was not until late December that the legislature passed a bill for frontier cavalry, allowing Texans who supported the Confederacy the opportunity to embrace military service close to home.[2]

Even though ammunition, horses, shelter, pack mules, and cooking supplies were initially scarce, Duff's Rangers enthusiastically answered the legislators' call for volunteers to serve in the newly created frontier regiments. They were fully prepared to confront the Plains Indians of Texas. However, border savagery soon demanded less vigilance than protecting the state from internal treachery; by the new year, it was evident that homebred traitors were as dangerous to the Confederacy as the most errant Indians.[3] Secession had sired them. Since February, Lincolnites, including E. J. Davis and A. J. Hamilton, had canvassed pro-Union counties in search of support. Though Davis and Hamilton eventually fled the state to join the U.S. Army, authorities considered the dissidents they left behind especially troublesome.[4]

Particularly troubling to Texas Confederates were recalcitrant merchants and entrepreneurs. With the continued devaluation of Confederate scrip, the Rebel government lacked financial stability. As the war continued to drain the South's coffers of hard currency, states like Texas had to purchase supplies and pay troops in Confederate scrip. Because the notes did not retain their value, many storekeepers simply refused to accept them as payment. When Confederates later forced them to take the near worthless notes, shopkeepers raised the prices of their goods in an attempt to offset potential losses in profit.[5] For Texas Confederates, such actions were tantamount to treason. Commenting on the merchants' practices, Col. Henry McCulloch raged, "Others are . . . using their utmost exertions to break down the currency of the country . . . some . . . have arms and other supplies for sale, and ask us twice as much for them in our currency as they would in gold or silver . . . . Our friends do not act in this manner, and these men are our enemies."[6]

McCulloch's frustration moved Gen. Hamilton P. Bee, new commander of the submilitary district of the Rio Grande, to action. In the first weeks of June, he dispatched James Duff and his Partisans to enforce martial law in the Hill Country, specifically targeting "merchants who denigrate the currency of the Confederate States."[7] Duff's presence had an immediate impact on the Central Texas region. Reporting on his actions in and near Fredericksburg, the captain stated, "I . . . instructed Lieutenant Lilly to wait on Mr. F. Lochte, a wealthy merchant of the place who had bought largely the produce of the county, and who would not sell for paper currency, and inform him that I required fifty bushels of corn. After some little hesitation he agreed to furnish it. After this I had no difficulty getting forage and all necessary supplies."[8]

Just as damaging to the Confederate cause was the perceived slander spread by businessmen like F. W. Doebbler and Julius Schlickum.[9] In the provost marshal's presence, one client confronted Schlickum, stating, "I have heard you advise people not to take Confederate Money. [You] advised me not to take it. [You] told me if I had any, I had better get shut of it, as it would be worth nothing in a short time. That the U.S. Army was getting the best of us and we would be whipped in soon and the money would be worthless."[10] Others testified that Schlickum "never appeared to believe anything coming from the Confederates, but on the contrary would always credit the news from our enemies. . . . I have always supposed him to be against us. He was not in the habit of presenting our successes in a fair light."[11] In a final damning criticism, witnesses claimed that the merchant was "opposed to the institution of slavery."[12]

Anti-abolitionists commonly expressed criticism of most of the foreign-born population in the Fredericksburg area years prior to the war. But once the war began, a significant number of Germans, especially those residing in Comal and Austin counties, proved their loyalty to the Confederacy by eagerly volunteering for Southern military units. Nevertheless, other German-speaking immigrants in the Hill Country refused to aid the Rebel cause.[13] In 1862 the *San Antonio Herald* printed that "the young men of that area held a meeting recently in which they resolved that as they were better farmers than the old men, they would remain at home, and let the old men go to the war. The latter held a meeting and resolved that as the young men refused to fight, they also would remain at home."[14] Sarcasm fell flat, however, in the face of the danger such dissidents posed, especially when many Texans were worried about potential Yankee invasions of their state. Because many noncombatants were young and in the fullness of their manhood, staunch Southerners soon accused them of treasonous acts, especially if compared to the starving remnants of Gen. H. H. Sibley's Army of New Mexico just returning from the West in defeat.[15]

Sickened by Sibley's stragglers, still reeling from the imposition of conscription, and shocked at the losses of Fort Donelson and New Orleans, Confederate sympathizers in San Antonio had lived in dread since the spring, when they discovered public broadsides advocating a Unionist revolt. Calling for the death of civic leaders, the leaflets urged "all German brothers" to "hang [the Texans] by their feet and burn them from below."[16] Vague distrust quickly exploded into blind rage against the German immigrants, especially those in the Hill Country.

James M. Norris, commander of the frontier cavalry and charged with security from the Red River to the Rio Grande, showed his ire as he struggled with procuring weapons, rationing limited supplies, and protecting settlers from renewed Indian attacks.[17] "If those persons who are talking so loudly of protecting the frontier," he wrote, "could be placed in the ranks of the Army of the Brave and Noble Sons of the South now battling for our rights, they would be much better employed than holding meetings and passing resolutions to fight the South."[18]

Norris's complaints, however, paled in comparison to those of Charles DeMontel, commander of D Company, responsible for patrolling some of the most ruggedly forested canyon lands of Texas. Aroused by a traitorous letter sent to one of his men and disturbed about Unionist ties to Bexar and Medina counties, DeMontel seethed when a sighting of a supposed band of Comanche warriors turned out to be a group of Germans staying in the mountains to avoid the Confederate draft. The Rebel soldiers were concerned because the foreigners were "well-mounted . . . [and] armed to the teeth," and he feared his men's vulnerability to Union men in the region.[19] Additionally, DeMontel reported,

"They are getting very bold [and] they speak of the table having turned and of hanging all secessionists. One of them remarked . . . the other day that the[re] were 300 of them in Medina County sworn . . . to fight us."[20]

It was gentle-natured Robert Beckham, brigadier-general of Thirty-first Brigade, Texas State Troops, however, who made the danger real. His plaintive comments about men "having gone away, but not to war," reinforced reports that nearly eight hundred draft evaders were in Gillespie and Kerr counties alone. Such defiance, coupled with information that "the population of Gillespie County . . . has already established a sort of scouting system . . . for the protection of the frontier," set off alarm bells.[21] Martial trial commissioners had long been hearing rumors of a secret organization of Unionists in the hills, stockpiling provisions, and "threatening the lives of those who did not believe as they did about Political matters."[22] The possibility that it not only existed but had militarized posed a major threat—a threat that intensified with the death of Basil Stewart.

Born in Scotland but employed as a herder near Fredericksburg, Stewart had attempted to escape conscription on the grounds of his foreign citizenship. With his case rejected, he became a Confederate spy and infiltrated the secret Unionist sessions, reporting on their activities. Within weeks, he was shot down, ambushed while driving a herd of cattle for a local rancher.[23] Numerous attempts by his employer to find the killers failed, but the slaying did confirm Confederate fears. The Scotsman's murder, combined with beatings of Southern sympathizers and sightings of horsemen traveling by night, suggested organized insurrection. Within a week, General Bee ordered Duff and his men back into the Hill Country.[24] Bee reported to his superiors that he had "appointed Captain Duff provost-marshal for the . . . disaffected . . . counties" and had instructed him to "declare martial law, . . . [to] require all good and loyal citizens to return . . . to their homes, . . . and to send out scouting parties into the mountain districts with orders to . . . break up any encampments and depots as had been reported to exist there."[25] To aid his efforts, Bee also increased the number of men stationed in the area. Duff now had four mounted companies under the command of Capt. John Donelson at his disposal. [26]

Accordingly, Duff marched his men to the Pedernales River, set up camp, and officially proclaimed martial law, "giving the inhabitants three days to come in and take the oath of allegiance to the Confederacy." That the time limit was too restrictive for outlying settlers to meet was implicit in the order; once the three days elapsed, Duff would have cause to treat them as traitors, and he did. Soon, troops were scouring the countryside, wagoners were bringing in prisoners, and squads were setting up guard tents.[27]

The wagons, however, hauled mostly women and children, who were quickly dispatched to San Antonio or Fredericksburg; consequently, the guard tents housed few inhabitants. Slowly, among troopers lounging along the river, a sense of foreboding began to spread. Only certain cronies of the commander ever seemed to go on bushwhacker raids, and they were pillaging far more than the provision depots that General Bee had ordered Duff to target.[28] "[At] what had been a well-cultivated little farm," a Ranger remembered, "the crops were trampled and destroyed, and not a living thing was to be seen on the place . . . the poor little furniture in the living room, and the loom in the kitchen, had been smashed . . . even the bee-hives . . . were overturned and empty . . . . All this had been done by some of our marauding parties by our Captain's orders. It made one utterly ashamed to be serving with such men."[29]

The shame spread with rumors of Duff's penchant for violence. He issued a standing order to his men "that he wanted no prisoners brought into camp," and that he believed "in converting Union men to the true faith [only] by means of the halter [noose]." Stories abounded of captives being "quietly taken away, and hanged at some distance from the camp." In the edgy atmosphere, local disdain toward Duff's Rangers and their commander intensified.[30]

But revulsion was thrust aside when word came that Unionists, nearly one hundred strong, had left their mountain hideout to head west, hoping to connect with Federals in Mexico. Under orders to arrest "any person . . . attempting to escape from the state," Captain Donelson organized a pursuit party. "We [were] in high spirits," one Southerner recalled. "[W]e had soon tired of inaction, and here was a chance of a fight against men who really were . . . against our country, and were well armed too."[31] On August 2, the men secured their mounts, packed victuals for a seven-day scout, and got a good night's sleep. The next morning detachments from Duff's company, Davis's state troops, and Donelson's Rifles set off behind First Lt. Colin D. McCrae, heading toward the Rio Grande to stop the Union sympathizers. [32]

Meanwhile, among the fugitives, a sense of exultation filtered through the ranks as the young men, leading spare mounts and pack mules, left Turtle Creek—fifteen miles west of Kerrville and a safe distance from Duff's Pedernales camp—on August 1. Months of tension—capped by accusations of cowardice, betrayal, and murder—culminated in their decision to leave Texas; within a fortnight all would be in Mexico where most planned to join the wartime U.S. Army.[33] It had been a hard choice—but necessary. In spite of best efforts to preserve peace in the Hill Country, pro-Confederates forced their hand.[34] What the United States had given them would have to be fought for, even if that meant leaving. And, as promised, the generosity of their adopted country had been bountiful. For those fleeing high taxes and food shortages in the fatherland, the United States had been an economic Eden. Here, urbanites like Philip Braubach drove stagecoaches; linen weavers like August Hoffman hauled freight; Julius Schlickum maintained a dry goods emporium;

Ferdinand Doebbler ran a tavern; and Wilhelm Boerner farmed an estate worth over $1,000.[35]

But secession savaged this high-ridged *marktgarten*. Shortly after the beginning of the war, military fines were crippling long-distance wagoners, and prohibition was closing local breweries. It was the downslide from coins to Confederate notes, however, that augured lasting economic ruin.[36] More and more worthless with each military defeat, such bills courted disaster for honest tradesmen, who needed to balance their depreciation with the increasing value of hard stock. The only solution, inflation, incurred the ire of citizens and military commanders alike, leaving the storekeepers scapegoats for the losses of the South. Castigated, assailed, and finally arrested, merchants like Schlickum and Doebbler were forced to the hills to escape men like James Duff.[37] In the company of other dissenters, the businessmen took cold comfort in evading their pursuers as news of homestead pillaging penetrated their hideouts.[38] Ironically, the Rangers' atrocities served to strengthen support for the Union and the constitutional freedoms that it protected. Belief in individual rights had led many immigrants like Edward Degener to risk the grueling voyage from Europe so that his sons could attain "minds free from prejudice . . in their own study of right and truth." To this end, schools and study centers had emerged in the earliest settlements along the northern Guadalupe, where young boys attended lessons in the morning and listened to their fathers discuss politics at night. To persons fleeing the reach of Prussian repression, the free inquiry and debate extant in the hinterlands of Texas were an untrammeled delight.[39]

It was the German-speaking immigrants' devotion to constitutional freedoms that caused many pro-slavery Texans to suspect them of engaging in abolitionist activities during the 1850s. By the middle of the decade, the two most important regional publications were the *New Braunfels Zeitung* and the *San Antonio Zeitung*, and both presses urged their readers to gather in open assemblies and to be active politically.[40] During the 1856 presidential election, the *New Braunfels* editor encouraged his community to "meet together . . . to agree . . . among ourselves . . . . The presidential election is the next opportunity in which we can test our strength . . . . It must and shall not find us unprepared, and unorganized."[41] Accordingly, German-speaking citizens from around the state met in San Antonio to codify their beliefs. But the convention participants soon found themselves in a firestorm as their ideas became public.[42] What was their transgression? A simple statement of principle written into the *Der Freie Verein* platform: "Slavery is an evil, the abolition of which is a requirement of democratic principles." Immediately following was an endorsement of states' rights and a series of other reforms unrelated to slavery, but the damage had been done. One pro-slavery advocate demanded to know, "Who are the Germans of Texas . . . and what are they doing? . . . . Verily, [they] have departed from every rule of propriety . . . and gone astray."[43]

The emancipation declaration rapidly became a target for every Know-Nothing, nativist, slaveholder—and conservative *Deutschlander*—in Texas, and when the editor of the *San Antonio Zeitung* supported it with editorials in German and English, he became a target.[44] Less than a year later, his publishing house was ransacked and razed. Southern Democrats and pro-slavery advocates showed little sympathy for the newspaperman's plight. Almost approvingly, one opposing editor stated that "the printing office of the *San Antonio Zeitung* . . . has been destroyed by the citizens of that town. The *Zeitung* has for some time past advocated doctrines entirely contrary to the spirit of our institutions. Generally speaking, we are opposed to mobs, but . . . this is one case where the nature of the circumstances will . . . justify their course."[45]

As the Civil War approached, liberal editors became even more vulnerable. In one instance, members of the Knights of the Golden Circle forced James P. Newcomb to stop publication of the *Alamo Express*, a paper that was highly critical of the secessionists. In another, authorities arrested S. A. White, editor of the *Victoria Advocate*, because of his protest against the use of martial law in his region.[46]

In this politically charged environment public expression and temperament became damaging evidence in treason trials. One defendant was arrested for having "something to say on all passing events.[47] Another was imprisoned for his ability to "to create discontent and dissatisfaction."[48] It even became a crime to have strong opinions. A prisoner was held for being "active in speaking his mind . . . [and] calculated to do the government infinite harm."[49] In many cases, due process was simply dead. The testimony of terrorized farmers, disgruntled associates, arrant debtors, and bribed spies held unchallenged sway in the martial law courts of San Antonio.[50] Occasionally no evidence of any kind was presented. "The proof in this case is so clear and explicit that the accused is not only a Black Republican, but that he is always active in disseminating his opinions," one judge stated, "that it is not thought necessary to recite particular occasions or acts."[51]

As freedom disappeared, a vengeful bloodlust took its place, trumpeted by one of the South's most outspoken papers. The editor of the *Weekly Texas State Gazette* reminded his readers, "There may be [yet] a few free soil dregs in our midst . . . . Fortunately there will be no difficulty ascertaining who they are. . . . Unless they immediately renounce their errors, and in good faith espouse the cause of their country, there is no telling how soon it may be deemed necessary to treat them as tories, spies, and traitors. . . . [T]he action of loyal citizens should be prompt and decisive."[52] What "prompt and decisive" meant was illustrated three months later with the report of a double hanging of "two doubtful characters" in Corpus Christi.[53] In spite of its cover as a military execution, the incident reeked of vigilantism, strongly countenanced by the leading newspapers in the state. The *Galveston Tri-Weekly News* commented, "We notice that summary justice is occasionally meted out to Lincoln sympathizers in various parts of Texas. . . . In times of peace no one can be more opposed than ourselves to visiting the death penalty upon even the most flagrant crimes, without the regular formality of legal trial, but at such a time as this . . . we . . . do not hesitate to say that the summary execution of the spies and traitors detected in our midst is a necessity. . . . [T]heir lives are justly forfeited to the country."[54]

Unwilling to forfeit their lives, but equally unwilling to sacrifice loyalty, Hill Country Unionists had early hoped to serve as range riders for the state, avoid conscription, and protect property—all at the same time. Their opportunity came with the Comanche incursions after the Federal troop withdrawal. In addition, indicted but unprosecuted members of the Waldrip gang intensified their border banditry, riding in packs at night and using the darkness for farm invasion and murder.[55]

Outrages were rampant—and seemingly unavenged. Trying to prevent more, the state set up district militia companies alongside the ranger borderland patrols, with orders for their brigadier generals to commission local leaders as enrolling officers. One of Beckham's choices for the Hill Country's Thirty-first Brigade, Jacob Kuechler, was a Union activist, however, and when he blatantly restricted his unit to known abolitionists, ultra-Southerners were incensed.[56]

"It is customary when Co[mpanies] are to be raised," one claimed, "to give notice. When this company was raised none could find it out, except those who were to join it, and persons who made inquiries, were told falsehoods as to the time and place of meeting. In place of holding their meetings at Fredericksburg, they went to Comfort . . . I never had any list of men in my hands showing the progress made by the accused in raising the company.[57]

Convinced, correctly, that an unstated purpose of the division was for the Unionists to enroll "and then when the Yankees come . . . join them," over a hundred angry protesters petitioned a revocation of Kuechler's commission—to which Lubbock speedily agreed. Branded a traitor and frustrated in his attempt to spread dissent, Kuechler took to the hills; refusing entry into a new Confederate-driven regiment, many of his young recruits joined him.[58]

Discouraged and disheartened—an earlier move to join with Austin Federals having foundered in March—proud Lincolnites made one more effort, this time to free Northern prisoners of war on their way to Louisiana. Failure there, and the collapse of a last attempt to legitimately organize for frontier defense, left them desperate.[59] They had quietly militarized in late spring, asserting their goal of taking only "such actions as might peaceably . . . protect their families . . . and to secure . . . members . . . from being disturbed and compelled to bear arms against the Union." But it was not long before some abandoned their own vow, physically attacking secessionists and assassinating Basil Stewart. By midsummer, military authorities had declared the Hill Country in open rebellion. Duff's raiders were wrecking households and fugitive living was taking its toll on the dissidents. The time had come for Hill County Unionists to meet officially one last time.[60]

This time nowhere near the number attended as had flocked to earlier secret meetings. On July 4, 1862, all hope of remaining in Texas, albeit in hiding, had cheered over five hundred faithful at Bear Creek, off the north fork of the Guadalupe River. By the end of the month, however, that dream had vanished. Any chance of restoring the rights of free individuals would have to come from a United States invasion, and the only way to insure that was to join the Federals in Mexico.[61] This was the hardest choice many of these young men would ever make—indeed, it was so wrenching that on July 31 fewer than ninety showed up at Turtle Creek, ten miles southwest from Kerrville and hidden deep in the hills. When Fritz Tegener sounded the command the next afternoon, only some sixty fell in behind him.[62]

Resolute in their decision, provisioned with supplies stockpiled for weeks, and buoyed by Governor Lubbock's thirty-day reprieve to any dissident willing to leave the state, the riders following Fritz Tegener were scions of some of the earliest families in the area. Gottlieb Stieler's eldest son, Henry, was there, as were the sons of Heinrich Steves and August Vater. Edward Degener's firstborn, Hugo, rode as company lieutenant, along with his younger brother, Hilmar; neighbor Pablo Diaz; and veteran frontiersman John Sansom.[63] Others in the division included Comfort businessman Ernest Cramer, county freight hauler August Hoffman, former cavalryman Henry Schwethelm, and escaped activist Jacob Keuchler, now serving as captain and scout. Tegener himself, part of the Comfort community since 1854 and a staunch Unionist, had been elected regimental commander. Charismatic, authoritative, and approachable, he seemed the perfect leader.[64] With him and his stalwarts cantering a steady twenty miles a day, heading southwest toward a border crossing below San Felipe del Rio, August 6 should have seen them well into Mexico.[65] But they never made it that far; five days into the expedition, Tegener's troops had not yet reached the Nueces River. Carefully pacing down canyons and creek beds along the Medina River before crossing to the Frio, they elected to proceed slowly, protecting their unshod pack mules from the rocky terrain—and playing like schoolboys on an outing.[66] "They were in no particular hurry," one of the men remembered, "and . . . jogged along at the rate of only five to ten miles a day. . . . Some of them, being fond of wild honey, searched for wild hives of bees, and took things easy in a general way."[67]

The leisurely pace soothed any sense of urgency, and, as they neared the border, the young Unionists compounded their carelessness by neglecting to post a rear guard, accosting an associate on the trail to take his supplies, and stopping at one spot for several days to conduct target practice. Soon the lackadaisical pace and brazen acts aroused misgivings that even the addition of four more fugitives on the eighth day of their journey could not calm. By the time the dissidents forded the west fork of the Nueces, anxiety had become full-fledged anger that flared at the next bivouac, approximately fifty miles from the border.[68]

Problems in camp began when the commander—about one hundred and fifty yards from the river in a tolerably open place—declared the group would stay there for the next thirty-six hours. Incensed, Henry Schwethelm vigorously protested that "they had been dallying along too easily." Taken aback, Tegener agreed to leave at dawn. But Schwethelm's sense of danger afflicted only a few; the majority of the party mocked his caution.[69]

By the time the horses had been pastured, however, an inner wariness seemed to replace earlier exuberance. Eating their fill at the campfires, the youths worked off the tension by wrestling, then turned to speechmaking, extolling the fatherland and America and refugeeing to Mexico. As a grand finale, August Hoffman remembered, they gathered together and, reprising choral parts practiced since childhood, harmonized on their most-loved folksongs.[70]

As the men prepared to bed down for the night, John Sansom reflected on reports made early that day of scouts seeing strangers in the distance. The sightings were quickly dismissed, but they now haunted him.[71] Before making his way to his bedroll, the frontiersman quietly quizzed Tegener once more. "Are you entirely satisfied, Major," he asked, "that our boys saw no strangers around this evening?" Tegener responded, "Of course I am . . . . Why do you ask?" Sansom quietly answered, "Because . . . I fear they did see strangers, and if they did, it means harm to us."[72] Taking heed, Tegener agreed to confer with his lieutenants once again, seeking out Keuchler and Degener in the night. After a brief conference, the major returned totally convinced "that no strangers were anywhere around."[73] Reluctant but subdued, Sansom prepared his bedroll, lay down, and dropped off to sleep.

Sansom and Schwethelm's fears quickly proved valid. By the time the Unionists were in their deepest slumber, four units of Rebel Texans were readying to attack. Even though Tegener and his men had at least thirty miles and two days' ride on them, Colin McRae and his command caught up with them at the west branch of the Nueces. McRae had driven his men, pushing hard down the Guadalupe and across its southern branch until they reached the timberlands. There they halted just long enough to prepare victuals for a three days' ride, striking out again at sunrise. The Confederates continued to advance, trailing down canyons, clambering up rockslides, and traveling by full moon. Reaching a waterhole at the head of the Frio River in half the time taken by the Unionists, they watered thirsty horses, filled canteens, and pushed on again.[74] Two more days found them across the main Nueces tributary in the mountains bordering Mexico. "[Now] we were nearing the Rio Grande, and if we were to catch the Germans, we must keep on without pause," one recalled. A half day later, "our scouts came hastening back to report that our long stern chase was at an end." The camp of the bushwhackers was just three miles away.[75]

Discovery was almost inevitable once the outriders climbed a tall bluff overlooking the Nueces' western fork. On its farther bank lay the Unionists, surrounded by thick masses of cedar trees, almost two hundred horses, and virtually no guards.[76] Ordering his men to hold their positions, the lieutenant and his subalterns advanced to reconnoiter the enemy campsite. Returning to base, McRae made plans to divide his command into two equal divisions, placing one to the right of the Germans on the edge of a dense cedar brake, and stationing the other in another thicket about forty yards to their left.[77] The plan was seconded by McRae's lieutenants, who directed the men to dismount and take shelter in a ravine running at right angles to the river. There they wrapped themselves in blankets, waited for midnight, and wondered if the Germans would put up a fight."[78] One Confederate soldier thought that the Unionists "would get over into Mexico if they could, but if caught would fight desperately. They had, no doubt, heard of the character and the doings of our commander, and would sell their lives dearly rather than fall into his hands."[79]

Well might they fear James Duff, whether in person or by proxy. Superior over McRae as well as Donelson, the provost marshal had not accompanied this particular expedition. But he had appointed a protégé to command his detachment, Second Lieutenant Edwin Lilly. Nicknamed "Luck" by a chronicler, Lilly was "unscrupulous . . . sharp . . . [and] would cheat his own father—if he could."[80] Riding with this Duff doppelgänger was Charles Burgemann, the eastbound friend Tegener's men had waylaid earlier. Although a Unionist who had been "at many of the meetings and . . . confided in," Burgemann was infuriated at losing his goods and seized the opportunity to regain them, even when it meant betraying old friends.[81]

Speculation waning, the troopers in the crevice drifted into a cramped sleep. Then around midnight, they awoke, checked their rifles, and discarded their hats. With white handkerchiefs wrapped round their heads, the entire company started down the sides of the chasm in single file, padding over breakneck rubble and along steep slides. "Silence had been strictly enjoined," one remembered, "so that as we slowly crept up and down those dreadful rocks, not a whisper was heard, nor a sound was audible save the tramp of feet or the noise of a falling stone."[82] "Into the bed of the stream we slid, one by one . . . . Though no word was spoken, one could see the intense excitement of the men as they paused for a hurried drink of water, and clutched their rifles and crept stealthily on."[83]

Illustration 4 The Battle of Nueces, August 10, 1862, at the Nueces, by C. H. Clauss, 1888. *Courtesy Roy O. Perkins III and Comfort Historical Museum.*

On solid ground again, the soldiers broke into two groups, one to slide through the cedar brake until emerging on the far side of the sleepers, the other to line up on the near side, within rifle range of the camp. Deploying successfully, the men were lying down to wait for a dawn attack when a sudden shot cracked the silence. A Unionist horse guard had wandered too deeply into the far thicket and stumbled over a Rebel. Forgetting all orders to kill silently, the Southerner fired his gun, downing the picket, and startling the entire camp. Immediately, "sixty or more Confederates . . . rose from their blankets and rushed pell-mell over a space of open ground to a part of their command which lay under the cedars some sixty yards south." There they regrouped and attacked the campsite.[84]

The Unionists erupted from their sleep in an immediate panic, running "hither and thither in great confusion . . . like a swarm of bees." Tegener quickly restored order and repulsed the Rebel attack, then led a countercharge. But the fire from the Texans was deadly; the major and two of his men fell wounded, and Ernest Bosler, another guard, died in crossfire. Then, as quickly as the initial shock, silence descended, and for almost an hour, nothing but nervous potshots punctuated the darkness.[85]

The lull gave John Sansom time to reconnoiter the Confederate position. Scrunching down in the brush, he crept around the well-armed Rebels until he reached a northwest point, and then crawled back into camp. His report was no more welcome than his conclusion: to withdraw. "I . . . went to . . . Major Tegener," he later recalled, "who . . . had not relinquished command . . . I at once advised . . . that if they wished to continue the fight, the Unionists should abandon their present position and select one where they would be less exposed to the fire of the enemy [and] . . . have a better chance to [do] damage."[86] Bleeding profusely and propped between pallet and saddle, Tegener gave the proposal a spiritless assent, but withheld orders. His lieutenant Hugo Degener was even more hostile. "Withdraw!" he exclaimed. "Never! Our two guards have been killed, Major Tegener and two others of our comrades wounded, and if we leave here, they will get our horses, our rations, and all our equipage. I would rather fight here until every man of us is killed than to go anywhere else."[87] Another lieutenant, Ernest Cramer, was less adamant, but just as resolute. "I had given my word to . . . cover the right wing and was fully determined to stay." Caught up in acrimony, aware of their vulnerability but hesitant to incur further fire, the Union men dithered. Some slipped over to their horses and tied them nearby; a few fortified their positions with bedrolls and sacks of flour. Some covered the bodies of the dead—all waited.[88]

With the dawn, the Rebels attacked. "Three times they assailed us," Cramer recalled, "each time, we drove them back."[89] "The defenders . . . dared us to come on," remembered a Southerner. "They even threatened to charge out . . . [at our] party."[90] Standing up, firing, and shouting as they ran, "*Laszt uns unser Leben so teuer wie möglich verkaufen* (Let us sell our lives as dearly as we can!)," the Germans nearly stopped their opponents. Only Lieutenant Harbour's steely command, "They are giving way, boys, come on, charge!" rallied the Texans to turn and counterattack.[91] "On our side, the bullets were whistling pretty thickly over the heads of six or seven of us who were fighting together," one Rebel related. "Very cautiously then, now crawling, now dodging behind trees, [we] worked [our] way up to the edge of the mott in which the camp stood. . . . There for a brief space we kept up a galling fire on the defenders."[92]

One by one, Unionists deserted their posts. "After the second attempt to take our camp nearly half of our men could not face the fight any longer," revealed one. "We held out until the sun shone over the mountain. Then we ran away, about thirty of us," added another. "By the end of the day . . . only 32 were [still] with us," recounted a third. Many who remained were dying: Henry Marckwardt and Albert Bruns, Hugo Degener and Hilmar Degener, Emil Shreiner and Pablo Diaz.[93]

Finally, the rest decided to withdraw. "We now knew," Jacob Kuechler recalled, "that we could not hold our position any longer, and the time had arrived to leave our camp."[94] The decision was not easy. "The [enemy] had at first continued to shoot at those lying there," August Hoffman added, "otherwise certainly still more of us would have remained."[95] Nevertheless, the

Unionists retreated. One of their numbers described the fallback, "the wounded who could walk left camp first and we followed, guarding the rear."[96] "When I saw Major Tegener and the survivors of his command leave the camp and the Confederates take possession of it," John Sansom wrote later, "I . . . mounted my horse and rode . . . to a high bluff in a cedar-brake which overlooked the later battleground . . . . [H]ere I remained until about 10 o'clock A.M. watching the Confederates as they stood and walked about the camp and its dead and wounded. . . . Then . . . dazed by a tragedy that had robbed of their lives nineteen vigorous young men, and wounded . . . six, I rode away."[97] Had Sansom remained in his overhead loft just a little longer, "dazed" would have been the mildest of his feelings. Heretofore, the engagement between the Unionists and Confederates had been a straightforward battle between equals, albeit enemies. Even the injured Germans left behind merited the victors' respect. "They had fought a good fight," a secessionist recorded, "and bore themselves so pluckily. . . . We bound up their wounds, and gave them water, and laid them as comfortably as we could in the shade. Poor creatures, how grateful they were!"[98]

But Lilly, Duff's lieutenant and confidant, soon ended that. Hill Country days of "no quarter" had not passed, and while Commander McRae lay with the rest of Rebel wounded, his subordinate persuaded the Germans to move into better shade, a short distance away.[99] One trooper remembered hearing "the sound of firing . . . a little way off. I though at first they were burying some of the dead, but it didn't sound like that. . . . so I seized my rifle and ran in the direction of the firing. Presently I met a man coming from it who . . . said, 'You need't be in a hurry, it's all done; they shot the poor devils, and finished them off.' 'It can't possibly be they have murdered the prisoners in cold blood,' I said, not believing even Luck [Lilly] would be guilty of such an atrocious crime. 'Oh, yes; they're all dead . . . and a good job too!'"[100]

The outrage did not find its way into McRae's official report, nor did the fact that the bodies of all the slain were left unburied, "stripped of their clothing . . . piled up one over the other in a large heap," for the next three years. Not until six months after Lee's surrender did Edward Degener, William Boerner, Gottlieb Stieler, and Ed Steves arrive on the bank of the western Nueces to gather up their sons' remains and take them home.[101]

Despite the massacre on the river, the execution of nearly ten more of Tegener's men in the next few weeks, and a literal bloodbath among civilians in succeeding months, Unionist sentiment remained strong.[102] As the war ended its second year, one local conscription officer along the lower Guadalupe was forced to request additional military support. The officer wrote that "there is . . . a spirit of insubordination among the Germans in this region [and] they are remarkably stubborn." But the governor's visit helped restore calm there, while the relieving of Duff and his successor, Donelson, from provost command initi-

Illustration 5 Funeral of German patriots at Comfort, Texas, August 20, 1865. *Courtesy
Library of Congress.*

ated a working truce in the hills.[103] Those still hiding in the mountains, including survivors of the Nueces battle, were allowed to enlist in a frontier company;
some, like August Hoffman, began hauling freight again.[104]

In time, other survivors, like John Sansom and Henry Schwethelm, returned
to their homes. Each had managed to enlist in the Federal army after all—
Schwethelm in New Orleans, Sansom in Mexico. Together with nine of their
original comrades, they served with honor in the First Texas Cavalry until the
end of the war.[105]

On August 10, 1866, in the small community of Comfort, people gathered
from miles around to dedicate a monument to the youths who had left for
Mexico just four years earlier. On one side of the limestone memorial were their
names; on the other, their reason for dying: *Treue der Union.*[106]

Notes

1   R. H. Williams, *With the Border Ruffians,* ed. E. H. Williams (Lincoln: University
of Nebraska Press, 1982), 235–36; Samuel P. Hopkins, "When the Texans Went
to War Once Before," comp. G. A. McNaughton, *San Antonio Express,* January 13,
1918, p. 24.

2   Williams, *Border Ruffians,* 189–91, 195, 197–99, 224–26; Ralph A. Wooster,
Texas and Texans in the Civil War (Austin: Eakin Press, 1995), 15–18; *An Act
to Provide for the Protection of the Frontier,* 9th Texas Legislature, December 21,
1861, Ranger Correspondence, Texas Adjutant General's Department, Archives

and Information Services Division, Texas State Library and Archives Commission (hereafter cited as ARIS-TSLAC); Robert P. Felgar, "Texas in the War for Southern Independence," (Ph.D. dissertation, University of Texas, Austin, 1935), 68–71. Born around 1828 in Scotland, Duff enlisted as a private in the U.S. Army in 1849. Court-martialed and convicted of desertion, his sentence was remitted, and he served until his discharge five years later. He became a successful businessman in San Antonio until secession; by June of 1862 he had founded Duff's Partisan Rangers, a part of the Texas Frontier Cavalry. His company was one of the many independent frontier units formed in Texas's early Confederacy, subject to the rules and regulations of the Confederate States Army but under the control of state authorities. See *An Act to Provide for the Protection of the Frontier of the State of Texas,* 9th Texas Legislature, December 21, 1861, Ranger Correspondence, Texas Adjutant General's Department, ARIS-TSLAC; James Duff, Enlistment Papers, U.S. Army, 1798–July 14, 1894, Adjutant General's Office, RG94, National Archives, courtesy of Paul Burrier; "Proceeding of General Court Martial," June 9, 1849, Fort Smith, Arkansas, Court-martial files, U.S. Army, 1798–July 14, 1894, Adjutant General's Office, GG49, National Archives, courtesy of Paul Burrier; "Special Order #9," Brigadier General Arbuckle, October 23, 1849, Fort Smith, Arkansas, U.S. Army, 1798–July 14, 1894, Adjutant General's Office, National Archives, courtesy of Paul Burrier; Brig. Gen. Robert Beckham to J. Y. Dashiell, June 2, 1862, New Braunfels, Texas, Texas State Troops, Thirty-first Brigade, General Correspondence, Texas Adjutant General's Department, ARIS-TSLAC; "Dissolution of Partnership," *San Antonio Herald,* March 15, 1862, p. 2; *San Antonio Herald,* May 10, 1862, p. 2; Alwyn Barr, ed., "Records of the Confederate Military Commission in San Antonio, July 2–October 10, 1862," *Southwestern Historical Quarterly* (hereafter cited as *SHQ*) 70 (July 1966): 94; Frank W. Heintzen, "Fredericksburg, Texas, during the Civil War and Reconstruction" (Ph.D. dissertation, St. Mary's University of San Antonio, 1944), 38–39.

3   Col. James M. Norris to Governor F. Lubbock, Camp Verde, April 19, 1862; Norris to Dashiell, Fort Belknap, Texas, April 23, 1862; Col. A. G. O'Bencham to Col. J. Y. Dashiell, Fort Belknap, Texas, May 17, 1862, all in General Correspondence, Texas Adjutant General's Department, ARIS-TSLAC; "An Act," *The Weekly (Austin) Texas State Gazette,* January 18, 1862, p. 2; Col. H. E. McCulloch to Maj. S. B. Davis, March 3, 1862, *The War of the Rebellion: A Compilation of the Official Records of the Union and Confederate Armies* (hereafter cited as *OR*), comp. Robert N. Scott (Washington, D.C.: U.S. Government Printing Office, 1880–1901), 1, 9:701.

4   *The Weekly (Austin) Texas State Gazette,"* March 22, 1862, p. 2; Wooster, *Texas and Texans in the Civil War,* 110–11; Claude Elliott, "Union Sentiment in Texas, 1861–1865, *SHQ* 50 (April 1947): 451; *San Antonio Herald,* July 26, 1962; Mary Jo O'Rear, "E. J. Davis Home of Corpus Christi" (seminar project, Texas A&M University-Corpus Christi, 1975), 3. Despite a 76 percent majority in favor of secession, the state vote taken on February 23, 1861, showed significant sections against dissolution. These included northern Red River counties (including Col-

lin, Cooke, and Grayson), western Hill Country counties (including Gillespie, Mason, and Blanco), and the frontier Uvalde and Medina counties. See A. R. Williams and W. M. Holmes, "Secession Movement in Texas," in *Historical Atlas of Texas* (Norman: University of Oklahoma Press, 1989), 39; Walter Buenger, *Secession and the Union in Texas* (Austin: University of Texas Press, 1984), 174–75; R. L. Biesele, *The History of the German Settlements in Texas, 1831–1861* (San Marcos: Southwest Texas State University, 1987), 206.

5   Williams, *Border Ruffians*, 231; "Domestic Enemies," *Weekly (Austin) Texas State Gazette*, March 22, 1862, p. 2; "Down with Them!" *San Antonio Semi-Weekly News*, June 2, 1862, p. 1; *San Antonio Semi-Weekly News*, June 16, 1862, and July 31, 1862, p. 2.

6   Col. H. E. McCulloch to Maj. S. B. Davis, March 3, 1862, *OR*, 1, 9:701.

7   Brig. Gen. H. P. Bee to Capt. S. B. Davis, October 21, 1862, *OR*, 1, 53:454; Wooster, *Texas and Texans*, 94; "General Orders, #13," *San Antonio Herald*, June 7, 1862, p. 2; Walter D. Kamphoefner, "New Perspectives on Texas Germans and the Confederacy," *SHQ* 102 (April 1999): 450; Alwyn Barr, ed., "Records," *SHQ* 70 (July 1966): 94.

8   Capt. J. A. Duff to Maj. E. F. Gray, June 23, 1862, *OR*, 2, 4:786.

9   F. Fresinius deposition, "Records," *SHQ* 73 (July 1969): 84; Erastus Reed testimony, "Records," *SHQ* 71 (October 1967): 254.

10   Seaman Field deposition, "Records," *SHQ* 71 (October 1967): 256.

11   Erastus Reed testimony, "Records," *SHQ* 71 (October 1967): 253.

12   Ibid., 253–54.

13   Joseph Graham testimony, "Records," *SHQ* 71 (October 1967), 255; Heintzen, "Fredericksburg, Texas," 6–7; "Letter from New Braunfels"; *Galveston Tri-Weekly News*, September 24, 1861, p. 2; *Galveston Tri-Weekly Telegraph*, April 12, 1862, p. 1; Martin Hardwick Hall, *Sibley's New Mexico Campaign* (Albuquerque: University of New Mexico Press, 2000), 168–69, 185–86; Kamphoefner, "New Perspectives," 447; Stephan Schwartz, *Twenty-two Months a Prisoner of War* (St. Louis: AF Nelson, 1892), 135–36, *Google Book Search*, http://books.google.com/books?vid=OCL23589620&1a (accessed June 27, 2007); Buenger, *Secession*, 178–79; Joe Baulch, "The Dogs of War Unleashed: The Devil Concealed in Men Unchained," *West Texas Historical Association Yearbook*, 126–41, http://digital.library.schreiner.edu/sldl/pdfa/Baulch.pdf (accessed September 27, 2006), 127.

14   *San Antonio Herald*, May 31, 1862, p. 2.

15   Capt. W. P. Graves to Major DeBray, August 24, 1861, Kemper City, Texas, General Correspondence, Texas Adjutant General's Department, ARIS-TSLAC; *Weekly (Austin) Texas State Gazette*, March 22, 1862, p. 2; "Soldiers of the Lower Grande," *San Antonio Semi-Weekly News*, July 7, 1862, p. 1; Col. H. E. McCulloch to Maj. S. B. Davis, March 3, 1862, *OR*, 1, 9: 701; Col. H. E. McCulloch to Maj. S. B. Davis, March 25, 1862, *OR*, 1, 9:704; "Latest from the West," *San Antonio Herald*, June 21, 1862, p. 1; "To the Citizens of Caldwell, Austin, Victoria, Milam, Angleton . . . and other Counties," *San Antonio Herald*, July 4, 1862, p. 1, and August 2, 1862, p. 1; Williams, *Border Ruffians*, 234. Gen.

H. H. Sibley's early war effort to take New Mexico and Arizona for the South concerned Texans. Although victorious in two major battles, the Confederates were unable to maintain a secure supply line, and by June 1862, Sibley was retreating. With almost a thousand imprisoned, sick or dead, the survivors' trek to San Antonio was desperate, " many of them . . . a-foot . . . ragged . . . and hungry." See Hall, *Sibley's New Mexico Campaign*, xvi, 141, 147; also Don E. Alberts, *The Battle of Glorieta: Union Victory in the West* (College Station: Texas A&M University Press, 1998), and Donald S. Frazier, *Blood and Treasure: Confederate Empire in the Southwest* (College Station: Texas A&M University Press, 1995).

16   *San Antonio Herald,* August 2, 1862, p. 1; "Still Another Confederate Disaster," p. 1, and "The Bad News," "Call on Texas for 15,000 More Troops," *San Antonio Herald,* March 1, 1862, p. 2; "Our Situation," *Galveston Tri-Weekly News,* May 3, 1862, p. 1; "The Conscription Law," *San Antonio Semi-Weekly News,* June 19, 1862, p. 1; Felgar, "Texas in the War," 85–86; Col. H. E. McCulloch to Maj. S. B. Davis, March 25, 1862, *OR,* 1, 9:705.

17   Norris to Dashiell, April 19, 1862, April 20, 1862, from Camp Verde, April 23, 1862, from Camp San Saba, General Correspondence, Texas Adjutant General's Department, ARIS-TSLAC.

18   Norris to Dashiell, May 22, 1862, Camp San Saba, General Correspondence, Texas Adjutant General's Department, ARIS-TSLAC.

19   "General Order #4," April 23, 1862, Camp San Saba, Texas, General Orders 1862, Ranger Correspondence, Texas Adjutant General's Department, ARIS-TSLAC; DeMontel to Dashiell, May 31, 1862, Camp Verde; DeMontel to Norris, May 17, 1861, Fort Belknap; DeMontel to Dashiell, May 31, 1862, Camp near Camp Verde; DeMontel to Norris, July 4, 1862, Camp McCord, all from General Correspondence, Texas Adjutant General's Department, ARIS-TSLAC.

20   DeMontel to Dashiell, April 13, 1862, Camp near Camp Verde, General Correspondence, Texas Adjutant General's Department, ARIS-TSLAC.

21   Brig. Gen. Robert Beckham to J. Y. Dashiell, March 28, 1862, May 13, 1862, June 7, 1862, June 29, 1862, July 1, 1862, all from New Braunfels, Texas, Texas State Troops, Thirty-first Brigade, General Correspondence, Texas Adjutant General's Department, ARIS-TSLAC.

22   Gen. Hamilton P. Bee to Capt. S. B. Davis, October 21, 1862, *OR,* 1, 53:454–55; Erastus Reed testimony, Julius Schlickum testimony, "Records of the Confederate Military Commission," *SHQ* 71 (October 1967): 254, 257.

23   Beckham to Dashiell, April 20, 1862, and April 26, 1862, New Braunfels, Texas, Thirty-first Brigade, Texas State Troops Correspondence, Texas Adjutant General's Department, ARIS-TSLAC; William Banta and J. W. Caldwell, *Twenty-seven Years on the Texas Frontier* (Council Hill, Oklahoma: L. G. Park, 1893, 1933), 186; Adolf Paul Weber, *Die Deutsche Pioniere: Zur Geschichte des Deutschthums in Texas,* trans. Helen Dietert (San Antonio, Texas: Selbstverlag des Verfassers, 1894), from the Jacob Keuchler Biographical File, Center for American History, University of Texas at Austin, Austin, Texas, 12–13, courtesy of Paul Burrier; August Siemering, "Die Deutschen in Texas Waehrend des Buergerkriege (The Germans in Texas

during the Civil War, Taken from the Records of Judge August Siemering, 1876),"
trans. Helen Dietert and Ronnie Pue, *Der (San Antonio) Freie Presse für Texas,* May
29, 1923, included in compilation by Paul Burrier, 2004, p. 24, courtesy of Paul
Burrier.

24   "500 Hundred Dollars Reward," *San Antonio Herald,* July 26, August 2, 1862,
     p. 2; Heintzen, "Fredericksburg, Texas," p. 44–45; Baulch, "The Dogs of War
     Unleashed," 131; Charles Nimitz testimony, "Records," *SHQ* 71(October 1967):
     263–64; "Who Are They?" *San Antonio Semi-Weekly News,* July 14, 1862, p. 2;
     San Antonio Herald, July 26, 1862, p. 1; Williams, *Border Ruffians,* 235–36; Hop-
     kins, "When the Texans," p. 24.

25   Gen. Hamilton P. Bee to Capt. S. B. Davis, October 21, 1862, *OR,* 1, 53:454–55.

26   Ibid.

27   Williams, *Border Ruffians,* 235–37; Gen. Hamilton P. Bee to Capt. S. B. Davis,
     October 21, 1862, *OR,* 1, 53:454–55; Heintzen, "Fredericksburg, Texas," 46–47.

28   Williams, *Border Ruffians,* 236–37; Heintzen, "Fredericksburg, Texas," 47–48.
     "Bushwhacker raids" were forays into the foothills to flush out malcontents and
     deserters.

29   Williams, *Border Ruffians,* 238.

30   Williams, *Border Ruffians,* 236, 258–59; testimony of E. Degener, "Records,"
     SHQ 73 (October 1969), 251; Hopkins, "When the Texans," p. 24; Heintzen,
     "Fredericksburg, Texas," 47.

31   Special Orders 5–9, Headquarters to Capt. H. T. Davis, July 22, 1862, Camp
     Collier, Special Orders 1862, Texas Adjutant General's Department, ARIS-
     TSLAC; Camp Pedernales Post Returns Report, August 1862, National Archives;
     Williams, *Border Ruffians,* 238.

32   First Lt. C. D. McRae to Maj. E. F. Gray, August 18, 1862, *OR,* 1, 9: 614;
     Baulch, "Dogs of War Unleashed," 133; Shook, "Battle of the Nueces," 36; Janet
     B. Herell, ed., *Texas Confederate Soldiers* (Wilmington, North Carolina: Broad-
     foot, 1997), 21.

33   John W. Sansom, "Battle of Nueces River in Kinney, Texas, August 10, 1862, as
     Seen and Reported by John W. Sansom," Texas State Library, Austin, Texas, 4, 13;
     Ernest Cramer to his parents, October 30, 1862, Monterrey, Mexico, *Germans in
     the Civil War* (Chapel Hill: University of North Carolina Press, 2006), ed. Walter
     Kamphoefner and Wolfgang Helbich, trans. Susan Carter Vogel, 431, courtesy
     of Gregory Krauter and Comfort Heritage Foundation; Jacob Keuchler to Guido
     E. Ransleben, *A Hundred Years of Comfort in Texas,* ed. Guido Ransleben (San
     Antonio: Naylor, 1954, 1974), 96; Henry Schwethelm, "The Story of the Nueces
     Massacre as Told by Henry Schwethelm," *Frontier Times* 29 (September 1952),
     file 3593, Kilgore Files, Special Collections Room at Texas A&M-Corpus Christi
     (cited hereafter as SCR), 343; Siemering, "Die Deutschen in Texas," *Dur Freie
     Presse für Texas,* June 8, 1923, p. 33 in compilation.

34   Cramer to parents, 431; Sansom, "Battle of Nueces River," 2–3; Siemering,
     "Die Deutschen in Texas," *Dur Freie Presse für Texas,* June 8, 1923, p. 27 in
     compilation.

35   Tyler Anbinder, *Nativism and Slavery: The Northern Know Nothings and the Politics of the 1850s* (Oxford: Oxford University Press, 1992), 7–8; David R. Hoffman, ed., "A German-American Pioneer Remembers: August Hoffmann's Memoir," *SHQ* 102 (April 1999): 490–91, 494, 495; Charles Schwartz testimony, "Records," *SHQ* 71 (October 1967), 267; F. Fresenius testimony, "Records," *SHQ* 73 (July 1969), 83–84; Joseph Graham testimony, "Records," *SHQ* 71 (October 1967), 255; U.S. Department of Commerce, Bureau of the Census, *Eighth Census of the United States, 1860* (June 11, 1860).

36   Beckham to Dashiell, April 7, April 26, May 3, June 3, June 6, June 7, 1862, New Braunfels, Texas, Thirty-first Brigade, Texas State Troops Correspondence, Texas Adjutant General's Department, ARIS-TSLAC; "Letter from New Braunfels;" Hoffman, "A German-American Pioneer," 498.

37   Testimony of E. Degener, "Records," *SHQ* 73 (October 1969), 251; "Headquarters, General Military District of the Rio Grande, San Antonio, Texas, May 14, 1862," *San Antonio Herald,* June 7, 1862, p. 2; "Headquarters, Trans Mississippi District, San Antonio, July 1, 1862," *San Antonio Herald,* July 12, 1862, p. 2; "Notice from the People's Store," "Price Current," *San Antonio Semi-Weekly News,* July 31, 1862, p. 2; *San Antonio Herald,* August 2, 1862, p. 2; Barr, "Records," *SHQ* 71 (October 1967), 260; Baulch, "Dogs of War Unleashed," 130.

38   Cramer to parents, 430.

39   Ransleben, *A Hundred Years,* 64–66, 80–81; Biesele, *History of the German Settlements,* 171–72; Adalbert Regenbrecht, "The German Settlers of Millheim before the Civil War," *SHQ* 20 (July 1916), 28, 31; Heintzen, "Fredericksburg, Texas," 17.

40   Biesele, *History of the German Settlements,* 223–25; Heintzen, "Fredericksburg, Texas," 3.

41   Heintzen, "Fredericksburg, Texas," 4–5.

42   Ibid., 8; Biesele, *History of the German Settlements,* 199–200.

43   Heintzen, "Fredericksburg, Texas," 8.

44   Ibid., 5–10; Biesele, *History of the German Settlements,* 198–99, 225; Biggers, *German Pioneers,* 51.

45   La Grange (Texas) Paper, June 30, 1855, p. 3, quoted in Biesele, *History of the German Settlements,* 225.

46   Stephan Schwartz, Twenty-two Months, 52–53; Claude Elliott, "Union Sentiment in Texas, 1861–1865," *SHQ* 50 (April 1947): 451–52; Felgar, "Texas in the War," 336–37; *San Antonio Semi-Weekly News,* July 14, 1862, p. 2; *San Antonio Herald,* July 12, p. 2, and July 26, 1862, p. 1.

47   Charles Nimitz testimony, "Records," *SHQ* 71 (October 1967): 262.

48   Judge Advocate submitting, "Records," *SHQ* 71 (October 1967): 257–58.

49   Judge Advocate submitting, "Records," *SHQ* 71 (October 1967): 275.

50   Testimony of E. Degener, "Records," *SHQ* 73 (October 1969): 250; Capt. James Duff to Maj. E. F. Gray, June 23, 1862, OR, 2, 4:786; Nimitz testimony, "Records," *SHQ* 71 (October 1967): 262–63, 266, 270–71, 275; Frederic Dambach testimony, "Records," *SHQ* 71 (October 1967), 258–59; Williams, Border Ruffians, 237.

51   Judge Advocate, "Records," *SHQ* 71 (October 1967), 275.

52   "Domestic Enemies," *Weekly (Austin) Texas State Gazette*, March 22, 1862.

53   "Summary Justice," *San Antonio Herald*, May 31, 1862.

54   "Traitors and Spies," *Galveston Tri-Weekly News*, June 2, 1862.

55   Sansom, "Battle of Nueces River," 2; August Hoffman in Ransleben, *A Hundred Years*, 87; Heintzen, "Fredericksburg, Texas," 21, 43–44; "Indians," *San Antonio Herald*, November 2, 1861; "The Recent Indian Raid," *San Antonio Herald*, January 25, 1862; *Galveston Tri-Weekly News*, January 28, 1862; Depositions of Frau Grobe and of John Dietz, April 4, 1862, and of Wilhelm Jung, April 9, 1862, Gillespie County, General Correspondence, Texas Adjutant General's Department, ARIS-TSLAC; Felgar, "Texas in the War," 158, 164, 337–40; Biggers, *German Pioneers*, 66–67, 70; Heintzen, "Fredericksburg, Texas," 65–67.

56   Beckham to Dashiell, January 5, January 9, January 21, March 28, 1862, New Braunfels, Texas, Texas State Troops, Thirty-first Brigade, General Correspondence, Texas Adjutant General's Department, ARIS-TSLAC; Cramer to parents, 429; Siemering, "Die Deutschen in Texas," *Dur Freie Presse für Texas*, May 29, 1923, p. 23 in compilation; Heintzen, "Fredericksburg, Texas," 21–22; Elliott, "Union Sentiment,"463; Baulch, "Dogs of War Unleashed," 127–28; Felgar, "Texas in the War," 80–81.

57   Nimitz testimony, "Records," *SHQ* 71 (October 1967), 262–63.

58   Wolman testimony, 261, Fresenius testimony, 264, Nimitz testimony, 262, all in "Records," *SHQ* 71 (October 1967); Cramer to parents, 429; Siemering, "Die Deutschen in Texas," *Dur Freie Presse für Texas*, May 29, 1923, p. 23 in compilation; Beckham to Dashiell, June 28, 1862, New Braunfels, Texas, Texas State Troops, Thirty-first Brigade, General Correspondence, Texas Adjutant General's Department, ARIS-TSLAC; Heintzen, "Fredericksburg, Texas," 21–22; Elliott, "Union Sentiment," 463; Baulch, "Dogs of War," 127–28.

59   Cramer to parents, 430; Schwartz, Twenty-two Months, 89–90, 92–93; Siemering, "Die Deutschen in Texas," *Dur Freie Presse für Texas*, May 29, 1923, pp. 25–26 in compilation; Beckham to Dashiell, May 13, 1862, New Braunfels, Texas, Texas State Troops, Thirty-first Brigade, General Correspondence, Texas Adjutant General's Department, ARIS-TSLAC; Heintzen, "Fredericksburg, Texas," 25–26, 32–33.

60   Heintzen, "Fredericksburg,"43– 45, 49; Sansom, "Battle of Nueces River," 2–4, 12; Cramer to parents, 430–31; Siemering, "Die Deutschen in Texas," *Dur Freie Presse für Texas*, May 29, 1923, p. 24 in compilation; Ransleben, *A Hundred Years*, 105; Baulch, "Dogs of War Unleashed,"130–32; Felgar, "Texas in the War," 342–43; Cramer to parents, 430–31. Also see Cramer to parents, 430–31; testimony of Degener, "Records," *SHQ* 73 (October 1969), 264; Hoffman, "A German-American Pioneer," 495; Jacob Keuchler to James Newcomb, Ransleben, *A Hundred Years*, 96–97; Henry Schwethelm, "The Story of the Nueces Massacre, as Told by Henry Schweithelm," *Frontier Times* 29 (September 1952), 339; Fritz Tegener to August Dücker, August 23, 1875, Austin, Texas, trans. Helen Dietert, Comfort Heritage Foundation, courtesy of Gregory Krauter.

61   Sansom, "Battle of Nueces River," 2–3; Cramer to parents, 431; Siemering, "Die Deutschen in Texas," *Dur Freie Presse für Texas*, June 9, 1923, p. 27 in compilation; Felgar, "Texas in the War," 342–44; Biggers, *German Pioneers*, 57–58; Heintzen, "Fredericksburg, Texas," 43, 49.

62   Sansom, "Battle of Nueces River," 4; Felgar, "Texas in the War," 344; Claude Elliott, "Union Sentiment," 465; "German Military Commands," http://rm.wanderer.org/info/dictionary.html (accessed May 9, 2007). The number of the Unionists going to Mexico is uncertain. Sansom reported 61, Keuchler 62, Hoffman 63, Schwelthelm and Cramer 68. Fritz Tegener was adamant the number was 65. See Keuchler to Newcomb in Ransleben, *A Hundred Years*, 96; Hoffman, "A German-American Pioneer Remembers," 495; Schwelthelm, "Story of the Nueces Massacre," 330; Cramer to parents, 431; Tegener to Dücker, August 23, 1875.

63   No one has located this document. See Baulch, "Dogs of War Unleashed," 132. However, its effect cannot be negated; not only did most Unionists believe they had thirty days to leave Texas, some even read the proclamation, possibly an outdated decree from 1861. See Robert G. Schulz, Jr., "The Nueces Massacre, also known as the Battle of the Nueces," http://www.hal-pc.org/~dcrane/txgenweb/nueces.htm (accessed September 25, 2006); also Sansom, "Battle of Nueces River," 10–11; Schwethelm, "Story of the Nueces Massacre," 339; Keuchler to Newcomb in Ransleben, *A Hundred Years*, 96–97; Heintzen, "Fredericksburg, Texas," 49–50; Felgar, "Texas in the War," 348–49.

64   Department of Commerce, U.S. Census Bureau, 8th Census of the United States, 1860 (June 11, 1860); Sansom, "Battle of Nueces River," 2–4, 6, 8; Cramer to parents, 428, 431; Tegener to Dücker, August 23, 1875; Hoffman, "A German-American Pioneer Remembers," 496; Schwethelm, "Story of the Nueces Massacre," 339; Siemering, "Die Deutschen in Texas," *Dur Freie Presse für Texas*, June 8, 1923, p. 27 in compilation; Ransleben, *A Hundred Years*, 24, 96–97; Biggers, *German Pioneers*, 57-58; Heintzen, "Fredericksburg, Texas," 43, 49; Biesele, *History of the German Settlements*, 175, 177; Felgar, "Texas in the War," 342–44.

65   This is estimating approximately one hundred miles from Turtle Creek to the Mexican border and assuming that the contingent would travel at least twenty miles per day. See Schwethelm, "Story of the Nueces Massacre," 339.

66   Cramer to parents, 431; Hoffman, "A German-American Pioneer Remembers," 496; Schwethelm, "Story of the Nueces Massacre," 339; Keuchler to Newcomb in Ransleben, *A Hundred Years*, 96–97.

67   Schwethelm, "Story of the Nueces Massacre," 339.

68   Keuchler to Newcomb in Ransleben, *A Hundred Years*, 97; Tegener to Dücker; Sansom, "Battle of Nueces River,"4; Weber, *Die Deutsche Pioniere*, 13; Siemering, "Die Deutschen in Texas," *Dur Freie Presse für Texas*, June 8, 1923, p. 27 in compilation; Williams, *Border Ruffians*, 239; Schwethelm, "Story of the Nueces Massacre," 339–40.

69   Sansom, "Battle of Nueces River," 4–5; Schwethelm, "Story of the Nueces Massacre," 339–40.

70   Sansom, "Battle of Nueces River," 5–6; Cramer to parents, 431; Hoffman, "A German-American Pioneer Remembers," 496; Hoffman in Ransleben , *A Hundred Years*, 87–88.

71   Hoffman in Ransleben *A Hundred Years*, 87–88; Hoffman, "A German-American Pioneer Remembers," 496; Warren Schellhase, ed., The Edited Journal of Fritz Schellhase, Gottfried and Sophie Schellhase Family, http://tuffie0.tripod.com/journaloffritrzschellhase.htm (accessed June 5, 2007).

72   Sansom, "Battle of Nueces River," 5–6.

73   Ibid., 6.

74   Williams, *Border Ruffians*, 237–40.

75   Ibid., 240–44.

76   Ibid., 244; Hoffman, "A German-American Pioneer Remembers," 496; Keuchler to Ransleben, A Hundred Years, 97; Sansom, "Battle of Nueces River," 4–5.

77   First Lt. C. D. McRae to Maj. E. F. Gray, August 18, 1862, *OR*, 1, 9:615; Williams, Border Ruffians, 244–45.

78   Ibid., 241, 245; 1st Lt. C. D. McRae to Maj. E. F. Gray, August 18, 1862, *OR*, 1, 9:615.

79   Williams, Border Ruffians, 241, 245.

80   Williams, Border Ruffians, 226, 230, 244–45; Hoffman, "A German-American Pioneer Remembers," 498; 1st Lt. C. D. McRae to Maj. E. F. Gray, August 18, 1862, *OR*, 1, 9:614–15; Camp Pedernales Post Returns Report, National Archives; Robert Shook, "The Battle of the Nueces, August 10, 1862," *SHQ* 46 (April 1963), 36–37, 40; Baulch, "Dogs of War Unleashed," 133. In his memoirs, R. H. Williams used aliases for superiors he disliked: General Bee was called "Wasp," Captain Duff was "Dunn" and Junior 2nd Lieutenant Lilly was "Luck." Also see Edwin Lilly, Thirty-third Regiment, Texas Cavalry, Service Records, War Department Collection of Confederate Records, National Archives, courtesy of Paul Burrier; Siemering, "Die Deutschen in Texas," *Dur Freie Presse für Texas*, June 8, 1923, p. 28 in compilation.

81   Sansom, "Battle of Nueces River," 4; Williams, *Border Ruffians*, 237; Siemering, "Die Deutschen in Texas," *Dur Freie Presse für Texas*, June 8, 1923, pp. 27–28 in compilation; Ransleben, *A Hundred Years*, 121; Heintzen, "Fredericksburg, Texas," 51; Felgar, "Texas in the War," 344. There may have been another "guide" in McRae's division as well, a straggler captured by McRae's men and compelled to reveal the Unionists' route. Also see Schwethelm, "Story of the Nueces Massacre," 339; Schwethelm to Ransleben, *A Hundred Years*, 90–91.

82   Williams, *Border Ruffians*, 245–46.

83   Ibid.

84   Williams, *Border Ruffians*, 246; Sansom, "Battle of Nueces River," 6–7; 1st Lt. C. D. McRae to Maj. E. F. Gray, August 18, 1862, *OR*, 1, 9:615; Cramer to parents, 431–32; Siemering, "Die Deutschen in Texas," *Dur Freie Presse für Texas*, June 8, 1923, p. 28 in compilation.

85   Sansom, "Battle of Nueces River," 7; Williams, *Border Ruffians*, 246–47; Schwethelm, "The Story of the Nueces Massacre," 340.

86   Sansom, "Battle of Nueces River," 8.

87   Ibid., 9.

88   Cramer to parents, 432; Sansom, "Battle of Nueces River," 9; Siemering, "Die Deutschen in Texas," *Dur Freie Presse für Texas*, June 8, 1923, p. 28 in compilation.

89   First Lt. C. D. McRae to Maj. E. F. Gray, August 18, 1862, *OR*, 1, 9:615; Cramer to parents, 432.

90   Williams, *Border Ruffians*, 247.

91   Hoffman in Ransleben, *A Hundred Years*, 88; Williams, *Border Ruffians*, 247; Sansom, "Battle of Nueces River," 9.

92   Williams, *Border Ruffians*, 247.

93   Keuchler to Newcomb in Ransleben, *A Hundred Years*, 96; Hoffman, "A German-American Pioneer Remembers," 497; Cramer to parents, 432; Sansom, "Battle of Nueces River," 13.

94   Keuchler to Newcomb in Ransleben *A Hundred Years*, 97.

95   Hoffman, "A German-American Pioneer Remembers," 497.

96   Keuchler to Newcomb in Ransleben, *A Hundred Years*, 97.

97   Sansom, "Battle of Nueces River," 10.

98   Williams, *Border Ruffians*, 248.

99   First Lt. C. D. McRae to Maj. E. F. Gray, August 18, 1862, OR, 1, 9:616; Camp Pedernales Post Returns Report, August 1862, National Archives; *San Antonio Semi-weekly News*, August 25, 1862, p. 2.

100   Williams, *Border Ruffians*, 249–50; Sansom, "Battle of Nueces River," 10, 13; Heintzen, "Fredericksburg, Texas," 53–54; Felgar, "Texas in the War," 345.

101   Cramer to parents, 433; Sansom, "Battle of Nueces River," 11–13; Schwethelm, "Story of the Nueces Massacre," 341; Ransleben, *A Hundred Years*, 93–94; Schellhase, The Edited Journal of Fritz Schellhase. What was reported was that the defenders had asked no quarter. The lieutenant listed two fatalities of his own, eighteen wounded, and a conspicuous lack of commendations. See 1st Lt. C. D. McRae to Maj. E. F. Gray, August 18, 1862, *OR*, 1, 9:615–16; Hopkins, "When the Texans," 24.

102   Thomas C. Smith, *Here's Yer Mule: The Diary of Thomas C Smith, 32nd Texas Cavalry, C.S.A.* (Waco, Texas: Little Texan Press, 1958), 19–20; Howard Henderson to J. W. Sansom in Ransleben, *A Hundred Years*, 119–20; Siemering, "Die Deutschen in Texas," *Dur Freie Presse für Texas*, June 8, 1923, pp. 30–31 in compilation. Numbers vary. Where Sansom totaled nineteen killed at the battleground and nine executed subsequently, Siemering listed fifteen dead or wounded on the Nueces and eight later rounded up and hanged. Schwelthelm also counted twenty-three in toto. Among the Confederates, McRae enumerated thirty-two Union dead, as did another battle veteran, W. J. Edwards. Hopkins cited thirty enemy killed, while Williams estimated a stunning eighty. Among those attempting again to cross to Mexico ten weeks later, Sansom lists six deaths in both his memoirs, although Ransleben's edition adds two to his list; Weber's account cites seven. See Sansom, "Battle of Nueces River," 10, 13; John Sansom, The Mas-

sacre on the Nueces River: The Story of a Civil War Tragedy, as Related by R. H. Williams and John W. Sansom (Grand Prairie, Texas: Frontier Times Publishing House, n.d.), http://texashistory.unt.edu/permalink/meta-pth-2409:2 (accessed September 16, 2006), 32, 35–36; Ransleben, *A Hundred Years*, 114; Schwethelm, "Story of the Nueces Massacre," 340, 341; Siemering, "Die Deutschen in Texas," *Dur Freie Presse für Texas*, June 8, 1923, pp. 29–30 in compilation; 1st Lt. C. D. McRae to Maj. E. F. Gray, August 18, 1862, *OR*, 1, 9:615; W. J. Edwards testimony, "Records," *SHQ* 73 (October 1969), 252; Hopkins, "When the Texans," p. 24; Williams, *Border Ruffians*, 248; Weber, *Die Deutsche Pioniere*, 14–15; Felgar, "Texas in the War," 346–48.

103   Four months after the August 10, 1862, battle, Duff and his men were officially mustered into the Confederate States service as Duff's Battalion of Partisan Rangers, serving both at Fort Brown and then later in Gonzales County. Within a year of war's end, however, Duff was indicted in Kendall County for his part in a lynching. Arrested for another killing in Arkansas, he escaped to Denver, then London, and finally died in France. See General Orders #1, Brig. Gen. H. P. Bee, January 2, 1863, San Antonio, Texas; James Duff to Captain E. P. Turner, August 24, 1863, San Antonio, Texas; and Duff to Turner, April 4, 1864, Camp on Lavaca; all in James Duff, Thirty-third Regiment, Texas Cavalry, Service Records, War Department Collection of Confederate Records, National Archives, courtesy of Paul Burrier. See also *State of Texas v. James Duff and Richard Taylor*, December 5, 1865, January 13, 1868, March 21, 1877, Kendall County Files, courtesy of Paul Burrier; "Duff, the Rebel Butcher of Western Texas," *San Antonio Daily Express*, August 3, 1869, p. 2; Heintzen, "Fredericksburg, Texas," 56–57; D. S. Stanley, *Personal Memories of Major General D. S. Stanley* (Cambridge, Massachusetts: Harvard University Press, n.d.), 234–35, courtesy of Paul Burrier. McRae's "guides" to the Nueces were also dead, and the straggler, according to Schwethelm, killed during the battle. See "The Story of the Nueces Massacre as Told by Henry Schwethelm," 340. Burgemann, injured in the fighting, died in Mexico, see *San Antonio Weekly News Herald*, August 25, 1862, p. 2; Camp Pedernales Post Returns Report, August 1862, National Archives; Ransleben, ed., A Hundred Years, 121.

104   Enrolling Officer A. J. Bell to Maj. J. P. Flewellen, November 28, 1862, *OR*, 1, 15:887; Maj. J. P. Flewellen to Capt. E. P. Turner, December 4, 1862, *OR*, 1, 15:886; Hoffman, "A German-American Pioneer Remembers," 498, 499; Lt. Col. H. L. Webb to Captain E. P. Turner, February 18, 1863, *OR*, 2, 4: 981; Siemering, "Die Deutschen in Texas," *Dur Freie Presse für Texas*, June 8, 1923, pp. 30–31 in compilation; Camp Pedernales Post Returns Report, August and September, 1862, National Archives; Heintzen, "Fredericksburg, Texas," 56; Felgar, "Texas in the War," 349–51, 354–56.

105   Sansom, "Battle of Nueces River," 13–14; Schwethelm, "Story of the Nueces Massacre," 342–44.

106   "Loyal to the Union." Schwethelm to Ransleben, *A Hundred Years*, 93–94.

Chapter 7

Without a Fight: The Eighty-four-day Union Occupation of Galveston, Texas

by Donald Willett[1]

Galveston is a feisty little seaport with a colorful and bizarre history. In the early 1800s, the island was the home port for the United States' most famous pirate, Jean Lafitte. At the turn of the century, the city survived the greatest natural catastrophe in North American history, the Hurricane of 1900. Forty-seven years later, the famous port in the Gulf of Mexico had a bird's eye view of the greatest man-made catastrophe in North America, the Texas City explosion of 1947. The port city was an active participant in the American Civil War. During the war, Confederate and Union forces fought a pitched battle for control the city. The Battle of Galveston was the most important military action of the Civil War in Texas. Details of the actual battle (when the Confederates recaptured Galveston) are well documented by Edward Cotham, Jr., in *Battle of the Bay: The Civil War Struggle for Galveston* (1998) and by Donald Frazier in *Cottonclads!: The Battle of Galveston and the Defense of the Texas Coast* (1998). Both historians admirably describe the military aspects of the event.[2] From their studies, we learn that on New Year's Day, 1863, Texas Confederates used a two-pronged attack to defeat Union naval and army forces that occupied the "Queen City of the Gulf." One prong marched across the wooden railroad bridge onto the island and attacked Union forces located near the harbor front. The second prong, made up of the famous Texas cottonclads, steamed down Galveston Bay from Houston, sailed into the harbor, captured one Federal warship, forced the retreating naval forces to scuttle their flagship and strand their army colleagues, forcing them to surrender unconditionally to the numerically superior Confederate forces. While both Cotham and Frazier provide an excellent account of the military operations involved in the battle, they do not detail the occupation of Galveston. This study attempts to fill that void.

When the Civil War commenced, the port of Galveston was the engine that powered the Texas economy and cotton was its fuel. Galveston was the most populous and wealthy city in Texas. It also was one of the largest ports on the Gulf of Mexico and the gateway to Texas and the western Confederacy. If President Abraham Lincoln hoped to reunite the Union, his troops needed either to

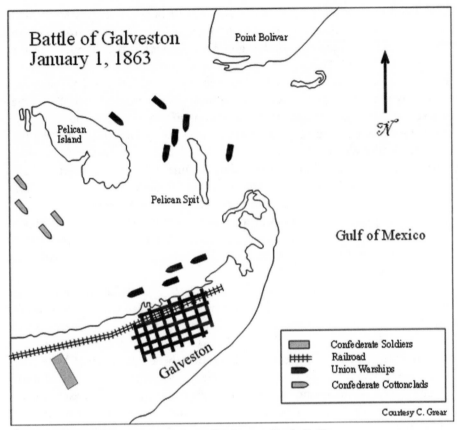

Battle of Galveston
January 1, 1863

Point Bolivar

Pelican
Island

Pelican Spit

Gulf of Mexico

Galveston

	Confederate Soldiers
	Railroad
	Union Warships
	Confederate Cottonclads

Courtesy C. Grear

Map 1 Battle of Galveston, January 1, 1863. *Courtesy Charles D. Grear.*

neutralize or capture the Queen City of the Gulf. If the Confederacy hoped to earn independence it had to keep all its seaports, including Galveston, open to foreign commerce.

When the war began, the Confederacy placed General Paul Octave Hébert in charge of military operations in Texas.[3] Hébert, a former governor of Louisiana, was a graduate of West Point and a veteran of the Mexican-American War with a solid reputation as an engineer.[4] When Hébert arrived in Galveston he was disturbed by what he saw. The city was a soldier's nightmare. It contained no military installations, no military materiel, nor a fortress to deter Union blockading vessels or repel an enemy attack. In Hébert's opinion the city was virtually undefendable.[5] This pessimistic attitude colored his attempts to defend the city from Union attack.

Hébert tried to remedy this situation by constructing several artillery positions along the beachfront, one near the Galveston side of the railroad bridge, and one on Pelican Spit, a small sandbar that guarded the entrance to the harbor.

He placed his beachfront cannons at Twenty-first Street, Fifteenth Street, and the largest at Fort Point, across the entrance to Galveston Bay from Pelican Spit.[6] Later he constructed another gun emplacement at the other end of the island near San Luis Pass.

He believed that the railroad bridge that connected Galveston to the mainland was the real key to defending Southeast Texas from invasion. On the Galveston side of this bridge his engineers constructed an artillery position near Eagle Grove. He hoped these guns would keep the Federals from shelling the bridge. He also cleared an area on the mainland side of the bridge and named this installation, located near present-day Virginia Point, Fort Hébert. If Federal troops ever threatened the harbor he could fall back in an orderly fashion, defend the railroad bridge, and protect the city of Houston from Union attack. But for the present his main concern was Galveston. The Louisianan hoped that this show of force would keep Union vessels at bay and prevent them from attacking the city. These hastily built emplacements bought Galvestonians one year of relative peace.

The Civil War came to Galveston on July 2, 1861. That morning locals walking on the beach spied the ominous silhouette of two Union naval vessels on the horizon. The steamship *South Carolina* and the schooner *Dart* were the first Union vessels to blockade Galveston. The next day the *Dart* reconnoitered the gulf side of the island looking for Rebel emplacements. When the small gunboat passed the Twenty-first Street battery the boys in gray lobbed a cannon ball at the enemy vessel. It quickly returned fire. This exchange of fire acted like a magnet for both sides. The *South Carolina* soon came to the aid of the smaller vessel. The local citizens, hoping to get a better view of this exciting event, packed their picnic baskets and scurried toward the beach and into harm's way. As the artillery duel commenced, one of the Union shells exploded over a large group of spectators. This wayward shot killed one local and sent a large percentage of the population fleeing to the relative safety of Houston.

Like it or not, the city of Galveston was now on the front line of the American Civil War. Life on the island would never be the same. Soon other units from the Union's Western Gulf Squadron began to tighten the blockade along the Texas coast. These ships ranged up and down the Texas coast from Sabine Lake to Brownsville. They chased, usually with little success, an occasional blockade-runner. Most importantly the blockade interrupted the unimpeded flow of raw materials and manufactured goods and reduced it to a trickle. The Union blockade slowly strangled the life's blood out of the economy of Texas and transformed Galveston from a dynamic and prosperous seaport into a dormant and impoverished enclave. The Confederates, lacking a viable navy, could only stand by and helplessly watch their cause slowly die.

This waiting game soon settled into a monotonous routine. Each day Federal vessels cruised up and down Galveston Island making sure to stay out of the range of Confederate cannons. The Rebel artillerist followed the movement of each vessel hoping it might come into firing range. None ever did. At night the Union navy vessels anchored offshore while the Confederates patrolled the beachfront in search of Union landing parties. They never came ashore.

The first hint that Union forces would conduct serious military operations against Galveston occurred on May 17, 1862. Two days earlier two Union vessels, the *Santee*, a propeller-driven warship and the *Sam Houston*, a wooden schooner, had appeared on the horizon. Capt. Henry Eagle, the commander of the two blockaders, informed the Confederate commander of Galveston that "in a few days the naval and land forces of the United States Government will appear off the town of Galveston to enforce its surrender." As a humanitarian gesture Eagle pleaded, "To prevent the effusion of blood and destruction of property which would result form the bombardment of your town I hereby demand the surrender of the place with its fortifications and all batteries in its vicinity with all arms and munitions of war."[7] Eagle allowed the Confederates twenty-four hours to answer.

General Hébert, who had earlier moved his headquarters to San Antonio, still believed that Galveston was indefensible. Upon learning of this threat his first instinct was to cut and run. He initially ordered military forces on the island to prepare to evacuate the island if an overwhelming force appeared. In particular he wanted the army unit on Pelican Spit to spike their guns, quietly evacuate their camp but leave their flag atop its flagpole. Hébert decided he would simply abandon the city without a fight before he would officially surrender it to the enemy.[8]

On May 19 Captain Eagle informed foreign consuls in the city "that four days will be allowed you from this date in which to remove your families and property. After that time the bombardment will commence at my earliest convenience."[9] This second message apparently stiffened Hébert's resolve. The general remarked, "From the tone of Captain Eagle's dispatch the inference is that he may again send a peremptory demand of surrender. There is to be no surrender on any circumstances. There may be an abandonment in face of a superior force, but nothing else."[10] However, in five months Hébert would disobey his own command.

One last time, on May 22, Captain Eagle informed the consuls that he could no longer assure their well-being during the upcoming bombardment. As the time drew near for the Union navy to commence its attack, Confederate defenders vowed to "give the frigate [*Santee*] a warm reception" if it dared to enter Galveston harbor.[11] One Galvestonian applauded Captain Eagle's bravado and mocked General Hébert's apparent timidity when he noted, "If the

Federal commander can intimidate the authorities and consuls of Galveston to vacate the city and make a surrender by threats alone, he may perform the same operation before every seaport of the Confederacy, and thus save his government all the expense of sending out fleets of gun boats and other armed vessels to accomplish the same end."[12] Just as the Rebels braced for the expected blow, Captain Eagle and his tiny fleet headed eastward toward the Mississippi River and another assignment. It was all a bluff! Galveston was still safe. Instead of attacking Galveston, the *Santee* and the *Sam Houston* ran out of food and left the area in search of something to eat.[13] Everyone knew that the enemy would someday attack Galveston. But they would not do it this day.

Quickly the situation returned to normal. Union naval vessels continued to blockade Galveston. Confederates continued to defend their city. However, something was different. Soon new blockaders replaced the *Santee* and the *Sam Houston* but they were larger and more heavily armed warships. Galvestonians did not know it but there had been a change of command and a change of strategy. The new commodore was newly promoted William B. Renshaw, a favorite of Adm. David Glasgow Farragut, the commander of the West Gulf Blockading Squadron. And the new strategy encouraged the West Gulf Squadron to attack and hold Texas coastal ports.

Confederate policy toward Galveston also changed. Since the time of the Republic, small wooden schooners shuttled between Houston and Galveston carrying food and other necessities to the island city. Suddenly without warning military authorities ordered these small boats to cease their supply runs to the island. Soon foodstuffs became scarce and tempers flared. The local newspapers published desperate pleas for food and supplies to lessen this new burden upon the island soldiers and their families. One islander angrily noted: "It seems rather a hard case for the Island City to be blockaded on one side by our enemies and, on the other side, by our friends."[14] An uneasiness blanketed the city.

In September Admiral Farragut ordered Commander Renshaw to "proceed down the coast of Texas with other vessels, keeping a good lookout for vessels running the blockade, and whenever you think you can enter the sounds on the coast and destroy the temporary defenses, you will do so and gain the command of the inland navigation." He reminded the young commander that "Galveston appears to be the port most likely for you to be able to enter, if the forts are not too formidable."[15] In short order Union vessels captured Sabine Pass and Corpus Christi, but Confederate defenders in Corpus repulsed the invaders.[16] This new Union activity flustered Confederate authorities. With coastal artillery in short supply and the Confederate navy nonexistent, there was only one thing Confederate authorities could do—threaten the Yankee invaders with biological warfare. Shortly after Union forces commenced their raids on the Texas seaboard, local newspapers began to report an epidemic of yellow fever up and down the coast.

According to journalists, yellow jack first struck Sabine City, near Sabine Pass, on September 10. One week later the fever appeared in Indianola. By the end of September, the "black vomit" struck Brownsville. In early October it spread to Matagorda. Rumors even suggested that the disease was present in Galveston Bay.[17] Should Renshaw attack the Texas coast and possibly spread an epidemic of yellow fever throughout the United States Navy? Or should he continue the already successful blockade strategy?

This impasse ended abruptly on October 4, 1862. That morning, eight Union blockading vessels appeared upon the horizon. The *Harriet Lane*, a converted mail carrier named after President James Buchanan's niece, entered Galveston harbor under a flag of truce. A messenger from the vessel informed city officials that Capt. William B. Renshaw wished to discuss terms for the surrender of the city of Galveston. After waiting several hours for a reply, the *Harriet Lane* retreated toward the gulf. Five Union vessels returned to the harbor. To convince his enemies that he was serious, Renshaw ordered his ships to bombard the Confederate batteries at Fort Point and Pelican Spit. A few well-placed Union broadsides transformed these Rebel strongholds into piles of rubble. Having gained the upper hand, Renshaw demanded the immediate unconditional surrender of the city. Confederate officials responded that they could not surrender because yellow fever had spread throughout the city. Renshaw rethought his unconditional surrender demand and instead granted city officials four days to evacuate the civilian population but maintain the military status quo. After that he promised to level the city if it did not surrender.[18]

For the next ninety-six hours civilians fled their homes while military forces stripped the city of anything that could aid the enemy. General Hébert, who still resided in San Antonio, ordered his soldiers to remove the remaining Confederate artillery to Virginia Point, on the mainland, but continue to defend the small Confederate artillery position at Eagle Grove.[19] For the first time since the Texas Revolution in 1836, Galveston looked like a ghost town.

On October 9, 1862, the unspeakable happened. Union officials rowed ashore and accepted the peaceful surrender of the city. For the only time in its history, "foreign" troops occupied the Queen City of the Gulf. News of the fall of the city sent a shockwave throughout the state. In a land that defined itself by armed resistance against overwhelming odds, unconditional surrender without a show of force was unthinkable. As one Galvestonian succinctly stated, "We look upon the tame surrender of Galveston to a few ferryboats as anything but creditable."[20] However, another islander had a different view. He reasoned that Galveston did not really surrender to the enemy. Military and civil leaders simply abandoned the city and the "enemy took possession of the place much in the same way [the pirate Jean] Laffite did some 45 years ago."[21]

Most Galvestonians blamed the military for their homelessness and suffering. To them military authorities were "either imbecile or neglectful" in their attempt to procure naval artillery to defend the city. Earlier, locals noted that a "number of influential citizens foreseeing that the place might be taken by a mosquito fleet, such as that which has now seized the key to Texas, raised a sum of money and sent a committee to Richmond to procure guns sufficient to prevent such a shameful disaster." This committee convinced Confederate officials to release twelve cannons for the defense of Galveston. These Texans transported the weapons to the Texas border. Much to their surprise, military authorities stopped them and confiscated the guns. After a "timely remonstrance," the soldiers allowed some cannons to continue to the island. Without sufficient weaponry, reasoned these gentlemen, Galveston was doomed. These angry citizens concluded: "Had the people of Galveston been left to liberty to defend their city, and the key to our state, without interference from military authorities, they would have had the cannon where they should have been and would have fought them too with sufficient effect to have kept out such a contemptible fleet as has now poured this burning indignity upon us." Instead, Galveston's defenders surrendered the city and removed the cannons, "along with the contents of the Galveston icehouse," to Virginia Point for safekeeping.[22]

For the governor of Texas, Francis Lubbock, news of the capitulation of Galveston was too much to bear. Earlier, in a message to the people of Texas, Lubbock noted, "I would rather see the city [Galveston] one blackened ruin than that a miserable, fanatical, abolition horde should be permitted to occupy it, gloating over their gains and laughing to scorn our abandonment of so important a strategic point."[23] This patriotic speech certainly reinforced the sagging morale of many Texans. For Galvestonians, however, the thought of a Texas governor who wanted to burn their beautiful city to the ground did not sit well. Strangely, after the war Lubbock moved to Galveston and served in city government for several years.

Around nine o'clock in the morning, the Federal fleet entered Galveston harbor and anchored near the wharves. At one o'clock in the afternoon, Commodore Renshaw's flagship, the *Westfield*, a converted New York City ferryboat, fired three shots, signaling that Renshaw was ready to accept the surrender of the city. The newly elected mayor pro tem and city council rowed to the flagship and met Renshaw, who informed the civil authorities that, for the present, he did not intend to occupy fully the city. For now, he meant to "hoist the U.S. flag upon the public buildings and that the flag should be respected." He warned the leaders that he would not tolerate another New Orleans-like reception. If anyone fired on his troops or ships or disrespected them or the flag in any manner, he would "hold the city responsible and open his broadsides . . . instantly" on the city and that he would keep his gun "shotted and double shotted for that purpose." He finished his harangue by noting that it was the "determination of his government to hold Galveston at all hazard until the end of the war, and that [the Confederates] could not take the port from him without a Navy." Once this meeting concluded, the mayor and his friends returned to shore, their heads held low. One hundred and fifty bluejackets and Marines, led by Capt. Jonathan Wainwright, the captain of the *Harriet Lane,* and "including about a half a dozen 'negroes'" rowed ashore, marched to the United States Custom House and raised the Stars and Stripes above the building. About a half an hour later, at around three o'clock that afternoon, they lowered the flag and returned to their ships.[24] Thus began the Union occupation of Galveston.

As the Federal occupation commenced, an eerie status quo evolved. During the day downtown Galveston and the harbor belonged to the Union. Each morning a detachment of sailors rowed ashore and raised the Stars and Stripes over the customhouse. Small detachments patrolled Strand and Ship's Mechanic streets and searched for possible Rebel activity. With most of the stores closed and the civilian population relocated inland, Galveston looked like a ghost town. At twilight another detachment of sailors rowed ashore, marched to the customhouse and lowered the Stars and Stripes. They quickly returned to the harbor and rowed back to their ship.

When Commander Renshaw first came ashore he quickly concluded that he had been bamboozled. As late as October 5, while lying at anchor in Galveston harbor awaiting the evacuation of Galveston, Renshaw believed that there was an epidemic of yellow fever in Galveston. Because of this outbreak he suspected that Admiral Farragut would not allow him to go ashore. Instead he expected to be harassed "in the extreme" by an estimated 5,000 Confederate troops on the mainland side of the railroad bridge.[25] In fact, that year yellow jack did not visit the Texas coast and Confederate troops did surprisingly little until the day of the battle.

Renshaw also discovered that the Rebels had broken their pledge to maintain the military status quo during the evacuation of the city. They had successfully removed all cannons from the city, save one, to Virginia Point. The remaining cannon was an X-inch Columbiad that Union naval fire disabled when Union naval vessels first entered Galveston Bay. However, the commodore learned that the Rebels left several "Quaker cannons" (tree trunks painted black and made to look like cannons) throughout the island. These facsimiles fascinated Renshaw. In a letter to Adm. David Porter, Renshaw noted that as he entered the harbor, "On Pelican Island there were two 'busters' looking right down the harbor . . . They are full sized X-inch Columbiads, beautifully made and finished so perfectly that at twenty-five yards you couldn't tell them from guns of approved patterns." He so loved these Quakers that he mounted one of them "on the forward part of the hurricane deck" of his flagship.[26] Tragically, this *faux* cannon must have been the last thing Renshaw saw before the scuttling charge that he lit on his flagship exploded prematurely and killed him. Had United States naval intelligence thoroughly examined Texas newspapers they would have known that the *Galveston Weekly News*, during the *Santee* affair, unwittingly admitted the existence of Quaker cannons on the island. The paper rather foolishly noted, "She [the *Sam Houston*] ran casually down along the beach and quite close in as if to draw the fire of our batteries and thus learn what guns and what quakers we had in position."[27]

The United States Navy did not possess detailed maps of Galveston harbor. To remedy this, Commodore Renshaw immediately ordered his men to sound the waters in and around the harbor. Their operations ventured into Galveston Bay as far as Redfish Bar, on the northern side of Pelican Spit. These activities attracted the Confederates' attention. What were the Federals planning? One Rebel journalist reasoned, "We believe the ferry boats will run on any depth of water where our river steamers can go."[28] Was Houston the Union's next target? Apparently the bluejackets' mapping efforts were terribly inaccurate. When the Battle of Galveston commenced, Commodore Renshaw grounded his flagship, the *Westfield*, on an oyster reef near Pelican Spit. The captain of the *Owasco*, a Union "90-day gunboat," while trying to aid the recently captured *Harriet Lane*, misjudged the width and depth of the ship channel, and could not maneuver his vessel. Unable to bring his guns to bear, he had to back his ship out of a fierce firefight with Confederate sharpshooters and leave the *Harriet Lane* in enemy hands. Were inaccurate charts another reason Union forces lost the Battle of Galveston?

Several problems soon arose. One concerned the status of runaway slaves in Texas. On September 22, 1862, President Abraham Lincoln issued the Emancipation Proclamation. He gave the Confederates until January 1, 1863, to end the rebellion and save the institution of slavery. If they did not surrender before the new year, Lincoln promised to free all slaves in Confederate territory. Therefore, while Union forces occupied Galveston the Federal government acknowledged the existence of slavery in the South. Early in the war, Union Gen. Benjamin Butler formulated the Union policy toward runaway slaves. After the Battle of Big Bethel (June 10, 1861), several slaves took refuge behind Union lines at Fortress Monroe, Virginia. When the slave owners demanded that Butler return their property he informed the Southerners that the fugitives were "contraband of war" and now belonged to the Federal government. Shortly after the surrender of Galveston, Captain Renshaw faced a similar dilemma.

Early on October 13, four slaves escaped by boat to Galveston. The following morning, the small white skiff tied up to the *Harriet Lane* and the four fugitives boarded the Union warship. That afternoon, the owners, a Dr. Stone and a Mr. Miller, demanded that Captain Renshaw return the runaways and the boat

that the slaves had stolen. Renshaw informed the Rebels that he would release
the runaways "with their consent, but not without" and ordered the two men to
return the following day. The next day the slave owners left Galveston a second
time with neither their boat nor their chattel.[29]

From October 13 until the new year, Federal policy toward runaway slaves
in Texas did not treat these fugitives as contraband of war. Renshaw instead
viewed them as chattel who could return to their owners if they wished to continue lives as slaves. Ironically, while classifying these men as runaway slaves,
Renshaw also believed that they did not possess any constitutional rights or freedoms. Shortly after this incident Renshaw arrested several "negroes" and forced
them to work without pay on new fortifications on Pelican Spit.[30] In Galveston
and elsewhere, combatants from both sides were willing to sacrifice their lives
to defend their views of slavery. But neither side believed that the slave's life
was worth respecting. Yankee or Rebel, it did not matter who was in charge in
Galveston; both considered themselves superior to the African American people
of Galveston. It mattered little to them whether the blacks they came into contact with were free or slave.

From sunset to sunrise Galveston Island belonged to the Confederacy. Day
and night Southern spies roamed freely throughout the city. Southern cavalry
traversed the island and continually reconnoitered Union activities around
the harbor. The Texans even maintained a permanent military presence on the
island, a small fort at Eagle Grove they used to protect the island side of the
railroad bridge from Union attack.

The capture of Galveston earned General Hébert a one-way trip out of
Texas. He returned to his home state where he commanded the subdistrict of
North Louisiana. Two days after the surrender of Galveston, Hébert's replace-
ment arrived in Texas. From the moment he appeared, Gen. John Bankhead
Magruder captivated the citizens of Texas.

A native of Virginia, Magruder graduated from West Point in 1830.[31]
Although an average student, Magruder excelled in the theater arts. Some cadets
believed his acting revealed a flair for the dramatic. Later, his battlefield tactics, including those in Galveston, seemed to confirm these observations. Fellow officers nicknamed Magruder "Prince John" because of his gentlemanly airs
and elegant clothing. He fought during the Mexican-American War under Gen.
Zachary Taylor in northern Mexico and with Gen. Winfield Scott in central
Mexico. Magruder earned a reputation as a brilliant artillery officer and a hard
fighter. When his home state seceded, Magruder resigned his commission in the
United States Army and offered his services to the state of Virginia. Magruder's
first assignment was command of Confederate forces on the Yorktown peninsula.
On June 9, 1861, he fought and won the Battle of Big Bethel, the first land battle
of the Civil War. After the battle the Confederate government promoted him

to brigadier general. Next, General Magruder constructed an elaborate series of trenches and earthworks between Yorktown and the James River. He hoped this would deter any Union attempt to stage an invasion from Fortress Monroe on the tip of the Yorktown Peninsula toward the national capital at Richmond.

In April of 1862 General George McClellan landed over 100,000 Union soldiers at Fortress Monroe. This marked the beginning of the famous Peninsula Campaign. Facing McClellan were 10,000 Rebels led by John Bankhead Magruder. Quickly, Prince John put his theatrical training to good use. He lined his trenches with hundreds of Quaker cannons and ordered his troops to march in circles, sound their bugles, and occasionally lob a cannonball at the fortress. By engaging in such activities, the Confederates attempted to conceal their inferior troop strength and thereby delay a Federal attack. The ruse worked. For a month the timid McClellan refused to leave the fort and engage the enemy. Eventually, McClellan left the relative safety of Fortress Monroe and slowly marched up the peninsula. His army came within eyesight of the Confederate capital in Richmond. Then two events occurred that changed forever the Civil War career of Prince John. First, a serious wound to Gen. Joe Johnson, the commanding Confederate general, forced the Rebel leaders to place Robert E. Lee in charge of the army. Second, General McClellan ordered part of his army to cross the Chickahominy River. This was all General Lee needed to take the offensive. He took most of his troops and attacked the smaller number of Union troops who had crossed the river. Lee ordered Magruder and his 25,000 troops (men had been added to his command since the beginning of the campaign) to stop McClellan and his 65,000 soldiers from capturing Richmond.

Once again, Prince John used his flair for the dramatic to achieve the impossible. Around the clock his soldiers marched in circles, blew their bugles, and feigned artillery bombardments and massed attacks. This clever deception so unnerved McClellan that he ordered his army to withdraw. Thus began the Seven Days Campaign (June 25–July 1) and the end of Magruder's military career in Virginia.

With the Union army in full retreat, Lee ordered Magruder to pursue vigorously the enemy. Magruder caught up with the Federals near Savage's Station but he did not begin his attack until late in the afternoon. His ineffective use of troops allowed the Yankees to slip away unscathed. Magruder next met his opponent at Malvern Hill. Lee ordered Magruder to lead a frontal attack on this strongly defended position. Well-placed Union artillery slaughtered his men. Like Pickett's charge at Gettysburg, Prince John's assault up Malvern Hill was a tragic disaster. Lee relieved Magruder of his command and the Confederate army shipped Prince John to Texas.

Almost from the moment Union sailors captured Galveston, rumors of an impending Confederate attack circulated throughout the city. This hearsay quickly unnerved Captain Renshaw and caused his men to develop itchy trigger fingers. An example of this itchy-trigger-finger syndrome was the signal-light affair. One evening Union sentries spied a series of flashing lights from a downtown residential area. Believing that these flickers were signals to Confederate forces at Virginia Point, the Federals fired several warning shots at the house and sent a squadron of bluejackets to question the occupants. The sailors arrested the elderly homeowner and escorted him to a Union warship. Under cross-examination the gentleman denied that he spied for Confederate forces but noted that his house contained no ceiling between the second floor and the attic. He argued that the signal lights were nothing more than shadows of family members who walked in front of the lighted candles on the second floor. After further interrogations and an inspection of the house Commander Renshaw let the old man go home.[32]

A second example of this syndrome was "The Battle with the Butchers." Each night after the capture of Galveston, Union lookouts noticed a number of mysterious lights in an area west of the city cemetery. The sound of horse-drawn wagons further convinced the Federals that this region on the outskirts of the city was the staging ground for a Confederate attack. Locals tried several times to convince the invaders that the lights came from an open-air slaughterhouse. Each night when the lights became visible navy sharpshooters peppered the area with minié balls. On October 28 a marksman shot a lantern from a butcher's hand and killed his horse. A second shot almost hit the butcher's sleeping daughter. The next morning the angry butchers informed the navy that there would be no more fresh meat on their dinner tables until the firing ceased. This Battle with the Butchers resulted in a crushing Union defeat. After several days of government rations Captain Renshaw relented and promised to allow these men to work in peace.[33] Ironically, during the Battle of Galveston General Magruder used the open-air slaughterhouse to stage his ground troops.

A third example of this syndrome focused on "One-Armed Tom." Almost daily Rebel sympathizers scouted the Union positions. The most famous of these spies was "One-Armed Tom" Barnett, a Mexican War veteran who had lost an arm to an enemy cannonball. For several weeks after the capture of Galveston, Barnett reconnoitered the downtown area and reported to Confederate leaders at Virginia Point. On December 1 Barnett began his rounds armed with a shotgun and a belly full of moonshine. Unwittingly, he stumbled onto a Union sentry stationed near the wharves. When ordered to halt, Barnett told the Yankee to "go to hell" and the two men exchanged fire. Upon hearing the shots, gun crews from two Union warships turned their cannons upon the city. The broadsides slightly damaged several buildings, including the Italian fruit stand, but caused no casualties. However, one overly eager journalist from Houston later reported that "one woman had her clothes torn off, but escaped injury."[34] The mystery woman never complained to local authorities and the Federals never captured "One-Armed Tom." After the war, Barnett joined the Galveston police force and enjoyed his new status as a local war hero.

Since his command did not include any foot soldiers or Marines, Renshaw believed that his sailors, even though they possessed greater firepower than the Rebels, could not repel an enemy attack. His second in command, Capt. Jonathan M. Wainwright, captain of the *Harriet Lane*, concurred. In a November 4 letter to Gen. Benjamin Butler, the commander of the Department of the Gulf in New Orleans, Wainwright observed, "Though the town is under our guns, we have no force to occupy it, and feel the want of some troops sadly. The place can easily be held by a regiment, with the aid of one or two vessels in the harbor . . . The town is well built, containing many fine stores and dwelling houses, together with other structures which could be converted into quite formidable strongholds, and easily held against anything less than artillery, from which the guns of our vessels would prove ample protection."[35] Several times, Renshaw wrote Admiral Farragut, and implored Butler to ask, to send soldiers to Galveston.

To keep the Confederates off guard, Renshaw authorized a number of raids and undercover operations in and around the bay. Some worked. Some did not. Sometime before November 14 Renshaw sent a Federal launch to Redfish Bar. Once there Federal troops captured a small schooner, the *Governor Runnels*, loaded with wood and sailed her to Galveston.[36] Renshaw feared that somehow the enemy would use the dark of night to sneak some cannons onto the island and attack his ships, a premonition that later proved correct. To lessen this possibility, on November 19 he sent a raiding party to Fort Point to torch the remaining wooden structures. The ensuing bonfire "burnt until late at night."[37] The most successful raid occurred the next day. That evening four launches from the *Westfield* and the *Owasco* rowed into the bay toward Redfish Bar and Half Moon Shoals. The object of their pursuit was a small Confederate schooner named the *Sheldon*. The bluejackets easily boarded and captured the ship and sailed her into the harbor. The next morning Renshaw found seventy to eighty bales of cotton in her hold.[38] Other undercover operations were not as successful.

After the surrender of Galveston, a small trickle of Union sympathizers, free and slave, straggled into Galveston and sought Federal protection. At one point approximately fifty to sixty people, including a "few negroes about 30 or 40 in all" lived near the wharves.[39] Apparently Renshaw periodically sent small launches to specified rendezvous points to ferry these Unionists from the mainland to the island. On November 13 the Federal warship closest to the harbor entrance lowered a launch. It rowed to a mysterious skiff floating near the tip of Bolivar Peninsula. Three men from the skiff, deserters from a Partisan

Illustration 6 Confederate lookout located at Bolivar Point. *Courtesy Library of Congress.*

Rangers unit stationed up the bay at Clear Creek, boarded the Union craft and it returned to the Yankee vessel. With its cargo safely aboard, the Union launch again returned to Bolivar Point. Unfortunately, it landed almost directly in front of a Confederate scouting unit. In the firefight that ensued, two Union navy men died and five others surrendered. The Confederates sustained no casualties.[40]

The desertion of the Partisan Rangers to the Union side raises several interesting questions. The odds that the Federal launch randomly rendezvoused at night in Galveston Bay near Bolivar Point with a passing skiff filled with Confederate deserters are rather high. It is more likely that this chance meeting was a planned rendezvous worked out between Federal officials in Galveston and Union sympathizers in the Galveston Bay area. An operation like this requires relatively sophisticated planning. A nighttime waterborne rendezvous involves a timeline, accurate maps and charts, good piloting skills, preordained signal lights and passwords and a well-laid-out course line for each boat to steer. Is it possible that an organized underground resistance movement of Unionists and Abolitionists existed in the Galveston-Houston area during the war? Did they keep in constant contact with Northern operatives before and after the surrender of Galveston? Also, why did the Union launch return to Bolivar Point after it delivered the Texas deserters to the Union navy? Were they looking for another group of discontented Texans to ferry to Galveston?

The most daring, but unsuccessful, raid occurred south of Galveston. On November 27 raiders from the Federal warship *Morning Light* rowed up Cedar Lake, near the entrance of the San Bernard River, and attacked a local salt-works. They demolished the equipment, burned the surrounding buildings, and destroyed several tons of salt. The next day they attacked another smaller salt factory four miles down the lake. The Federals landed two launches with thirty-four troops. There to greet them was a unit of Confederate cavalry and foot soldiers. Caught in a vicious crossfire, the Federals fled to their boats. According to local sources, only "three of thirty four men got out of the launches, and they with assistance only; and it is supposed that the balance were either killed or badly wounded." According to the Federal report, the Confederates killed one bluejacket, seriously wounded five others, captured one, and "about every one [else] . . . was slightly wounded."[41]

On December 18, 1862, Maj. Gen. Nathaniel Banks, the new commander of the Department of the Gulf in New Orleans, ordered Col. Isaac Burrell, the commander of the newly formed Forty-second Massachusetts Infantry to pro-ceed immediately to Galveston with all available men. Three days later, 260 army troops departed the Crescent City. On Christmas Eve they arrived at the entrance to Galveston harbor.

When he arrived, Burrell expected to bivouac his troops in the middle of the harbor on Pelican Island. This small island possessed comfortable military barracks and was relatively safe from a Confederate attack.[42] When the remain-der of his regiment rendezvoused, Burrell could move his troops onto Galveston and establish control of the city. Commodore Renshaw, however, insisted that Burrell station his men at Kuhn's Pier, a four-hundred-foot-long and twenty-foot-wide tee-head pier on Eighteenth Street. Renshaw assured Burrell that in case of an attack, a navy vessel would remove his soldiers from the pier in five minutes.[43] This order was the first of several mistakes by Renshaw that ulti-mately cost him his life.

The next morning, as soon as the troops disembarked at Kuhn's Pier, things began to go wrong. Burrell quickly discovered that longshoremen in New Orleans inadvertently loaded the wrong type of ammunition onto his transport vessel. If attacked, only one-third of his troops would have enough musket balls to protect themselves.[44] And Kuhn's Pier would be a nightmare to defend.

Colonel Burrell concentrated his defenses on the large two-storied ware-house located at the end of the pier. He converted the storehouse into a barrack and a hospital and ordered his men to pile sacks of plaster up the inside wall facing the city. He hoped this would protect his troops from enemy fire. Next, his soldiers ripped up some planking on the pier closest to the shore and used it to construct a barricade for the sentries. He later established another barricade at the other end of the pier adjacent to the tee head.[45] He hoped these modifications would deter a frontal attack by the Rebels.

Satisfied with his defensive preparations, Burrell scouted the city and the nearby Confederate positions. The railroad bridge fascinated him. He wondered why Renshaw made no serious attempt to capture or destroy the only avenue of attack open to Rebel forces on the mainland. Earlier, Union sailors filled the *Governor Runnels*[46] with combustible material and converted her into a fire ship. Then Renshaw countermanded his orders to fire the bridge and ordered his sailors to unload the vessel and use it as a target ship in the channel. Also, the Rebel light-artillery position at Eagle Grove was within range of naval artillery and yet the bluejackets fired a few salvos at the fort to get the range but never tried to destroy the battery or damage the bridge. On the eve of the Battle of Galveston, the only route on and off the island remained in Confederate hands.

The Confederate government placed General Magruder in command of the district of Texas, New Mexico, and Arizona. Since the Confederate defeat at Glorieta Pass, near Santa Fe, New Mexico, left New Mexico and Arizona in Union hands, Magruder only had to worry about defending the Lone Star State. The key to securing Texas and the entire Trans-Mississippi theater of the war, in Prince John's opinion, was Galveston Bay. "Whoever is master of the railroads of Galveston and Houston is virtually master of Texas."[47] In Magruder's mind, his course of action was clear. He had to attack Galveston and recapture its railways.

The Magruder battle plan consisted of a two-pronged attack upon Federal occupational forces in Galveston. The land force, consisting of troops and field artillery, would, under the cover of darkness, cross the two-mile-long railroad bridge, march another two miles over open ground, evade enemy detection, enter downtown Galveston, and position themselves and their field pieces near the waterfront. The naval fleet would steam down the bay from Houston and position itself just out of sight of the Federal fleet. At the appointed time, the land troops would attack the army position at Kuhn's Pier and hope to divert the navy's attention from the seaward approach to Galveston. Once the navy focused its firepower upon the attacking Rebels, the Confederate fleet would assault and capture the *Harriet Lane* and turn its guns upon the other enemy vessels. The attack was a bold but risky plan. As one military historian noted, "None but a Magruder would have attempted such a hazardous undertaking; it was contrary to all the maxims of scientific warfare. But the battle plan was no more bold or unconventional than Prince John himself."[48]

Now that he had his plan, all Magruder needed were some ships and soldiers and a little bit of luck. Most of the soldiers came from New Mexico. In

December of 1861 Gen. Henry Sibley had launched an ill-fated campaign from Texas into New Mexico. He hoped that the military conquest of that state would bind New Mexico to the Confederacy. A crushing defeat at Glorieta Pass ended any hope of victory and forced the ragtag army of Texas volunteers to retreat to the Lone Star State. By the time Magruder arrived in Texas, Sibley's Texas Brigade found itself bivouacked on the banks of Buffalo Bayou, not far from Houston. Magruder soon enlisted these soldiers in his crusade to liberate Galveston.[49]

The ships came from Galveston Bay. Magruder took command of four small steamboats and ordered shipyard workers to convert two of these paddle wheelers into cottonclads capable of capturing the fifteen warships in the Federal fleet. Prince John selected Leon Smith, an old friend, to supervise this difficult task. Smith first wandered the sea as a young man and on the eve of the Civil War captained sailing ships in the New York City–to–Galveston trade.[50]

Smith instructed the workers to fasten five-hundred-pound cotton bales around the engine, boilers, and machinery of three of the boats. He hoped the bales would protect the ships from Union cannon fire and serve as a platform for army sharpshooters. He then ordered laborers to rig boarding planks, similar to the ancient Roman *corvus,* from the king post of his two largest vessels, the *Neptune,* an old wooden mail packet, and the *Bayou City,* a wooden paddle-wheel bay boat.[51] Leon Smith used this device to board quickly the *Harriet Lane* and overpower its crew. He proclaimed the boats ready for war after workmen mounted a thirty-two-pounder on the bow of the *Bayou City* and two twenty-four-pound cannons on the bow of the *Neptune.* Silhouetted against a setting sun, the Galveston Bay flotilla was an impressive sight.[52]

Originally, Magruder scheduled the attack upon Galveston for December 27, 1862. He had to postpone the assault four days because the cannons for his ships did not arrive on time. On New Year's Eve Prince John informed his commanders it was time to march on Galveston and drive the Yankees into the sea. With Magruder's coded order, "The Rangers of the Prairie send greetings to the Rangers of the Sea," the Confederate naval vessels commenced their attack on the Federal ships in Galveston.[53] By the time the smoke cleared over Galveston, the impossible had occurred. For the first time since the War of 1812, enemy forces boarded and captured a United States naval vessel, the *Harriet Lane.* For the only time in American naval history, an enemy force used an ancient Roman naval boarding device, the *corvus,* to capture an American warship. For the only time during the Civil War, a United States naval squadron deserted army troops on shore and made no attempt to rescue them. This action allowed Confederate troops to force these unfortunate soldiers on Kuhn's Pier to surrender unconditionally. While abandoning Galveston, the Union navy scuttled its flagship, the *Westfield,* and fled the battle scene under a white flag. Once the Union fleet passed the horizon and the coast was clear, Galveston became the only Confederate port during the Civil War temporarily to break the Union blockade and the only Southern port that the South ever recaptured. Union forces never attacked Galveston again. When the war ended in 1865, Galveston was the only major seaport still in Southern hands.

Notes

1. The author wishes to thank the Texas A&M University at Galveston Research Office for generous financial assistance that allowed him to travel to the National Archives in Washington, D.C., and the Lorenzo de Zavala State Archives in Austin, Texas.
2. Edward Cotham, Jr., *Battle of the Bay: The Civil War Struggle for Galveston* (Austin: University of Texas Press, 1998); Donald Frazier, *Cottonclads!: The Battle of Galveston and the Defense of the Texas Coast* (Abilene, Texas: McWhiney Foundation Press, 1998).
3. Samuel Boyer Davis, General Order No. 1, September 18, 1861, *The War of the Rebellion: A Compilation of the Official Records of the Union and Confederate Armies* (hereafter cited as *OR*), comp. Robert N. Scott, (Washington, D. C.: U.S. Government Printing Office, 1880–1901), 1, 4:106.
4. George W. Cullum, *The Biographical Register of the Officers and Graduates of the U.S. Military Academy* (Boston: Houghton Mifflin, 1893), 1, biography no. 1017.
5. P. O. Hébert to Secretary of War, September 27, 1861, *OR*, 1, 4:112–13.
6. George R. Wilson, Order No. 34, October 11, 1861, *OR*, 1, 4:117.
7. Joseph Cook to Hébert, May 17, 1862, *OR*, 1, 9:710.
8. Ibid., 711.
9. Ibid.
10. Ibid., 712.
11. Ibid.
12. Galveston *Weekly News*, May 21, 1862.
13. Henry Eagle to David G. Farragut, June 4, 1862, *The Official Records of the Union and Confederate Navies in the War of the Rebellion* (hereafter cited as *OR Navies*) (Washington, D. C.: U.S. Government Printing Office, 1899–1908), 1, 18:536.
14. Galveston *Weekly News*, July 9, 1862.
15. Farragut to W. Renshaw, September 19, 1862, *OR Navies*, 1, 19:213.
16. Ibid., 253–54.
17. Articles on this "epidemic" of yellow fever can be found in the Galveston *Weekly News*, September 10, 1862, September 17, 1862, October 8, 1862, and October 15, 1862.
18. Renshaw to Farragut, October 5, 1862, *OR Navies*, 1, 19: 254–60, contains Captain Renshaw's report.
19. Ibid., 262–63, contains Col. Joseph J. Cook's report. He commanded Confederate troops on the island. His immediate superior was Col. X. B. DeBray, who commanded Confederate forces in and around Galveston Bay. Apparently, Cook's men

were quite thorough in stripping the city. Proudly Cook reported, "All machinery of any value was removed. The civil authorities removed all the county records of every kind and all records of the city corporation and of the district court. The railroad company removed all their material of every kind and by 11 a. m. of the 8th we had removed all Government property of any value except the X-inch gun at Fort Point."

20. *Galveston Weekly News,* October 22, 1862.

21. Ibid., October 15, 1862.

22. Ibid. Apparently, Galvestonians believed that removing all ice-cold malted beverages from the island was a military necessity.

23. Francis R. Lubbock, *Six Decades in Texas; or, Memoirs of Francis Richard Lubbock, Governor of Texas in War Time, 1861–63, A Personal Experience in Business, War, and Politics* (Austin, Texas : B. C. Jones, 1900), 350.

24. *Galveston Weekly News,* October 15, 1862.

25. Capt. William Renshaw to Adm. David Porter, October 5, 1862, M 625, Area Files, Area 6, Porter Papers, Naval War Records, Roll 58, National Archives, Washington, D.C. There were fewer than 500 troops at Virginia Point.

26. Ibid.; Renshaw to Farragut, October 8, 1862, *OR Navies,* 1, 19:255.

27. *Galveston Weekly News,* May 21, 1862.

28. *Galveston Weekly News,* October 22, 1862.

29. Ibid.

30. Ibid.

31. This short overview of John Bankhead Magruder's military career comes from Thomas M. Settles, "The Military Career of John Bankhead Magruder" (Ph.D. diss., Texas Christian University, 1972), and Paul D. Casdorph, *Prince John Magruder: His Life and Campaigns* (New York: John Wiley, 1996).

32. *Galveston Daily News,* February 17, 1929.

33. J. W. Moore, Acting Mayor, City of Galveston, to Commander of the USS *Harriet Lane* [Capt. Jonathan M. Wainwright], October 28, 1862, M 625, Area Files, Area 6, Naval War Records, Roll 58, National Archives, Washington, D.C.

34. *Galveston Weekly News,* December 3, 1862, December 10, 1862; Charles Hayes, *Galveston: History of the Island and City* (Austin, Texas: Jenkins , 1974), 542–45.

35. *Galveston Weekly News,* January 21, 1863.

36. Ibid., November 19, 1862.

37. Ibid., November 26, 1862.

38. Ibid. One correspondent thought that the ship was named the *Brazoria.*

39. Ibid.

40. Ibid.

41. Ibid.; Report of Acting Master Dillingham, November 28, 1862, *OR Navies,* 1, 19:380–83.

42. N. P. Banks to Isaac Burrell, December 1862, *OR,* 1, 15:201–2.

43. Charles Bosson, *History of the Forty-second Regiment, Infantry, Massachusetts Volunteers, 1862, 1863, 1864* (Boston: Mills, Knight, 1886), 70–71.

44. Col. Isaac Burrell, Report, December 29, 1862, *OR,* 1, 15, 27:204–5.

45. Ibid.

46. *Galveston Weekly News*, November 19, 1862.

47. *OR*, 1, 26:261.

48. Settles, "Military Career of John Bankhead Magruder," 238.

49. S. S. Sanderson to J. B. Magruder, January 2, 1863, *OR*, 1, 15:922.

50. J. B. Magruder to James A. Sheldon, January 6, 1863, *OR*, 1, 15:931–32.

51   The *corvus* was a Roman naval boarding device first used in the first Punic War
     against Carthage. The Greek historian Polybius first described the *corvus* in
     volume three of his work, *The Histories*. According to Polybius the *corvus* was a
     four-foot-wide and thirty-six-foot-long boarding plank that Roman naval archi-
     tects attached to the bows of their warships. When dropped on an enemy's ship
     the *corvus* allowed Roman legionnaires to board the vessel and engage in hand-to-
     hand combat and to turn the ship into a floating battlefield.

52   C. G. Forshey to X. B. DeBray, December 25, 1862, *OR*, 1, 15:908.

53   Hayes, *Galveston: History of the Island*, 552.

Chapter 8

"Nothing but Disaster": The Failure of Union Plans to Capture Texas

by Edward T. Cotham, Jr.

From the outset of the Civil War, the Lincoln administration was pressured to launch a campaign to capture Texas. Many of these pleas were prompted more by economic considerations than by strategic thinking. In November 1861, for example, Massachusetts Governor John Andrew wrote the secretary of the navy at the urging of what he called "some of our most practical, experienced, and influential business men" to recommend that "the Federal Government should make its next demonstration upon the coast of Texas, the State easiest to take and hold, with larger public consequences dependent upon such action than any other."[1]

As Governor Andrew's plea suggested, Union strategy with respect to the capture of Texas seemed at first glance easy to formulate and implement. One look at a map confirmed that Texas included almost one-fourth of the entire Confederate coastline. The sheer length of this shoreline meant that any particular point along it was likely to be lightly defended. All that was needed, it seemed to Northern politicians and business interests alike, was for military planners to select a landing site and descend upon it with a large body of troops. This beachhead would then be used as a base of operations from which to launch a major campaign that would quickly subdue Texas.

If Union strategy was deceptively simple in that it seemed only to require a successful strike at a single place along the Texas coast, Confederate strategy was complicated in that it seemed to require the successful defense of all potential landing points along that same vast coast. Gen. Paul Hébert, who was placed in charge of the Confederate Department of Texas near the outset of the war, warned his superiors in September 1861 that he found the Texas coast "in almost a defenseless state, and in the almost total want of proper works and armaments." Recognizing that his enemy had the advantage of choosing where and when he would strike, and that the Texas coast provided numerous potential landing sites, Hébert placed on the record his firm conviction that "the task of defending successfully any point against an attack of any magnitude amounts to a military impossibility."[2]

As it turned out, Northern optimism about capturing Texas and Southern pessimism about defending it were both misplaced. Texas would not turn out to be "the State easiest to take and hold," as Governor Andrew had so confidently predicted. Equally erroneous was General Hébert's dire prediction that defending Texas was a "military impossibility." Instead, as one historian has observed, "the Texan defense of the seacoast between 1861 and 1865 proved to be one of the most brilliant unsung feats of any Confederate state during the war."[3]

Starting in August 1862, and continuing through 1863, Texas was the target of an almost unending series of raids, attacks, and full-scale invasion attempts, almost all of which can be summed up in one word: disaster. This is not just the verdict of historians. Adm. David Glasgow Farragut used the word "disaster" so frequently in his official reports concerning events in Texas that the secretary of the navy came to expect it. As Farragut stressed to Cdre. Henry Bell, his hand-picked commander of the naval forces off Texas: "Don't have any other disaster if possible, for they are abusing us enough at home."[4]

Things had not always looked so bleak for Union hopes in Texas. The summer of 1862, for example, had ended on a relatively optimistic note. Lt. John W. Kittredge, in charge of U.S. naval forces in the vicinity of Aransas Bay, grew tired of blockading the bays of South Texas and attempted to capture the port city of Corpus Christi. On August 12, Kittredge guided his fleet of small ships into Corpus Christi Bay and threatened to bombard the city. During the night of August 15, a Confederate force under the command of Maj. Alfred Hobby moved three guns into the remains of an old fortification dating from the Mexican War near the water's edge and at dawn opened fire on the Union fleet. The battle for Corpus Christi had begun.[5]

The surprised Federals eventually returned fire, doing very little damage to the Confederate gunners or their fort. In his official report, Kittredge claimed that he had silenced the enemy's guns several times during the day, but chose to withdraw out of range at nightfall. Several days following this engagement, Kittredge landed a small party with a howitzer and tried to take the Confederate battery by using this land force in combination with a naval bombardment. A timely charge by Texas cavalry, however, scattered the Union land force, causing it to retreat to the safety of the Union ships.[6]

Although the attempt to take Corpus Christi had failed, Kittredge's demonstration served notice that Texas ports were under the continuing threat of capture from Union blockaders. But that threat would have to come from a different Union officer. About a month after his unsuccessful attack on Corpus Christi, Kittredge was lured ashore and fell into a Confederate trap. Upon hearing that Kittredge had been captured, Admiral Farragut chose not to characterize this embarrassing incident as a disaster. Instead, he reported to Secretary of the Navy Gideon Welles that Kittredge had "succeeded very well" at Corpus Christi since the blockaders continued to blockade the entrance to Corpus Christi Bay.[7]

The next Union operation off the Texas coast was at Sabine Pass, and it turned out to be significantly more successful than Kittredge's attack at Corpus Christi. On the morning of September 23, 1862, two small steamers arrived off of Sabine Pass under the command of Acting Master Frederick Crocker. An aggressive commander by nature, Crocker quickly calculated that conditions favored an attack, and decided to capture Fort Sabine, the Confederate fort guarding the entrance to Sabine Pass.[8]

Most of a day was lost getting the Union ships over the sandbar at the entrance to the pass. The extensive oyster-shell reefs and narrow channels near the entrance to the pass made it difficult to maneuver the ships close to the Confederate fort, but late on the afternoon of September 24 the expedition reached sufficiently close range to commence firing. This bombardment lasted until early evening when it was suspended because the enemy was not returning fire.[9]

Dawn on September 25 brought the Union expedition a pleasant surprise. Captain Crocker went ashore under a flag of truce and discovered that during the night the Confederates had evacuated Fort Sabine. The fort's garrison had been decimated by an epidemic of yellow fever.[10] The capture of Sabine Pass had cost Northern forces not a single casualty. Crocker proudly boasted to Admiral Farragut: "I have the honor to report the entire success of our expedition to Sabine Pass. The town is in our possession and the battery . . . entirely destroyed without the loss of a single man on our side."[11]

By the end of September 1862, Sabine Pass and the entrance to Corpus Christi Bay were in Union hands. But the main port of Texas, Galveston, was still under Confederate control. To remedy that vexing situation, Cdre. William B. Renshaw was sent to Texas near the end of September with a variety of vessels that had seen service on the Mississippi as part of the mortar flotilla. Admiral Farragut instructed Renshaw to "proceed down the coast of Texas with the other vessels, keeping a good lookout for vessels running the blockade, and whenever you think you can enter the sounds on the coast and destroy the temporary defenses, you will do so and gain the command of the inland navigation." In case Renshaw had missed the hint, Farragut reiterated that Galveston should be the target "if the forts are not too formidable."[12]

As it turned out, the forts at Galveston would not prove much of an obstacle for Renshaw. Faced with limited resources, General Hébert elected not to seriously oppose the Union navy's entrance into Galveston Harbor. He chose instead to put up only token resistance when Renshaw's force arrived on October 4, 1862. Renshaw discovered that the "formidable-looking battery" at the entrance to the harbor possessed only one real gun, the remainder being wooden replicas or Quakers.[13]

After a four-day evacuation period, Union forces entered Galveston without resistance and the city fell into Union hands. With Renshaw's conquest of Galveston, the Texas Gulf Coast seemed to be securely in Federal hands. Farragut proudly reported to Washington that "I am happy to inform you that Galveston, Corpus Christi, and Sabine City and the adjacent waters are now in our possession." The only thing left to do, he reported, was to garrison the captured towns. "All we want, as I have told the Department in my last dispatches, is a few soldiers to hold the places, and we will soon have the whole coast."[14]

Farragut's bold prediction in October 1862 that he would soon have possession of the entire Texas coast was both premature and inaccurate. Within two months the admiral's plans for Union domination began to completely unravel, to be replaced by a steady stream of disasters that rekindled Confederate hopes. Several factors contributed to this change of fortunes. First, the Confederates managed to capture several expeditions sent ashore by Union blockaders. These incidents naturally made the officers in charge of the blockading force cautious and nervous about their security. Next, an attempt by Commodore Renshaw to seize control of the ports in Matagorda Bay was frustrated when a small force of Confederate artillery drove off two Union gunboats at the Battle of Port Lavaca (October 31–November 1, 1862). Finally, Union spies located in several different parts of Texas reported that Confederate forces (both army and navy) were preparing to attack the blockaders. Faced with a variety of real and imagined threats, Union commanders began to pull back at every port from Sabine Pass to the Rio Grande, leaving the Texas coast once again largely in Confederate hands.[15]

Although Admiral Farragut dismissed the threats reported by his commanders in the fall of 1862 as enemy propaganda and wishful thinking, there was indeed a Confederate threat assembling in Texas. A new commander, Maj. Gen. John Bankhead Magruder, arrived in Houston in November 1862 and began making plans to recapture Galveston, the key to the survival of the Confederacy in the West. As Magruder wrote to Lt. Gen. E. Kirby Smith, "In my judgment, Texas is virtually the Trans-Mississippi Department, and the railroads of Galveston and Houston are virtually Texas. For whoever is the master of the railroads of Galveston and Houston is virtually master of Texas, and this is not the case with any other part of Texas."[16]

Because of Galveston's importance, General Magruder elected to quickly undertake operations to regain control of the city. On the morning of January 1, 1863, a small force of Confederate artillery and cottonclad gunboats drove the U.S. naval force out of Galveston Harbor, in the process causing the destruction of Cdre. William B. Renshaw and his flagship. In one of the most dramatic and unique battles of the war, Galveston was recaptured by the Confederacy, the only major port recovered by Southern forces during the war. Magruder became the hero of the hour. Both the Confederate Congress and the Texas legislature lost no time in passing resolutions congratulating the general on a "brilliant" victory.[17]

From the standpoint of U.S. military officials, the defeat at Galveston was one of the greatest debacles of the war. Admiral Farragut later called the battle the "most unfortunate" and "most shameful" incident in the entire history of the U.S. Navy. It was not only a symbolic defeat. Noting that Galveston as a military target on the coast was second in importance only to New Orleans and Mobile, Gen. Nathaniel Banks would later confess to the secretary of war that the loss of Galveston was "the most unfortunate affair that occurred in the [Department of the Gulf] during my command."[18]

For a few weeks after the battle it appeared that the Confederate recapture of Galveston might be only a temporary victory. Another large Federal fleet arrived off the entrance to Galveston Bay, this time under the direction of Cdre. Henry Bell, and made preparations to again enter the harbor and seize the town. But just before Bell was about to launch his assault, the Confederates had yet another amazing stroke of luck. On January 11, 1863, the Confederate commerce raider CSS *Alabama* arrived off of Galveston and lured the USS *Hatteras* away from the rest of the Federal fleet. In a battle that lasted less than twenty minutes, the *Alabama* sank the *Hatteras*, and with it the Union's plans for recapturing Galveston.[19]

In reporting the loss of the *Hatteras* to Washington, Farragut used language that would soon become a continuing refrain: "It becomes my painful duty to report still another disaster off Galveston."[20] The shocking loss of the *Hatteras*, and fears that the *Alabama* might still be lurking in the vicinity, made Commodore Bell pause to reevaluate his whole strategy for recapturing Galveston. Confederate engineers in the Island City took full advantage of this delay and quickly built up an immense series of fortifications that completely surrounded the town and included an ingenious line of batteries protected by iron casemates. By the end of the month, Commodore Bell and his superiors had given up plans to recapture Galveston.[21]

Admiral Farragut knew that the Confederate success using improvised naval forces at Galveston would lead to another such attack. He wrote to another officer that "there appears to be a vein of ill luck upon us, so look out for it. They will now be emboldened by their success and try it again."[22] Farragut thought that the next attack would be at Mobile, but once again he had underestimated his adversaries. The Confederates would indeed "try it again" using cottonclad warships, but it would be even sooner and closer than Farragut had expected. The blockade at Sabine Pass was about to be tested.

Shortly after Galveston was recaptured, Maj. Oscar M. Watkins was sent to the Sabine River near the town of Orange and began assembling a force of cottonclads to attack the Union blockaders.[23] Watkins took charge of two river steamers, the *Uncle Ben* and the *Josiah H. Bell*, and began equipping them for battle. Under Capt. Charles Fowler's direction, the decks of the ships were lined with cotton bales, a strategy that had proven successful during the recapture of Galveston.[24] It took a week to make final preparations, but on the morning of January 21, 1863, the Confederate fleet was finally ready to attack. Unfortunately, the commander who had put the expedition together was not fit to command it. Watkins apparently had a drinking problem and when the time came to get under way, he was so inebriated that the sharpshooters and crew were relieved to see Captain Fowler take control of the expedition.[25]

As the two Confederate cottonclads steamed out of Sabine Pass at daylight on the twenty-first of January, Captain Fowler spotted two Union blockaders lying at anchor offshore. The larger of these two ships, the *Morning Light*, was slightly larger than the *Josiah Bell* and mounted eight guns.[26] The second blockader, a small schooner named the *Velocity*, was originally a British ship that had been captured four months earlier trying to run the blockade. Like the *Uncle Ben*, it mounted only two small guns.[27]

As the Confederate cottonclads made their appearance, the Union blockaders quickly set their sails and prepared to make a run for it. But as luck would have it, the wind was light and eventually the Confederate armada closed to effective firing range. The first shots from both sides were short and, as the wind began to pick up, it appeared that the Union ships might make good on their escape. But the breeze suddenly stopped and the Confederate gunners took full advantage of these conditions, repeatedly striking the rigging of the *Morning Light*, disabling some of its guns and gun ports, and doing significant damage to the ship's internal supports.[28]

As the range between the vessels narrowed, the Confederate sharpshooters opened fire on the crippled *Morning Light*, sweeping its deck with deadly fire. Capt. John Dillingham, the Union commander, issued pikes to his crew to enable them to repel boarders. But the withering fire directed at Dillingham's vessel from the Confederate sharpshooters eventually forced the Union crewmen to take shelter below decks. Finally concluding that he had no choice, Dillingham surrendered. The fight lasted approximately two hours, ending about twenty-eight miles southwest of the entrance to Sabine Pass. The Confederates had only one man slightly injured in the battle. They captured 109 prisoners and returned to Sabine Pass with both of the captured Union ships as prizes. It was a spectacular victory.[29]

January 1863 turned out to be the high-water mark for the Confederacy in Texas. Three separate times during that month, Confederate newspapers rushed to report dramatic successes, beginning with the shocking recapture of Galveston, followed ten days later by the *Alabama*'s sinking of the *Hatteras*, and then ten days later the capture of the Union blockaders at Sabine Pass. The elation of January, however, soon gave way to the realities of a series of crushing Confederate defeats during the summer of 1863. July alone saw the surrender of Southern fortresses at Vicksburg and Port Hudson, as well as the defeat of Robert E. Lee's Army of Northern Virginia at Gettysburg. Texas was still in Confederate hands, but a threat loomed on the horizon.

Confident that the tide of war was at last beginning to flow in the North's favor, military strategists in Washington began to plan a major fall campaign. Two options soon emerged. The Federal forces freed up on the Mississippi by the fall of Vicksburg could be transported out of the mouth of the river and then moved either east to attack Mobile or west to invade and occupy Texas. An informal survey was taken and planners in the U.S. Army and Navy reached a consensus (a rarity) on the strategy that should be followed. From Gen. Ulysses S. Grant to Adm. David G. Farragut, military experts favored a movement east to attack the important Confederate port at Mobile.[30]

Despite the military's near unanimous support for a movement east against Mobile, Abraham Lincoln overruled his advisers and directed that the force instead proceed west to attack Texas. It was not that Lincoln believed that Texas was a more important military target than Mobile. In fact, his decision to launch an attack against Texas had almost nothing to do with military considerations. Instead, the president had become convinced that a Federal presence on Texas soil was essential to prevent the French government from using the Civil War as a diversion to separate Texas from the Union. Lincoln's decision was probably also helped along by powerful business and political interests in the North that continued to pressure him to set up Texas as a secure zone from which cotton could be exported to idled textile mills in New England.[31]

Having made the decision to invade Texas, Lincoln left to his generals the decision of where precisely to begin the invasion. Like the president, General-in-Chief Henry Halleck knew little of Texas and decided to leave the detailed planning of the campaign to the general in command of the Department of the Gulf. Thus, it finally fell to Maj. Gen. Nathaniel Banks in New Orleans to plan the Texas campaign.[32]

Banks looked at maps of Texas and carefully evaluated all of the potential invasion routes. From a strategic standpoint, it was apparent that the main target of any invasion force sent to Texas needed to be Galveston and the railroad connections at nearby Houston. If the Federals could control this vital transportation network, Banks reasoned, they would for all intents and purposes control Texas. Because Union spies reported the fortifications surrounding Galveston to be greatly strengthened, however, General Banks quickly devised a plan that would involve the capture of Galveston and Houston through an indirect approach. Instead of recapturing Galveston first and then using it as a

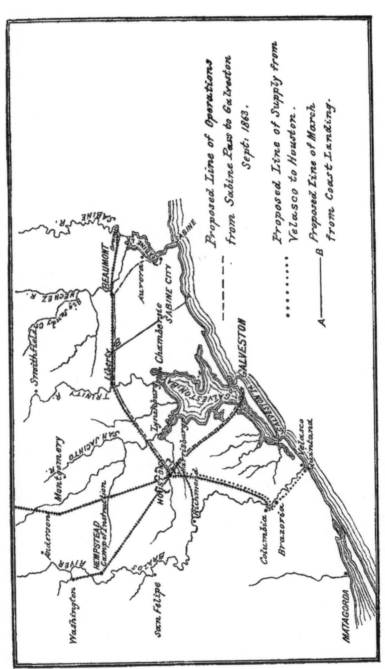

Map 2 Proposed line of operations from Sabine Pass to Galveston, September 1863. *Courtesy Edward T. Cotham, Jr.*

base of operations to proceed against Houston, Banks planned to take Houston first and then cut Galveston off from the rest of Texas.[33]

The problem with the back-door plan to take Galveston was that it required a long approach over enemy territory. It was at this point that Sabine Pass entered the picture. As shown on the map that General Banks sent to President Lincoln explaining his invasion plan (map 2), the overland approach to Houston required use of the railroad line that stretched west from the Louisiana border to Houston.[34] The most convenient landing point close to the eastern terminus of the railroad was just below Sabine City, a small town near the entrance to Sabine Pass. General Banks believed a landing at this point would face no serious resistance, making it the perfect place to begin his Texas campaign. He issued orders to transport a large force to Sabine Pass before the enemy could make preparations to receive it.[35]

In charge of this force was Maj. Gen. William B. Franklin. The infantry force that Franklin was to command included almost 20,000 men from the Nineteenth Corps. The available troop transports, however, would only accommodate a fraction of these men. As a result, it was decided to land the force on Texas shores in a series of successive waves. Franklin would accompany the first wave of approximately 5,000 men.[36]

General Banks knew there was a Confederate fort near the mouth of Sabine Pass that would have to be subdued before his Texas expedition could safely land. To deal with this obstacle, Banks asked for the U.S. Navy's help. Acting Volunteer Lt. Frederick Crocker was assigned to use his small fleet of gunboats to capture the fort and secure a landing site. His force consisted of the *Clifton*, a New York ferryboat converted into a gunboat, and three other shallow-draft gunboats (*Sachem*, *Arizona*, and *Granite City*).[37]

Although the original plan called for all of the Union forces to be in position to launch a surprise attack at dawn on September 7, it proved impossible to coordinate the necessary ship movements and it was not until after nightfall that Crocker and the rest of the expedition finally assembled off the entrance to Sabine Pass. By this point it was clear that the attack on the Confederate fort could not have the originally intended element of surprise. But with a relatively large force and four gunboats, Crocker and Franklin were still confident that they could seize their objective and get the Texas expedition off to a successful start the next day.[38]

The Confederate fort that Crocker faced at dawn on September 8 was not the same one that he had overcome so easily in the fall of 1862. The earlier fort (Fort Sabine) had been abandoned by the Confederates and a replacement (Fort Griffin) had now been constructed at a site farther from the entrance to the pass. Fort Griffin had a triangular shape with a 100-yard sawtooth edge that was designed to fit along the shore of a point near the northern end of an

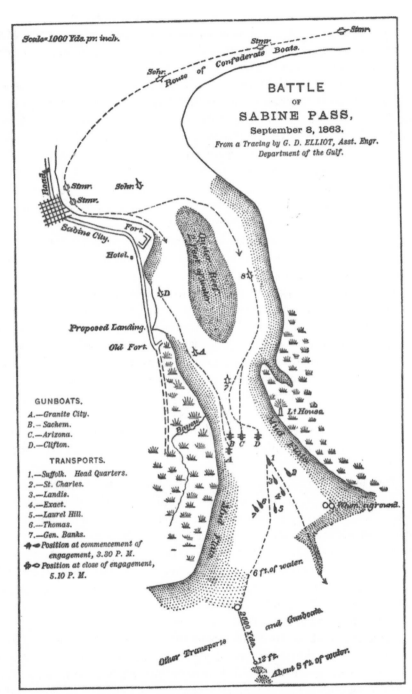

Map 3 Battle of Sabine Pass, September 8, 1863. *Courtesy Edward T. Cotham, Jr*

oyster-shell reef (map 3). The fort's guns overlooked the western or Texas channel as well as the eastern or Louisiana channel on the far side of the reef. Made primarily of local materials like earth and shell, the fort was reinforced by a core of wood and railroad iron.[39]

The Confederate defenders in Fort Griffin consisted of the Davis Guard, a military and social organization formed in Houston before the war. The Davis Guard had been mustered into Confederate service as Company F of Cook's First Texas Heavy Artillery. Named after Jefferson Davis, the company consisted primarily of Irish dockworkers and laborers from Houston and Galveston. As the Union expedition approached, Lt. Richard "Dick" Dowling, a twenty-six-year-old Houston saloonkeeper, was in command of the Davis Guard. The Guards, as members of the company were known, liked and respected Dowling. A quiet man with a great sense of humor, Dowling was capable of getting more from these men than a more conventional commander. That did not mean they were easy to command. On the contrary, they were a rowdy bunch who made a habit of fighting and riotous behavior.[40]

As they practiced their loading and firing drills almost endlessly in the heat of the summer of 1863, Dowling and the Guards watched the construction of Fort Griffin (the fort they were to occupy) with great interest. To assist them in finding their targets, Maj. Julius Kellersberg, the Confederate engineer in charge of East Texas, painted a white line down the barrel of each of their large guns. He then had white wooden stakes driven at strategic places in the channels where the enemy's ships could be expected to come during any attack. With practice, Dowling and his gunners became highly proficient at aiming their guns at the various markers and shifting their fire rapidly between them. This practice would be critical to the outcome of the battle that was about to take place.

Dawn broke on September 8, 1863, to find a very busy scene at the entrance to Sabine Pass. From the parapet of Fort Griffin, Dowling studied the more than twenty ships comprising the Federal fleet through his binoculars and realized that he and his fewer than fifty men were in a perilous position. His orders permitted him to retreat if confronted by a superior enemy force. Outnumbering him more than a hundred to one, the force that he was watching certainly seemed to qualify as a superior force by any definition, but Dowling was not prepared to give up his position without a fight. In an unconventional move, Dowling decided to put the question to a vote.

Accounts differ as to the discussion among Dowling and his men and there is unfortunately no clear record of the arguments that were used to ultimately persuade the men to stay and tend their guns. But it is likely that some of the discussion involved the large number of Irishmen who had fought and died at the Alamo less than thirty years before. In fact, it is certain that the Alamo was on the mind of Dowling and the Guards as they made their collective decision to stay and fight. Dowling's official report states that the men formally adopted as their motto in the coming battle "Victory or death," the closing words in the last letter that William B. Travis sent from the Alamo.[41] Having made their decision and drawn their own line in the sand, the determined men of the Davis Guard made their final preparations and awaited the Federal onslaught.

At about 6:30 a.m. on September 8, Crocker took the *Clifton* (his flagship) and deliberately steamed within easy range of the Confederate fort, inviting its fire so that he could get a better idea of the range and accuracy of its guns. Since there was no reply, Crocker decided to anchor and fire some of his long-range guns to see if he could provoke the fort's defenders into some return fire. By 7:30, the *Clifton* had fired twenty-six shells at Fort Griffin, most of which landed either well behind or in front of the fort. Acting in accordance with his orders, Dowling did not fire a single shot, leaving a baffled Crocker no option but to retire with little more information about the capabilities of the foe he was facing than when he had commenced his reconnaissance.[42]

Anticipating no immediate threat from the Confederate fort, Crocker summoned the rest of the expedition to come over the sandbar at the entrance to Sabine Pass. It took until almost four o'clock in the afternoon to get the troops in the seven transports comprising the advance force into the pass and into position to cooperate with Crocker's attack. Many of the transports and supply ships were still outside of the bar when the battle eventually erupted.[43]

To prepare the final battle plan, a general council of war had been held at about noon on board the transport *Suffolk*. The original plan of attack, blessed by Cdre. Henry Bell before the expedition left Louisiana, had called for Crocker's naval force "to make the attack alone, assisted by about 180 sharpshooters from the army, divided among his vessels; and having driven the enemy from his defenses, and destroyed or driven off the rams, the transports are then to advance and land their troops."[44] That plan, however, had been based on the assumption of a surprise dawn attack, an element of the strategy that was now impossible to achieve.

Since surprise was now out of the question and the arms and capabilities of the Confederates in Fort Griffin were still a mystery, the plan of attack was amended to provide that the army would now be an active participant. While the gunboats attacked the fort, the army was supposed to land a party of about 500 skirmishers under the command of Gen. Godfrey Weitzel. This force was to move rapidly forward and assist in driving the Confederate defenders out of their fortifications. Such an attack was expected to be particularly effective since it required the fort's defenders to choose between firing their guns at the gunboats to the east or at Weitzel's infantry force, which would be attacking from the south.[45]

Crocker's plan for attacking Fort Griffin called for the gunboat *Sachem* to steam rapidly up the Louisiana channel followed by the *Arizona*. The *Clifton* itself would move up the Texas channel very slowly, waiting for the enemy to respond to the movement in the Louisiana channel, which was intended mainly as a diversion. Crocker intended from the beginning to lead the main attack himself from the deck of the *Clifton*. He planned to make a dash up the Texas channel in *Clifton* the moment the enemy's guns were turned upon the *Sachem* and the *Arizona*.[46]

At 3:30 p.m., Crocker sent the "up anchor" signal to the rest of his gunboats. Ten minutes later, the *Clifton* started its slow move to the entrance to the Texas channel while the *Sachem* got underway up the Louisiana channel.[47] Dowling and his men noticed the movement toward them almost immediately. Seeing that the ships in the Louisiana channel would reach the fort first, Dowling quickly positioned his guns to point at their pre-selected targets in that channel. As the *Sachem* steamed within 1,200 yards of Fort Griffin, Dowling gave the order to fire, and the six Confederate guns finally unleashed their full fury. A brisk exchange of fire followed between the *Sachem* and the defenders of Fort Griffin.[48]

When the *Sachem* reached a point about halfway up the oyster bank separating the two channels, an almost perfectly aimed shot entered the ship's steam engine machinery and burst its steam dome. The rupture of the steam dome sent clouds of steam cascading through the interior of the ship, scalding and killing crewmen where they worked. The steam then poured out the hatches to injure the sharpshooters and crewmen on deck. Acting Volunteer Lt. Amos Johnson, who was in command of the *Sachem*, later reported that the explosion on his vessel killed or seriously wounded thirty-two men, including several members of the 161st New York Volunteers who were serving on his ship as sharpshooters. Johnson was not ashamed of his ship or its performance in this action, later reporting that "my officers and men behaved well during the fight up to the time of the explosion taking place, which seemed to have such [a] demoralizing effect upon the greater part of the crew that many of them deliberately jumped overboard."[49]

With its steam engine now inoperative, the *Sachem* was incapable of further movement up the pass toward the Confederate fort. Captain Johnson dropped anchor and gave orders to continue firing. Unfortunately, Johnson discovered that his orders to the gun crew could not be obeyed because they had joined the increasing exodus of men who had jumped overboard to escape the dangerous cloud of steam that still shrouded the ship. For the time being, Johnson and his ship were helpless and the stage would shift to the Texas channel. The Louisiana channel portion of the Federal attack plan had failed.[50]

As the diversionary attack up the Louisiana channel was reaching its dismal climax, the attack up the Texas channel was just getting started. At first, it appeared that this part of the Federal attack might be more successful. When the *Sachem* and the Confederate fort began exchanging fire, Captain Crocker could see that the fort's guns were all trained on the Louisiana channel as he had anticipated. Making full use of this diversion, Crocker gave the order for the *Clifton* to begin its dash up the Texas channel under a full head of steam. Although Crocker's ship was firing at the Confederate fort as it made this dash, it was doing little real damage. The Confederate engineers had deliberately sited Fort Griffin on a point that was dead ahead of any ships coming up the pass, thus precluding an approaching enemy from aiming any guns at the fort other than those located in the forward part of the vessel.

As the *Clifton* reached the halfway mark up the Texas channel, Crocker's plan quickly began to fall apart. The Louisiana channel diversion failed to achieve its purpose when the Confederates rapidly disabled the *Sachem* and had plenty of time to swing their guns around to cover the Texas channel. Dowling's instructions were to aim first at the wheelhouses of approaching ships in order to disable their steering and navigation. This objective was accomplished when a fortunate shot from the Confederate battery severed the Union vessel's tiller rope, causing it to become unmanageable and run aground about 500 yards below the fort.[51]

Running aground made the *Clifton* an easy target for Dowling's gunners and it was soon hit with a shot that penetrated the ship's steam boiler. As with the damage to the steam machinery on the *Sachem*, clouds of steam soon made the interior of the *Clifton* uninhabitable and poured out the top, chasing the sharp-shooters from the upper deck, and further damaging the ship. One of the forward guns was hit by a shot, disabling it, and wounding a number of crewmen. In addition, the nine-inch pivot gun suffered so much damage that the crew could only fire it using a hatchet.[52]

At this point, Crocker knew that his only hope was to hold out until the army landed and managed to rescue his vessel by capturing the fort. To gain time, he and his crew continued firing from their disabled ship for almost half an hour, repeatedly loading grapeshot in an unsuccessful attempt to drive the Confederate defenders from their guns. Crocker himself went forward both to direct the fire and encourage his men to hold out for a while longer. While he was in the midst of this brave display, an officer approached and informed the captain that further resistance was futile and that he had taken it into his own hands to haul the flag down to start the process to signal surrender.[53]

Although outraged by his subordinate's presumption, Crocker eventually had to concede that the man was right. At first he ordered the flag hoisted again, but quickly realized that he had neither the men nor the guns to continue the fight. Looking behind him, he was disgusted to observe that General Weitzel and his infantry force had never even landed and were not coming to his assistance as agreed.

Over in the Louisiana channel, Crocker could see the *Sachem* disabled and the *Arizona* retreating. Clouds of steam were still billowing out of the *Sachem* as well as his own ship, and the waters of the pass were filled with injured and dying men.[54] Seeing no alternative, Crocker made preparations for the *Clifton's* surrender and began the unpleasant task of destroying both his signal book and official papers.[55] Over on the *Sachem*, Captain Johnson had also begun to destroy his signal book, flood his magazine, and disable his largest gun. Upon seeing the white flag flying on the *Clifton*, Johnson also hoisted a white flag and surrendered his ship.[56]

The battle was over. Dowling checked the time and recorded that from the time he fired his first shot until the surrender of the gunboats only forty-five minutes had elapsed. Looking around to see how his men had fared in the battle, Dowling was amazed. As Capt. Frederick Odlum, Dowling's immediate superior, reported: "Our loss was, strictly and positively, nobody hurt. Not a single man received even a scratch, and the fort but very slightly injured, and the contents entirely uninjured." Calling the battle "a glorious and honorable little affair," Odlum confessed that "it does really seem that Providence has kindly favored us in this affair."[57]

The side that Providence seemed not to favor in this battle viewed the results of the battle quite differently. Secretary of the Navy Gideon Welles ordered a court of inquiry regarding what quickly became known as "the disaster at Sabine Pass" and wrote with obvious restraint that "the disastrous results and total failure of the Sabine Pass expedition is a source of regret."[58] All in all, the U.S. Navy lost two gunboats mounting thirteen guns, together with their crews and accompanying sharpshooters. The actual number of Union casualties (killed, wounded, captured, and missing) was about four hundred.[59]

News of Dowling's remarkable victory spread through the South like wildfire. The fall of 1863 was a time of great stress in every corner of the Confederacy. The Confederate government was desperately in search of heroes, and Dick Dowling and his little band of Irishmen made ideal candidates. Gen. Hamilton Bee expressed the sentiments of many when he wrote tendering his "congratulations on the brilliant affair at Sabine. It has inspired us all."[60]

The victories in Texas throughout the first nine months of 1863 that so inspirited Southerners had quite a different impact on Northern morale and strategy. At the end of January 1863, a month that had brought three separate embarrassing defeats for the navy, Admiral Farragut lamented to a friend that "I have nothing but disaster to write the Secretary of the Navy."[61] The failure to capitalize on successful landings at Galveston and Sabine Pass meant that the Federals would waste most of another year attempting to capture the Lone Star State. First, General Banks would send an expedition down to the mouth of the Rio Grande and attempt to fight his way up the Texas coast to Galveston. When that campaign was too slow in producing results, Banks would come back to his original goal of attempting to capture East Texas, this time with a disastrous campaign up the Red River in Louisiana. That campaign, which never even reached Texas soil, cost the Federals thousands of casualties and undoubtedly prolonged the war.[62]

In the end, Federal campaigns to capture Texas turned out to be some of the least productive military operations of the Civil War. Adm. David Porter accurately summarized them as "melancholy" and suggested with ample justification that they were "badly managed."[63] Time and again, promising avenues of attack were squandered, leading to captured vessels and heavy casualties. Military planners in Washington, particularly the high command of the U.S. Navy, came to expect that reports from Texas would begin by describing yet another frustrating disaster. In fact, the very word "disaster" came to be synonymous with Union naval operations in Texas. It would not be until the summer of 1865 that Union forces would end this parade of disasters and finally gain control of the Texas coast.

Notes

1   J. Andrew to G. Fox, Boston, November 27, 1861, *The War of the Rebellion: A Compilation of the Official Records of the Union and Confederate Armies* (hereafter cited as *OR*), comp. Robert N. Scott (Washington, D.C.: U.S. Government Printing Office, 1880–1901), 1, 15:412.

2   P. Hébert to the Secretary of War, Galveston, September 27, 1861, *OR*, 1, 4:112.

3   Dave Page, *Ships versus Shore: Civil War Engagements along Southern Shores and Rivers* (Nashville: Rutledge Hill Press, 1994), 347.

4   D. Farragut to H. Bell, New Orleans, February 6, 1863, *Official Records of the Union and Confederate Navies in the War of the Rebellion* (hereafter cited as *OR Navies*) (Washington, D.C.: U.S. Government Printing Office, 1894–1922), 1, 19:603–4.

5   Norman C. Delaney, "Corpus Christi: The Vicksburg of Texas," in William N. Still, John M. Taylor, and Norman C. Delaney, *Raiders and Blockaders: The American Civil War Afloat* (Washington, D.C.: Brassey's, 1998), 151–60.

6   J. Kittredge to G. Welles, Off Corpus Christi, August 12, 1862, *OR Navies*, 1, 19:151–52; J. Kittredge to G. Welles, Off Aransas, August 20, 1862, *OR Navies*, 1, 19:160–61.

7   D. Farragut to G. Welles, Pensacola Bay, October 15, 1862, *OR Navies*, 1, 19:253.

8   Report of F. Crocker, Off Calcasieu Lake, October 2, 1862, *OR Navies*, 1, 19:217–18.

9   Report of L. Pennington, Sabine Pass, September 29, 1862, *OR Navies*, 1, 19:221–22; Report of Q. Hooper, Sabine Pass, October 5, 1862, *OR Navies*, 1, 19:220.

10   Report of Q. Hooper, Sabine Pass, October 5, 1862, *OR Navies*, 1, 19:220.

11   Report of F. Crocker, Off Calcasieu Lake, October 2, 1862, *OR Navies*, 1, 19:217–19.

12   D. Farragut to W. Renshaw, Pensacola Bay, September 19, 1862, *OR Navies*, 1, 19:213.

13   W. Renshaw to D. Farragut, Off Galveston, October 5, 1862, *OR Navies*, 1, 19:254–55.

14   Report of D. Farragut, Pensacola Bay, October 15, 1862, *OR Navies*, 1, 19:253–54.

15   H. Washburn to J. Dillingham, USS *Morning Light*, November 28, 1862, *OR Navies*, 1, 19:382; Report of A. Johnson, Aransas Bay, December 8, 1862, *OR Navies*, 1, 19:396; R. Law to W. Renshaw, At Sea, December 7, 1862, *OR Navies*, 1, 19:394–95; Edward T. Cotham, Jr., *The Southern Journey of a Civil War Marine: The Illustrated Note-Book of Henry O. Gusley* (Austin: University of Texas Press, 2006), 114–16.

16   J. Magruder to E. Smith, Beaumont, September 26, 1863, *OR*, 1, 26, 2:261.

17   J. Magruder to S. Cooper, Galveston, February 26, 1863, *OR*, 1, 15:216; Edward T. Cotham, Jr., *Battle on the Bay: The Civil War Struggle for Galveston* (Austin: University of Texas Press, 1998), 132.

18   Report of N. Banks, New York, April 6, 1865, *OR*, 1, 26,1:7; D. Farragut to T. Bailey, Mississippi, Above Port Hudson, April 22, 1863, *OR Navies*, 1, 20:157.

19   Report of H. Bell, Off Galveston, January 13, 1863, *OR Navies*, 1, 19:508–9; J. Stancel to N. Banks, New Orleans, January 15, 1863, *OR Navies*, 1, 19:509–10; Cotham, *Battle on the Bay*, 143–47.

20   D. Farragut to G. Welles, New Orleans, January 15, 1863, *OR Navies*, 1, 19:506.

21   Cotham, *Battle on the Bay*, 143–47; Report of H. Bell, Galveston, January 18, 1863, *OR Navies*, 1, 19:508–9; D. Farragut to G. Welles, New Orleans, January 21, 1863, *OR Navies*, 1, 19:552–53; Edward T. Cotham, Jr. *Sabine Pass: The Confederacy's Thermopylae* (Austin: University of Texas Press, 2004), 68–71; D. Farragut to G. Welles, New Orleans, January 15, 1863, *OR Navies*, 1, 19:506.

22   D. Farragut to J. Alden, Off New Orleans, January 5, 1863, *OR Navies*, 41, 19:489–90.

23   Report of O. Watkins, Sabine Pass, January 23, 1863, *OR Navies*, 1, 19:564.

24   William Wiess, "First Federal Defeat at Sabine Pass," *Confederate Veteran* 20, (March 1912): 108–9.

25   K. D. Keith, "The Memoirs of Captain Kosciusko D. Keith," *Texas Gulf Historical and Biographical Record* 10, (November 1974): 60–61.

26   Paul H. Silverstone, *Civil War Navies: 1855–1883* (Annapolis, Maryland: Naval Institute Press, 2001), 103; "The Naval Fight Off Sabine," report from the *Houston Telegraph*, January 25, 1863, *OR Navies*, 1, 19:571.

27   F. Crocker to D. Farragut, Off Calcasieu Lake, October 2, 1862, *OR Navies*, 1, 19:218–219; Report of Surgeon Sherfy, Champaign City, Illinois, April 12, 1864, *OR Navies*, 1, 19:560.

28   Report of Surgeon Sherfy, Champaign City, Illinois, April 12, 1864, *OR Navies*, 1, 19:558–62; Report of O. Watkins, Off Sabine Pass, January 23, 1863, *OR Navies*,

1, 19:564–66; "The Naval Fight Off Sabine," from the *Houston Telegraph*, January 21, 1863, *OR Navies*, 1, 19:570–73; Report of Zack Sabel in Francis Lubbock, *Six Decades in Texas; or, Memoirs of Richard Francis Lubbock* (Austin: Ben C. Jones, 1900), 459–60.

29 O. Watkins to E. Turner, Houston, March 14, 1863, *OR Navies*, 1, 19:570; Wiess, "First Federal Defeat at Sabine Pass," 109; "The Naval Fight Off Sabine," report from the *Houston Telegraph*, January 25, 1863, *OR Navies*, 1, 19:570–73.

30 U. S. Grant, "Chattanooga," in Robert U. Johnson and Clarence C. Buel, eds., *Battles and Leaders of the Civil War: Grant-Lee Edition* (1887–1888; repr., Harrisburg, Pennsylvania: Archive Society, 1991), 3, part 2:679–80; Chester G. Hearn, *Admiral David Glasgow Farragut: The Civil War Years* (Annapolis, Maryland: Naval Institute Press, 1998), 171–75.

31 Cotham, *Sabine Pass*, 83–85; J. Andrew to G. Fox, Boston, November 27, 1861, *OR*, 1, 15:412–13; A. Lincoln to U. S. Grant, Washington, August 9, 1863, *OR*, 1, 24, 3:584.

32 H. Halleck to N. Banks, Washington, August 6, 1863, *OR*, 1, 26,1:672.

33 N. Banks to H. Halleck, New Orleans, August 15, 1863, *OR*, 1, 26,1:683.

34 N. Banks to A. Lincoln, New Orleans, October 22, 1863, *OR*, 1, 26,1:290–92.

35 Ibid.; Report of N. Banks to the Secretary of War, New York, April 6, 1865, *OR*, 1, 26,1:18–19.

36 N. Banks to H. Halleck, New Orleans, September 5, 1863, *OR*, 1, 26,1:286.

37 Report of H. Bell, New Orleans, September 4, 1863, *OR Navies*, 1, 20:515–16.

38 Cotham, *Sabine Pass*, 108–9.

39 Ibid., 71–76; H. Thatcher to E. Canby, New Orleans, May 31, 1865, *OR*, 1, 48, 2:692.

40 Andrew Forest Muir, "Dick Dowling and the Battle of Sabine Pass," in Ralph A. Wooster, ed., *Lone Star Blue and Gray: Essays on Texas in the Civil War* (Austin: Texas State Historical Association, 1995), 177–89.

41 Report of R. Dowling to F. Odlum, Sabine Pass, September 9, 1863 (hereafter cited as "Dowling Report"), *OR Navies*, 1, 20:560; Joe B. Frantz, "The Alamo," in Seymour V. Connor et al., *Battles of Texas* (Waco, Texas: Texian Press, 1967), 13; Cotham, *Sabine Pass*, 122–23.

42 Second Report of F. Crocker, Edgartown, April 21, 1865 (hereafter cited as "Second Crocker Report"), *OR Navies*, 1, 20:544–48; Dowling Report, *OR Navies*, 1, 20:559.

43 Second Crocker Report, *OR Navies*, 1, 20:546; Report of W. Franklin to N. Banks, On Board S.S. *Suffolk*, September 11, 1863, *OR Navies*, 1, 20:528.

44 Report of H. Bell to G. Welles, New Orleans, September 4, 1863, *OR Navies*, 1, 20:515.

45 Second Crocker Report, *OR Navies*, 1, 20:545; Report of W. Franklin to N. Banks, On Board S.S. *Suffolk*, September 11, 1863, *OR Navies*, 1, 20:528; Report of G. Weitzel to W. Hoffman, On board SS *Suffolk*, September 11, 1863, *OR Navies*, 1, 20:531; Report of J. Taylor contained in extract from papers of H. Bell, n.d., *OR Navies*, 1, 20:551.

46 Second Crocker Report, *OR Navies,* 1, 20:546.

47 A. Johnson to H. Thatcher, New Orleans, March 4, 1865, *OR Navies,* 1, 20:553; Dowling Report, *OR Navies,* 1, 20:559.

48 Ibid.

49 A. Johnson to H. Thatcher, New Orleans, March 4, 1865, *OR Navies,* 1, 20:553.

50 Ibid.; Statement of J. Taylor in extract from papers of H. Bell, undated, *OR Navies,* 1, 20:551; Cotham, *Sabine Pass,* 130–33.

51 Cotham, *Sabine Pass,* 135–37; Report of F. Odlum to A. Mills, Sabine Pass, September 8, 1863, *OR Navies,* 1, 20:557; Dowling Report, *OR Navies,* 1, 20:559.

52 Dowling Report, *OR Navies,* 1, 20:559.

53 Ibid.

54 Ibid.; Report of F. Crocker, Houston, September 12, 1863, *OR Navies,* 1, 20:539–41.

55 Second Crocker Report, *OR Navies,* 1, 20:547.

56 Report of A. Johnson to H. Thatcher, New Orleans, March 4, 1865, *OR Navies,* 1, 20:553.

57 F. Odlum to A. Mills, Sabine Pass, September 9, 1863, *OR Navies,* 1, 20:558; Dowling Report, *OR Navies,* 1, 20:559.

58 G. Welles to H. Bell, Navy Department, October 2, 1863, *OR Navies,* 1, 20:538; G. Welles to H. Bell, Navy Department, October 9, 1863 [second letter of that date], *OR Navies,* 1, 20:538.

59 F. Odlum to A. Mills, Sabine Pass, September 9, 1863, *OR Navies,* 1, 20:558; L. Smith to E. Turner, Sabine Pass, September 8, 1863, *OR Navies,* 1, 20:556.

60 H. Bee to E. Turner, Fort Brown, September 18, 1863, *OR,* 1, 26, 2:237.

61 D. Farragut to J. Alden, New Orleans, January 27, 1863, *OR Navies,* 1, 19:584.

62 Ludwell H. Johnson, *Red River Campaign: Politics and Cotton in the Civil War* (Kent, Ohio: Kent State University Press, 1993), 278–79; Report of N. Banks, *OR* 1, 26, 1:7, 18–20.

63 David D. Porter, *Naval History of the Civil War* (Secaucus, New Jersey: Castle, 1984), 347.

Chapter 9

Hide Your Daughters: The Yankees Have Arrived in the Coastal Bend, 1863

by Charles D. Spurlin

At the outbreak of the American Civil War in April 1861, Texas policymakers considered Matagorda Bay, a major inlet in Southeast Texas separated from the Gulf of Mexico by Matagorda Peninsula and Matagorda Island, as a likely place for enemy activity. A contributing factor for this view was an article that appeared in the *New York Commercial Advertiser* shortly after President Abraham Lincoln proclaimed a blockade of Southern ports. The newspaper stated that unless Matagorda Bay, Galveston, Brazos Santiago, and the mouth of the Rio Grande were blockaded the Federal government could not expect success in foiling Confederate trade. The principal reason the paper gave for listing Matagorda Bay was the extensive shipment of goods passing over the bay's water from the ports at Indianola and Port Lavaca, or Lavaca, as the town was known at the time.[1]

In 1861, Indianola with its deepwater facilities was a significant Texas port, rivaling Galveston for the importation and exportation of products such as cotton, wool, hides, salt, machinery, sugar, molasses, corn, wine, clothing, lumber, and furniture. Some overly optimistic prognosticators even foresaw Indianola eventually surpassing Galveston in shipping. Less consequential than its sister community, but, nevertheless, another vital shipping point was Port Lavaca, a light-draught port situated several miles up the coast from Indianola along the adjoining Lavaca Bay. Besides its attraction as a respectable seaport, Port Lavaca was located on the south end of the San Antonio and Mexican Gulf Railway that extended from the town some twenty-five miles westward to Victoria on the Guadalupe River. The railroad caused many locals to speculate that Port Lavaca was an ideal location for a Federal invasion.[2]

Initially, the role of defending Matagorda Bay was left to the men stationed at Fort Washington, an earthen bastion built during the Texas Republic era on the northeastern tip of Matagorda Island facing the Gulf of Mexico. However, Col. Robert R. Garland, commander of the Sixth Texas Infantry Regiment stationed at Camp Henry E. McCulloch near Victoria, inspected the facility in December 1861 and deemed it indefensible from a Federal assault. Consequently, upon his recommendation, the bulk of the troops manning the fort were shifted two miles northward to a site below Saluria at the mouth of Pass Cavallo opposite Pelican and Bird islands. The new location was named Camp Esperanza (Hope). Although there is no definitive answer why the encampment was so named, one explanation is the island had a considerable number of drought-resistant esperanza plants. During this time, the area was experiencing a severe drought, and residents were hoping it would end soon.[3]

Transforming Camp Esperanza into Fort Esperanza fell to Maj. Caleb G. Forshey, a Confederate artillery and engineer officer for coastal defense. Construction of the new facility began in early 1862 and was largely accomplished over objections of their owners by some thirty impressed slaves working alongside Confederate soldiers. Building the fort proved to be a slow process due to such factors as inclement weather and the slowness in acquiring necessary construction material, but eventually the fortification was completed. The defensive facility was constructed of sand reinforced with timber procured from a logjam at the mouth of the Colorado River, and held together by shellcrete, a material made of pulverized seashells that resembled concrete. In order to protect the fort from a flank attack, as well as from an assault from the rear by land, numerous rifle pits dotted with unsophisticated redoubts were excavated for a quarter of a mile. As an added protection from a possible Federal assault, in the spring of 1863, mines, or torpedoes, were placed in the channel separating the bar at Pass Cavallo and Fort Esperanza, near the fort's trenches, in the artificial strait between Port Lavaca and Powder Horn, and outside the mouth of the Guadalupe River. None of the mines, however, proved effective against the forthcoming Federal attack on the installation.[4]

By the end of July 1863, Union political leaders began serious discussions on the invasion and occupation of Texas. President Lincoln in a note to Secretary of War Edwin M. Stanton on July 29 wrote, "Can we not renew the effort to organize a force to go to Western Texas? Please consult with the General-in-Chief on the subject. If the Governor of New Jersey shall furnish any new regiments, might not they be put into such an expedition. Please think of it. I believe no local object is now more desirable." Why the urgency to establish the Federal presence in the Lone Star State? Apparently, there is a twofold answer. One, and perhaps the most important consideration, was the French occupation of Mexico City in June of 1863 and the perceived possibility that France's Louis Napoleon III and the Confederacy would unite against the United States. A second factor was the political pressure brought to bear on Federal officials by influential Republicans during the summer of 1863 to establish a loyal government in Texas, the only Confederate state completely void of Union troops.[5]

During the afternoon of July 31, 1863, in the War Department Building, a meeting consisting of Secretary of War Stanton; Maj. Gen. Henry W. Halleck, general-in-chief and military advisor to Lincoln; and Secretary of Navy Gideon Welles was held to discuss the Texas question. Deciding where troops should enter the Lone Star State was at the heart of the talks. Halleck expressed the opinion that the invasion should take place at Galveston. Welles expressed a contrary view by proposing Indianola. His suggestion seemed rather odd to Halleck since he was oblivious to the seaport's existence. The secretary of the navy hastily explained the advantages Indianola had over Galveston. He maintained the town was closer to the state capital and the Rio Grande, it would better accommodate large warships, and it would be easier to seize. Before the meeting broke up, the group sided with Halleck, agreeing that the final decision should be left to Maj. Gen. Nathaniel P. Banks, commander of the Department of the Gulf, who would oversee the invasion. At 12:30 p.m. on August 6, Halleck telegraphed Banks that the movement against Texas should be made "with the least possible delay." Furthermore, the general-in-chief stated, "Do this by land at Galveston, at Indianola, or at any other point you may deem preferable."[6]

In the meantime, Banks expressed his opinion to higher authorities that since Vicksburg had been seized in early July 1863, the next military objective should be Mobile. His view was shared by Maj. Gen. Ulysses S. Grant. The day before Halleck sent his telegram to Banks, Lincoln, believing it necessary to express his thoughts on the matter, wrote to Banks and commented, "Recent events in Mexico, I think, render early action in Texas more important than ever." On August 9, the president sent a letter to Grant expounding on the need to establish a foothold in Texas. Lincoln in the missive stated that a military movement against Mobile seemed "tempting" to him as well if it were not for the "recent events in Mexico, I am greatly impressed with the importance of re-establishing the national authority in Western Texas as soon as possible."[7]

Having been given the authority to decide where the Federal presence should be established in Texas, Banks selected Houston, reasoning that the town "would place in our hands the control of all the railway communications of Texas; give us command of the most populous and productive part of the State; enable us to move at any moment into the interior in any direction." Furthermore, he maintained that from Houston the troops could be withdrawn to Galveston, which could easily be fortified with a minimal number of men, and thus permit the bulk of his department to move against Mobile. After giving thought to various plans of attack on Houston, Banks concluded that a land force supported by naval vessels would enter Texas by way of the Sabine River and move along the coast to the Bayou City.[8]

All did not go well for the Union invasion expedition. In September 1863, the Federals were soundly defeated at Sabine Pass by a Confederate contingent under the command of Lt. Richard W. "Dick" Dowling, a twenty-four-year-old native Irishman and tavern owner. As a result of Dowling's victory, the Yankee soldiers involved in the episode never embarked from their troopships and returned to New Orleans without ever stepping on Texas soil.[9]

Following the debacle at Sabine Pass, Banks considered an overland movement by way of the Bayou Teche. The route proved to be impractical as the Federal troops discovered that it was "without supplies of any kind, and entirely without water." Banks finally decided to send an expedition of some 7,000 men, comprising the Thirteenth Army Corps, under the command of Maj. Gen. Napoleon J. T. Dana, a veteran of the Peninsula and Antietam campaigns, to occupy the lower portion of the Rio Grande. As perceived by the commanding general, the troops could advance from the Rio Grande up the coast and seize Houston and Galveston from "below instead of above."[10]

Once the ships in Banks's expedition were assembled, the vessels embarked from Louisiana for the Rio Grande on October 26, 1863. When the task force arrived in the open gulf waters, the ships were placed in two rows approximately a mile apart. Space for the troops on the transports was at a premium. The soldiers were so cramped that some of the men claimed they did not have enough room to lie comfortably on the decks. For the first couple of days, the weather was pleasant and the water calm, deteriorating, however, at approximately 4:30 a.m. on October 30 when a cold front swept across the gulf. The surf became extremely treacherous, scattering the ships from their defined formation and leading to tormenting thoughts among many of the soldiers and sailors that the ships might vanish beneath the ocean. So powerful were the swells lambasting the vessels, several of the small ships were severely damaged to the point they had to be towed by other vessels in the fleet. Seasickness among the soldiers became epidemic as the waves tilted the ships from side to side, the bows rising from the raging water and just as quickly lunging harshly back from whence they came. Intensely frightened for their safety, "men lashed themselves to the sides with ropes." Believing their lives were in peril, some of the officers in the Fifteenth Iowa Regiment desperately sought to have their vessel sail "under the guns of the rebel forts on the coast, as, in their view, a Texan prison must be even more hospitable than a watery grave." The request was rejected by the regiment's commander. As the situation became more and more critical, it became imperative to lighten the ships by dumping overboard "bulky articles," mules, horses, "battery wagons, artillery equipments, and other property" to prevent them from sinking. The move was successful, for only three vessels were lost, and not a single person. Soldiers aboard the doomed ships were safely transported to other vessels.[11]

One of the unfortunate ships was the *Union*. After it became evident the *Union* was going to be unable to stay afloat, the captain of the *Empire City* quickly "ordered a boat to be lowered and manned. . . .This, with the life-boat from the Union rescued the crew" and African American soldiers. Five trips were required to remove the men to safety. During the evacuation, a number of the soldiers aboard the *Union* were paralyzed by fear, becoming "unable to spring into the boats as they approached the side of the vessel" and, therefore, were thrown overboard with the hope and anticipation that those in the lifeboats would pluck them from the water. Unbelievable as it may seem, all the men were retrieved without a single loss of life.[12]

On November 1, Banks's expeditionary force of approximately 4,500 men arrived off of Brazos Island, near the mouth of the Rio Grande, and began to make preparations to land on Texas soil. The following day at noon the *General Banks* followed closely by the *Clifton* reached the island. Of utmost importance for the Union soldiers was to raise the Stars and Stripes over the island. The first Federal unit to land was the Nineteenth Iowa Regiment. The men of the regiment proudly asserted that the standard given to Company A by J. J. Bishop and several ladies of Keokuk, Iowa, "was the first to wave on Texas soil in this portion of the State." However, according to the chronicler of the Fifteenth Maine Regiment, this honor belonged to the men of the Maine regiment when Pvt. James R. Oliver of Company B climbed to the roof of a building and vigorously waved Old Glory, receiving "the tumultuous cheers of the soldiers on the vessels within view of the very romantic and inspiring spectacle." Regardless of which regiment flew the colors first, Banks sent a message to Lincoln stating, "The flag of the Union floats over Texas today."[13]

Throughout the disembarking, the Union troops did not receive any opposition from the Confederates. Even though the soldiers did not have to engage their enemy, they experienced a variety of difficulties during the landings, resulting in loss of the lives of several soldiers. One major problem was the draught of the transports being too great to permit them to enter shallow water, requiring the soldiers to be transported to shore in rowboats. During the landings, four of the rowboats capsized when they were unable to overcome a sandbar. One of the mishaps produced the death of seven soldiers and two crewmen from the *Owasco*. In another incident, after the survivors of a capsized boat were picked up, they and their rescuers attempted to land in nearby Mexico but were turned away by Mexican officials. Meanwhile, other rowboats became grounded on sandbars and were unable to proceed to shore, posing a hardship on the shorter men who were required to wade in water up to their armpits. Also, the difficulties associated with transporting the horses to land caused a problem during the landing of the troops. Because there was an insufficient amount of gear to properly unload the animals, some of the horses were thrown overboard with the handlers' expectation that all of the horses would swim to shore. A number of the animals, however, swam in the opposite direction and drowned in the Gulf. Despite the adversities, by November 3, virtually all the troops were ashore, and several of the regiments after securing necessary rations commenced to move

Illustration 7   Soldiers digging trenches at Point Isabel, Texas. *Courtesy Library of Congress.*

against Brownsville, arriving in that town three days later without encountering any resistance from the Confederates.[14]

While Union detachments made their way to Brownsville, other Federal units moved up the coast. On November 6, General Dana ordered the Twentieth Iowa Regiment under the command of Maj. William G. Thompson to board the schooner *Emma Amelia*, proceed to Point Isabel, and secure the town. Occupation of the community was accomplished without any difficulties.[15]

The next item on the expedition's agenda was to seize the Confederate sand embankment on Mustang Island, impractically characterized as Fort Semmes. Manning the fortification were fewer than one hundred Texans, mostly from the Twenty-fourth Battalion, State Troops, under the command of Maj. George O. Dunaway from Lavaca County. Included in the defensive structure was an artillery battery led by Capt. William H. Maltby, a resident of Corpus Christi. Unfortunately, when the weapons (a 12-pounder, an 18-pounder, and a 24-pounder) were mounted on their wooden platforms, they were positioned to fire upon enemy ships that attempted to enter Corpus Christi Bay, making them virtually useless against the pending land attack.[16]

Brig. Gen. Thomas E. G. Ransom, a well-respected officer in command of the Third Brigade, Second Division, was assigned the responsibility of capturing the fortification. During the military operations on Mustang Island, the Third Brigade consisted of the Thirteenth and Fifteenth Maine regiments, two companies from the Twentieth Iowa Regiment, First Engineers, Corps d'Afrique, and two boat howitzers. Arriving at the southern end of the island at sunset on November 16, the Union troops immediately started toward the Confederate defenses, a distance of twenty-two miles. Marching rapidly through the night hours with skirmishers in the forefront followed by troops manually pulling two 24-pounder Parrott guns, the command halted at 4:00 a.m., four miles from the fort, and rested until daylight before resuming the advance.[17]

The Texans were oblivious to the presence of Federal troops until the enemy was spotted by a lookout stationed about a mile from the fort. Afterwards, approximately forty Confederate skirmishers were dispatched to meet the foe. When the enemy soldiers were within a thousand yards of the Texans, the Federals opened with a volley from their rifles, causing the skirmishers to retreat to the confines of Fort Semmes. One of the Confederate participants in the engagement later remarked that "their long range guns sent minnie bullets whizzing past the ears of the Texans; who on account of the distance were precluded from replying with any effect, as their bird guns would not have proved effective . . . at a greater distance than fifty yards." Meanwhile, General Banks, who was aboard the flagship *McClellan,* observed with satisfaction the unfolding of the assault on the fort. As Ransom's men formed into a line of battle in preparation to charge the stronghold, the Federal gunboat *Monongahela* fired several eleven-inch shells into the earthwork, panicking the defenders. Realizing they were outgunned and outmanned with zero chance of being reinforced, Major Dunaway, over the objections of Lt. Michael L. Stoner from Victoria, who was convinced that an effective withdrawal could be made to the mainland, chose to acquiesce unconditionally rather than put up a fight. A white shirt, therefore, was placed on the end of a bayonet and extended skyward for the advancing Federals to see. Surrendering to the Federals were nine officers and eighty-nine men. In addition to the prisoners, Maltby's unspiked artillery pieces, small arms, several horses and mules, one schooner, and ten small boats were seized. The latter items were particularly gratifying acquisitions for the Federals since they were woefully short of light-draught vessels that were necessary to ply the water between the barrier islands and the coastal lands.[18]

Within hours after Ransom's troops occupied the fort, the general began to receive reinforcements. Being exhausted from the forced march up the island, the Union soldiers in the original contingent were allowed to take a break before resuming their forward advance. The downtime was especially welcomed by the troops who had developed blisters on their feet from marching through the loose, shifting island sand and who desperately needed the opportunity for the sores to heal. Meanwhile, Maj. Gen. Cadwallader C. Washburn arrived on Mustang Island and assumed command of all the Federal forces in that vicinity. On November 22, Ransom, who had been reassigned as a brigade commander, and his contingent were ferried to St. Joseph's Island where they encamped and spent the night. Early the next morning the Federal troops resumed their trek northward, reaching Cedar Bayou, the inlet separating St. Joseph's Island from Matagorda Island, about noon.[19]

Before the troops crossed Cedar Bayou, Maj. Charles Hill with a small detachment of Confederate soldiers appeared with a white flag at the southern tip of Matagorda Island. Capt. C. S. Illsley, commander of the Fifteenth Maine

Regiment, selected Sgt. James Saunders to cross the bayou and parley with the Texans. Stripping himself of his outer clothing and weapons, Saunders waded into Cedar Bayou and commenced to swim to Matagorda Island. After reaching the island, he was interrogated by Hill as to what happened to the Confederate garrison on Mustang Island. Of particular importance to the major was to find out if there was any truth to a rumor that prisoners had been mistreated and "two citizens of Texas had been hung in the rigging of" a Federal ship. Saunders, either not having an appropriate answer or thinking it improper for him to respond to the query, refused to disclose any information to Hill. Highly agitated, the major pressed the sergeant for a response, and an argument between the two soldiers ensued, whereupon Hill pulled his revolver and shot Saunders, slightly wounding the unarmed man. The Union soldiers on St. Joseph's Island witnessed the incident and reacted by immediately opening fire upon the Confederate detachment, mortally wounding Hill. The Texans retaliated with a few random rounds of their own before hastily retreating, leaving the major's body to be retrieved by the Federals.[20]

During the Federal advance up the coast, Magruder made appeals for additional men, warned citizens of the dastardly consequences to their property should the Federal forces be victorious, and ordered the destruction of material items that conceivably could be utilized by the Union invasion force. In the meantime, while Federal operations on Mustang Island progressed, Col. William R. Bradfute, commander of the Confederate coastal defenses, boarded the steamer *Cora* with a company from the Eighth Texas Infantry Regiment, slipped by enemy naval vessels, and made his way to Fort Esperanza. To bolster the defenses at the bastion, Col. Stephen H. Darden, commander of the Fifth Infantry Regiment, Texas State Troops, with three small companies was dispatched to the location. At the same time, Bradfute, while visiting Port Lavaca on November 24, issued a call for every minuteman in the vicinity, estimated to be between seventy-five and one hundred men, to report for service. Meanwhile, Magruder ordered Col. Peter C. Woods's Thirty-sixth Texas Cavalry Regiment and Col. Charles L. Pyron's Second Texas Cavalry Regiment to proceed to Fort Esperanza, but the fortification was abandoned before the two regiments could reach it. Also detailed to the area was Gen. Hamilton Bee who had been unable to counter the Federal occupation along the Rio Grande. Not knowing that Fort Esperanza had been vacated when he issued the order, Magruder directed Bee to concentrate his forces at Indianola and to take personal command of the units, so the enemy could be stopped from entering the port town "and cutting off our troops—getting on the inside."[21]

As the Texas military detachments were being shuffled, a rumor spread like wildfire through the communities west of the Colorado that the area was going to be abandoned to the invading enemy forces. To counter the hearsay, Magruder issued a public proclamation denying it. Blaming the falsehood on the enemy as a propaganda tactic to persuade the people to disregard their responsibilities as soldiers and citizens, the commanding general assured the inhabitants that the area would be defended "to the utmost of his ability." Even though troops would provide support to defeat the enemy, Magruder remarked that the residents could best protect their families by taking up arms against the invading foe "and to retard his progress into the heart of the country." He further stated that "all minute-men, all exempts—in short, every man capable of bearing arms west of the Colorado—are now urged by every consideration of honor, duty, and interest to arm themselves with such weapons as they can procure," and report to Bee "either at Larco Creek, low down on the San Antonio River, or at Victoria."[22]

Presumably to encourage the citizenry along the coast to join the efforts to impede the Federal advance, Magruder increased the anxiety level in an already fearful populace by claiming in another public proclamation primarily aimed at planters in the coastal counties that the invading Federals had brought with them "five thousand to ten thousand muskets with which to arm the slaves against their masters." To prevent this from happening, he called upon the planters who lived along the navigable portions of the waterways and within fifty miles of the coast from Corpus Christi to Galveston to voluntarily remove their slaves to the interior. If they did not, Confederate cavalry, out of military necessity, "in haste and without regard" to the slaves' "well being" would do so. Reminding the slave owners of the Emancipation Proclamation's intent and the "utter disregard of all social rights" by Lincoln's "minions," Magruder contended there was "no room for hope, even to the most credulous, to save their property, and especially their negroes." Because of the military exigency, the commanding general let it be known that if items that could benefit the enemy, such as "jewels, plate, linen and other valuables, and particularly wagons, horses, mules and vehicles of every kind," were not removed, they would be destroyed by his troops. "Save him this painful necessity," Magruder pleaded, "and remove your negroes beyond the reach of the enemy without a moment's delay." Showing supreme confidence in his military forces, the commanding general remarked that he expected to ultimately "drive the 'Vandals' back to their ships."[23]

While Magruder was dispatching public proclamations, the lead Federal troops with some difficulty crossed Cedar Bayou on November 25 and began inching their way northward toward Fort Esperanza. Aware of the Union's presence on Matagorda Island, Bradfute on November 26 appealed to Magruder for additional troops, so he could "meet them down on the island, and not wait for them to attack the fortification." At the time of the colonel's plea, the possibility existed that the enemy might flank the fort and isolate it from the mainland by landing at Lamar and proceeding to take Indianola and Port Lavaca. Engaging the enemy before it reached Fort Esperanza, the colonel reasoned, would prevent the success of the flanking maneuver. The coastal commander also pointed out to Magruder that the garrison needed more ammunition to defend itself against a "vigorous attack, should it last for any length of time." Both requests, for reinforcements and for ammunition, were not fully satisfied. Well aware of Bradfute's predicament, Magruder authorized the colonel to abandon the fort should it become "untenable." Before doing so, however, Bradfute was directed to spike the "heavy cannon" and to destroy all unmovable objects.[24]

After General Ransom's brigade crossed Cedar Bayou, it proceeded up Matagorda Island some seven miles where it encamped and waited the arrival of the First Brigade, First Division commanded by Col. Henry D. Washburn. At the time, the First Brigade was made up of the Thirty-third Illinois Regiment, the Ninety-ninth Illinois Regiment, the Eighth Indiana Regiment, the Eighteenth Indiana Regiment, the Twenty-third Iowa Regiment, and the Seventh Michigan Battery. Around midnight, Colonel Washburn's unit, which also had a hard time crossing Cedar Bayou, reached Ransom's position. During the morning of November 26, the combined troops broke camp and resumed their trek toward the fort. Upon the completion of roughly twenty-three miles, the Federal soldiers again bivouacked. On November 27, Maj. Gen. Cadwallader C. Washburn, overall commander of the Union forces on Matagorda Island, directed Ransom to march his Third Brigade up the center of the island while Colonel Washburn's detachment took a parallel route abutting the coastline running along the gulf.[25]

Between 11:00 a.m. and noon, Colonel Washburn's brigade reached the lighthouse near Fort Esperanza and waited until Ransom's brigade arrived at its assigned position. Soon after the Federal troops halted, a reconnoitering party was sent to probe the outer defenses of the Confederate fort. As the detachment carried out its task, it had a brisk, but rather short, firefight with Confederate pickets, forcing the Texas soldiers after they had counterattacked to retreat inside the fortification. In the skirmish, the Confederates suffered an undetermined number of casualties while two Union men were wounded, one mortally. After the engagement, the patrol cautiously moved onward until it came within three hundred yards "of the outer work of the enemy—a heavy earthwork, extending from the bay to a lagoon." Having acquired the desired information, the reconnaissance group started to withdraw when it was shelled by Fort Esperanza's 128-pounder and the 24-pounders. The Federal soldiers succeeded in reaching their main line without any of them being injured.[26]

Subsequently, Fort Esperanza's artillery targeted Colonel Washburn's brigade. All the shells fell harmlessly, but they did, nevertheless, produce amusement for the Federal troops. During lulls between the firing of the rounds, Union soldiers waved their hats and hands and yelled loudly to encourage the gunners to hurry up and fire again. Some of the men nonchalantly attempted to snag a cannonball in the air with a hat. Others mimicked the enemy artillerymen by holding a rifle "in a horizontal position, while three or four of his merry comrades came up and went through all the motions of loading an eleven inch cannon." Upon completing the act of loading the weapon and pretending to fire it, the "soldiers would loudly cheer, as though they believed the shot had dismounted the rebel cannon." Apparently, genuinely amused at the Federal antics, the Confederate artillerymen got into the spirit of the fun and turned their largest weapon in the direction of the gulf and fired a few shots. When the shells hit the water, they produced a large spray before traveling a distance bounding and "skipping and playing across the smooth water." In appreciation of the Confederate water show, the Federal soldiers gestured their gratitude with body motions.[27]

Sometime around 2:30 a.m. on November 28, a cold front composed of wind, rain, sleet, and sporadic snowflakes swept across Matagorda Island. Although the adverse weather conditions caused discomfort for the Confederates, the Union troops who were spread out on the coastal prairies with little protection from the elements suffered the most from the norther. A Yankee soldier who was on picket duty when the cold front hit, remarked, "Each blast seemed to be a piece of sharp frozen steel that cut us through and through." The Federal troops who did not have tents, and there were a considerable number, dug holes in the sand for protection. Unfortunately, these temporary cavities soon filled with sand, requiring the men "to dig out again almost immediately or be smothered by the drifting sand." Whoever was fortunate enough to have a "dog tent" shared the shelter with as many comrades as could fit into it, whether enlisted men or officers. Because of the bad weather, military confrontations between the two sides on November 28 were largely limited to brief skirmishes that produced no casualties and an occasional random shot from the fort. On the next day, however, military action intensified significantly as the Union brigades went on the offensive to seize Fort Esperanza.[28]

Before midnight on November 28, Federal artillery was moved forward despite the frigid temperature and placed in firing positions aimed at the fortification. The deployment was made without being detected by the stronghold's defenders. At daybreak on November 29, the Union artillerists commenced to shell the unsuspecting Confederates. Meanwhile, Federal infantry along with additional artillery advanced, intensifying the offensive and driving the Texans from the rifle pits located on the outer perimeter of the fort. The Union batteries lobbed shells into the bulwark with uncanny accuracy, causing the fort's gunners to take shelter, virtually eliminating counterfire. Whenever the Confederate artillery fired in retaliation, solid balls were used rather than anti-personnel ammunition, permitting the advancing soldiers to dodge the incoming rounds and, thus, suffer no casualties. Absent in the cannonading of Fort Esperanza were the Union gunboats. The cold front that hit the coast produced gale-force winds that prohibited the vessels from maneuvering into position to use their weapons or even from entering Matagorda Bay. Conceivably, if the navy had entered into the fight with its heavy guns and had been able to sail into the bay, the fort would have suffered greater destruction, and the defenders would have been unable to escape, creating a strong possibility that the fort would have capitulated earlier. Even without the added firepower, the Federals made substantial progress up the island, occupying Fort Esperanza's outer defenses and securing positions for a final push the next day.[29]

With the approach of darkness, the Union troops halted and prepared to bivouac for the night. As the soldiers settled down for what they hoped would be a peaceful rest after a tiring day of marching and fighting under less-than-desirable weather conditions, they were startled sometime between 12:30 and 1:00 a.m. on November 30 by the noise of an explosion emanating from Fort Esperanza. Realizing almost immediately the sound came from an exploding magazine inside the fort, and surmising the structure was being abandoned, Federal skirmishers rushed toward the bastion. As the Union soldiers expected, they found the garrison had withdrawn. Not realizing the Texans had actually vacated the fort some three hours before the explosion, a detachment was ordered to overtake the retreating enemy, but it soon discovered the Confederates had already escaped by means of a rope ferry, extending from the island to the mainland. By the time the pursuing Federals reached the ferry, the Texans had cut the rope, "allowing the floating bridge to swing around upon the shore." However, not all the Confederates managed to make it off the island safely. Eight men had remained behind to set fire to the fort's munitions, but before they could do so, Federal troops arrived and captured six of the Texans.[30]

When the first Union soldiers who arrived at Fort Esperanza were about to enter the fortification, a magazine exploded, slightly injuring several men from the falling debris. Throwing caution to the wind, a few of the men pressed on into the abandoned earthwork, being greeted with additional bursting munitions, burning timbers, and blazing cotton bales. All but the foolhardy remained outside, huddling near the outer walls for protection from flying timbers and other airborne items until the fires were exhausted. The sight of exploding ammunition "was a fire-work exhibition never excelled" and would be long remembered by the eyewitnesses. Miraculously, none of the soldiers were killed. Clearly, the Confederates who were given the task of destroying the arsenal did a haphazard job. Mistakenly, they "calculated on the fire burning through the woodwork of each magazine until the powder was reached" rather than igniting a powder trail that ran directly to the separate chambers.[31]

When it was comparatively safe enough for the Federal troops to enter Fort Esperanza, they found one dead, unburied Confederate soldier and an appreciable amount of "valuable property in the shape of ordnance and other stores," including one spiked 128-pounder Columbiad, and seven spiked 24-pounder siege weapons. Casualty figures for the two contending forces during the fighting on Matagorda Island were slight. The Confederate losses were one killed and ten captured whereas the Federals reported one killed and ten wounded.[32]

An unidentified correspondent in a letter sent from Port Lavaca to a Houston newspaper a few days after he and other defenders had vacated Fort Esperanza provided insight into the defensive shortcomings of the fortification and the rationale behind its evacuation. According to the author of the article, the fort was perfectly located, noting that it was constructed to counter an attack by water. Unfortunately, the Federals attacked by land. Furthermore, the individual stated, the enemy artillery was substantially better and was accurate to the point that "almost every shell dropped into the fort." Deeply concerned that rounds would penetrate the magazines causing them to explode, the writer added, the soldiers had to abandon the idea of taking refuge in the adjoining bombproof bunkers for they became "the most unsafe places in the fort; in fact, the only safe place about it was the parapet." Moreover, the defenders were woefully undermanned and poorly trained to withstand an assaulting force of several thousand superiorly armed men, many of whom were combat veterans. Additionally, the correspondent remarked, to have stayed on the island any longer would have made a retreat impossible, maintaining that with improving weather conditions enemy naval vessels could have entered Matagorda Bay and cut off the escape routes.[33]

With Fort Esperanza firmly under the control of the Federal troops, Col. Henry D. Washburn sent a detachment at daylight on November 30 to McHenry Island to take "possession of a small earthwork containing one 24-pounder gun, considerable ammunition, and some garrison equipage." Because driftwood, drinkable water, and grass were more plentiful on Matagorda Peninsula than on Matagorda Island, elements of Union regiments on orders from Maj. Gen. Cadwallader C. Washburn began to disembark on December 1 at Decrow's Point, located on the southern end of the peninsula, where they encamped. An additional factor for the general's decision to deploy troops on the peninsula was the impression he had at the time that a movement was going to be conducted toward Houston and Galveston. By stationing troops at Decrow's Point, General Washburn contended he would eliminate "the very tedious job of ferrying" forces from Matagorda Island to that location when the decision to go on the offensive was made. As events unraveled, no such order was ever given. Federal dominance of Matagorda Bay was further solidified when Maj. Gen. Fitz Henry Warren with the First Brigade, First Division occupied Indianola on December 23. Warren had previously seized the port town for a brief time on December 13, raising the American flag before departing. The residents were initially frightened

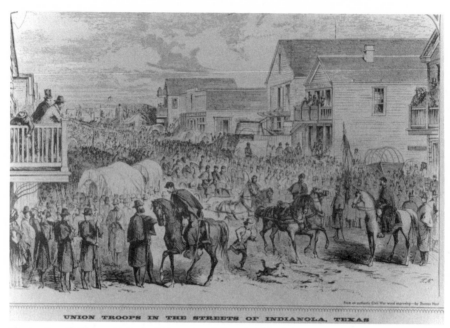

Illustration 8 Union troops in the streets of Indianola, Texas. *Courtesy Victoria College/University of Houston-Victoria Library.*

when the Federal troops entered the community since they accepted at face value Magruder's various public proclamations claiming the enemy was barbaric. However, by the time Indianola was evacuated on March 15, 1864, the local inhabitants, except for the most diehard advocates of the Confederacy, considered the Union occupiers in a much more favorable light. Amazingly, no one in Indianola notified the Confederate military that the Federal troops had pulled out and relocated on Matagorda Island. The withdrawal was discovered by happenstance three days later by patrolling Texas cavalry.[34]

Throughout the remainder of 1863, Federal troops continued to arrive in the Matagorda Bay region. General Washburn reported from Fort Esperanza on December 15 that he had 6,321 men under his command. Additional units arrived after the turn of the year, but shortly thereafter the numbers began to decline as Federal regiments were reassigned to Louisiana where they participated in Banks's doomed spring offensive to invade East Texas. While the Yankees were encamped on Matagorda Island, the fort was reconstructed and major improvements were made in its defensive capacity. All the work put into Fort Esperanza, however, was for naught. When the U.S. forces departed on June 15, 1864, they demolished much of the structure to prevent its reoccupation by their enemy. Col. George W. K. Bailey, the last officer in charge of the fort, reported that he took with him "all valuables, together with the heavy guns" previously seized. "I burnt everything combustible," Bailey noted, "except the private dwelling of Colonel Forrester [Foster], and blew up the forts." Throughout the remainder of the Civil War, Fort Esperanza was largely neglected and never resumed its previous role as a protector of the Texas Coastal Bend. Today, the site lies offshore, the casualty of shore erosion.[35]

Notes

1   The author wishes to thank Jo Ann Spears, Shirley Parkan, Lou Ellen Callarman, Sheron Barnes, Gayle Hardcastle, and Pat Spurlin for their assistance during the writing of this work. Brownson Malsch, *Indianola: The Mother of Western Texas* (Austin, Texas: Shoal Creek Publishers, 1977), 115, 152; Linda Wolff, *Indianola and Matagorda Island, 1837–1887* (Austin, Texas: Eakin Press, 1999), 4, 45.

2   Dermot H. Hardy and Ingham S. Roberts, eds., *Historical Review of South-East Texas* (Chicago: Lewis Publishing, 1910), 1:97; *Victoria Advocate*, October 19, 1861; Victoria City Council Minutes, January 19, 1861, February 11, 1861, March 19, 1861, microfilm, Victoria Public Library, Victoria, Texas.

3   Bill Winsor, *Texas in the Confederacy: Military Installations, Economy and People* (Hillsboro, Texas: Hill Junior College Press, 1978), 8–9, 17–18, 23, 36–37; R. R. Garland to Boyer Davis, December 6, 1863, D. D. Shea to Samuel Boyer Davis, December 6, 1861, *War of the Rebellion: A Compilation of the Official Records of the Union and Confederate Armies* (hereafter cited as *OR*), comp. Robert N. Scott (Washington, D.C.: U.S. Government Printing Office, 1880–1901), 1, 4:153, 155–156; Malsch, *Indianola*, 159–60; Wolff, *Indianola*, 46.

4   Occasionally, Fort Esperanza was referred to in Confederate correspondence as Fort DeBray in reference to Col. Xavier Blanchard DeBray, commanding officer of the military subdistrict located in Houston. C. G. Forshey to W. W. Hunter, February 2, 1862, Dan D. Shea to W. W. Hunter, February 3, 1862, *Official Records of the Union and Confederate Navies in the War of the Rebellion* (hereafter cited as *OR Navies*) (Washington, D. C.: U.S. Government Printing Office, 1894–1922), 1, 17:165–67; Forshey to Davis, February 2, 1862, February 19, 1863, *OR*, 1, 53:779–80, 788; Shea to Edmund P. Turner, January 15, 1863, Forshey to John B. Magruder, March 2, 1863, *OR*, 1, 15:949–50, 1001–2; D. Bradbury to James Duff, January 9, 1864, *OR*, 1, 34, 2:854–55; Leon Smith to Commanding Officer at Indianola, Texas, August 10, 1863, *OR*, 1, 26, 1:171; Special Order No. 140, May 23, 1863, H. Mercer to Shea, June 4, 1863, Turner to [Hamilton] Bee, June 9, 1863, Turner to W. R. Bradfute, August 7, 1863, *OR*, 1, 26, 2:16–17, 37, 42, 151–52; Winsor, *Texas*, 17–18; Joe Petty Jr., ed., *Victor Rose's History of Victoria County* (Victoria, Texas: Book Mart, 1961), 31; Wayne McAlister and Martha McAlister, *Matagorda Island: A Naturalist's Guide* (Austin: University of Texas Press, 1993), 69–70; William H. Chenery, *The Fourteenth Rhode Island Heavy Artillery (Colored)* (New York: New York Negro Press, 1969), 22.

5   Roy P. Basler, ed., *The Collected Works of Abraham Lincoln* (New Brunswick, New Jersey: Rutgers University Press, 1953), 6:354–55; Gregory Davis, *Benjamin*

Franklin Martin, A Union Soldier (n.p.: privately printed, 1997), 389; James G. Hollandsworth, Jr., *Pretense of Glory: The Life of General Nathaniel P. Banks* (Baton Rouge: Louisiana State University Press, 1998), 135; Ben M. Hobratsch, "Yorktown on the Rio Grande: Texas Hopes for French Intervention during the Civil War," *Journal of South Texas* 18 (Fall 2005): 261–64.

6   Davis, *Benjamin Franklin Martin*, 393; *OR*, 1, 26, 1:672.

7   Basler, ed., *Collected Works*, 7:364, 374.

8   Banks to E. M. Stanton, April 6, 1865, *OR*, 1, 26, 1:18–19; Hollandsworth, Jr., *Pretense of Glory*, 136.

9   Ralph A. Wooster, *Texas and Texans in the Civil War* (Austin, Texas: Eakin Press, 1995), 88–92; Paul D. Casdorph, *Prince John Magruder: His Life and Campaigns* (New York: John Wiley, 1996), 253–55); Banks to Stanton, April 6, 1865, *OR*, 1, 26, 1:18–19; Alwyn Barr, "Texas Coastal Defense, 1861–1865," *Southwestern Historical Quarterly* (hereafter cited as *SHQ*) 65 (July 1961): 25–27.

10   Banks to Stanton, April 6, 1865, *OR*, 1, 26, 1:19–20; Hollandsworth, Jr., *Pretense of Glory*, 139–41; *Philadelphia Daily Evening Bulletin*, November 10, 1863; Murphy Given, "Banks Leads Union Invasion of South Texas," *Corpus Christi Caller*, November 6, 2002; Jerry Thompson, *A Wild and Vivid Land* (Austin: Texas State Historical Association, 1997), 109; Laura Snyder, "The Blockade of the Texas Coast During the Civil War" (master's thesis, Texas Technological College, 1938), 99; Wooster, *Texas*, 94.

11   Henry A. Shorey, *The Story of the Maine Fifteenth* (Bridgton, Maine: Press of the Bridgton News, 1890), 54–55; *Philadelphia Daily Evening Bulletin*, November 16, 1863; A. T. Mahan, *The Navy in the Civil War: The Gulf and Inland Waters* (New York: Scribner's, 1885), 3:188; James S. Clark, *The Thirty-fourth Iowa Regiment: A Brief History* (Des Moines, Iowa: Watters-Talbott; 1892), 17; Davis, *Benjamin Franklin Martin*, 404; Givens, "Banks," *Corpus Christi Caller*, November 6, 2002.

12   *Philadelphia Daily Evening Bulletin*, November 16, 1863.

13   As of October 31, 1863, the Rio Grande expedition force consisted of 6,998 men. However, only 4,416 soldiers were present for duty. Shorey, *Story*, 55–56; *Philadelphia Daily Evening Bulletin*, November 16, 1863; Thompson, *Wild*, 109; Banks to Charles P. Stone, November 2, 1863, November 4, 1863, Magruder to W. R. Boggs, November 21, 1863, Abstract from Returns of the Department of the Gulf for October 1863, John Bruce to N. B. Baker, December 1, 1863, *OR*, 1, 26, 1:396–98, 425, 432, 783; Fitzhugh, "Saluria," *SHQ* 61:95; Stephen A. Townsend, *The Yankee Invasion of Texas* (College Station: Texas A&M University Press, 2006), 16–17; Nannie M. Tilley, ed., *Federals on the Frontier: The Diary of Benjamin F. McIntyre, 1862–1864* (Austin: University of Texas Press, 1963), 249; Chester Barney, *Recollections of Field Service with the Twentieth Iowa Infantry Regiment* (Davenport, Iowa: privately printed, 1865), 245.

14   Townsend, *Yankee*, 18; *Des Moines Daily Statesman*, November 22, 1863, November 24, 1863; *Philadelphia Daily Evening Bulletin*, November 16, 1863, November 21, 1863; Shorey, *Story*, 57.

15   Banks to Stanton, April 6, 1865, William Hyde Clark to Major Thompson, November 15, 1863, *OR*, 1, 26, 1:20, 788–89.

16   Banks to H. W. Halleck, November 18, 1863, T. E. Ransom to August W. Sexton, November 18, 1863, E. R. Tarver to A. G. Dickinson, November 21, 1863, Banks to Stone, November 17, 1863, *OR*, 1, 26, 1:409–10, 426, 438, 803–4; Barr, "Texas," *SHQ* 65:28; *New York Herald*, December 7, 1863; *Philadelphia Daily Evening Bulletin*, December 3, 1863, December 13, 1863; Mahan, *Navy*, 3:188; *Des Moines Daily Statesman*, December 5, 1863; Winsor, *Texas*, 9; William Allen and Sue Hastings Taylor, *Aransas: The Life of a Texas Coastal County* (Austin, Texas: Eakin Press, 1997), 141–42; Petty, Jr., *Victor Rose's*, 23–24.

17   Petty, Jr., *Victor Rose's*, 23–24.

18   Ibid.

19   Shorey, *Story*, 60–61; Ransom to William H. Morgan, December 6, 1863, *OR*, 1, 26, 1:427.

20   John Ireland to Bradfute, November 23, 1863, *OR*, 1, 26, 1:447; Shorey, *Story*, 62.

21   Bee to Turner, November 19, 1863, Bradfute to Turner, November 24, 1863, *OR*, 1, 26, 1:436, 445; Bee to Turner, November 24, 1863, Turner to Bee, November 30, 1863, *OR*, 1, 26, 2:443, 460; Casdorph, *Magruder*, 261; Fitzhugh, "Saluria," *SHQ* 61:96–97.

22   Bee to Turner, November 21, 1863, *OR*, 1, 26, 1:437; Magruder to the Citizens of Western Texas, November 27, 1863, *OR*, 1, 26, 2:452–53.

23   Philadelphia *Daily Evening Bulletin*, January 4, 1864.

24   Bradfute to Turner, November 26, 1863, J. A. Murray to Turner, November 26, 1863, Magruder to E. Kirby Smith, November 27, 1863, *OR*, 1, 26, 2:447–49.

25   Stone to C. C. Washburn, December 5, 1863, H. D. Washburn to G. Norman Lieber, December 3, 1863, Ransom to William H. Morgan, December 6, 1863, *OR*, 1, 26, 1:420–21, 427.

26   H. D. Washburn to Lieber, December 3, 1863, *OR*, 1, 26, 1:421; Isaac H. Elliott, *History of the Thirty-third Regiment Illinois Veteran Volunteer Infantry* (Gibson City, Illinois: Press of the Gibson Courier, 1902), 53; Albert O. Marshall, *Army Life; From a Soldier's Journal* (Joliet, Illinois: privately printed, 1883), 322.

27   Marshall, *Army Life*, 326–27.

28   Ibid., 327–28; Elliott, *History*, 53; Shorey, *Story*, 64; H. D. Washburn to Lieber, December 3, 1863, Ransom to Morgan, December 6, 1863, *OR*, 1, 26, 1:421, 428.

29   Shorey, *Story* 64–65; Elliott, *History*, 53; Marshall, *Army Life*, 327–28, 330; H. D. Washburn to Lieber, December 3, 1863, Ransom to Morgan, December 6, 1863, *OR*, 1, 26, 1:421–22, 428; J. H. Strong to H. H. Bell, November 29, 1863, *OR Navies*, 1, 20:702; Dupree, *Planting*, 76.

30   H. D. Washburn to Lieber, December 3, 1863, Ransom to Morgan, December 6, 1863, *OR*, 1, 26, 1:422, 428; George P. Finley to Turner, November 30, 1863, OR, 1, 26, 2:458; Smith to Magruder, November 30, 1863, *OR Navies*, 1, 20:853; Shorey, *Story*, 65; Eudora I. Moore, "Reminiscences of Indianola, Tex.,"

Confederate Veteran 31 (January 1923): 16; *New York Herald*, December 13, 1863; J. S. Clark, *The Thirty-fourth Iowa Regiment: A Brief History* (Des Moines, Iowa: Watters-Talbott, 1892), 18.

31   Marshall, *Army Life*, 331–34; Strong to Bell, November 30, 1863, *OR Navies*, 1, 20:702.

32   Townsend, *Yankee Invasion*, 30; H. D. Washburn to Lieber, December 3, 1863, *OR*, 1, 26, 1; 422; Shorey, *Story*, 65.

33   Houston *Tri-Weekly Telegraph*, December 5, 1863; Marshall, *Army Life*, 337–38.

34   C. C. Washburn to Stone, December 14, 1863, *OR*, 1, 26, 1:849, 853; Duff to J. E. Slaughter, March 18, 1864, *OR*, 1, 34, 2:1058; *Diary of William Warner Reid*, http://www.mkwe.com/ohio/pages/Reid-03.htm; Townsend, *Yankee Invasion*, 35.

35   C. C. Washburn to Stone, *OR*, 1, 26, 1:860; George W. K. Bailey to George B. Drake, June 22, 1864, *OR*, 1, 34, 1:1011.

Chapter 10

Red and White Fighting the Blue: Relations between Texans and Confederate Indians

by Charles D. Grear

Civil War historians have traditionally focused on battles in the Eastern and Trans-Appalachian theaters of the war, leaving the impression that the war was fought by white men in blue and gray uniforms. Primarily, this assumption is true; white men did make up the bulk of both the Union and Confederate armies. However, in the Trans-Mississippi Theater of the war, the organization of armies was more complex. In the Indian Territory, present-day Oklahoma, raids and battles raged between Northern and Southern soldiers with their American Indian counterparts, Pins (Union) and Half-bloods (Confederate), and African Americans. During 1864, the Fifth Texas Cavalry Brigade, better known as Gano's Brigade, a motley group of Confederate Texans led by Brig. Gen. Richard Montgomery Gano, fought side by side with the Indian brigade led by Cherokee Chief Brig. Gen. Stand Watie in the Indian Territory. This chapter examines the relationship between the white and Indian soldiers, particularly the Cherokee, and provides a much-needed study into the role of race relationships in the Trans-Mississippi during the Civil War. Specific aspects include how they interacted, how well they fought as a division, and their reaction to fighting black Union soldiers.[1]

The Indian Territory contained reservations for the Indian Nations removed by the United States government during the Trail of Tears in the 1830s. Among the tribes relocated, the Cherokees, Creeks, Choctaws, Chickasaws, and Seminoles were the most populous. At the outbreak of the Civil War, the Choctaws and Chickasaws immediately joined the Confederacy and many of the Creeks and Seminoles followed. A feud among the Cherokees, the largest and most powerful of the Indian Nations, delayed their decision, which eventually widened a rift that already existed among their people. Before the start of the war, a feud had developed within the Cherokee Nation between the factions of Chief John Ross and Chief Stand Watie. Their main dispute originated in 1835 when a group of Cherokee men, one a brother of Watie, favored the Cherokee resettlement in the Indian Territory. The Watie faction signed the Treaty of Echota over the protests of Ross and his followers, essentially giving the Indian Removal Act of 1830

Illustration 9 Brig. Gen. Stand Watie. *Courtesy Massachusetts MOLLUS Photograph Collection, U.S. Army Military History Institute, Carlisle Barracks, Pennsylvania.*

legitimacy. This treaty defined the two opposing factions within the Cherokee Nation, the Pins and the Half-bloods. The dispute between the two groups eventually developed into a blood feud that continued until the Civil War, resulting in the murder of leaders from both sides, including Watie's brother.

Chief Ross, a Cherokee elite of Scottish decent, organized and led the Keetoowah, or the secret society of the Pins, named for the crossed pins they wore on their coat lapels and calico shirts. Membership in the society consisted mainly of full-blooded Cherokees. Supported by abolitionists from the North, the Pins followed a more northern lifestyle, except their leader Ross, who owned over a hundred slaves.[2]

Watie, a lawyer, businessman, and leader in the Cherokee Nation, who served as speaker on the Cherokee National Council, led the other faction, composed mostly of mixed-blood Cherokees. Degatada (Watie's Indian name, meaning to stand firm) was born near present-day Rome, Georgia, to a mother who was half Indian and half white and an Indian father who converted to Christianity. Watie's role in Cherokee politics, his mixed heritage, and education made him a natural leader of the group of men that opposed Ross. The men he led identified more with the Confederacy because they felt oppressed by the Pins that controlled the Cherokee Nation, similar to the South's view of the abolitionists and Republicans in the North. Additionally the Half-bloods developed ties to Southern businessmen through commercial hunting, the raising of livestock, the commercial farming of cotton, membership in the Masonic Order and Protestant churches, and their increasing reliance on the institution of slavery. Watie's men even organized themselves and joined the secret military society called Knights of the Golden Circle. The purpose of the society was to establish a Southern slave empire from Central America through the Caribbean basin. This attracted the half-blooded Cherokees because, if they could be part of the empire, they would be free from the control of the Pins and maintain the institution of slavery in their nations.

In the one hundred years before the Civil War, slavery became ingrained in Indian society. Native Americans belonging to the Choctaw Nation owned 2,297 slaves, Creeks owned 1,651 slaves, Chickasaws 917, and the Cherokees owned the most slaves with 2,504. The Seminoles were the only exception, owning no slaves. Like other Southern slave owners, the Native American slaveholders inherited the racial prejudices of the institution, denying blacks, both slave and free, basic civil liberties afforded to the poorest in their society.[3]

On August 12, 1861, Watie's Half-bloods joined the Confederacy after Confederate agent Albert Pike negotiated a peace treaty with the five Indian Nations. Pike succeeded in obtaining Indian support for the Confederacy and agreements that they would not attack frontier settlements. At the same time the Indians chose sides, Federal troops abandoned the Union fortifications located in the territory. Thus the Confederacy gained control of the land just north of the Arkansas River in 1861, including Fort Gibson, which was the strongest military port in the Indian Territory. However, the Union army quickly made plans to recapture the area.[4]

In early 1863, the Confederacy lost over half of the Indian Territory because of two Union raids from Kansas, the most costly culminating at the Battle of Honey Spring on July 17, 1863. Watie and the Confederate Cherokees suffered tremendously from these raids because they lost control of the Cherokee Nation in the northeastern corner of the Indian Territory and nearly sixteen thousand Cherokees became refugees, including the families of the soldiers fighting under Watie. The raids generated suffering and privation for the refugees and depleted the territory of its food and livestock. However, it also created a difficult situation for the Union soldiers occupying the land because it forced them to ship in all of their supplies by boat or wagon, thus making the Union positions vulnerable to Confederate raids.[5]

Also, at the outbreak of the Civil War, Federal soldiers abandoned forts located on the Texas frontier. This opened the way for Comanches and Kiowas to raid isolated farms along the periphery of settled Texas. Through these raids the Plains Indians hoped to reclaim lands lost to white settlers, especially in the Northern Subdistrict of Texas. On one occasion, a band of raiders came within twenty-five miles of Fort Worth. Combating the Indian depredations, Texas Governor Francis R. Lubbock created the Twenty-ninth Texas Cavalry to defend the North Texas frontier settlements. By March 1863 the Native American threat to the Lone Star State subsided and the regiment received a transfer to the Indian Territory to defend North Texas from an expected Union offensive that spring. By August 1863, Confederate commanders reinforced the Twenty-ninth Texas with three Confederate units, the Thirtieth Texas Cavalry; the First Regiment, Arizona Brigade; and Krumbhaar's Battery. Collectively, these units formed Gano's Brigade. Confederate authorities initially placed the brigade under the command of Brig. Gen. Smith P. Bankhead.[6]

The brigade suffered from many demoralizing problems. The morale of the men had plummeted because many rushed into volunteering in the army to avoid conscription. Desertion and lack of discipline continued to plague the brigade through the rest of the summer and fall of 1863. To resolve this problem, Brig. Gen. Henry McCulloch, the new commander of the Northern Subdistrict of Texas, relieved Bankhead from command of the brigade on October 16, and replaced him with Brig. Gen. Richard Montgomery Gano who officially took command on October 24.[7]

Gano, a native of Bourbon County, Kentucky, moved to Grapevine, Texas, in Tarrant County in 1857, where he distinguished himself as a doctor, pioneer, cattleman, and Indian fighter. Early in the war Gano raised a squadron of Texas cavalrymen to fight for his home state of Kentucky. While fighting with Brig. Gen. John H. Morgan as commander of the Seventh Kentucky Cavalry in the Western Theater, Gano rose through the ranks from captain to acting brigadier general.[8]

In June 1863 Gano fell ill from "valvular heart disease with hypertrophy." Pronounced unfit for duty, Gano returned home to recuperate. By July, Governor Lubbock placed Gano, who made a miraculous recovery, in command of all the cavalry in the Texas state troops. On October 10, Gano arrived in Bonham, Texas, where McCulloch encountered problems with the unruly nature of the Fifth Texas Cavalry Brigade. Instead of having Gano command the state troops, McCulloch instructed him to command the insubordinate brigade.[9]

With his newly expanded brigade, Gano marched his men to Doaksville, Indian Territory, to obtain new uniforms and prepared them for winter camp at Laynesport, Indian Territory. While in winter camp, Lt. Gen. Edmund Kirby Smith, commander of the Trans-Mississippi Department, placed Maj. Gen. Samuel Bell Maxey in command of all the Confederate Indians and Gano's Brigade. Maxey, a close friend of Smith, inherited two major problems in the Indian

Illustration 10 Brig. Gen. Richard Montgomery
Gano. *Courtesy Texas Heritage Museum.*

Territory: his command did not have enough soldiers to adequately defend the
territory against a Union invasion and it lacked the necessary provisions to feed
and cloth not only for Bell's troops but also for the families of their Indian allies
who had been displaced by the Union advance. Sympathetic to the Indians,
Maxey spent most of his tenure as commander of the Indian Territory successfully gathering provisions for his soldiers and their displaced families through
raids on Union supply trains.[10]

After spending the winter in Laynesport, the men of Gano's Brigade and
the Indian Brigade prepared themselves for the spring campaigning season of
1864. Before this time the two groups of Confederates had limited contact
with each other. Besides Gano consulting with Watie, the contact between
the men initially was limited to actual combat situations. While fighting the
enemy, relations between the two groups were amiable. The major battles the
men fought together included Poison Spring in Arkansas and Flat Rock and
Cabin Creek in the Indian Territory. The actions of the men demonstrate their
ability to unite for the defense of their homes and families in the Indian Territory and Texas. Additionally, both sides displayed their reactions to fighting
against African Americans in the Union Army at Poison Spring and Flat Rock.

But once there was a lull in fighting, the Texans and Indians would often fight each other.

The first major engagement that these men fought together was the Battle of Poison Spring. Maxey received letters from Maj. Gen. Sterling Price, Confederate commander of Arkansas, asking for assistance in the defense of the state from the Union army's advance from Fort Smith and Little Rock in the Red River Campaign. Missing most of the heavy fighting, the Texans and Indians arrived in time to provide the finishing stroke to the Union advance held up in Camden, Arkansas. Within the first day of occupying Camden, the Union soldiers consumed most of their forage and food supplies for the army. Not able to receive supplies from Fort Smith, Little Rock, or by water, the Union commander sent men to scour the countryside, where they found an ample amount of corn near Poison Spring.[11]

On April 17, two days after entering Camden, a detachment was sent out to acquire the stores of corn near Poison Spring. Col. James M. Williams of the First Kansas Colored Volunteer Infantry commanded this detachment. William's detachment included five hundred men from the First Kansas Colored Volunteer Infantry, along with smaller detachments of Kansas cavalrymen and artillerymen from Indiana. The total size of the force numbered 695 men, 2 guns, and 198 wagons. This foraging party traveled eighteen miles down the road toward Washington, while Williams dispatched a hundred wagons in every direction to procure corn. By midnight, all of the wagons returned full of corn and the men camped for the night.[12]

The foraging party did not escape the attention of the Southern army. Col. Colton Greene discovered this detachment and reported to Maj. Gen. John S. Marmaduke. The major general immediately organized a small force to attack the exposed Union detachment. With additional information about the Union strength, Marmaduke felt that his force was too small to engage the Federals and returned to camp. After they returned, Marmaduke requested all available troops, including Gano's and Watie's brigades, be ready to attack by 8:00 a.m.[13]

The combined Confederate force completely routed the Union foraging party. Fearful of an attack from Camden, the Confederates secured the train and prepared to leave. The brigades re-formed along with 170 wagons and all of the captured Union artillery. The engagement at Poison Spring represented a complete success for the Confederates in the Trans-Mississippi. For Gano's and Watie's troops, the battle marked the first time that most of these men fought together.[14]

A week before the battle of Poison Spring, a well-publicized massacre of Federal soldiers occurred at Fort Pillow, Tennessee. Lt. Gen. Nathan Bedford Forrest, a commander notorious for his ferocity, killed a significant number of black Union soldiers after they had surrendered or had been wounded. That did not

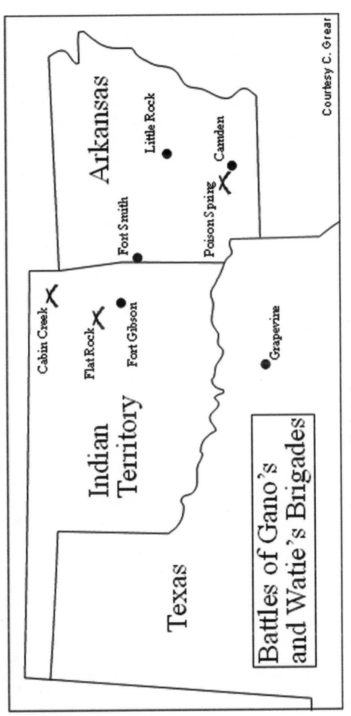

Map 4 Battles of Gano's and Watie's Brigades. *Courtesy Charles D. Grear*

prove to be the only time such actions occurred. At the Battle of Poison Spring, a significant number of African American soldiers received no quarter from the attacking Confederates. Accounts from both sides confirm the overwhelming number of soldiers from the First Kansas Colored Volunteer Infantry murdered by Confederates while they retreated, surrendered, and lay wounded. That pattern reoccurred throughout the war at places such as Milliken's Bend, Saltville, and Petersburg. Poison Spring was not an exception, although it became the greatest atrocity towards African American soldiers in the Trans-Mississippi.[15]

The total Union loss in the engagement included 122 killed, 97 wounded, and 81 missing. The First Kansas had 438 men participate in the engagement. Among its ranks, the black regiment lost 117 killed, 65 wounded, and only 4 captured. That represented 42 percent of the regiment, an extremely high percentage for any engagement. Maj. Richard G. Ward of the First Kansas reported, "We were obliged to bring our wounded away the best we could, as the Rebels were seen shooting those that fell into their hands."[16] The Confederates overwhelmed the Union troops, leaving very little opportunity for the wounded to escape. Another description describes how the white Confederate soldiers drove the captured wagons over the wounded black soldiers and execution squads went about the field killing those whose wounds were so severe that they couldn't be moved.[17]

In addition to the Federals, the Confederates also mentioned the event. General Price reported: "The enemy were completely routed, leaving nearly 500 dead (mostly negroes) on the field."[18] Another report by Brig. Gen. William Cabell, who participated in the engagement, stated, "The number of killed of the enemy was very great, especially among the negroes."[19] The Confederates did not kill all the African American soldiers taken as prisoners. The difference in the number of white prisoners and black prisoners shows how the Rebels treated the two races. Out of sixty-two Union prisoners, fifty-eight were white, and only four were black. This clearly demonstrates that the Confederates gave less quarter to the African American soldiers since within the Union force there were five black soldiers to every two white.[20]

The atrocity did not end with the killing of the African American soldiers but continued after they died. An account found in a clipping from the *Washington (Arkansas) Telegraph* stated that "the Choctaws buried a Yankee soldier in an ordinary grave. For a headstone, they sat up a stiff dead negro buried to the waist. For a foot stone, another negro reversed, out from the waist to the heels."[21] According to Confederate Capt. William A. Miler's account, the Indians mutilated the bodies of the dead African American soldiers: "[A] regiment of Indian troops, who wanted to scalp the negroes, but not being allowed to do so, they cut off their noses, and had great stringers of them until the smellers got too offensive." Both groups of Confederates participated in the slaughter and mutilation.[22]

Gano's Brigade participated in this atrocity with members having their own reasons for their actions. Before Gano took command of the brigade, some of the regiments previously fought against the First Kansas. One regiment in particular was Col. Charles DeMorse's Twenty-ninth Texas. DeMorse was in command of General Gano's brigade during the engagement, because the general received a bullet wound to his left elbow in an earlier skirmish, which might have helped lead to the massacre. DeMorse and the Twenty-ninth Texas had fought the First Kansas at Honey Springs a year earlier in the Indian Territory. In the engagement, the regiment met decisive defeat, DeMorse received a wound, and the regiment suffered a high number of casualties. Yet the African Americans did not kill a single wounded or captured Texan at Honey Springs. Nevertheless, when the two sides met on the battlefield in Poison Spring, DeMorse's men sought revenge on the soldiers. According to the colonel, "few prisoners were brought in by my command."[23]

Another reason the Texans participated in the killing may have been their background. Texans had become notorious for not following orders that went against their personal liberties. That seemed especially true for the Thirtieth Texas, which six months prior to the engagement received a poor review and in another instance the commanding colonel disarmed an entire company. The poor review resulted from the lack of discipline the men displayed. Without discipline, low morale could infect a unit making it difficult to prevent the soldiers from doing as they pleased to the black troops. Consequently Confederate soldiers saw black troops as their enemy and as a symbol of an endless and increasingly unpopular war. The fear of slave revolt in the South could have created part of the emotional reaction to armed black soldiers. Also, the Rebel soldiers, both Texan and Indian, did not consider ex-slaves as legitimate foes because many still viewed them as slaves, socially beneath them.[24]

For the Union army, the Battle of Poison Spring demoralized its soldiers by keeping vital supplies from reaching their camps. Facing starvation, the invading army retreated to Little Rock. With the threat to southern Arkansas dissipated, General Smith relieved the Texans and Indians from duty in Arkansas on April 28. The two brigades returned to the Indian Territory as victors.[25]

The lull in fighting created tension between the two groups over perceptions the Texans had on the Indian population. Many of the Texans resented fighting for a people they felt had questionable loyalties. Throughout the course of the Civil War numerous Indians defected from Watie's Brigade to the Union army or waited for Union occupation in 1863 to join the home guards. William Steele, a Texan who fought in the Indian Territory before Gano's men arrived, stated: "Their allegiance to the Government seems to be regarded more in the light of a voluntary contribution on their part, susceptible of being withheld, at their option, than the performance of an obligatory duty. In order to acquire the reputation derived from success, it is necessary to . . . coax and demagoguize with the Indians."[26] Coupled with the sense of distrust was the Indians' strange behavior, such as their fifteen-minute war cry; their appearances, especially with battle paint; and the burden the refugee population placed on their supplies, causing a large number of Watie's men to desert to care for their families. Though the Indians were successful on the battlefield, the Texas soldiers perceived them as "wholly unreliable as troops of the line. The officers, as a general rule, are ignorant, void of moral tone of character and indisposed to enforce discipline among their men."[27]

Another factor that created disgust among some of the Texans was Maxey's promotion of Watie to brigadier general. Many Texans did not agree, Colonel DeMorse being the most vocal. DeMorse venomously protested about "the old question of the relative grade of races." The Texas colonel reasoned that:

> The Indian is physiologically recognized as an inferior race, and I respectfully protest against the decision of the major-general commanding this district as one to which no white officer, . . . , can submit. . . . no Indian commander is qualified by attainments for such duty as the regulations of the army call for, is superadded the well-known mental incapacity of that people to direct operations which require promptness and concentration of mind. . . . I ask respectfully to be immediately relieved from duty in this district, as I shall not, . . . subordinate myself to an individual of an inferior race.[28]

Never before had DeMorse expressed ill feelings towards the Indians that he served with during the past year. The idea of white supremacy was prevalent among the American population during the decade preceding the Civil War. Anglo Americans accused people of different races or ethnic groups of retarding the advancement of civilization. Even though the men would fight on the battlefield for the common cause of the Confederacy, DeMorse's tirade reveals that other social issues lay just below the surface, waiting to erupt.[29]

After the men returned to the Indian Territory, they camped at Fort Towson. There they recovered from the fight at Poison Spring and assumed garrison duty at the fort. These problems did not last long when in July General Maxey ordered Gano's Brigade, in cooperation with General Watie's Confederate Indians, to make a demonstration on a lightly garrisoned Fort Smith. Maxey recognized Fort Smith's reliance on overland routes and considered this demonstration necessary, not to conquer the Federal soldiers stationed there, but to cut them off from their supplies and starve them out that section of Arkansas.[30]

Maxey's plan consisted of keeping Watie's troops on the Limestone Prairie, which would check any Union attempt to advance south. With the Indian force holding the Federal soldiers in the forts, Price and his men in Arkansas could cut off the supply trains from Little Rock. This left the supply trains from Fort

Gibson. With the depleted number of soldiers in Fort Smith, the escorts would not be strong enough to face Gano's Brigade. If this starvation plan could be accomplished, it could result in the evacuation of both Fort Smith and Fort Gibson and keep the Texans and Indians separated until the controversy over Watie's promotion cooled.[31]

Also, Maxey hoped that the siege of Fort Smith would ease tensions beginning to arise within the First Indian Brigade. The Indians within his division became upset since they had not received payment in months and their families faced starvation in refugee camps. Attacking Fort Smith offered an opportunity to capture much-needed supplies. The raid, which culminated at Massard Prairie, achieved a complete success. Not only did Maxey's troops rout the enemy, but they also captured a large store of supplies. The spoils of the fight included "about 200 Sharp's rifles, and about 400 six-shooters, a number of horses, some sutler's stores, [and] camp equipage."[32] The objects that the men could not carry off, they destroyed so the enemy could not use them again. Beyond the material success of the raid, Confederates made it harder to defend Fort Smith. It forced Brig. Gen. John M. Thayer to relocate his scouting posts closer to the fort, limiting his ability to watch enemy movements. Maxey commented: "I do not believe the enemy will now throw out anything more than a reconnaissance in force."[33]

Maxey allowed the men and horses of Gano's and Watie's brigades to rest and recuperate in separate camps from their demonstration on Fort Smith at Camp Pike, Indian Territory, during August. The men did not rest long before receiving orders to participate in a raid in their own district. Similar to their demonstration on Fort Smith, the Confederates attempted to starve out the Federal troops stationed at Fort Gibson, Indian Territory. If the men could succeed in capturing enough food and supplies, the Union threat in the Indian Territory could be reduced significantly and the soldiers and refugee Indians could survive the fall and winter.[34]

They planned to launch the raid into the northeast Indian Territory to disrupt the Union supply route between Fort Gibson and Fort Scott. Additionally, they planned to attack Fort Gibson if it was not heavily defended.[35] Aside from providing badly needed supplies to the Confederate troops, the raid would serve as a diversionary demonstration for General Smith. The commander of the Trans-Mississippi ordered a Confederate force under General Price to advance on Kansas City and Fort Leavenworth to stir up Union citizens in Missouri and Kansas. He hoped that this would cause the citizens to petition Abraham Lincoln for additional troops, and force the president to divert troops from Maj. Gen. William Tecumseh Sherman's army, which was marching through the South, thereby slowing down and weakening Sherman's attack on Atlanta and his march to the sea.[36]

With the new raid planned, Generals Gano and Watie met on September 12, 1864, to work out the tactical details of the raid. During the meeting Watie waived rank in Gano's favor and gave the overall command of the raid to Gano since the majority of the force were Texans. The Confederates left Camp Pike on September 14, with 1,200 men in the Texas brigade and 800 Confederate Indians in Watie's Brigade.[37]

Two days into the raid, Gano halted his force at Sand Town Ford on the Verdigris River to plan an attack on a Union hay camp eight miles away at Flat Rock. Flat Rock lay only fifteen miles west of Fort Gibson under the command of Capt. Edgar A. Barker. To protect the hay camp, Barker commanded a detachment of 125 soldiers from the Second Kansas Cavalry and First Kansas Colored Volunteers. Gano and Watie quickly organized and launched their attack.[38]

After thirty minutes Barker found himself being attacked from four directions, Confederate soldiers within 200 yards of his lines, and "completely overwhelmed and surrounded, and my position every moment becoming more and more untenable."[39] Barker attempted an escape with all his mounted men, leaving the dismounted men of the Second Kansas Cavalry and all the First Kansas to fend for themselves. With approximately forty men, Barker charged through a weak spot in Watie's line. This escape attempt was futile since only fifteen of the men managed to escape to Fort Gibson. Captain Barker was one of the lucky few.[40]

After Barker's escape from Flat Rock, the remaining soldiers, especially the black infantry, rallied under Lt. Thomas B. Southerland. The Federal soldiers kept repelling the Confederates for two hours until they ran out of ammunition. When they ran out of ammunition, the Confederates charged into the Union camp "capturing all of the white soldiers remaining there, and killing all the colored soldiers they could find. Only four out of thirty-seven of them [African American soldiers] succeeded in making their escape."[41] While capturing Federal soldiers, Howard Holden from Gano's Brigade captured a Union soldier who turned out to be his brother John Holden. Predictably he received quarter.[42]

It was almost dusk when the fighting stopped and the massacre began. Mounted Indians with guns ready began to trot their horses through the rows of uncut hay and tall weed patches, shooting down the black soldiers like hunting game. Some of the infantrymen rose from the hay crying, "O! Good Master, save and spare me," but each received a bullet from the Confederate Indians. Some of the African American soldiers submerged themselves in the open small pools of water with only their noses exposed to air. Most of these men received the same fate as the others when Rebel soldiers dragged their bodies out of the water.[43] Jefferson P. Blaze of the Thirtieth Texas described the killing of the black soldiers, "The water was red with the blood of the dead negroes. The few Indians who were along with the army dragged the bodies from the water and took all that was of any value from them."[44] Four black soldiers escaped by concealing themselves in the water and used water lilies, overhanging willow branches, and prairie branches to conceal their noses. When night came, they crawled out of the water and escaped in the dark.[45]

After Gano's men subdued all the Union soldiers, they proceeded to capture and destroy all of the camp and garrison equipage, company books, all the ordnance, a thousand tons of hay, mowing machines, and wagons. The Confederates also captured twenty-five horses, twelve mules, and two six-mule wagons and harnesses. While the Confederates collected and destroyed the supplies, captured Union soldiers told about a big wagon train that left on September 12 from Fort Scott to resupply Fort Gibson.[46]

The number of casualties in the fight dramatically differed between the two opposing forces. Barker's force suffered forty men dead and sixty-six men wounded, missing, or captured. Only nineteen men escaped unharmed from the confrontation. The Confederates on the other hand only suffered three men wounded, none mortally. With nearly all of his force intact, Gano's men finished destroying the supplies until darkness set in and camped on the battlefield for the night. The following day the entire Confederate force continued north to intercept the Federal wagon train moving to Fort Gibson.[47]

The Federal wagon train, the prize Gano and Watie sought, was under the command of Maj. Henry Hopkins of the Second Kansas, from the same regiment as the men engaged in the fight at Flat Rock. During the first part of September, the wagon train had been loaded with as many supplies as the animals could bear at Fort Scott, Kansas, and by September 12 the wagon train had left for Fort Gibson. The train numbered 300 wagons: 205 government wagons, four government ambulances, and ninety sutler wagons. The initial escort consisted of fifty mounted men and thirty dismounted men of the Second Kansas, sixty mounted and seventy dismounted men of the Fourteenth Kansas Cavalry, and ten mounted and forty dismounted men of the Sixth Kansas Cavalry. A few days later the size of the force increased to 360 men with the arrival of a hundred Union Cherokee Indians from the Second Indian Regiment and the Third Indian Regiment. Along with the reinforcements, Hopkins received a dispatch from Col. C.W. Blair, the commander of Fort Scott. The dispatch warned Hopkins of a Confederate movement north of the Arkansas River. Hopkins responded to the dispatch by asking Blair for as many troops as could be sent to reinforce the train, because he feared that the Confederate force would attack and overwhelm him.[48]

On September 17, the day after the fight at Flat Rock, Hopkins and the wagon train established their camp for the night, fifteen miles north of Cabin

Creek. That night he received a dispatch from the commanding officer of Fort Gibson, Col. S. H. Wattles, giving a more detailed description of Gano's force. The note stated that the Confederate force numbered 1,200 to 1,500 men and was moving toward Cabin Creek. Wattles also ordered Hopkins to move his command to Cabin Creek immediately, await further orders, and informed him that reinforcements were en route.[49]

By 9 a.m. the next morning, Hopkins and the wagon train arrived at the military crossing and stockade at Cabin Creek. At the stockade were 140 Pin Cherokees from the Third Indian Regiment under the command of Lt. B. H. Whitlow and 170 Pin Cherokees of the Second Indian Regiment commanded by Lt. John C. Palmer. With the addition of these soldiers, Hopkins' entire force consisted of 120 mounted white cavalry, 140 dismounted white cavalry, 30 mounted Cherokees, and 330 dismounted Cherokees, totaling 610 men.[50]

On the same morning, Gano proceeded with four hundred Texans and two artillery pieces toward Cabin Creek, leaving General Watie in command of the reserve troops at Wolf Creek. Gano discovered the supply train near the stockade and reconnoitered the enemy's position. Realizing the Union force outnumbered the Texans, the commanding general sent a courier to Watie ordering him to bring the rest of the command to his position.[51] Gano's courier reported on how he found the Indians when he arrived at Wolf Creek:

> Eager yet nervous, they made "medicine" and tried to recall old battle omens of their vanished long-house culture. Too bad the hated "pins" and their abolitionist Keetowah medicine men were on the other side! The country hereabouts had been unlucky for Confederate Indians. Stand Watie's attack on July 17, 1863, had failed. Was his "medicine" wrong? Indians in the ranks discussed this seriously when Greenbrier Joe saw a vision—a white deer near the encampment. He believed this a "sign" of victory, and the column was confident as it rode away to meet Gano.[52]

Watie arrived just after midnight of September 19. With his force now complete again, Gano immediately moved the entire command forward. Within half a mile of the stockade, Gano formed his men into battle lines with Watie forming his troops to the left.[53]

After a brief delay, the Confederates "closed in until near enough to hear shouting and laughter within the palisades. . . . In the darkness the raiders shouted taunts at them, and the Indians in the barricade replied. The turkey-gobble challenge shuddered back and forth. No Cherokee of spirit could ignore that call of their blood."[54] Some of the Cherokees individually advanced in front of their regiments challenging the Pins to fight and attempting to rally their fellow Cherokee warriors to advance with them. There was no general engagement in the darkness.[55]

When the daylight broke across the horizon, Gano wasted very little time getting his men into action. Gano ordered the Indian regiments to attack the Federal position. The Indians succeeded in driving the Union soldiers back 150 yards before the attack became bogged down. Seeing the attack stalled, Gano led the Thirtieth Texas in a charge only to be repulsed. When the Texans retreated, Gano replaced the Indians, who ran out of ammunition, with detachments from all of the Texas regiments.[56]

With the bulk of Gano's force charging the Union right, Hopkins moved the majority of the Federal front to face the attacking Rebels. This allowed the Confederate artillery to induce a destructive fire upon the Union flank so that "crash after crash of shell swept Yankees, negroes, Pins, and mules away from the land of the living, while every regiment and company poured in volley after volley, and the brave Indians, having replenished with ammunition, came again to work."[57] Gano created a crossfire between the cavalry and the artillery. This crossfire pushed the Federal troops out of their fortifications and around 9 a.m. the field belonged to the Confederates.[58]

Without reinforcements and artillery Hopkins knew he could not hold his position. Since the Confederate charge on the right cut the Union force off from the main road, Hopkins ordered his men to retreat east along the Grand River. This route led the Federal soldiers away from the attacking Rebels under a smoke screen produced by the Texans' cannons. The Federals left almost all of the wagons in Confederate hands and their retreat only concluded when the force arrived at Fort Gibson at 7 a.m. on September 21, two days later.[59]

With the fighting ended, the Confederates began to examine their treasure. The Rebels discovered they captured over one and a half million dollars' worth of Federal property. The Indians on the other hand, as described by Capt. Curtis Johnson of the Fifteenth Kansas Cavalry, captured "part of the train, in which were sutlers' wagons, they procured liquor, and after becoming intoxicated slaughtered indiscriminately."[60] In their drunken state, they began to kill wounded prisoners and mutilated the dead Union soldiers. After getting tired of preying on the bodies of Union soldiers, they proceeded to throw captured property over the bluffs in the creek, just for the sheer joy of seeing the destruction of the objects.[61]

Being far behind enemy lines, Gano ordered his force to quickly secure all functioning wagons with healthy mules and load them with as much of the captured supplies as they could handle. At the completion of loading the supplies, the force moved out. The Confederates burned all the broken wagons and the ones that could not be taken, along with everything left in the stockade. In short time, Gano and his force overcame their difficulties and loaded 130 wagons, harnessed 740 mules, and left Cabin Creek.[62]

The capture of the wagon train and the destruction of the hay ricks by the Texans and Indians caused a tough winter for the Union soldiers and their horses. Besides making the Federal soldiers suffer a little more in the winter, the force also "cut off communication between Forts Gibson and Smith"[63] and hampered the Union's ability to resupply the forts. Being isolated and having difficulty obtaining supplies had a bad effect on the Union army's morale and prevented it from invading southern Indian Territory and North Texas.[64]

Soon after the raid, paranoia among the Union officers in the Indian Territory began to set in. Thayer began to see armies where armies did not exist. "My present information leads me to believe that the enemy, under Generals Cooper, Gano, and Stand Watie will attempt to take the next train that is sent from Fort Scott, and they will probably throw a force of 3,000 or 4,000 men north of Arkansas for that purpose."[65] Gano and Watie had just arrived at Camp Pike the day before and there was not a single Confederate command near Fort Gibson. Another idea that influenced the Union army's worries was overestimation of the number of Confederate troops in the Indian Territory. Federals estimated that Gano's Brigade contained approximately 2,850 men and Watie's Brigade 3,950. The actual numbers were well below half the amount the Union commanders believed.[66]

Though the raid produced good results for the Indian Territory, it did not help the greater Trans-Mississippi Department. All the hard marching wore out the Indians' horses. A month later when General Smith called upon Watie's Brigade to support Price's return to Confederate territory, it could not because the exhausted horses needed more time to recuperate.[67]

Overall the raid through the Union-held Indian Territory achieved success. General Maxey, concerned with the successes of the raid, expressed excitement about the cooperation between the brigades, stating that the series of brilliant victories . . . north of the Arkansas River, by the troops under the leadership of the gallant and chivalrous Gano and the noble old hero, Stand Watie [were successful]. . . . Throughout the expedition I am rejoiced to say perfect harmony and good will prevailed between the white and Indian troops, all striving for the common good of our beloved country. . . . The major-general commanding deems this a fit occasion to say that not the least of the glorious results of this splendid achievement is the increased good will of the Indian and white troops toward each other, and the increased cheerfulness and confidence of all in their prowess and ability to whip anything like equal numbers.[68]

In his report Gano complimented Watie for being "by my side at Cabin Creek, cool and brave as ever."[69]

The raid at Cabin Creek boosted the morale of both the Texans commanded by Gano and the Indians led by Watie. The men enjoyed new clothes, shoes, and a sufficient amount of food for the winter. Despite the praise, problems developed between the Texans and Indians while in winter camp. Before the winter of 1865, the men only interacted during combat and never during a prolonged period, such as a winter camp. As a result of a difference in cultures, lack of discipline, and alcohol, drunken brawls between Indians and whites frequently occurred. In an attempt to solve the problem, DeMorse suggested separation of the two brigades and wrote a protest to Maxey. DeMorse's protest repeated the view he wrote about Watie's promotion the previous spring. Within days Maxey had DeMorse arrested and court-martialed. The court-martial found DeMorse guilty of writing derogatory literature about the character of the Indian allies, and suspended his rank and pay for six months. Before the six-month suspension ended, the war concluded so the South granted DeMorse an honorable discharge.[70]

Little did the men of both brigades know that the next year would be more difficult; Gano would leave the department of the Trans-Mississippi, the Texans were transferred to the Lone Star State, and that their raid at Cabin Creek was the last successful expedition north of the Arkansas River in the Indian Territory. As the war concluded, Watie was the last Confederate general to surrender his soldiers, capitulating to the enemy on June 23, 1865. With the war concluded, life for the Confederate Indians and their families remained in turmoil. Every aspect of the Indian Territory was touched by the war. Returning soldiers and families found their homes destroyed, family members killed, resources lost, and most troubling, the Indian Nations remained divided. Watie's life after the war embodied what the rest of the Indians experienced. The general lost a son, his livelihood, and home. He spent his last years trying to rebuild his life and died on September 9, 1871, with the sovereignty of his nation reduced by the Federal government during Reconstruction.[71]

In the later part of the war the relationships between white and Indian soldiers deteriorated, most notably among the enlisted soldiers and those whose earlier assignments had been to fight Indians. DeMorse personified this situation especially since Maxey promoted Watie to brigadier general, a rank above the Texan. Some Texans, mainly those in higher positions, such as Gano and Maxey, noticed the importance of the Indians in maintaining a fighting force in the Indian Territory and established good relationships. Despite their differences, the men fought well as a joint unit against the Union army, fulfilling their goals of retarding the encroachment of the Northern army from gaining more control of the Indian Territory and threatening North Texas. Still, during lulls in action, the men's racist views threatened to divide them. In the end both groups of men suffered during Reconstruction—the Indians more than the Texans.

Notes

1   This article will focus more on the Cherokee Nation because it was the largest and the leadership of Stand Watie had a direct impact on its role in the Confederacy. Frank Cunningham, *General Stand Watie's Confederate Indians* (Norman: University of Oklahoma Press, 1998), 28–29.

2   Clarissa W. Confer, *The Cherokee Nation in the Civil War* (Norman: University of Oklahoma Press, 2007), 19, 22, 33; Cunningham, *General Stand Watie's Confederate Indians*, 28–29.

3   Being of mixed blood provided opportunities of education, personal wealth, and business experience through a white father and a position in the tribe through an Indian mother. Additionally, children of mixed parents learned English more easily since it was stressed in the household. Cunningham, *General Stand Watie's Confederate Indians*, 4, 28–29, 39; Donald S. Frazier, *Blood and Treasure: Confederate Empire in the Southwest* (College Station: Texas A&M University Press, 1995), 13; John C. Waugh, *Sam Bell Maxey and the Confederate Indians* (Fort Worth, Texas: Ryan Place, 1995), 29–30; Confer, *The Cherokee Nation in the Civil War*, 9–10, 13–14, 23–27.

4   Charles M. Hubbard, *The Burden of Confederate Diplomacy* (Knoxville: University of Tennessee Press, 1998), 45; Waugh, *Sam Bell Maxey and the Confederate Indians*, 32–34; Louise Horton, *Samuel Bell Maxey* (Austin: University of Texas Press, 1974), 34–35; Louise W. Horton, "General Sam Bell Maxey: His Defense of North Texas and the Indian Territory," *Southwestern Historical Quarterly* 74 (April 1971): 509.

5   Waugh, *Sam Bell Maxey and the Confederate Indians*, 32–34; Confer, *Cherokee Nation in the Civil War*, 89; Annie Heloise Abel, *The American Indian as Participant in the Civil War* (Cleveland: Arthur H. Clark, 1919), 243.

6   Laurence M. Hauptman, *Between Two Fires: American Indians in the Civil War* (New York: Free Press, 1995), 27; B. P. Galloway, ed., *Texas, the Dark Corner of the Confederacy: Contemporary Accounts of the Lone Star State in the Civil War* (Lincoln: University of Nebraska Press, 1994), 222, 228; Robert L. Kerby, *Kirby Smith's Confederacy: The Trans-Mississippi South, 1863–1865* (New York: Columbia University Press, 1972), 215–16; Dudley G. Wooten, ed., *Comprehensive History of Texas* (1898; Austin: Texas State Historical Association, 1986), 2:561; Ernest Wallace, *Charles DeMorse: Pioneer Statesman and Father of Texas Journalism* (Paris, Texas: Wright Press, 1985), 145; Ralph A. Wooster, *Lone Star Regiments in Gray* (Austin, Texas: Eakin Press, 2002), 192–94.

7   Gano did not officially hold the rank of brigadier general until later but received the title because he performed the duties of that rank. Cunningham to Magruder, 21 October 1863, U.S. War Department, *The War of the Rebellion: A Compilation of the Union and Confederate Armies* (hereafter cited as *OR*), comp. Robert N. Scott (Washington, D.C.: U.S. Government Printing Office,1880–1901), 1, 26, 2:342; Schaumburg to Boggs, 26 October 1863, *OR*, 1, 22, 2:1052; Wallace, *Charles DeMorse*, 144; Stephen B. Oates, *Confederate Cavalry West of the River* (Austin: University of Texas Press, 1961), 38; Galloway, *Texas, the Dark Corner of the Confederacy*, 8; Gano to Magruder, 12 August 1863, *OR*, 1, 26, 2:160; Kerby, *Kirby Smith's Confederacy*, 216–17.

8   Roscoe M. Pierson, ed., *John Allen Gano 1805–1887: A Collection Containing His Biographical Note Book No. 2 With Biographical sketches by James Challen, Richard M. Gano and W.C. Morro,* (Lexington, Kentucky: Lexington Theological Semi-

nary, 1982), 34; Terry Wolever, *The Life and Ministry of John Gano, 1727–1804*, (Springfield, Missouri: Particular Baptist Press, 1998), 438; Jerry B. Rushford, "Apollos of the West: The Life of John Allen Gano" (master's thesis, Abilene Christian College, 1972), 212–13, 214–15; Waugh, *Sam Bell Maxey and the Confederate Indians*, 72; S. M. Fields, "Texas Heroes of the Confederacy," *Dallas Times Herald*, May 10,1925; Margret Hancock Pearce, "The Gano Cabin History and A Story From Narratives," *Dallas Journal: Dallas Genealogical Society* (December 1996): 31–32; Waugh, *Sam Bell Maxey and the Confederate Indians*, 72.

9   Valvular heart disease with hypertrophy is the reduction of the valves in the heart combined with an enlarged heart. One could conclude he faked the disease to get transferred back to Texas. Ralph A. Wooster, *Lone Star Generals in Gray* (Austin, Texas: Eakin Press, 2000), 124; William C. Davis, ed., *The Confederate General*, (Harrisburg, Pennsylvania: National Historical Society, 1991), 154; Stephen Yancey to S. P. Bankhead, September 1, 1863, Record Group 109, Chapter 2, Vol. 132, Military Departments Letters Sent, District of Texas, New Mexico, and Arizona, June–September 1863, National Archives and Records Service, General Services Administration, War Department Collection of Confederate Records, National Archives, Washington, D.C.

10   Steele to Gano, November 7, 1863, *OR*, 1, 22, 2:1062; Maxey to Smith, January 15, 1864, *OR*, 1, 34, 2:876; Louise Horton, *Sam Bell Maxey: A Biography* (Austin: University of Texas Press, 1974), 10–11; Waugh, *Sam Bell Maxey and the Confederate Indians*, 14, 34; Horton, *Samuel Bell Maxey*, 35; Horton, "General Sam Bell Maxey: His Defense of North Texas and the Indian Territory," 509.

11   Ira Don Richards, "The Battle of Poison Spring," *Arkansas Historical Quarterly* 18 (Winter 1959): 339–40; Ludwell H. Johnson, *Red River Campaign: Politics and Cotton in the Civil War* (Baltimore: Johns Hopkins Press, 1958), 119.

12   Williams to Whitten, April 24, 1864, *OR*, 1, 34, 1:743–44.

13   Marmaduke to Belton, April 21, 1864, *OR*, 1, 34, 1:818–19; Walker to Ochiltree, 19 April 1864, *OR*, 1, 34, 1:849.

14   DeMorse to Ochiltree, April 21, 1864, *OR*, 1, 34, 1:846–47; Williams to Whitten, April 24, 1864, *OR*, 1, 34, 1:745–46; Gibbons to Williams, April 21, 1864, *OR*, 1, 34, 1:755; Marmaduke to Belton, April 21, 1864, *OR*, 1, 34, 1:819–20; Maxey to Belton, April 23, 1864, *OR*, 1, 34, 1:843.

15   Brian Steel Wills, *The Confederacy's Greatest Cavalryman: Nathan Bedford Forrest* (Lawrence: University Press of Kansas, 1992), 188–89; Hondon B. Hargrove, *Black Union Soldiers in the Civil War*, (Jefferson, North Carolina: McFarland, 1988), 58.

16   Ward to Williams, April 20, 1864, *OR*, 1, 34, 1:754; Hargrove, *Black Union Soldiers in the Civil War*, 58; Anne J. Bailey, "Was There a Massacre at Poison Spring?," *Military History of the Southwest* 20 (Fall 1990): 161.

17   Report of Colonel James M. Williams, April 24, 1864, *OR*, 1, 34, 1:746; Kerby, *Kirby Smith's Confederacy*, 312.

18   Price to Boggs, May 1864, *OR*, 1, 34, 1:781.

19   Cabell to Ochiltree, April 20, 1864, *OR*, 1, 34, 1:792.

20 Williams to Whitten, April 24, 1864, *OR*, 1, 34, 1:743–44.

21 As cited in Charlean Moss Williams, *Washington, Hempstead County, Arkansas* (Houston: Anson Jones Press, 1951), 98; Albert Castel, *General Sterling Price and the Civil War in the West* (Baton Rouge: Louisiana State University Press, 1968), 177.

22 Captain William A. Miler "Sixty-One to Sixty-Five," December 4–6, 1914, clipping from undetermined newspaper, Poison Spring file, Texas Heritage Museum, Hill College, Hillsboro, Texas.

23 Anne J. Bailey and Daniel E. Sutherland, eds., *Civil War Arkansas: Beyond Battles and Leaders* (Fayetteville: University of Arkansas Press, 2000), 218; Yeary, 250; James R. Wilmeth, "Thoughts and Things as They Occurred in Camp—A.D. 1864," personal diary, Special Collections, Brown Library, Abilene Christian University, Abilene, Texas.

24 Bailey, "Was There a Massacre at Poison Spring?" 160–66; Gregory J. W. Urwin, "'We Cannot Treat Negroes . . . as Prisoners of War': Racial Atrocities and Reprisals in Civil War Arkansas," *Civil War History* 42 (September 1996): 210.

25 Lonnie J. White, ed., "A Bluecoat's Account of the Camden Expedition," *Arkansas Historical Quarterly* 24 (Spring 1965): 86–87, 89; Williamson to Maxey, Special Orders No. 1, April 28, 1864, *OR*, 1, 34, 1:845–46.

26 William Steele to S. S. Anderson, February 15, 1864, Record Group 109, Chapter 2, Vol. 267, Military Departments Letters Sent, District of Indian Territory, October 1863–June 1864, National Archives, National Archives and Records Service, General Services Administration, War Department Collection of Confederate Records, Washington, D.C.; Confer, *Cherokee Nation in the Civil War*, 78.

27 William Steele to S. S. Anderson, February 15, 1864, Record Group 109, Chapter 2, Vol. 267, Military Departments Letters Sent, District of Indian Territory, October 1863–June 1864, National Archives, National Archives and Records Service, General Services Administration, War Department Collection of Confederate Records, Washington, D.C.; Confer, *Cherokee Nation in the Civil War*, 96, 98, 99, 100.

28 DeMorse to Cooper, July 3, 1864, *OR*, 1, 34, 4:699–700.

29 Allen C. Ashcraft, ed., "Confederate Indian Troop Conditions in August 1864," *Chronicles of Oklahoma* 41 (Winter 1963–64): 446; Reginald Horseman, *Race and Manifest Destiny: The Origins of American Racial Anglo-Saxonism* (Cambridge, Massachusetts: Harvard University Press, 1981), 297.

30 Boggs to Maxey, May 15, 1864, *OR*, 1, 34, 3:826; John C. Grady and Bradford K. Felmly, *Suffering to Silence: Twenty-ninth Texas Cavalry, C.S.A.*, (Quanah, Texas: Nortex Press, 1975), 145.

31 Edwin C. Bearss, "General Cooper's CSA Indians Threaten Fort Smith," *Arkansas Historical Quarterly* 16 (Autumn 1967): 257–62.

32 Maxey to Boggs, July 30, 1864, *OR*, 1, 41, 1:29.

33 Ibid.

34 Mamie K. Yeary, ed. *Reminiscences of the Boys in Gray, 1861–1865* (Dallas, Texas: Smith & Lamar / M.E. Church South, 1912), 219; Cooper to Scott, September 14, 1864, *OR*, 1, 41, 1:781.

35 Cooper to Scott, September 14, 1864, *OR*, 1, 41, 1:781.

36 Grady and Felmly, *Suffering to Silence*, 153; Wiley Britton, *The Union Indian Brigade in the Civil War*, (Ottawa, Kansas: Kansas Heritage Press, 1922), 435–36; E. Kirby Smith to President Jefferson Davis, March 11, 1865, Record Group 109, Chapter 2, Vol. 71.5, Military Departments Letters Sent, Trans-Mississippi Department, Confidential Letters and Telegrams Sent January–April 1865, National Archives and Records Service, General Services Administration, War Department Collection of Confederate Records, National Archives, Washington, D.C.; J. Bankhead Magruder to W. R. Boggs, October 15, 1863, Record Group 109, Chapter 2, Vol. 131, Military Departments Letters Sent, Department of Texas, October 1863, National Archives and Records Service, General Services Administration, War Department Collection of Confederate Records, National Archives, Washington, D.C.

37 Kerby, *Kirby Smith's Confederacy*, 354; Copper to Scott, October 1, 1864, *OR*, 1, 41, 1:783; Maxey to Boggs, October 7, 1864, *OR*, 1, 41, 1:780; Grant Foreman, *A History of Oklahoma*, (Norman: University of Oklahoma Press, 1952), 128–29.

38 Gano to Cooper, September 29, 1864, *OR*, 1, 41, 1: 788–89; Barker to Thomas, September 20, 1864, *OR*, 1, 41, 1: 771.

39 Barker to Thomas, September 20, 1864, *OR*, 1, 41, 1: 772.

40 Ibid.

41 Ibid.

42 Britton, *Civil War on the Border*, 245–46; Yeary, *Reminiscences of the Boys in Gray, 1861–1865*, 733.

43 Jay Monaghan, *Civil War on the Western Border 1854–1865*, (Toronto, Canada: Little, Brown, 1955), 307.

44 Yeary, *Reminiscences of the Boys in Gray, 1861–1865*, 46.

45 Britton, *Civil War on the Border*, 246–47; Urwin, "'We Cannot Treat Negroes . . . as Prisoners of War,'" 210.

46 Barker to Thomas, September 20, 1864, *OR*, 1, 41, 1:772.

47 Ibid.; Gano to Cooper, September 29, 1864, *OR*, 1, 41, 1:789; Watie to Cooper, September 21, 1864, *OR*, 1, 41, 1:784, 789.

48 Hopkins to Thomas, September 22, 1864, *OR*, 1, 41, 1: 76667.

49 Ibid.

50 Ibid.

51 Gano to Cooper, September 29, 1864, *OR*, 1, 41, 1: 789.

52 The date July 17, 1863, refers to the battle of Honey Springs where Watie and the Confederate Indians suffered a major defeat, allowing the Union army to control more of the Indian Territory. Monaghan, *Civil War on the Western Border 1854-1865*, 307.

53 Gano to Cooper, September 29, 1864, *OR*, 1, 41, 1:789; Stewart Sifakis, *Compendium of the Confederate Armies: Texas* (New York: Facts on File, 1965), 39–87; Watie to Heiston, October 3, 1864, *OR*, 1, 41, 1:786; Hauptman, *Between Two Fires*, 54.

54 Monaghan, *Civil War on the Western Border, 1854–1865*, 308.

55 Hopkins to Thomas, September 22, 1864, *OR*, 1, 41, 1:768; Cunningham, *General Stand Watie's Confederate Indians*, 156.

56 Yeary, *Reminiscences of the Boys in Gray, 1861–1865*, 724; Gano to Cooper, September 29, 1864, *OR*, 1, 41, 1:790.

57 Gano to Cooper, September 29, 1864, *OR*, 1, 41, 1:790.

58 Ibid.

59 Hopkins to Thomas, September 22, 1864, *OR*, 1, 41, 1:769.

60 Curtis to Morris, September 20, 1864, *OR*, 1, 41, 1:774.

61 Federal reports of the casualties do not specify the number of men killed, wounded, or captured. Gano to Cooper, September 29, 1864, *OR*, 1, 41, 1:790–92; Yeary, *Reminiscences of the Boys in Gray, 1861–1865*, 351; Monaghan, *Civil War on the Border*, 309.

62 Watie to Heiston, October 3, 1864, *OR*, 1, 41, 1:787; Monaghan, *Civil War on the Western Border, 1854–1865*, 309.

63 Yeary, *Reminiscences of the Boys in Gray, 1861–1865*, 309.

64 Thayer to Steele, September 24, 1864, *OR*, 1, 41, 3:341.

65 Thayer to Halleck, September 29, 1864, *OR*, 1, 41, 3:475.

66 Thayer to Lacey, October 15, 1864, *OR*, 1, 41, 3:882.

67 Kerby, *Kirby Smith's Confederacy*, 355; Grady and Felmly, *Suffering to Silence*, 167.

68 General Orders No. 61, October 7, 1864, *OR*, 1, 41, 1:793.

69 Gano to Cooper, September 29, 1864, *OR*, 1, 41, 1:791.

70 Wallace, *Charles DeMorse*, 151, Ralph A. Wooster, *Lone Star Regiments in Gray* (Austin, Texas: Eakin Press, 2002), 204; Grady and Felmly, *Suffering to Silence*, 182–86. DeMorse to Cooper, July 3, 1864, *OR*, 1, 34, 4: 699–700; DeMorse to Cooper, October 1864, *OR*, 1, 34, 4:700.

71 Wallace, *Charles DeMorse*, 151, Wooster, *Lone Star Regiments in Gray*, 204; Confer, *The Cherokee Nation in the Civil War*, 145, 147, 149, 158; Cunningham, *General Stand Watie's Confederate Indians*, 210–12; Horton, "General Sam Bell Maxey: His Defense of North Texas and the Indian Territory," 521.

Chapter 11

Defending the Lone Star: The Texas Cavalry in the Red River Campaign[1]

by Gary D. Joiner

In March 1864, Union forces began the fifth attempt to invade Texas in fewer than fifteen months. The commander of the Union Department of the Gulf, based in New Orleans, was Maj. Gen. Nathaniel Prentiss Banks. With aspirations for the presidency, he was at that time arguably more popular than Abraham Lincoln. Banks needed a stunning, or at least well-publicized, victory to vault him into office. The Union navy had failed at Galveston Bay on New Year's Day, 1863.[2] Banks's Nineteenth Corps commander, Maj. Gen. William Buel Franklin had failed miserably at Sabine Pass on September 8, 1863.[3] He failed again in October and November during the Texas Overland Expedition.[4] The fourth attempt at least landed troops on Texas soil, this time on the barrier islands along the coast and at Brownsville during November 1863, but no meaningful attempt was made to strike inland.[5] The fifth expedition was the Red River Campaign, resulting in the largest combined-arms operation west of the Mississippi River during the Civil War. All of these events convinced Texans that they were high on the priority list for Union invasion and they were not mistaken.

Most Texans at the time believed, and rightly so, that the battle to save Texas should be fought in Louisiana. Once the war came to the Pelican State in 1862, Texas became the obvious target of Union aspirations. Writing in 1863, John E. Hart of the Fourth Texas Cavalry wrote, "The battles of Texas will be fought in Louisiana . . . And there it behooves us to strike for our homes."[6] This need to protect Texas from invaders outside its borders perhaps strikes at the core of the Texas psyche during the nineteenth century and in some deep-seated ways still exists. Texas was, of course, annexed as an independent nation. That fact has never strayed far from the center of Texan social and political thought (if there ever was something akin to a consensus on such matters.) As one Texas cavalryman wrote after the war, "To us, Texas was the 'nation': to her alone we owed allegiance. We were *allied* with other Southern States, not indissolubly *joined*."[7]

The vast size of Texas and relatively large distances between towns spawned the need for cavalry units. Although there were some famous infantry units that served far from home, such as John Bell Hood's Texas Brigade of the Army of

Northern Virginia, the state produced more cavalry regiments than any other Southern state. Most of these served in the Trans-Mississippi Department, primarily in Louisiana, Texas, and in the Indian Territory. The remainder served in the southeastern states of Tennessee, Mississippi, Georgia, and the Carolinas.[8] It became difficult to obtain and train mounts as the war progressed and at least one-third of these units were dismounted, though they retained their cavalry-unit designation. During the Red River Campaign, the majority of forces arrayed against the Union invaders were Texans. Some, such as Maj. Gen. John G. Walker's First, or Texas, Division of the Army of Western Louisiana, were already deployed in Louisiana.[9]

Most of the cavalry units were held in Texas by the district commander, Maj. Gen. John Bankhead Magruder. Magruder did not want to release his highly mobile force until he was absolutely certain that the invasion up the Red River was not an elaborate feint to draw attention from the major assault, which he thought might be Galveston or Matagorda Bay.[10] When requested to release the cavalry for use by Maj. Gen. Richard Taylor, the district commander for western Louisiana, Magruder sent them, but the bulk of the cavalry were positioned so far south, around Hempstead west of Houston, that they almost arrived too late to help stem the tide of the Union forces.

Leading the cavalry was newly appointed Bvt. Maj. Gen. Tom Green, already famous as something of a hero in Texas. Green was a graduate of the University of Tennessee and Princeton College in Kentucky. Following graduation he moved to Texas where he practiced law. Green joined the Texas forces during the Texas Revolution and helped man one of the famous cannons called the "Twin Sisters" at the Battle of San Jacinto. Once hostilities began during the Civil War, Green offered his services and entered as a colonel, attached to Henry H. Sibley's Brigade. In this command, he saw action in New Mexico. He also was the hero in the repulse of Union forces at Galveston on January 1, 1863. Fearless, intrepid, sometimes reckless, and hard-driving, he was one of Richard Taylor's favorite officers.[11] Green was also loved and admired by his men, asking much from them and they responded in kind.

His cavalrymen and mounted infantry were famous for their individuality and the variety of their weapons and gear. Some were disciplined cavalry troopers but many others were not. Most brought their own weapons and some had to be given guns when they arrived in Louisiana. Though typically hard to define this group, most had bandolier belts crossed over their chests and carried bowie knives for close-in fighting. Many wore sombreros and sported long, drooping handlebar mustaches. They rode with abandon and could be compared to Russian Cossacks.[12]

Green's Cavalry Corps was divided into divisions. The first was actually a brigade led by Brig. Gen. Hamilton P. Bee. This was composed of the First Texas

Cavalry, led by Col. Augustus C. Buchel; the Twenty-sixth Texas Cavalry, led by Col. Xavier B. DeBray; and Terrell's Texas Cavalry, led by Col. Alexander W. Terrell.

The other component was Major's Division led by Brig. Gen. James P. Major. This division consisted of two brigades. The first, Lane's Brigade, led by Col. Walter P. Lane, was comprised of the First Texas Partisan Rangers, led by Lt. Col. R. P. Crump; the Second Texas Partisan Rangers, led by Col. Isham Chisum; the Second Regiment, Arizona Brigade, led by Col. George W. Baylor; and the Third Regiment, Arizona Brigade, led by Lt. Col. George T. Madison. The second brigade was led by Col. Arthur P. Bagby. This brigade was comprised of the Fourth Texas Cavalry, led by Col. William P. Hardeman; the Fifth Texas Cavalry, led by Maj. Hugh A. McPhaill; the Seventh Texas Cavalry, led by Lt. Col. Philemon T. Herbert, Jr.; and the Thirteenth Texas Cavalry Battalion, led by Lt. Colonel Edward Waller, Jr.[13]

Perhaps the most unusual of these commanders was Col. August Buchel, late of the Prussian army. He commanded a regiment of cavalry raised from the town of New Braunfels. Because the German immigrants felt they were fighting for their new homeland, they were particularly enthusiastic fighters. Their presence made President Lincoln's long-held idea of a German-Texas counter-revolution ring hollow.

Prior to the campaign, rumors intensified of the anticipated Union threat. Magruder repositioned forces to counter a threat from the east or south. He ordered his forces to gather in camps and areas where they might be deployed as rapidly as possible. Some of the units were originally stationed along the Gulf Coast, such as Company E of J. B. Likens's Thirty-fifth Texas Cavalry Regiment, part of Brig. Gen. Hamilton Bee's Brigade. The remainder of the Thirty-fifth Texas Cavalry was deployed nearby, in Matagorda County, countering a perceived threat to Matagorda Bay.[14] The regiment was sent to the Hempstead area on March 1. This was eleven days before the Union navy opened the campaign by entering the Red River. The distance was so great that the regiment did not reach the fighting until after the battles of Mansfield and Pleasant Hill. They did participate in the Battle of Blair's Landing and subsequent actions.[15]

The majority of the cavalry corps was encamped in and around Hempstead. This would provide access to Louisiana via any of the three branches of the Texas Trail. When Banks ordered the Texas Overland Expedition in 1863, Magruder took the extraordinary step of ordering outer defenses to be constructed just inside Louisiana along the Texas Trail fords across the Sabine. The earthworks were surveyed and constructed during the fall and winter of 1863–1864 by Confederate soldiers and enslaved African Americans under the command of Lt. Col. C. G. Forshey, chief consulting engineer of the District of Texas. The southernmost was at Niblett's Bluff near Vinton in Calcasieu Parish.

Next was the Burr's Ferry works in Vernon Parish almost due west of Alexandria. The northernmost were to be located at Logansport in DeSoto Parish, but the latter were apparently never constructed. All three were designed to be *têtes de ponts,* or heads of bridges.[16] Magruder believed that his cavalry would best be positioned at Hempstead to make a dash into Louisiana at Niblett's Bluff or, more likely, Burr's Ferry.[17] The cavalry was to act as a mobile strike force, seizing the bridgeheads, securing the border crossings, and finally, if circumstances permitted, riding as deeply as possible into Louisiana to interdict the Union forces. On March 6, upon request from Lt. Gen. Kirby Smith, the department commander based in Shreveport, Magruder ordered the Texas Cavalry Corps under Maj. Gen. Tom Green to Alexandria. The Union navy had not yet entered the mouth of the Red River, but word of the massing of vessels at Vicksburg and the concentration of troops near New Iberia and Brashear City (present-day Morgan City) in southern Louisiana, had reached the Confederate commanders. Green's route was to proceed from Hempstead, "via Montgomery, Woodville, Burkeville, Huddleston, and Hurston, La. [probably Hinestown] to Alexandria, La."[18] This was the Burr's Ferry route. The Union navy moved so quickly in taking Alexandria on March 15 that Green was diverted north to Hemphill, and from there crossed into Louisiana at Logan's Ferry at Logansport. This diversion forced a hard ride through downpour-soaked roads as they moved around the Sabine River swamp to link up with Richard Taylor. Taylor, always high-strung, was anxious that his cavalry would not meet him in time to stop the Union advance before it reached a point where it could spread out on more than one road. That point was the town of Mansfield in DeSoto Parish, only forty miles south of Shreveport. Green rode his men hard. He crossed the Sabine River into Louisiana at Logansport with the bulk of his force on April 6. After a short rest at the village and college campus at Keachi, they joined Taylor at Pleasant Hill and then rode ahead to find the location and activities of the Union forces.

Green's arrival was critically important to Taylor. The aggressive Texan cavalrymen would perform the true task of cavalry—reconnaissance and intimidation. Without them, Taylor had little chance of slowing the Union column until he was prepared to meet them. He could not readily identify which units he would be fighting without the cavalry's assistance. It was Green's cavalry who confirmed Banks was using only one line of approach and that he had stupidly hindered his own cavalry by forcing them to stay with their train. Advance parties of the cavalry had first encountered the Union column near Crump's Corners (modern-day Bellemont). They then retrograded, only annoying the Union cavalry. On April 7 three miles north of Pleasant Hill, the Union Nineteenth Corps Cavalry Division ran into four regiments of Green's cavalry at Wilson's Farm.[19] Green chose to change his tactics and charged the Union cavalry. The

Illustration 11 A critical moment in the Red River Expedition of April 1864. *Courtesy Library of Congress.*

Union cavalry commander, Brig. Gen. Albert Lindley Lee, could not accurately estimate their numbers. He formed his men on both sides of the road and set up his howitzers to provide support.

Green charged and forced the Union right back several yards, the Rebels attacking with their customary Rebel yell. The first brigade of Union mounted infantry came up and fired a volley into the Confederate ranks, which then fell back into the field. Trees on Lee's right still contained an unknown number of Rebels keeping up a withering fire. There was no way to charge them in the dense woods. The Confederates fell back and Lee had held his ground.[20] Union casualties were seventy killed and wounded in an action that lasted half an hour.[21] While the fight was unfolding, the Federal column ground to a halt. Although the battle was small compared to other actions during the campaign, it was very important to the Confederates. Green forced the Union cavalry into a new mind-set. From this point, Lee was leery of every rise of ground and turn in the road. The Union cavalry was much more cautious. Green effectively slowed the Union column to a crawl giving Taylor enough time to prepare his forces for the next day. He identified which Union units were in the lead of the column and how they would fight. While gaining this information he intimidated his opponents, making them apprehensive.

The Union cavalry slowly rode another four miles to Carroll's Mill. As Lee's cavalry neared the mill, Green's Texans again made a demonstration, which forced them to come into battle order. After a brief skirmish in the diminishing twilight, the Rebels melted into the woods. Lee posted pickets and finally halted for the night.[22] With constant skirmishing, a frustrated Lee pushed the Confederate cavalry screen back six miles on the morning of April 8.

Illustration 12 The war in Louisiana—Commodore Porter's fleet before Alexandria, March 26. *Courtesy Library of Congress.*

Green's mission was not to bring on a full-scale battle, but to buy Taylor time. He did this with alacrity. Sometime between noon and 1 p.m., Lee and his men emerged from a thick woods and found themselves at an intersection of the road on which they were traveling and one that went to the Red River. The intersection was called Sabine Crossroads. The Confederate cavalry that had been a constant menace for the last two days seemed to disappear.

Gen. Albert Lee, at the head of his column, moved another three-quarters of a mile to the edge of a huge clearing, 800 yards deep and 1,200 yards across, at the slope of a ridge called Honeycutt Hill.[23] Confederate skirmishers were there in force. This was a portion of Green's cavalry. Lee looked up at the long slope of the hill and expected the Confederates to use the same hit-and-run tactics that had plagued his troops the previous day. As Lee and his small infantry support moved forward, the riders gave way. The Union cavalry and infantry units moved to take the ridge. As Lee rode to the crest of the hill, he saw the bulk of the Confederate army west of the Mississippi drawn up in a line of battle all across his front on both sides of the road and extending down and past his right flank.[24]

Green divided his force to protect the wings of Taylor's army, which had formed into an L configuration about three miles in length from tip to tip. Separated by several hundred feet and to the left and right of the infantry was the bulk of the Texas cavalry, positioned in three tiers on the left flank and in a single line on the right.[25] After four hours in which both sides watched each other intently and the Federals brought troops forward, the Confederates charged. Green and the bulk of his units on the Confederate left flank enfiladed the Union position and effectively forced the Union line to roll back upon itself rather than extending their own positions outward. The regiments led by Hamilton Bee on the Confederate right flank became lost in the woods and played little part in the fighting.

The force of the attack by the Louisiana and Texas divisions and the pressure placed upon the Union flanks destroyed the Union position in less than an hour. Confederate infantry and cavalry pursued the Union soldiers to their fallback position at the crossroads and it too collapsed in less than twenty minutes. The fighting ended with the Confederates controlling the only water near the battlefield, but unable to drive the Federal forces from a ridge after a pursuit of three miles.

Richard Taylor was aware of the presence of Union warships and transports on the Red River. He had received reports that Adm. David Dixon Porter commanded a "fleet of about thirty vessels of which only five were loaded with troops—the others being gunboats and transports loaded with stores."[26] Taylor was certain that the fleet would withdraw once learning of the army's flight to Grand Ecore and he wanted to cut communications between the Federal army and navy.[27]

Always audacious, Taylor had never abandoned his dream of recapturing New Orleans. If he could keep the Federal army and navy separated, perhaps both could be destroyed in detail. Taylor knew that on April 9, the Federal fleet had sailed past Grand Bayou Landing heading toward Shreveport, well beyond the support of the army.[28] He saw an opportunity to capture the Federal fleet but understood that his soldiers had to battle a major mental obstacle: "the ideas prevailing in the first years of the war about gunboats. . . . [It] was popularly believed that the destructive power of these monsters were not to be resisted."[29]

That night at 1:30 a.m., Taylor wrote orders to Maj. Gen. John G. Walker sending Green and his cavalry to Blair's Landing in an attempt to cut off the Union navy. This mission had to wait, for later that day at the Battle of Pleasant Hill, Green and his men held the Confederate left flank and eventually cut off an escape route between Banks's army and the fleet. Where the Battle of Mansfield was a major Confederate victory, the Battle of Pleasant Hill was a bloody stalemate. The Union commanders could not agree on the next course of action and General Banks decided to retreat to Grand Ecore on the night of April 9–10 along the same road on which his column had ascended. As Banks evacuated, Green's orders from the night of April 8–9 were executed. He and about 2,500 cavalry rode to Blair's Landing on the Red River, which was due west of Pleasant Hill and approximately 45 miles north of Grand Ecore.

The Union flotilla was moving downstream upon receiving word of Banks's defeat at Mansfield. Early on the morning of April 12, they sorted out their convoy, repaired several damaged vessels and headed downriver. The fleet that Green was attempting to interdict consisted of the lightest draft, but heavily armed, contingent of 104 vessels brought up the river by Admiral Porter It consisted of one ironclad, two monitors, a timberclad, and several tinclad vessels. The monitors were the *Osage* and the *Neosho*. Each was equipped with two

11-inch naval smoothbore guns in a single turret mounted at the bow. These sister ships were the only stern-wheel monitors built during the war. Despite their great weight, the *Osage* and the *Neosho* needed only four-and-a-half feet of water beneath their decks to float. However, the huge turrets in their bows and massive armored engine houses in their sterns made the vessels unwieldy and difficult to steer in tight places. The ironclad was the *Chillicothe*. Two side wheels and two screw propellers drove this hybrid. She required almost seven feet of water below the waterline to get underway.[30]

The *Lexington*, built in 1860, was one of the oldest warships in the inland fleet. As a timberclad side-wheeler, the *Lexington* used thick layers of wood to protect her from enemy guns. She required six feet of water to keep her afloat.[31]

Porter also selected the *Fort Hindman* and the *Cricket*, two tinclads with thinner armor, approximately one-half to three-quarters of an inch thick. The *Fort Hindman* required just two feet of water to float. The *Cricket* was a stern-wheeler and had a draft of four feet.[32]

The remainder of the U.S. Navy's contingent consisted of the tugboats *Dahlia* and *William H. Brown* and the supply transport *Benefit*. Of the three, *William H. Brown* was the only one armed.[33]

These vessels guarded and herded the army's transports, at least twenty boats. The quartermaster's boats held supplies for the main column and 1,600 men of the XVII Corps under Brig. Gen. T. Kilby Smith. Smith armed most, if not all, of these boats with army field cannons mounted on the decks. He also placed bales of cotton and sacks of oats on the decks from which his men could fire in relative safety.[34]

At daylight on April 11, Taylor ordered Col. Arthur Bagby to take Sibley's Brigade and an artillery battery and intercept Porter at Grand Bayou Landing. Bagby left Mansfield and marched fifteen miles before reaching Bayou Pierre.[35] During the day Bagby learned that a detachment of Union cavalry had marched north to meet the fleet, no doubt to warn the Yankee sailors that the army had withdrawn.[36] Bagby conducted a night crossing of the bayou and pushed on to the Red River, arriving at midnight only to discover that Porter's fleet had already passed downriver. This was a very difficult operation due to the swollen waters of the bayou. Bagby decided to rest his men a few hours before continuing the pursuit.[37]

The same day Taylor dispatched Bagby to the Red River, Tom Green directed forward operations at Pleasant Hill. At 4:00 p.m., Green sent Brig. Gen. Hamilton P. Bee to pursue Banks.[38] Bee took several veteran regiments from his own and Brig. Gen. James P. Major's divisions plus one section of artillery and set out after the Federal army.[39]

Following Bee's departure, Green received orders from Taylor to intercept the Union fleet at Blair's Landing, eighteen miles east of Pleasant Hill. Taylor impressed upon Green the importance of arriving at the landing before the fleet passed downriver.[40] At 6:00 p.m., Green gathered the cavalry remaining in Pleasant Hill, the Twenty-third Texas—newly arrived from the Lone Star State—the Thirty-seventh Texas, and the brigade of Col. William H. Parsons, and set off for Blair's Landing. Green also sent word to the untested Thirty-sixth Texas, somewhere between Mansfield and Pleasant Hill, to join him.[41]

Taylor promised Green ample artillery support, knowing that Confederate success depended on it.[42] He dispatched artillery batteries under John A. A. West, M. V. McMahon, and William G. Moseley to Blair's Landing.[43] However, the recent hard fighting had left many of the Confederate batteries short of horses and the ability to rapidly move their cannons.[44]

Green's command traveled much of the night, arriving at John Jordan's ferry on Bayou Pierre before sunrise. The Confederates bivouacked the remainder of the night. To prevent alerting any Federals in the area, Green refused to allow his troopers to build any campfires.[45]

On April 12, the Rebels continued hunting the Union fleet. At daybreak, Green sent scouts ahead to locate the Federal fleet and any Union land forces that might be in the area.[46] During the morning, Col. Peter C. Woods's Thirty-sixth Texas cavalry regiment and five howitzers of John A. A. West's artillery battery also arrived at Jordan's Ferry. When the scouts returned, they reported no Federal infantry but they had located three wooden vessels and one gunboat near Blair's Landing. According to the scouts, the gunboat was aground. Believing the boats to be nearly helpless, Green decided to attack the Federals at the landing, where the river was relatively narrow and gave him the best opportunity to create a bottleneck that would prevent other Federal vessels from passing downstream. He ordered the time-consuming process of shuttling his men across the bayou.[47]

While Green made preparations for an attack, Arthur Bagby had his men in the saddle and riding south.[48] Traveling cross-country, the command maintained a brisk pace but was unable to overtake the retreating Union navy for much of the day.[49]

Deciding that it would take too much time to shuttle his entire command across the bayou, Green chose to leave the majority of the horses behind.[50] He ordered company commanders to select every tenth man to stay behind and guard the camp, wagon train, and remaining horses.[51]

Once Green crossed the bayou, he dined with his brother-in-law Brig. Gen. James P. Major and Capt. Alexander P. Morse. The general spoke "freely of the danger of this attack; but felt the necessity of constant action, and knew that Gen. Dick Taylor was expecting great things of him."[52] Perhaps Green's apprehension was caused by his unfamiliarity with the new troops accompanying him or the fact that insufficient artillery had reached him. Whatever the reason, he expressed a longing for his former command—Sibley's Brigade and the Val Verde Battery—veteran soldiers he could rely on.[53]

By the time Green's command had crossed Bayou Pierre, it was late in the afternoon. From Jordan's Ferry, the Confederates marched four miles through a swampy wood before arriving at a slough at the edge of the Blair Plantation. As the column emerged from the woods, Col. William H. Parsons caught up with the commanding general.[54] Parsons had been delayed in Shreveport on army business but, not wanting to miss any fighting, had ridden forty miles to overtake his brigade.[55]

Green had known Parsons since the early 1850s, when "frequent social and official contact" had cemented a friendship.[56] However, they had not seen each other since before the war. After exchanging greetings, Green confided to Parsons, "I know you but I don't know your men."[57] Parsons assured his old friend that the men of Parsons's Brigade were honored to be fighting under Green's command and that the brigade deserved their reputation as veteran combat troops.[58]

Green's concerns were not entirely unfounded. Although Parsons's Brigade was an experienced combat unit, Alexander Terrell's Thirty-seventh Texas was relatively inexperienced, though the regiment had fought well at Mansfield and Pleasant Hill.[59] Peter Woods's Thirty-sixth Texas and Colonel Nicholas Gould's Twenty-third Texas had never been tested in combat.[60] West's artillery battery had been formed in December 1863 and it too had seen action at Mansfield and Pleasant Hill.[61]

Green and Parsons reconnoitered the area and found the situation much different than the scouts had reported.[62] The *Osage* had run aground near the landing despite being lashed to the transport *Black Hawk* earlier in the day to help the ironclad maneuver. The army transport *Alice Vivian*, loaded with nearly four hundred horses, had run aground and was stuck fast. Another army transport, the *Hastings*, had tied up to the landing to repair a wheel while the transports *Emerald* and *Clara Bell* attempted to tow the *Alice Vivian* off the sandbar. A seventh vessel, the wooden gunboat *Lexington*, was tied up to the east bank, above the *Alice Vivian*, to offer protection to the struggling ships. Most of the fleet was just upstream from the plantation house.[63]

The boats at Blair's Landing were part of the rear division of the Union fleet, commanded by Lt. Cdr. Thomas O. Selfridge, and had experienced problems all day.[64] Kilby Smith reported navigation on the Red River "exceedingly difficult" with nearly every transport in need of repairs.[65]

While the Federal fleet struggled on the river, Green contemplated his options. He was troubled by the lack of artillery and had hoped that rifled cannons, capable of smashing the hulls or penetrating vital areas of the floundering Federal fleet, would have reached Blair's Landing by now.[66] Uncharacteristically,

Green sought Parsons's opinion of the impending fight. "The moon is at its full: we are deficient in artillery, and the approach on ironclads may be made and we may retire if necessary without incurring serious loss in a night attack, as the initiative is in our hands," Parsons replied.[67] The sun would not set for nearly two hours and Green knew any delay would give the Federals a chance to discover the waiting Confederates. More time would also give the fleet a chance to free its grounded boats and escape. A less aggressive officer may have heeded Parsons's advice but Green decided to attack immediately. Because Parsons's Brigade made up the bulk of the attacking force, Green ordered Parsons to lead the attack against the fleet.[68] Brigadier General Major was placed in charge of a reserve of several hundred troopers and would be responsible for preventing any Union infantry from disembarking from the transports.[69]

To reach the landing, the Rebels had to cross a large, cleared field. A levee, about twenty feet above the water line, ran parallel to the riverbank. Between the levee and the forest was a fence-lined road, about five hundred paces from the landing.[70] The Blair family house, the slave quarters, and outbuildings also occupied the property.

As the Confederates deployed, Green rode over to the inexperienced Thirty-sixth Texas and, as one trooper recalled, "gave us a little talk and said we were about to perform one of the most glorious feats of the war."[71] West's howitzers were ordered to unlimber at the lower bend of the river, where they would be able to rake the decks of any ascending ship.[72]

The Confederates raced across the field, crossed the road, and sprinted toward the landing.[73] The Rebels searched the plantation buildings as they made their way toward the levee but found no Union infantry, though Parthenia Blair, wife of landowner James D. Blair, and her children were located inside the house.[74]

Most sailors aboard the Federal vessels could not see over the levee but the pilot of the *Black Hawk*, from his elevated position, reported a large force advancing from the woods. Many of Green's men were dressed in Union blue—the result of scavenging after the recent battles at Mansfield and Pleasant Hill—which initially confused the slow-to-respond Federals.[75]

Once the Confederates reached the levee, they ran along the bank and stopped directly in front of the ships, where they unleashed a withering fire.[76] Selfridge reported that "everything that was made of wood on the *Osage* and *Black Hawk* was pierced with bullets."[77] The *Black Hawk's* pilot could not leave the protection of the iron pilothouse, which was struck by at least sixty bullets.[78] Soldiers aboard the *Black Hawk* fled to the *Osage*. On the other boats, the Yankees scrambled for cover below deck or behind bales of cotton and hay or sacks of oats stacked on deck.[79] One Confederate remembered some Federals diving overboard and trying to swim to the opposite riverbank "but there was such a hail from the small arms that many a poor fellow never reached the shore."[80]

Though unable to maneuver easily, the warships *Lexington* and *Osage* began to return fire.[81] Green knew that he would be unable to capture the ships with small-arms fire alone and ordered West's howitzers nearer the landing. West unlimbered four hundred yards from the landing, the transport *Hastings*, "within point blank range."[82] The *Hastings* began to slip away from the landing.[83] West fired at the *Hastings* but the first shots fell short; the next few were too long.[84] Despite their great size, the Federal vessels proved difficult to hit because the low river caused them to be partially concealed and protected by the levee.[85]

The *Lexington* sailed upriver, engaging West's cannon with her 8-inch bow guns.[86] In fact, the Confederate artillery attracted most of the U.S. Navy's attention. By now, the transport *Rob Roy* had taken position astern of the *Black Hawk* and added the weight of four 30-pounder Parrott guns to the fight. A section of artillery aboard the *Emerald* began to direct its fire on West's guns too.[87] West was "exposed to a terrible fire" and in a short time many of his battery horses were killed, forcing the artillerists to manhandle the howitzers.[88] Eventually, one howitzer was put out of action and a caisson with ammunition was destroyed. Soon the ineffective Confederate artillery, already low on ammunition, retired from the field.[89]

As the fleet dueled with Green's artillery, a Federal transport rounded the bend above the landing and disembarked infantry on the eastern shore. The Union foot soldiers marched opposite the Confederate cavalry, took up positions in the dense tree line, and began sniping at any visible Confederates.[90] Most of the Rebels were too busy firing at the fleet to notice this new threat, which caused more casualties than did the naval batteries.[91]

While Green battled at Blair's Landing, Bagby's column continued to march south. Eventually, Bagby's troopers succeeded in passing several vessels. Yet, inexplicably, Bagby "seemed to think it not advisable to attack" and allowed the ships to continue unmolested.[92] A trooper from the Fourth Texas Mounted Volunteers confided that "it seems as if there was a lack of courage to do any certain thing."[93] Bagby halted for the day a short distance from Blair's Landing.

The strange battle between the Southern cavalry and the Northern navy raged for nearly one hour. Selfridge wrote that "the fire of 2,500 rifles at point-blank range, mingled with the slow, sullen roar of our two great guns, was something indescribable."[94] The *Lexington* consistently improved her aim while firing grape and shrapnel along the length of the Rebel line. A portion of the levee caved in under the fire of the Union warship.[95] Combining with the *Osage*, a deadly crossfire was poured on the Confederates.[96] The *Osage* "had expended every round of grape and canister, and was using shrapnel with fuzes cut to one second."[97] The Confederates began to take more and more casualties.[98]

Green, "who was here, there, and everywhere cheering and encouraging the men by deed and word," knew that the *Lexington* was vulnerable to small-arms fire when her portholes were opened to run out the big ship's guns.[99] But the Rebels' fire was not low enough to reach the portholes. Knowing that many in his command had never before faced gunboats, Green determined to provide the leadership and direction his men needed, despite warnings by some officers against his going into the fight.[100]

Dismounting near the Thirty-sixth Texas, Green urged the men to move nearer the edge of the levee where they could raise themselves up before firing, giving themselves a greater downward angle to fire into the portholes.[101] Suddenly a shell burst above Green and he disappeared in a cloud of smoke. When the smoke cleared, the general's lifeless body lay on the ground, his dead horse nearby.[102] He had been struck in the head by a piece of shrapnel and died instantly when a portion of his skull was torn away.[103] The same shot had severed the right arm of Lt. Col. Benton of the Thirty-sixth Texas and wounded several others in the area.[104]

The whole scene was too much for some of the Confederates. With Green's death, some of Gould's and Wood's troopers began to abandon their positions as rumors of an imminent retreat swept through the ranks.[105] Parsons, assuming the order was issued by the commanding general, located John Alexander Green, a member of Tom Green's staff and the general's brother.[106] "Great God, Colonel! What does this mean?" asked Parsons. "I am ordered by General Green to withdraw my men."[107] Colonel Green responded, "Sir, this cannot be, for my brother lies yonder dead."[108]

As the senior officer on the field, Parsons began issuing orders. As the Twelfth Texas abandoned the riverbank Parsons urged, "About face: the post of safety is the post of duty; forward!"[109] The regiment returned to the levee to continue the fight. The lopsided battle continued for another half hour but with the sun setting and victory all but gone, Brig. Gen. Major ordered the Confederates to retire.[110] The Rebels withdrew from the landing.[111]

Casualties on both sides were light. The Confederates suffered fourteen killed, thirty-nine wounded, and four missing.[112] As for Union casualties, Kilby Smith wrote, "My loss . . . is incredibly small."[113]

Colonel Parsons ordered an officer from the Thirty-sixth Texas to locate and remove Tom Green's body from the battlefield.[114] At the same time, and under "severe shelling" from the escaping Union fleet, most of the wounded Confederates were also evacuated from the battlefield.[115] Once again, the command crossed Bayou Pierre and camped for the night while a guard of honor watched the fallen general's body, which was taken by wagon to Austin, Texas.[116]

Following the action at Blair's Landing, the Texas cavalry performed valiant service, but the nature of the campaign was altered. Lt. Gen. Kirby Smith pulled Walker's Division and the small Arkansas and Missouri divisions out of Richard Taylor's forces and diverted them to Arkansas. This left Taylor with only the scarred remnants of the Louisiana Division, most of which were Texas troops under the Prince de Polignac, and the Texas cavalry, then under General Major, to hold off the vastly superior forces of the Union column.

The loss of Tom Green was almost impossible to overcome. Texas cavalry fought at the Battle of Monett's Ferry as part of the Arizona Brigade. Here, Hamilton Bee failed to trap the Union force at the ferry, which would have been possible despite his much inferior numbers. There were inadequate resources to trap either the Union army or navy and thus the Federal forces fled to Alexandria. The Union navy was nearly trapped and the Union army was anxious to leave as quickly as possible. Richard Taylor and his meager forces could only look at the Union defenses, but could do nothing to breach them. After dams were constructed by Col. Joseph Bailey, the Union navy escaped Alexandria, thwarting the possibility of self-destruction, to keep the fleet out of Confederate hands. Two more battles were fought during the retreat, an artillery engagement at Mansura and an infantry holding action at Yellow Bayou. The cavalry harassed the fleeing Union column during the entire retreat, but was not able to inflict any real damage against the large numbers of men they faced.

To many Texans, Tom Green served as a martyr to keep the invaders from the sacred soil of Texas. What is his legacy and that of the Texas Cavalry Corps and the other components of the Army of Western Louisiana? Texas and Louisiana troops could honestly say that they had protected their homelands of eastern Texas and the Red River Valley. They had driven out the Yankees, who would never make another attempt at invasion in that region for the remainder of the war. When the South was defeated and her armies shattered, they alone could claim this final victory.

Notes

1   Portions of this chapter appeared in the article "To Defend the Sacred Soil of Texas: Tom Green and the Texas Cavalry in the Red River Campaign" *East Texas Historical Journal*, 46 (Spring 2008): 11–27; Curtis Milbourn and Gary D. Joiner, "The Battle of Blair's Landing, *North and South* 9 (February 2007): 12–21.

2   Edward T. Cotham, *Battle on the Bay: The Civil War Struggle for Galveston* (Austin: University of Texas Press, 1998), passim.

3   Edward T. Cotham, *Sabine Pass: The Confederacy's Thermopylae* (Austin: University of Texas Press, 2004), passim; Brian Sayers, *On Valor's Side: Tom Green and the Battles for Early Texas* (Hemphill, Texas, 1999), 131–33.

4   Richard Lowe, *The Texas Overland Expedition of 1863* (Fort Worth, Texas: McWhiney Foundation Press, 1996), *passim*.

5   U.S. War Department, *The War of the Rebellion: A Compilation of the Official Records of the Union and Confederate Armies* (hereafter cited as *OR*) (Washington, D.C.: U.S. Government Printing Office, 1890–1901), 1, 26, 1:20–1.

6   Donald S. Frazier, "The Battles of Texas Will Be Fought in Louisiana": The Assault of Fort Butler, June 28, 1863," *Southwestern Historical Quarterly* (hereafter cited as *SHQ*) 104 (2001): 333–62.

7   Anne J. Bailey, *Texans in the Confederate Cavalry* (Fort Worth, Texas: McWhiney Foundation Press, 1995), 14.

8   Ibid., 16–17.

9   Richard Lowe, *Walker's Texas Division, C.S.A.: Greyhounds of the Trans-Mississippi* (Baton Rouge: Louisiana State University Press, 2004), passim; J. P. Blessington, *The Campaigns of Walker's Texas Division* (Austin: University of Texas Press, 1994), passim.

10   Paul D. Casdorph, *Prince John Magruder: His Life and Campaigns* (New York: John Wiley, 1996), 265.

11   Richard Taylor, *Destruction and Reconstruction: Personal Experiences in the Civil War* (New York: D. Appleton, 1890), 178; Francis R. Lubbock, *Six Decades in Texas* (Austin: Ben C. Jones, 1900), 536.

12   Taylor, *Destruction and Reconstruction*, 158; *OR*, 1, 34, 2:1029; Lubbock, *Six Decades in Texas*, 534–36; Johnson, Robert U. and Clarence C. Buel, eds., *Battles and Leaders of the Civil War* (Secaucus, New Jersey: Castle Books, 1986), 4:369.

13   Taylor, *Destruction and Reconstruction*, 158; *OR*, 1, 34, 2:1029; Gary D. Joiner, "The Red River Campaign of 1864 in the American Civil War," Appendix 2: Order of Battle of the Red River Campaign (Ph.D. diss., St. Martin's College, Lancaster University, United Kingdom, 2004).

14   Letter from Jefferson Morgan to his wife, Amanda Ann Sportsman Morgan, living at their home in Ellis County, Texas. See Gary D. Joiner, ed., *Little to Eat and Thin Mud To Drink: Letters, Diaries, and Memoirs of the Red River Campaigns, 1863–1864* (Knoxville: University of Tennessee Press, 2006), 143–46.

15   Ibid., and subsequent letters in the same collection.

16   Burr's Ferry nomination for inclusion in to the list of National Historic Places, 2004. The Burr's Ferry Earthworks were listed on the register June 22, 2004, as number 04000636.

17   Magruder's Special Order 66, March 6, 1864, *OR*, 1, 34, 1:1027.

18   Ibid.

19   U.S. Congress, *Report on the Joint Committee on the Conduct of the War, 1863–1866* (hereafter cited as *JCCW*), vol. 2, *Red River Expedition* (Millwood, New York: Krauss Printing, 1977), 185.

20   *OR*, 1, 34, 1:450, 616–17; *JCCW*, 2:58.

21   *JCCW*, 2:194.

22   Ibid.

23   John G. Belisle, *History of Sabine Parish Louisiana* (Many, Louisiana: Sabine Banner Press, 1912), 159.

24   Irwin, *Nineteenth Corps*, 299; *OR*, 1, 34, 1:291, 456; Taylor, *Destruction and Reconstruction*, 160–61; *JCCW*, 2:60–62.

25   *OR*, 1, 34, 1:563–64; Taylor, *Destruction and Reconstruction*, 162; Blessington, *Walker's Division*, 185–86; Gary D. Joiner, *Through the Howling Wilderness: The 1864 Red River Campaign and Union Failure in the West* (Knoxville: University of Tennessee Press, 2006), 84–86.

26   R. Taylor to S. S. Anderson, April 18, 1864, *OR*, 1, 34, 1:570.

27   Taylor to Anderson, *OR*, 1, 34, 1:570.

28   Ibid.

29   Taylor, *Destruction and Reconstruction*, 118.

30   Paul H. Silverstone, *Warships of the Civil War Navies* (Annapolis, Maryland: Naval Institute Press, 1989), 149.

31   Ibid., 158–59.

32   Ibid., 168, 170.

33   Ibid., 183; see Gary D. Joiner, *One Damn Blunder From Beginning to End: The Red River Campaign of 1864* (Wilmington, Delaware: Scholarly Resources, 2003), 137–38.

34   Joiner, *One Damn Blunder*, 139; see photograph of the *Fort Hindman*, Naval Historical Center photo no. NH 61569.

35   W. Randolph Howell, Diary, April 11, 1864, Howell (W. Randolph) Papers, Center for American History, University of Texas, Austin, Texas.

36   Taylor to Anderson, *OR*, 1, 34, 1:570.

37   Howell, Diary, April 11, 1864; Oscar Haas, *History of New Braunfels and Comal County, Texas, 1844–1946* (Austin: Steck, 1968), 86.

38   Alwyn Barr, "William T. Mechling Journal," copy in Shreveport Archives, Louisiana State University, Baton Rouge; Fredericka Meiners, "Hamilton P. Bee in the Red River Campaign of 1864," *SHQ* 78 (July 1974): 21–44, reprinted in Ralph A. Wooster, ed., *Lone Star Blue and Gray: Essays on Texas in the Civil War* (Austin: Texas State Historical Association, 1995), 297.

39   Barr, "Mechling Journal," 368; Meiners, 33.

40   Taylor to Anderson, *OR*, 1, 34, 1:571; Richard Taylor to Maj. Gen. John Walker, Mansfield, 1:30 [a.m. April 9, 1864], Walker Papers, Southern Historical Collection, Wilson Library, University of North Carolina, Chapel Hill, North Carolina.

41   Taylor to Anderson, *OR*, 1, 34, 1:571; B. P. Gallaway, *The Ragged Rebel: A Common Soldier in W. H. Parsons' Texas Cavalry, 1861–1865* (Austin: University of Texas Press, 1988), 86–87; John W. Spencer, *Terrell's Texas Cavalry* (Austin: Eakin Press, 1982), 42.

42   Taylor, *Destruction and Reconstruction*, 118; David D. Porter, *The Naval History of the Civil War* (New York: D. Appleton, 1886), 511–12.

43   Taylor to Anderson, *OR*, 1, 34, 1:571.

44   J. L. Brent to Maj. Gen. Taylor, April 14, 1864, in J. L. Brent, Letter Books, October 1862–May 1865, and Order Book, November 1864–May 1865, micro-

film, Perry-Castañeda Library, University of Texas, Austin, Texas; Chester Alwyn Barr, Jr., "Confederate Artillery in the Trans-Mississippi" (M.A. thesis, University of Texas, 1961), 150–51.

45   Carl L. Duaine, *The Dead Men Wore Boots: An Account of the 32nd Texas Volunteer Cavalry, C.S.A., 1862–1865* (Austin: University of Texas Press, 1966), 118; Gallaway, *The Ragged Rebel*, 90–91.

46   Duaine, *Dead Men Wore Boots*, 118; Gallaway, *Ragged Rebel*, 90–91.

47   Minetta Altgelt Goyne, *Lone Star and Double Eagle: Civil War Letters of a German-Texas Family* (Fort Worth: Texas Christian University Press, 1982), 130.

48   Haas, *History of New Braunfels*, 87; Howell, Diary, April 12, 1864.

49   Haas, *History of New Braunfels*, 87; Howell, Diary, April 12, 1864; Connie O'Donnell, ed., "The Diary of Robert Williams: Marches, Skirmishes, and Battles of the Fourth Regiment, Texas Militia Volunteers, October 1861 to November 1865," typed manuscript (photocopy), Harold B. Simpson Research Library, Hill College, Hillsboro, Texas: 67.

50   Tom Green Scrapbook, Sarah Riddell Manuscript Collection, Texas State Archives Commission, 10, Texas State Archives, Austin, Texas; Spencer, *Terrell's Texas Cavalry*, 42.

51   Gallaway, *Ragged Rebel*, 91.

52   Walter George Smith, *Life and Letters of Thomas Kilby Smith, Brevet Major-General, United States Volunteers, 1820–1887* (New York: G. P. Putnam's Sons, 1898), 117.

53   Ibid.

54   W. H. Parsons, *Condensed History of Parsons Texas Cavalry Brigade, 1861–1865, Together with Inside History and Heretofore Unwritten Chapters of the Red River Campaign of 1864* (Corsicana, Texas: n.p., 1903), 87.

55   Parsons, *Condensed History*, 87; Alwyn Barr, "The Battle of Blair's Landing," *Louisiana Studies* 2 (1963): 206.

56   Parsons, *Condensed History*, 87.

57   Ibid, 88.

58   Ibid.

59   Spencer, *Terrell's Texas Cavalry*, 2–42.

60   Bruce S. Allardice, "Curious Clash at Blair's Landing," *America's Civil War* (July 1997): 60.

61   Arthur W. Bergeron, Jr., *Guide to Louisiana Confederate Military Units, 1861–1865* (Baton Rouge: Louisiana State University Press, 1989), 26–27.

62   *Galveston (Texas) Tri-Weekly News*, June 3, 1864.

63   Smith, *Life and Letters of Thomas Kilby Smith*, 102; John A. Green, "Green, General Thomas," *Biographical Encyclopedia of Texas* (New York: Southern Publishing, 1880), 134; Allardice, "Curious Clash at Blair's Landing," 61.

64   Allardice, "Curious Clash at Blair's Landing," 61.

65   Smith, *Life and Letters of Thomas Kilby Smith*, 101–102.

66   Green, *Biographical Encyclopedia of Texas*, 134.

67   Parsons, *Condensed History*, 88.

68   Ibid.

69 Allardice, "Curious Clash at Blair's Landing," 60; Gallaway, *Ragged Rebel*, 93–94.

70 Goyne, *Lone Star and Double Eagle*, 130; Thomas O. Selfridge, Jr., *What Finer Tradition: The Memoirs of Thomas O. Selfridge, Jr., Rear Admiral, U.S.N.*, with a new introduction by William N. Still, Jr. (Columbia: University of South Carolina Press, 1987), 101.

71 Duaine, *Dead Men Wore Boots*, 118.

72 Green, *Biographical Encyclopedia of Texas*, 134.

73 Goyne, *Lone Star and Double Eagle*, 130.

74 Green, 135; Mamie Yeary, *Reminiscences of the Boys in Gray, 1861–1865* (Dayton: Morningside Press, 1986), 677; Melba Marguerite Gupton, "Teenie and Jim: Family Story of Parthenia Irvin (Rugeley) Blair and Col. James Douglas Blair, 2nd Louisiana Cavalry, Blair's Landing, Red River," typed manuscript (photocopy), 18, Tom Green Vertical File, Mansfield State Historic Site, Mansfield, Louisiana.

75 Selfridge, "The Navy in the Red River," 101–2.

76 Goyne, *Lone Star and Double Eagle*, 130.

77 Thomas O. Selfridge, "The Navy in the Red River," in *Battles and Leaders of the Civil War*, vol. 2, eds. Robert Underwood Johnson and Clarence Clough Buel (New York: Thomas Yoseloff, 1956), 363.

78 Selfridge, "The Navy in the Red River," 102–3; Green, 135.

79 Smith, *Life and Letters of Thomas Kilby Smith*, 102–3; Green, 135.

80 Yeary, *Reminiscences of the Boys in Gray*, 418.

81 Selfridge, "The Navy in the Red River," 102; Smith, 102.

82 Tom Green Scrapbook, 10; Parsons, *Condensed History*, 88; Goyne, *Lone Star and Double Eagle*, 130; Smith, *Life and Letters of Thomas Kilby Smith*, 102.

83 Selfridge, "The Navy in the Red River," 102; Smith, 102.

84 Smith, *Life and Letters of Thomas Kilby Smith*, 102.

85 Allardice, "Curious Clash at Blair's Landing," 61.

86 Bache to Porter, *ORN*, 1, 26, 1:50.

87 W. S. Hinkle to Richard Arnold, April 14, 1864, *OR*, 1, 34, 1:409; John H. Tiemeyer to Richard Arnold, April 18, 1864, *OR*, 1, 34, 1:385.

88 J. L. Brent, "Operations of the Artillery of the Army of Western Louisiana, after the Battle of Pleasant Hill, *Southern Historical Society Papers* 9 (1881): 257; Thomas Kilby Smith to Hough, April 16, 1864, *OR*, 1, 34, 1:381; Smith, 102.

89 Selfridge, "The Navy in the Red River," 102; Barr, "Blair's Landing," 207; Allardice, "Curious Clash at Blair's Landing," 61.

90 *Galveston (Texas) Tri-Weekly News*, June 3, 1864; Allardice, "Curious Clash at Blair's Landing," 62.

91 Green, *Biographical Encyclopedia of Texas*, 135.

92 Haas, *History of New Braunfels*, 87; Howell, Diary, April 12, 1864.

93 Haas, *History of New Braunfels*, 87.

94 Selfridge, "The Navy in the Red River," 103.

95 Parsons, *Condensed History*, 89; Bache to Porter, *ORN*, 1, 26, 1:50.

96 Parsons, *Condensed History*, 92; Bache to Porter, *ORN*, 1, 26, 1:50.

97 Selfridge, "The Navy in the Red River," 103.

98   Duaine, *Dead Men Wore Boots,* 118.

99   Tom Green Scrapbook, 10.

100 *Houston (Texas) Daily Telegraph*, April 22, 1864, typed manuscript (photocopy), Tom Green Vertical File, Mansfield State Historic Site, Mansfield, Louisiana.

101 Green, *Biographical Encyclopedia of Texas*, 135.

102 Gallaway, *Ragged Rebel,* 99; Allardice, "Curious Clash at Blair's Landing," 63.

103 Yeary, *Reminiscences of the Boys in Gray,* 172; Smith, 188.

104 Allardice, "Curious Clash at Blair's Landing," 63.

105 Gallaway, *Ragged Rebel,* 98–99.

106 Carolyn Hyman, "Green, John Alexander," *New Handbook of Texas* (Austin: University of Texas Press, 1996), 3:314.

107 Anne J. Bailey, *Between the Enemy and Texas: Parsons's Texas Cavalry in the Civil War* (Fort Worth: Texas Christian University Press, 1989), 175.

108 Bailey, *Between the Enemy and Texas,* 175. It appears the order to withdraw was given by Brig. Gen. James Major, following Green's death the ranking officer at Blair's Landing.

109 Parsons, *Condensed History,* 89.

110 *Houston (Texas) Daily Telegraph*, April 22, 1864; Green, 135.

111 Parsons, *Condensed History,* 89–90.

112 Barr, "The Battle of Blair's Landing," 208–9.

113 Smith, *Life and Letters of Thomas Kilby Smith,* 103.

114 Joiner, *Little to Eat,* 135–36.

115 Green, *Biographical Encyclopedia of Texas*, 135.

116 Ibid.

Chapter 12

Prison City, Camp Ford: Largest Confederate Prisoner-of-war Camp in the Trans-Mississippi

by James M. Smallwood

Once the Civil War began, both North and South established detention camps for captives. Well-known Confederate holding centers were in Richmond, Macon, Savannah, Raleigh, Goldsborough, and Andersonville, the last considered notorious because of its high death rate. In the Trans-Mississippi Theater, Camp Ford in Smith County near Tyler became the biggest of the prison camps west of the Mississippi. At one time it held more than 5,200 men, perhaps as many as 5,550 when it reached its peak occupation in May of 1864.[1] Four miles northeast of Tyler, Camp Ford originated as a training center for Confederate volunteers and, later, for conscripts. Established in April of 1862, it was named in honor of the noted Texan, Col. John S. Ford. Other temporary training sites once dotted the Smith County countryside, but Camp Ford, near Ray's Creek across from a freshwater spring and near the Tyler–Marshall Road, became a permanent installation when in 1863 it underwent a transformation and emerged as a prisoner-of-war site, one that had the lowest death rate of any large camp during the war.[2]

Southerners in the Trans-Mississippi had taken relatively few Union prisoners until Maj. Gen. John Bankhead Magruder recaptured Galveston on January 1, 1863. Then the numbers began to mount. Later that summer, associated with a campaign into Louisiana, yet more prisoners fell into Southern hands. The Trans-Mississippi needed a new site, and the command eventually chose Tyler's Camp Ford for at least five reasons. First, the place was already functioning as a training site and could furnish, marginally, enough guards to guarantee security. Second, Smith County had a sound economy, led by a flourishing agricultural sector oriented toward producing food crops and developing livestock herds; the area could thus both afford a site and feed its prisoners. Third, a Confederate supply depot was nearby. Fourth, Ford was near a good freshwater spring and freshwater creek. And, fifth, Smith County was remote enough to discourage escape attempts, yet close enough to Shreveport, Louisiana, to participate in prisoner exchange programs.[3]

Camp Ford's first prisoners, captured in Louisiana, arrived in July of 1863 accompanied by a contingent of the Walter P. Lane Rangers, headquartered in Harrison County. The Yankees numbered forty-eight, their ranks soon swelling to seventy-five. Originally held in Tyler in the Federal courthouse, the group was soon transferred to Camp Ford, which had no stockade and only thirty-eight guards. Many more men arrived before the year was out, including a bunch from Camp Groce, near Hempstead, when the Confederates abandoned that site.[4]

Ford's first long-term commandant, the West Pointer Col. R. T. P. Allen, had an outstanding military record. After fighting in the Second Seminole War, he joined the faculty at Allegheny College, later transferring to Transylvania College. In 1847 he founded Kentucky Military Institute. Some years later, his old friend the Reverend John Carner convinced him to come to Texas and found a military school in Bastrop. From there, he supported the secessionists but became horrified when he observed the actions of the first Texans to volunteer for Dixie's cause. They believed in neither discipline nor drill and had no real knowledge of warfare. They thought valor and devotion would win the war. Allen knew better. When the war came, Allen volunteered. His first activity was to write a guide for military training: *Manual of Instruction, Designed Especially for the Volunteers and Militia of Texas*, in which he argued that young men needed to spend at least one month in a camp of instruction before going to war. Later a combat officer, he was grievously wounded at the Battle of Milliken's Bend in June of 1863. When Colonel Allen recovered, command made him commandant of Tyler's Camp of Instruction in November of 1863 just as it was evolving into a prisoner-of-war camp, now having about 550 prisoners, most captured in a Louisiana campaign. Lt. Gen. Edmund Kirby Smith, who had been commander of the Trans-Mississippi since October of 1862, had issued Allen's orders on November 3, and the colonel arrived in Smith County on November 9.[5]

In coming to Camp Ford, Allen rode straight into trouble. The Yankee prisoners and Smith County civilians would give him all the headaches that he could endure. At issue was camp security: specifically, monitoring and firmly controlling the prisoners. Prior to his arrival, the seventy-five prisoners seemed to have the run of Smith County, their guards allowing them to roam around. Usually they were looking for food. Some surprised Mittie Marsh, whose husband was at war and whose farm was about five miles from Camp Ford, when they appeared at her door. On August 30, she wrote her soldier husband, Bryan Marsh, that "the Yanks do just as they please."[6] Matters became worse in late October. On September 29, 1863, Confederate Gen. "Fighting" Tom Green had led his forces to victory in the Battle of Morganza in Louisiana and after capturing a small brigade almost intact wound up with a grand prize: 468 prisoners. Green sent his prisoners to Camp Ford, the new additions arriving on

October 30. Now the camp was home to more than 500 men who had only sev-
enty-one inexperienced militiamen and one regular army lieutenant as guards.
The number of prisoners simply overwhelmed their keepers, especially in a holding area that did not even have a stockade. Lt. Col. J. B. Leake, then the ranking
Northern officer at the camp, noted that some men escaped almost daily.[7]

Smith County's Mittie Marsh again wrote her soldier husband, Bryan, telling him: "All of the Yankee prisoners were about to make there escape. [Forty-
eight] got away in one night. . . . The prisoners were going to unarm the guards
and go from camps to Tyler." Mittie continued, saying that the inmates threatened to burn Tyler to the ground. She concluded that she had "heard that their
600 more prisoners coming her I don't know what we'll do with them their will
be more Yankees than any thing else."[8]

Finally the guards decided to bring order to the camp and to ensure that
no more men escaped. They established a "deadline" of logs that ringed the
area where they held prisoners. The deadline was aptly named—if the prisoners went past a certain line, made from stacks of fallen timber, they were shot
to death. On November 11, Yankee Pvt. Thomas Moorehead was supposedly
waiting for wood and accidentally strayed past the deadline. Sentry Frank Smith
shot him stone dead, the ball passing through Moorehead and shattering the
arm of another prisoner. Because of the incident, angry Federals threatened to
kill their guards, sack Tyler, and leave the entire area in ashes. However, rumors
held that there was more to the Moorehead story than met the eye. It appeared
to be part of a larger escape attempt, three other men having already escaped
on November 8. To blunt the Federals' rage, Colonel Allen quickly convened a
court of inquiry, a panel that included at least one prisoner; he also invited all
Federal officers to witness the proceedings. Results of the four-day inquiry were
never made public, but Allen's quick action calmed the Yankees somewhat.[9]

During the inquiry, for some reason, Allen began to suspect that some area
Unionists were helping the prisoners who were trying to escape. He directed Sgt.
J. C. Curtis of Lane's Rangers to get into civilian garb, take the alias "Smith,"
pose as a Confederate deserter, and approach noted Unionists. Curtis sought
out two well-known supporters of the United States: George W. Whitmore and
George Rosenbaum. In talking with Whitmore and Rosenbaum, Curtis became
suspicious of them, whereupon Allen ordered their arrest. After lodging the two
men in the Tyler jail on November 17, guards moved them to Camp Ford a
week later.[10] All the while, Whitmore and Rosenbaum maintained that they
were innocent of any crime.

The Whitmore family, headed by patriarch John H. Whitmore, had a
farm south of Canton (later renamed Omen) in the southeastern part of Smith
County, the acreage also extending into Rusk County. George, one of John's
two sons, became an attorney and set up a practice in Marshall. In the late

1850s, he represented Harrison County in the legislature as a follower of Sam Houston. As the war approached, he warned Texans about the folly of following the Southern fire-eaters, who were determined to destroy the Union and who instead would only be able to destroy Dixie. The other Unionist, Rosenbaum of Van Zandt County, had once served as a district attorney for the Ninth Judicial District, which included Smith County.[11]

Meanwhile, the deserter "Smith" (né Curtis) resumed his investigation. He continued to observe the Whitmore family and hoped to detect any troublesome activities among them. What he learned was nothing short of astounding. After a last trip to the Whitmore farm, he gained the confidence of William H. Whitmore, George's brother. The spy learned some of the details of a plot to free all the prisoners. He came away from the Whitmore home with a gift of $150 in Confederate notes and five handguns. After Curtis made his report, Allen sent a squad to arrest William Whitmore. At first held in the Tyler jail, he was soon escorted to Camp Ford. Once there, he learned—just as his brother and Rosenbaum had learned—that he could not mingle with the Yankee prisoners, perhaps because local Confederate authorities feared that the trio might try to lead a revolt. Instead, guards lodged the three alleged conspirators not in the main camp but in the guardhouse, called the wolf pen, a fact suggesting that the local Unionists may have received harsher treatment than other prisoners. Whitmore and Rosenbaum remained in Camp Ford until July 5, 1864, when the Confederates transferred them to Camp Martin, just south of Rusk, where they remained until finally being freed in November.[12]

After the early escapes and the larger plot that failed, life in Camp Ford settled into something that could be called peaceful as most prisoners accepted their immediate fate. And the Whitmores and Rosenbaum did not remain completely isolated. Conscripts who deserted but were later captured soon joined the three in the wolf pen. Even the Union prisoners made contact each day by arranging for at least one man to commit a small offense and to be incarcerated in the pen for the day. Once there, the prisoner could console the two men and tell them the news about the outside world.[13] Meanwhile, various locals continued to express alarm about mass escapes and the devilry that such escapees could cause. The tense situation was such that Allen temporarily impressed dozens of male slaves (with their owners' consent) to construct a stout stockade to contain the bluecoats. Before the end of November, the laborers had completed an eighteen-foot-high split-log surround, which took in about four acres, to enclose the troublesome Union men.[14]

As the war continued, prisoner occupation of Camp Ford occurred in four distinct phases. First came the unenclosed camp from August of 1863 through early November. Second came the new stockaded camp from November of 1863 to April of 1864. Third was the great expansion of the stockade that came after

Illustration 13 Commissioned officers of the Nineteenth Iowa Infantry after their exchange as prisoners of war, New Orleans. *Courtesy Library of Congress.*

the Louisiana campaigns of 1864. The fourth phase began in October of 1864 as new exchanges took place and as the camp's population dropped from a high of more than 5,200 men to fewer than 3,000. It was the third phase that turned Camp Ford's routine into mayhem. The Union's Red River Campaign of 1864 caused alarm in Confederate Louisiana and Texas. Upon learning that the Federals were coming, Rebel commanders in the Bayou State moved approximately 700 prisoners from Shreveport to Tyler to get them away from the action. Next, the combined results of the battles of Mansfield and Pleasant Hill in April of 1864 were to greatly increase the Trans-Mississippi's number of prisoners. Maj. Gen. Richard "Dick" Taylor's men captured almost 4,000 Federals, most of whom wound up in Camp Ford, meaning that the stockade had to be enlarged. By mid-April, slave gangs had expanded it to the north and east. Now the stockade covered about eleven acres. Shaped like an irregular rectangle, the addition had six-foot walls built of split post oak trees. Workers also constructed three large log cabins to serve as quarters for the guards.[15]

After the big influx of new prisoners, the detainees at first built their own cabins, but lack of tools and the receding tree line brought change. The prisoners began banding together and building "shebangs," small structures that resembled earthen caves, wooden shacks, and pup tents. Capt. William May, a guest of Camp Ford from December of 1863 to June of 1864, witnessed the large influx and, later remembered that, in what he called "Prison City," shelter came in all shapes and sizes: "Here upright sticks sustain a simple thatch of leaves; there poles fixed slantwise and overlaid with bark, compose an Indian lodge. Some householders are satisfied with blankets stretched across two saplings." Continuing, he said that other men built "palisade mansions, eight feet square, with stakes, inserted in the earth, like picket fences, and covered with a roof of twigs. Another's dwelling is of basket-work wrought out of ashwood pellings; beyond this is a roof composed of oak slabs slanting from a mud-wall six feet high . . . plastered with a layer of clay." Down by the brook, May concluded, were "caverns, excavated in the clay . . . with steep earthen staircases entering to their subterrene apartments."[16]

Not only did the men provide their own shelters, but also they had wisely safeguarded their water supply and consequently their health. The inmates named Navy Capt. Amos Johnson of the USS *Sachem* to supervise the work to protect their water. Johnson then recruited a number of healthy inmates who built two wooden reservoirs to hold water from the clear spring adjacent to Ray's Creek. One reservoir held drinking water, the other was to be used for bathing. Also, Johnson located the reservoirs as far as he could from the latrines, which were located in the northeast corner of the camp.[17]

Although prisoners generally exhibited good morale, the character and actions of Commandant Allen and his wife, Julia, often boosted that morale. Colonel Allen, for example, allowed prisoners to have visitors, and both he and Julia often brought extra food for the men. One inmate, Capt. William F. McKinney of the Nineteenth Kentucky Infantry, recorded in his diary on April 28, 1864, that Mrs. Allen visited camp and donated "a nice mess of dried peaches." In his entry for May 7, the prisoner noted another of her visits, saying simply "provisions brought," as if such actions were a routine occurrence.[18] The Federals so liked Julia that they began calling her "Mother Allen."[19] One prisoner so appreciated Mother Allen that he dedicated a poem to her in the name of God. In his first four lines, Col. A. J. H. Duganne wrote:

All kindly acts are for the Dear Lord's sake
And His sweet law and recompense they claim,
 "I was in prison," thus our Savior spake,
And unto me you came.[20]

Mrs. Allen was not the only woman who befriended the inmates. The youthful Tyler belle Mollie E. Moore, poetess extraordinaire, did so, too, as did other local young ladies. Captain May commented on such fraternizing with civilians that Mother Allen brought to camp. "Often," he said, "our fiddler's skills" were needed, and on many a night men in camp heard the "thrum of stringed instruments [while] divers rebel dames and demoiselles . . . sit [and] chat with Yankee officers." The Smith County women listened to "Yankee songs, accompanied by Yankee fingers upon banjoes made by Yankee hands." When the fiddler played "Sounds from Home," the medley drew "tears from the eyes of the lady rebels." Usually, on such a night, once all visitors had gone, the men paired off and danced late into the approaching morn to the tunes of the fiddler, about which all May could say was, "Dance on, poor prisoners! Cheat your hearts out of loneliness."[21]

Occasionally, the men found ways to boost their morale and make a political statement at the same time. A few days before their July 4, 1864, celebration, certain prisoners stripped a small tree of all its branches and hung a cord from its top. Their jailors "never wondered at that," recalled one inmate, because "we were always doing queer things."[22] Then, on their designated day, *The Old Flag*, a camp newspaper put together by the aforementioned William May, circulated all day long during which men made speech after speech about their sacred Union. After a band concert and a sing-song, the fife, flute, banjo, and fiddle struck up "The Star-Spangled Banner." At precisely that moment, a thin, ragged man jumped out of a shebang and, quick as a wink, raised the flag of the Forty-eighth Ohio on the small tree: "Like a flash the flag of our Union sped up to the peak," said one Yank, "and waved triumphantly over that rebel prison pen! Such cheers as went up from those hungry throats! No rebel could have drowned it!"[23] Of course the guards rallied quickly and rode through the compound with sabers at the ready and ended what they considered an insulting incident. They also intended to find and to confiscate the flag, but inside one shebang, the thin, ragged man approached another inmate, a man in bed ill with fever. He got the sick man up and wrapped the banner around the man's wasted body. Then he helped the sick man get his garments back on and put him back to bed. A witness later asserted that the Rebel search did no good: "They never found that flag."[24] (The flag is now in possession of the Ohio State Historical Society).

Often prisoners found amusement by simply playing jokes or pranks on the guards. On a corner of one of the camp's main streets, so many men gathered to gamble that it was dubbed "Keno Corner." One Rebel adjutant named B. W. McEachern, of English heritage but not a native Southerner, was so fond of money that he remained in the compound after roll call and joined in the keno games and chuck-a-luck, a dice game. On some days he crowed because he had won, but he usually left enraged the next day after losing all his winnings of the day before. On many occasions, McEachern kept his side arms, two Colt revolvers, while with the men. One morning Robert Rogers of Ohio laid plans to steal the weapons. As a keno game went on, the adjutant became more and more absorbed with the play, and Rogers simply slipped the guns out of their holsters without the Rebel realizing it. McEachern eventually left the compound unarmed and unaware of it until he went into the commander's headquarters, where a cohort casually advised him that he had been robbed. Accompanied by a detachment of armed guards, the humiliated Confederate stormed back to Keno Corner to demand the return of the Colts. Surprisingly, not a single prisoner knew anything about the theft; they had not seen a thing. Frustrated by the prisoners' refusal to help him find his guns, the woebegone McEachern left in a huff, only to return later in the day and again demand his Colts. This time, he threatened to withhold rations, a move that would be life threatening to some of the sick men. Soon, the guns popped up, but the victim was never happy thereafter. Although he stopped gambling with the men, they forever after called him "Keno," much to his continuing disgust.[25]

To further boost morale, the men developed a Camp Ford "philosophy" that emphasized the positives of prison life and their eventual release. They illustrated their philosophy with a poem, "The Jolly Cock Robin":

A Jolly old Cock
Was case on a rock—
A rock jutting out on the sea;
And said he to himself
  "I'm cast on this shelf,
As merit is used to be!
I don't care a curse,
It might have been worse,"
Said this jolly old cock, said he;
  "I've still got a bunch
To serve for lunch,
And a capital view of the sea!
So I think I can die,
Without piping my eye"—
But a ship was just nearing the rock;
And he giggled with joy,
When the crew cried "Ahoy!"
And rescued this jolly old cock[26]

While excitement occurred on July 4 and a few other times, usually daily life inside the camp was boring and monotonous. Yet the men lived as best they could and made the most out of difficult circumstances. William May and several others left accounts that give much detail on daily life inside the stockade of what May called "Prison City." As historian Vicki Betts pointed out, the camp took on the appearance of a frontier town and developed many of the same services. The men called their central street Fifth Avenue, upon which, in the middle of the camp, was a canopy of pine boughs that sheltered a raised platform. It served as a marketplace and was also the place where guards delivered prison supplies. At the time May was writing, the daily menu consisted of beef, slaughtered by the inmates, and cornmeal, but local farmers added to the fare. They often came and brought their surplus foodstuffs to the market. To hear May tell it, the farmers gouged the prisoners, selling their goods at outrageous prices—sugar at $30 a pound, for example. But sometimes the men turned the tables on farmers who overpriced their goods. May recalled a day when a local producer entered the camp and came to the market to push his expensive sugar. Men charged the platform, scooped the sugar up by the handfuls from an open barrel, and ate it as they ran away. The raid came so fast and was over so quickly that the farmer could not even identify the villains. Other agrarians lost goods ranging from white flour to turkeys, from cornmeal to whiskey.[27]

The Union men got the best of another Smith County farmer who often came to Prison City to sell his produce on Fifth Avenue. Fearing theft, he usually waited outside until some jailors assembled to lead him into camp and to protect his goods while he was at the market. One day when the guards were slow to reach him, the farmer foolishly told the gatekeeper to forget the escort. He went in alone because he had made many trips and had never had trouble with the men. Once inside, he let all customers know that he had fresh cabbage for sale, along with sweet potatoes, a pair costing five dollars in Confederate scrip. The inmates quickly swarmed him and began helping themselves to the produce. When the now-panicked agrarian tried to get away by whipping his horse, the animal moved fast but the farmer on board his small wagon did not. Some prisoner had pulled the linchpins. Not only did the men get the rest of the produce, they also stole the farmer's straw hat and red bandanna and left the grower sitting in the dirt near the platform. Afterward, the thieves showed mercy by gently helping the farmer up and dusting him off. They restored his wagon to use and merrily sent him on his way. One Federal soldier said that the man was "the worst scared rebel in Texas." Local lore holds that the farmer left fast and never returned to Prison City. The guards saw all the tomfoolery but chose not to intervene, perhaps because they knew that the prisoners desperately needed food.[28]

Col. A. J. H. Duganne added his account of daily life in Prison City. Most men healthy enough to do so rose around daybreak. "Tatterdemalions roll out of burrowing places, creep up from the caves, and emerge from hut-openings," said the colonel. He described the men as "Red-capped Zouaves, wide-breeched; blue-bloused cavalry men, yellow trimmed: all hungry looking: sergeants with service stripes; jack-tars in holy-patched trousers . . . barefooted cannoneers—rank and file generally hatless, bootless, and shirtless . . . Motley's the only wear." Quoting Shakespeare, Duganne added: "Such costumes never were beheld before outside of Rag Fair or the 'Beggers' Opera.' I wish our Uncle Abraham, or Sam, could see this *sans culotte* procession march up Pennsylvania Avenue."[29] After seemingly the whole camp swarmed Fifth Avenue, Duganne mingled with the throng: "I pass the 'bakery' where an enterprising New Yorker sells his ten-cent leathery doughnuts and caoutchouc [rubberlike] grape-pies for a greenback dollar. I glance a moment at our 'jeweler's window, where a corporal

tinkers with watches; [and I] elbow through the crowd surrounding a Lieutenant's turning-lathe, which whorls out chessmen at three dollars a set."[30] So went
the early morn on a typical day in Prison City.

Although many prisoners remained as content as any prisoners could be,
over time, as the prison population went up, problems developed. The living
standards within the camp declined. Crowded conditions led to more sickness and disease. An epidemic of measles killed several prisoners. One detainee
lamented that the sick had no medicine. (The Union's naval blockade of the
South was partially responsible for that). He said that many new arrivals had
no shelters, nor enough to eat, and had no change of diet. He added that the
camp had become filthy. "Beef bones, rotten leaves, lice, hair, rags, filth of an
indescribable kind was," he complained, "all raked up in piles all over the camp.
The piles were full of maggots and were making life intolerable."[31]

Authorities did what they could to alleviate hardships. They directed the
construction of a small hospital nearby, but conditions remained crude, and
medicines were almost nonexistent, with the result that guards lodged only
dying men there. New prisoners still had no quarters awaiting them, and the
camp continued to stink miserably because of inadequate sanitation. Food
shortages continued to occur, and sufficient clothing became unavailable, as
half-nude men battled rain and cold weather. While maggots continued to feast
on garbage, the Union men built more shebangs, flattened tomato cans to use as
plates, and whittled wood in the shape of spoons.[32]

Always critical in the camp, the food shortages became more acute as time
went on. Standard rations at first included a pound of meat and a pint of cornmeal per day. But, eventually, the guards reduced quantities. Further, the meal
consisted not just of kernels but also of ground husks and cobs, and the coarse
substances caused disorders such as dysentery and diarrhea. Some woebegone
soldiers bartered their clothes for food. According to one Federal, others seemed
to go crazy. He added that "it was plain to be seen that we were becoming
weaker every day."[33]

Some of the keepers became scavengers for themselves and their captives,
procuring such items as rye for coffee. Some prisoners received passes to look
for wild onions to add to their meager fare. As the war neared its end, inmates
and jailors alike were hungry enough to plant gardens outside the stockade,
hoping for a good yield. Capt. J. M. McCulloch supervised prisoners who tried
to grow their own food. Despite such developments, scurvy became more common. Guards suffered along with the men because the Confederate Congress
had earlier stipulated that rations for prisoners of war would be the same as
those for Dixie's own enlisted men. When hunger reared its head, guards agonized along with their charges. Early on, the fact that Texas was not successfully
invaded insured that the Smith County bounty would prevent starvation, but

by 1864 shortages became more pronounced, especially after the number of inmates finally mounted to almost 50 percent of the county's entire population. Shortages created more hard times.[34]

Not all prisoners meekly accepted the fate of possible starvation, nor did they accept prison life in general. Many tried to escape, an activity that boosted camp morale in a way that the keepers hated. Some successful escapees made it to freedom after bribing a few guards. Others tried to forge their own passes to get out of the compound, a ploy that sometimes worked. Other men experimented with tunneling. Although a few men gained freedom in this manner, digging dirt remained mostly a waste of time. Some men tried a more direct method. They simply loosened enough of the camp's log walls to create a crawl space. After they were on the other side of the wall, they ran for the nearest woods. But most all of the attempts failed, in part because Union men were not familiar with East Texas geography and were easily caught. For example, fifteen men escaped together near the end of the war. They bribed a guard, one Giger, who let them out. But, unfortunately for them, they wandered around lost for days, and Confederate searchers recaptured thirteen of them before they even reached the Sabine River. Two, however, eluded the Rebel patrol and may have eventually reached New Orleans and safety.[35] On another occasion, C. D. Gibson of the Eighteenth Iowa Infantry led a three-man breakout. Within a short period of time, hounds led a posse headed by planter John Wiggins to the wayward trio before they crossed the Sabine. Gibson later recalled his first taste of Southern hospitality. Wiggins took the three prisoners to his plantation mansion and let them feast on pork and sweet potatoes before delivering them to military authorities the next day. During a return trip to Tyler in 1911, Gibson averred that the food he ate at the Wiggins place was the "best supper" he had ever had.[36]

Because of the filth in camp, in 1864 authorities allowed inmates to shovel the garbage into refuse carts that were dumped in the deep forest, well away from Prison City. Originally, the garbage was simply piled up around the interior of the camp, but the stink of it and the danger of epidemics finally forced the guards to allow prisoners to haul away the offal. That development led to the prisoners' "underground railroad," so named by the bluecoats because the cleanup activities led to many escapes. One or two men would lie down in a cart and cover themselves with blankets. Then their cohorts would shovel rubbish atop them. Because the keepers seldom followed the wagons all the way to the dumpsite, men could rise up, throw off the refuse, and run for freedom.[37]

Regardless of the escape method, runaways preferred to make their attempts on rainy nights because such weather would throw off the tracking hounds. But, again, once outside the walls, runners faced long odds because Union lines were so far away. Even so, historians Robert Glover and Randal Gilbert estimated that as many as one attempt in ten may have been successful, with the escapee making it back to Federal lines. One Yank who made it was Joseph T. Mills of the Seventy-seventh Illinois Infantry. Captured at Mansfield during the Red River Campaign, Mills had no intention of meekly accepting his fate. One day, while the attention of the guards was focused on a score of men out gathering wood, Mills and one comrade simply climbed the wall and jumped to freedom. With his break-mate, Mills then traveled more than 400 miles inside Confederate territory before reaching safe haven.[38]

Most runners failed to share that fate, especially after local Confederate authorities hired an old Indian as a tracker. The Indian used a pack of dogs numbering at least a dozen. If the animals discovered a scent, the Indian and his aides could catch a man afoot who had even as much as a three-day head start. One morning the dogs picked up a track at the very opening of an escape tunnel. Immediately the Native American blew a whistle to alert a bugler, who sounded the alarm. Quickly a squad of cavalry joined the tracker. Two hours later troopers returned with two escapees and by noon had herded eleven more back into the camp. On another occasion, during a nighttime thunderstorm, seven men from a Kansas outfit succeeded in climbing the walls and ran. Although they got as far as the Sabine River bottoms, hounds that usually chased runaway slaves rounded them up there. Rebel pursuers found all seven in one tree, clinging to the branches to escape the dogs.[39]

On March 14, 1864, the prisoners decided to entertain themselves and their guards by gathering together and singing popular songs of the era. The seemingly impromptu entertainment proved to be a diversion. While the event was staged and the guards distracted, fifteen men escaped by simply digging a log out of the stockade, crawling to the other side, and then running. Authorities captured thirteen of the escapees, but Capt. Robert Stott and Lt. J. D. Fry proved elusive enough to get to their own lines in Louisiana. Lt. E. J. Collins was not as lucky. On July 3, 1864, he ran, but hounds caught him and mauled him before the guards could get control of the dogs. By then, Col. J. P. Border was camp commandant. Irritated by the repeated escape attempts, he ordered guards to shoot any future escapees whether caught in the act of breaking out or recaptured later. Lesser but harsh punishments for runners included hanging prisoners by their thumbs or forcing them to stand in place for hours. Alternately, guards withheld the rations of returned escapees.[40]

Some men tried to tunnel their way out of Prison City. Most of the time, tunneling proved to be a waste of time, something often tried but seldom successful. An exception occurred in September of 1864. After weeks of tunneling, trying to get beyond the east wall of the stockade, on September 27, thirty-five prisoners broke out. Again, most were soon captured, but at least five managed to get to their own lines. Some other prisoners also tried tunneling in the fall of

Illustration 14 Non-commissioned officers of the Nineteenth Iowa Infantry after their exchange as prisoners of war, New Orleans. *Courtesy Library of Congress.*

1864, but an inmate informed the guards, who found the tunnel and collapsed it. (Why the inmate was a turncoat is unknown.)[41]

While chasing runaways and monitoring men inside the walls, guards watched conditions continue to decline through 1864. Food continued to be hard to come by, but prisoners continued to receive the same rations as their keepers. Meanwhile, Confederate officers became determined to do what they could to ease the burdens of both the prisoners and the guards. Authorities rekindled the exchange program that had earlier been discontinued. In July of 1864, 856 men at Camp Ford joined the first exchange. The Confederates took another 406 to Camp Groce, earlier closed but now reopened. In September, Confederate leaders paroled another 1,000. In February of 1865, commanders exchanged another 1,000. Such activity solved some of the problems that both Confederate soldiers and Smith County civilians had in trying to support Camp Ford. After the exchanges began, communal efforts resulted in the construction of better housing, as the prisoners built a few larger structures, such as log houses up to sixteen-feet square. The new edifices became most popular on cold, rainy nights, as up to thirty-five men might find temporary shelters in each one.[42]

Although exchanges continued, strained race relations marred the entire process. Confederate representatives constantly refused—until near the end of the war—to exchange blacks, nor would they exchange white officers who had commanded African American units. Black captives could be thankful that they at least had life, for many of their number were massacred whenever they fell into Southern hands. Although the massacre at Fort Pillow, Tennessee, remains the most famous incident, smaller episodes occurred in the Trans-Mississippi. Such an episode took place at Camp Ford where the fate of some black sailors hung in the balance. The senior Union naval officer at the camp now was Lt. Frederick Crocker who had commanded the USS *Sachem*, which Southerners had captured during the Battle of Sabine Pass. After he was exchanged, Crocker complained to superiors that the local Smith County Confederates still detained at least twenty-seven black sailors who were impressed as laborers, although in reality these men were treated like slaves. The Rebels refused to treat African Americans as prisoners of war, as had finally been agreed in October of 1864. Such black men just disappeared. Not even one of the twenty-seven men—they had probably been murdered—had their names appear on final exchange lists from May of 1865.[43]

After the war some of Camp Ford's ex-prisoners lodged serious complaints about their stay in Prison City, calling their treatment was part of a "hellish design" and part of a brutal system created to ensure that men would suffer and die. Except for the fate of the black prisoners mentioned above, such statements were exaggerations. Of the 5,200 (possibly 5,550) prisoners who once called Camp Ford home, only 286 (one source lists 289) died there (just more than 5 percent). Given a 15.5 percent death rate in all Southern prisons, Camp Ford's rate represented a very low tally. Northern prisons had a 12 percent death rate, and Ford's was, obviously, less than one-half of that.[44]

The end of Prison City came soon after Gen. Robert E. Lee surrendered at Appomattox. Rumors, started by local Confederate officials, had it that the Southern forces in the Trans-Mississippi might carry on the fight. Such news inflamed Camp Ford's remaining prisoners, who escalated their escape attempts. One hundred men, helped by a corporal of the guards, broke out in one massive effort. Such an event foreshadowed the general crumbling of Confederate authority. Rebel desertions, a major problem near the end of the war, became even more of a crisis. Looting and pillaging of government installations in Smith County became the order of the day.[45]

Given the general collapse, on May 13, Confederate authorities ordered that all Camp Ford prisoners be processed and paroled out. The next day, more keepers deserted. Now, only a few of the men of the Fifteenth Texas Cavalry remained as guards. Many of them passed their time whiskey-bound for several days and did not monitor the prisoners, some of whom joined their captors and stayed drunk as well. On May 17 the remnant of the Fifteenth Texas escorted the last 1,800 prisoners to Shreveport for processing and release. Soon, temporary occupation of Smith County began. Into Tyler rode Maj. Thomas D. Vredenburg, a veteran of Camp Ford who had earlier been exchanged. He headed a Union detail that reached the county in late June. By then local government had collapsed; all was chaos. While the major was helping to reorganize government with an eye toward law and order, some of his men knocked down part of the stockade. The rest would soon deteriorate. Prison City was no more.[46]

Notes

1   Randal B. Gilbert, "Notes on Camp Ford," copy in author's possession; James M. Smallwood, *Born in Dixie: The History of Smith County, Texas* (Austin, Texas: Eakin Press, 1999), 2 vols., 1:183. For more on Northern and Southern prisons, see William B. Hesseltine, *Civil War Prisons: A Study in War Psychology* (Columbus: Ohio State University Press, 1930) and William B. Hesseltine, ed., *Civil War Prisons* (Kent, Ohio: Kent State University Press, 1962). An older comparative work is Thomas A. Tripp's *Civil War Imprisonments: A Comparative Study of Prisons and Prisoners of Both Armies During the Civil War in the United States, 1861–1865* (privately published, 1928). For a contemporary study of camps in Dixie, see Allen O. Abbott's *Prison Life in the South: At Richmond, Macon, Savannah, Charleston, Columbia, Charlotte, Raleigh, Goldsborough, and Andersonville during the Years 1864–1865* (New York: Harper, 1865). For Andersonville, consult Ovid L. Futch, *History of Andersonville Prison* (Gainesville: University of Florida Press, 1968). For another case study, see Louis A. Brown's *The Salisbury Prison: A Case Study of Confederate Military Prisons, 1861–1865* (Wendell, North Carolina: Avera Press, 1980).

2   *Tyler Reporter*, June 27, August 1, 1861, copies in "Camp Ford," Vertical File, Archives, Smith County Historical Society, Tyler, Texas; Smallwood, *Born in Dixie*, 1:183–84. The classic work on the detention center is *Camp Ford, C. S. A.*, by F. Lee Lawrence and Robert W. Glover (Austin: Texas Civil War Centennial Advisory Committee, 1964). For a shorter summary, but one that provides new information, see Robert W. Glover and Randal B. Gilbert, "Camp Ford, Tyler, Texas: The Largest Confederate Prison Camp West of the Mississippi River," *Chronicles of Smith County, Texas* (hereafter cited as *CSC*) 28 (Winter 1989): 16–37. For a concise overview, see Vicki Betts, *Smith County, Texas, in the Civil War* (Tyler, Texas: Smith County Historical Society, 1978), 42–45.

3   Glover and Gilbert, "Camp Ford," 17–18; Gilbert, "Notes on Camp Ford," copy in author's possession; Thomas Ludwell Bryan, "The Old Stockade," *CSC* 12 (Summer 1973): 25; Smallwood, *Born in Dixie*, 1:184–85.

4   Glover and Gilbert, "Camp Ford," 17–18; Smallwood, *Born in Dixie*, 1:185.

5   Vicki Betts, "R. T. P. Allen: The Texas Years, 1857–1865," unpublished typed manuscript. Ms. Betts allowed me to use her material on Allen, and I am grateful for that favor. For Allen's orders from Kirby Smith, also see Randal B. Gilbert's booklet, *A New Look at Camp Ford* (Tyler, Texas: Smith County Historical Society, 2006), 5. Gilbert also has a section that discusses issues of prisoner exchanges and

paroles. Unfortunately, Gilbert does not attribute his sources, a blemish on an otherwise valuable work.

6   Mittie Marsh, quoted in Gilbert, *New Look*, 5.

7   Gilbert, *New Look*, 4–5.

8   Mittie Marsh to Bryan Marsh, November 12, 1863, Marsh Papers, Archives, Smith County Historical Society, Tyler, Texas.

9   Gilbert, *New Look*, 5–6; Smallwood, *Born in Dixie*, 1:186–87.

10 For more on Rosenbaum and "Smith," the supposed deserter, see Randal B. Gilbert, "The People are Relieved of their Fears: The Building of the Camp Ford Stockade," *CSC* 24 (Winter 1985): 3–5, 8; Smallwood, *Born in Dixie*, 1:188.

11 For more detail on Whitmore, see Randolph B. Campbell, *A Southern Community in Crisis: Harrison County, Texas, 1850–1880* (Austin: Texas State Historical Association, 1983), 164, 170, 173–75, 187–91, 209–10; Smallwood, *Born in Dixie*, 1:189. For a review of Whitmore's career, see Randolph B. Campbell, "George W. Whitmore: East Texas Unionist," *East Texas Historical Journal* 28 (Spring 1990): 17–27.

12 Gilbert, *New Look*, 8; Glover and Gilbert, "Camp Ford," 20–21; Gilbert, "The People are Relieved of their Fears," 2–7; Smallwood, *Born in Dixie*, 1:189.

13 William May, "Prison Papers," in *The Old Flag: Fiftieth Anniversary* (Department of Connecticut Grand Army of the Republic, 1914), copy in "Camp Ford," Vertical File, Archives, Smith County Historical Society, Tyler, Texas. May and others held a fifty-year reunion of the veterans in Camp Ford and published the above-cited booklet, the pages of which are unnumbered.

14 Sarah A. Carter to Milton Carter, Jr., November 15, 1863, in Andrew L. Leath, ed., "News from Flora, 1863: The Carter Letters," *CSC* 25 (Summer 1986): 28; Gilbert, "The People of Tyler are Relieved of Their Fears, 1–9; Glover and Gilbert, "Camp Ford," 20; Betts, *Civil War*, 42–43. For more on early escapes and attempted escapes from Camp Ford, see Kate Stone, *Brokenburn: The Journal of Kate Stone, 1861–1868*, ed. John Q. Anderson (Baton Rouge: Louisiana State University Press, 1955), 257–58.

15 Glover and Gilbert, "Camp Ford," 23–24, 30, 32; Gilbert, "Notes on Camp Ford," copy in author's possession; William W. Heartsill, *Fourteen Hundred and 91 Days in the Confederate Army*, ed. Bell Irvin Wiley (Jackson, Tennessee: McCowat-Mercer Press, 1953), 200; Bryan, "Old Stockade," 25; Betts, "R. T. P. Allen," 10. For the dimensions of the expanded camp, see Gilbert, *New Look*, 9.

16 William May, "Prison Papers," in "Camp Ford," Vertical File, Archives, Smith County Historical Society, Tyler, Texas.

17 Glover and Gilbert, "Camp Ford," 22–23, 26; Betts, *Civil War*, 43–44; Gilbert, *New Look*, 9.

18 McKinney, William F., "The Diary of Captain William F. McKinney," intro. and ed. by Randal B. Gilbert, *CSC* 25 (Summer 1986): 15–25.

19 Ibid., 23.

20 The poem is from A. J. H. Duganne's *Camps and Prisons*, quoted in James P. Douglas, *Douglas's Texas Battery*, ed. Lucia Rutherford (Tyler, Texas: Smith County

Historical Society, 1966), 139. Duganne's remembrance is also republished in *The Old Flag: Fiftieth Anniversary*, unnumbered pages, copy in "Camp Ford," Vertical File, Archives, Smith County Historical Society.

21 May, "Prison Papers," in *The Old Flag: Fiftieth Anniversary*, unnumbered pages, copy in "Camp Ford," Vertical File, Archives, Smith County Historical Society, Tyler, Texas.

22 Anonymous, quoted in *The Old Flag: Fiftieth Anniversary*, unnumbered page, copy in "Camp Ford," Vertical File, Archives, Smith County Historical Society, Tyler, Texas.

23 Ibid.

24 Ibid.; Smallwood, *Born in Dixie*, 1:197, 200.

25 John B. Beach, "Camp Ford Prisoner," manuscript, copy in "Camp Ford," Vertical File, Archives, Smith County Historical Society; A. J. Swanger to R. E. Francis, February 3, 1895, "Camp Ford," Vertical File, Archives, Smith County Historical Society, Tyler, Texas; Smallwood, *Born in Dixie*, 1:202–3.

26 "The Jolly Cock Robin," in "Notes Made by Captain May," *The Old Flag: Fiftieth Anniversary*, unnumbered pages, copy in "Camp Ford," Vertical File, Archives, Smith County Historical Society, Tyler, Texas.

27 May, "Prison Papers," ibid.

28 Beach, "Camp Ford Prisoner," manuscript, "Camp Ford," Vertical File, Archives, Smith County Historical Society, Tyler, Texas.

29 Augustine J. Duganne, *Camps and Prisons* (New York: n.p., 1865), 38081.

30 Ibid.

31 Aaron T. Sutton, *Prisoner of the Rebels in Texas: The Civil War Narrative of Aaron T. Sutton*, ed. David G. MacLean (Decatur, Indiana: American Books, 1978), 22.

32 Glover and Gilbert, "Camp Ford," 24–25; Bryan, "Old Stockade," 25–27; newspaper clipping, n.d., "Camp Ford," Vertical File, Archives, Smith County Historical Society, Tyler, Texas; Betts, *Civil War*, 43–44.

33 Sutton, *Prisoner in Texas*, 39.

34 Glover and Gilbert, "Camp Ford," *CSC*, 25; Bryan, "Old Stockade," *CSC*, 27; Betts, *Civil War*, 44–45; Sutton, *Prisoner in Texas*, 39; *War of the Rebellion: A Compilation of the Official Records of the Union and Confederate Armies*, comp. Robert N. Scott, (Washington, D.C.: Government Printing Office, 1880–1901), 2, 8:196.

35 McKinney, "McKinney Diary," ed. Gilbert, *CSC*, 21; Bryan, "Old Stockade," *CSC*, 26–27; Glover and Gilbert, "Camp Ford," *CSC*, 27–28.

36 *Tyler Daily Courier-Times*, April 14, 1911; McKinney, "McKinney Diary," ed. Gilbert, *CSC*, 21; Glover and Gilbert, "Camp Ford," *CSC*, 27–28.

37 Sutton, *Prisoner in Texas*, 24–26; newspaper clipping, n.d., "Camp Ford," Vertical File, Archives, Smith County Historical Society, Tyler, Texas.

38 Joseph T. Mills, "Civil War Memoir," manuscript, in "Camp Ford," Vertical File, Archives, Smith County Historical Society, Tyler, Texas; Glover and Gilbert, "Camp Ford," *CSC*, 27–29.

39 Sutton, *Prisoner in Texas*, 28–29.

40   McKinney, "McKinney Diary," ed. Gilbert, *CSC*, 18–20; Gilbert, *New Look*,
      16–18.

41   Gilbert, *New Look*, 16–18.

42   Newspaper clipping, n.d., "Camp Ford," Vertical File, Archives, Smith County
      Historical Society, Tyler, Texas; Glover and Gilbert, "Camp Ford," *CSC*, 24–25;
      Bryan, "Old Stockade," *CSC*, 25–27.

43   On the muddled confusion regarding black prisoners, see Glover and Gilbert,
      "Camp Ford," *CSC*, 30, 32–33.

44   Betts, *Civil War*, 77, 79; Smallwood, *Born in Dixie*, 1:210. Gilbert has a raw
      figure of 321 deaths but believes that number is an over-count because of the
      poor recordkeeping by the Quartermaster's Department. For example, some men
      were listed twice (some three times) on death rolls and, in other cases, the same
      deceased Yankee's name was listed on more than one grave. Gilbert notes these
      errors and estimates that the true figure would be approximately 289. See, Gilbert,
      New Look, 15–16. For a brief comparison of Northern and Southern prisons, but
      one that does not mention Camp Ford, see James M. McPherson, *Battle Cry of
      Freedom* (New York: Oxford University Press, 1988), 796–97, 800–2.

45   Betts, *Civil War*, 77, 79; Glover and Gilbert, "Camp Ford," *CSC*, 33–34.

46   Glover and Gilbert, "Camp Ford," *CSC*, 33–34; Smallwood, *Born in Dixie*,
      1:210–11.

Part IV

Political, Social, and Cultural Life during the War

Chapter 13

The Confederate Governors of Texas

by Kenneth E. Hendrickson, Jr.

In 1863 James P. Newcomb, the Unionist editor of the *San Antonio Alamo Express,* penned the following:

> The man who prophesies, even at this day, the end of the present troubles, risks his reputation for sanity, but if there is any certainty in Heaven or earth the present Southern Confederacy must perish—it is founded on no principles of liberty or right—it is the work of satanic ambition, and terrible will be its end.[1]

His words were prophetic, but in 1861 few would have believed it. Most Texans, including their political leaders, hailed secession as a step toward liberty and freedom—an escape from the exploitation of the "abolitionist hordes" of the

Illustration 15 Texas Governor's Mansion. *Courtesy Library of Congress.*

North. And so, the birth of the Confederacy was met with joy, a joy that would be short-lived. As the Confederacy began to crumble and decay, the burdens of leadership became almost unbearable. In Texas these burdens were borne, in part, by three men: Edward Clark, Francis R. Lubbock, and Pendleton Murrah. Each faced major problems and mounting stress, although it was Murrah who was most deeply affected.

This is their story.

In the wake of the Republican victory in the election of 1860 and the rise of the secessionist movement immediately thereafter, some were filled with grim foreboding. Among them was the old warrior Governor Sam Houston, who had long counseled that secession meant disaster. But few listened to him. The Texas Secession Convention convened as scheduled on January 28, 1861, and soon passed an ordinance proposing that the state leave the Union. Houston was asked to attend the meeting and did so, but was unable to affect the outcome. The ordinance went to the people on February 23, and passed by a vote of 46,129 to 14,697. There were numerous citizens who declined to vote and eighteen counties actually cast a majority vote of no, but the outcome was hailed by most. Once the secession ordinance passed, Houston recommended to the legislature that Texas decline to join the Confederacy, but instead remain independent. The convention, of course, rejected this proposal and passed an ordinance requiring all state officials to take an oath of allegiance to the Confederacy. After prayerful consideration on the night of March 25, Houston refused to take the oath on the following day. Immediately thereafter, the office of governor was declared vacant and Houston was ordered to vacate the mansion. Many years later, Unionist William Baker, a Presbyterian minister in Austin, remembered that fateful moment:

As I look back into the darkness of those days, the central figure of them all is that of the old governor sitting in his chair in the basement of the Capitol . . . sorrowfully meditating what it was best to do. . . . The officers of the gathering upstairs summoned the old man three times to come forward and take the oath of allegiance. . . . I remember as yesterday three calls thrice rejected. Sam Houston! Sam Houston! Sam Houston! But the old man sat silent, immovable, in his chair, whittling steadily on.[2]

In his last message to the legislature Houston accepted the will of the people, but declared the action of the convention illegal and maintained that all legal authority remained in his hands. But his declaration proved to be an empty gesture. He gathered his family together and vacated his office and the governor's mansion, never to return. On March 18, 1861, the very day that Houston submitted his last message to the legislature, Lieutenant Governor Edward Clark was sworn in as the first governor of the Confederate era.[3]

Clark was born in New Orleans on April 1, 1818. He was the nephew of a famous governor of Georgia and a descendant of George Rogers Clark of

Revolutionary War fame. Hence, he could claim to be a member of one of the South's most distinguished families, but by the time of his birth his father, Elijah, had fallen on hard times and was forced to move the family to Georgia. Elijah died in the early 1830s when Edward was a teenager, and shortly thereafter, he and his mother moved to Montgomery, Alabama. There, Edward studied law and was admitted to the bar. He married in 1840, but his wife, Lucy, soon died. Several months after his wife's death, Clark moved to Texas and opened a law office in Marshall. In 1849 he married Martha Melissa Evans who eventually bore him four children.

Meanwhile, Clark became active in public affairs. He was a delegate to the Constitutional Convention of 1845 and served in the first state legislature where he was appointed to numerous standing committees. After the outbreak of the war with Mexico, Clark volunteered for service and was made aide-de-camp to General J. P. Henderson, a former governor. During the war he was cited for his gallantry at the Battle of Monterrey. Returning to private life at the end of the war, Clark was elected to the state senate and then became secretary of state during the administration of Governor Elisha M. Pease. He left that position after Pease's retirement and was soon named commissioner of claims by the legislature. In 1859 he ran for lieutenant governor against Francis R. Lubbock and was elected. Unlike Sam Houston, the new governor, he was an avid supporter of the secessionist movement.[4]

By the time Clark assumed office, conflict between the United States and the newly formed Confederate States of America seemed inevitable, but Texas was ill prepared for the struggle. Despite the fact that U.S. forces withdrew, leaving most of their livestock and equipment behind, the state faced serious problems. Money was scarce and both the coast and frontier lay unprotected from possible attack by hostile Indians or U.S. forces. With respect to the financial crisis, Clark asked State Comptroller Clement R. Johns for advice and the latter responded by proposing that the legislature issue one million dollars worth of 8 percent bonds, increase the ad valorem tax from 12.5 cents to 16.5 cents, and double the poll tax from fifty cents to a dollar. Clark agreed and the legislature acted swiftly. The governor then appointed Ebenezer B. Nichols, a prominent Galveston businessman, to sell the bonds and purchase arms.[5]

Clark also turned his attention to defense. John S. "Rip" Ford, the famous Ranger, raised a regiment tasked with the defense of the Rio Grande borderlands, and Henry E. McCulloch organized another regiment to defend the northwest frontier. Meanwhile, Clark negotiated with the newly formed Confederate government in Montgomery concerning the vital matters of recruitment and defense. He called upon Secretary of War Leroy Walker to assure him that the Confederate government would bear the cost of frontier defense, but did not receive a satisfactory reply. At the same time, Walker asked Clark to call for volunteers to be drilled, equipped, and held in readiness. Clark agreed to Walker's request and on April 17, 1861, he issued a proclamation dividing the state into six military districts for purposes of recruiting and training volunteer units.[6]

On April 12, 1861, Confederate shore batteries at Charleston, South Carolina, opened fire on Fort Sumter and the Civil War began. No one knew how long and disastrous the war would be, but at the outset most Texans were eager to fight. On April 24, Clark issued a call for more volunteers and simultaneously began a search for more weapons and equipment to arm the volunteers. Thus far Ebenezer Nichols had had little success in selling Texas bonds, so the financial crisis continued. Nevertheless, later in the summer Clark, ever the optimist, appointed three additional purchasing agents to go in search of weapons for the troops. But at the same time he was inundated with pleas from people all over the state to provide them with weapons to defend themselves from possible attacks by U.S. troops or Indians.[7]

Shortly after Col. Earl Van Dorn, the newly appointed Confederate military commander of Texas, arrived in San Antonio, Clark began to correspond with him about the urgent need to defend the coast and the frontier. Van Dorn assured him that he had a plan. Clark was also concerned about the possibility of attacks by Mexican bandits along the Rio Grande, and wrote to the governors of Nuevo León, Coahuila, and Tamaulipas expressing his desire to continue friendly relations with their people. Meanwhile, Clark continued to enroll troops and search with little success for supplies. In June, in response to pressure from Confederate officials, he issued a proclamation establishing eleven new camps of instruction. Volunteers were to report to the camps for training while they waited for orders from the Confederate government. These men were required to furnish their own weapons and supplies. At the same time, Secretary of War Walker asked Clark to assist in finding supplies for the army and the governor responded by appealing to the people for help. He issued a proclamation calling upon Texans to form county committees and societies to collect blankets, comforters, and warm clothing for the troops fighting in Arkansas, Kentucky, and Virginia. He also informed Walker that wool could be converted into cloth by prisoners at the state penitentiary and soon quartermasters from most Southern states had contracted with penitentiary officials for such services. This practice continued until near the end of the war.[8]

Edward Clark hoped to be re-elected in August of 1861, but was not even endorsed by the state Democratic Party. The reason for this slight is not clear, especially since Clark had served effectively and was dedicated to the Confederate cause and the welfare of the state. The state Democratic Party, in fact, did not endorse anybody, so the campaign turned into a free-for-all involving three candidates: Clark, Lieutenant Governor Francis R. Lubbock, and General

Thomas Jefferson Chambers. All three promised to prosecute the war with vigor and to cooperate with the Confederate government, but it soon became clear that Lubbock was the favorite of the party leadership and most of the press. Even so, the election was close. Lubbock received 21,854 votes to 21,730 for Clark, while Chambers trailed with 13,733. Thus, Francis Lubbock was elected by a margin of 124 votes.[9]

Governor Clark deserves more attention than he has received from most Texas historians. As the first wartime governor, he faced enormous problems and coped with them reasonably well. Although he was unable to solve the financial difficulties he faced, he succeeded in providing the Confederacy with some 20,000 volunteers and worked hard to reorganize the state's militia system. At the same time he tried to observe the legal limitations of his office while of necessity exercising more power and authority than any previous governor.

After leaving office, Clark was commissioned a colonel in the Confederate army's Fourteenth Texas Infantry Regiment. This regiment was attached to Walker's Division in Louisiana in 1863 and 1864, and participated in the battles of Pleasant Hill and Mansfield in the Red River Campaign. Clark was wounded at Pleasant Hill and was soon discharged from the army. At the end of the war he fled to Mexico, fearing reprisals from the United States government. However, he soon returned to his home in Marshall where he engaged in some business pursuits and practiced law. He died on May 4, 1880, and was buried in Marshall.[10]

Francis R. Lubbock became the second Civil War governor of Texas in November 1861. He was born in Beaufort, South Carolina, on October 15, 1815, and received some education there, but was forced to go to work at an early age because of his father's death. After a short time as a hardware store clerk and manager of a cotton warehouse in Hamburg, South Carolina, he moved to New Orleans where he opened a drugstore. Soon he met, courted, and married Adele Baron, the daughter of a prominent cotton merchant.

In October 1836, Lubbock went to Texas in search of his brother Tom who had been fighting in the revolution. He found his brother and returned to New Orleans only to go back to Texas in January 1837. There he settled in the new town of Houston and went into the mercantile business. At the same time he became involved in politics and public service. He was chosen assistant clerk of the Texas House of Representatives in 1837 and became chief clerk in 1838. When Sam Houston assumed the presidency, he made Lubbock comptroller of the republic. During the presidency of Mirabeau Lamar, Lubbock returned to private life, but when Houston resumed the presidency in 1841, he asked Lubbock to resume his duties as comptroller. Lubbock agreed but soon resigned the post to become district clerk of Harris County. During the 1840s Lubbock operated a ranch south of Houston and continued to serve as district clerk. He was one of the organizers of the Democratic Party in Texas and in the mid-1850s parted ways with his old friend Houston in a dispute over the Know-Nothing movement. In 1857, Hardin Runnels defeated Houston in the race for the governor's chair and Lubbock defeated Edward Clark for lieutenant governor. Two years later, Runnels and Lubbock were defeated by Houston and Clark.[11]

As the dispute between the North and the South over slavery spiraled out of control in 1860, Lubbock traveled to Charleston, South Carolina, as one of Texas's eight delegates to the Democratic convention. After the convention split, he served as temporary chair of the faction that nominated John C. Breckinridge for president. He favored the breakup of the Union in the event of a Republican victory and when Lincoln won he made speeches and wrote letters urging secession. Then on April 18, 1861, he announced that he would run for governor. He had been urged by many friends to do this and firmly believed that he could be elected. But, when the state convention met in Dallas on May 27, there was no quorum, so the delegates who were present agreed to adjourn without making a nomination. This decision led to the three-man race in August that Lubbock won.[12]

Shortly after the election, Lubbock decided to visit Richmond, the new Confederate capital, to, as he put it, "better inform myself of public affairs." After a grueling trip, he arrived to find the city, "a-stir with warlike preparation . . . the air resonated with the blare of military music, Confederate flags floating from public and private buildings." He visited with President Jefferson Davis and concluded that he was "pre-eminently fitted for the high position to which he had been called by the unanimous voice of the South," a view that he never abandoned although he could not have been more wrong.[13]

Lubbock returned to Texas in October, settled affairs at his ranch, and journeyed to Austin. There, on November 7, 1861, he was sworn in as the second governor of Confederate Texas. In his inaugural address to the legislature he summarized his view of the conflict that had recently begun:

> It has been said, gentlemen, that this is a war for slavery. I tell you it's a war for liberty! Upon the issue of this war must depend our status in all time to come. We must either maintain our liberties by strong arms and stout hearts, or we must consent to become the most abject slaves of the basest, most corrupt, and vulgar despotism that ever clutched in its horrid grasp the liberties of a free people.[14]

He called upon his associates to support the troops, have faith in the Confederate government, and be prepared to make whatever sacrifices might be required to win. He promised a fair and impartial administration that would be dedicated to the benefit of all the people. He reminded the lawmakers that their most pressing immediate needs were to provide for more effective frontier and coastal defenses and to deal with the continuing financial crisis.[15]

On November 15, Lubbock again addressed the legislature, this time with specific recommendations for action. He proposed an increase in the ad valorem tax from 16.5 to 25 cents per $100 and the issue of non-interest-bearing treasury warrants. He also called for the development of a plan for frontier defense, a revision of the militia law to improve the system inaugurated by Governor Clark, the establishment of a state cannon factory, and the expansion of the penitentiary. The legislature soon set to work to deal with Lubbock's proposals. It passed a new militia act dividing the state into thirty-three districts and made all white males liable for military service. This law also provided for periodic military training and authorized the government to institute a draft by lottery if there were not enough volunteers. Later, Lubbock was to enforce this system vigorously, a policy that eroded his popularity. The legislature also created a frontier regiment whose companies were to be stationed at posts about twenty-five miles apart. The governor was authorized to petition the Confederate government in Richmond to take this unit into national service provided it would always be under state control and would never leave the state. In January 1862, the legislature accepted most of Lubbock's financial proposals. They raised the ad valorem and poll taxes and re-established a license fee to be imposed on doctors, lawyers, and dentists. Also, state treasury warrants and Confederate treasury notes were made receivable for state taxes and state lands.[16]

Early in January the acting Confederate Secretary of War, Judah P. Benjamin, proposed that Texas exchange 5 percent U.S. indemnity bonds held by the state for 8 percent Confederate bonds so that the U.S. bonds could be used by Richmond to purchase arms and ammunition. Lubbock agreed and asked the legislature to legalize the transaction. On January 11, the lawmakers complied by passing two laws. The first of these created the Texas State Military Board, consisting of the governor, the treasurer, and the comptroller. The board was authorized to replace any bonds held by the state with Confederate bonds. It was also empowered to issue $500,000 worth of state bonds to buy military supplies and to establish armament factories, but these efforts bore little fruit. The military board members had very little luck in their efforts to exchange Texas bonds for arms. The bonds, after all, were essentially worthless. The board was only slightly more successful in its attempt at another approach, which was to persuade planters to sell cotton to them in exchange for 8 percent state bonds. The state would then use the cotton to buy supplies from Mexico and Europe. As to the manufacture of arms, the board established a foundry and a cap and cartridge factory in Austin. The former produced only a few cannons, but the latter was a little more successful. Despite these problems, the board met constantly during Lubbock's administration trying desperately to carry out its mission. In the long run, however, it must be judged to have been a failure.[17]

Meanwhile, Lubbock had been devoting most of his time to defense needs. His concerns about the vulnerability of the state's long coastline, which stretched from the Sabine in the east to the Rio Grande in the west, was particularly acute. This vast region was ill prepared to defend against a seaborne attack—Galveston was especially vulnerable—and to make matters worse, Lubbock had no confidence in Brig. Gen. Paul O. Hébert, the new Confederate military commander in Texas. Hébert, from Louisiana, was an engineer, not a military tactician. Moreover, he lacked imagination and the intestinal fortitude required to meet and overcome major difficulties. When Lubbock wrote to Hébert inquiring about his plans, the general had no encouraging reply. He wrote that there were too few men and supplies available and that his responsibilities would probably drive him to an early grave.[18]

Replying to Hébert's pessimism, Lubbock said it would be better to destroy the city than to let it fall into enemy hands. When Galvestonians learned of this, many concluded that Lubbock was recommending that the city be burned. He hastened to deny this charge, but his fears were, in fact, soon realized. In May of 1862, Capt. Henry Eagle, in command of U.S. naval forces off Galveston, demanded the town's surrender. Hébert refused, but at the same time ordered all civilians to evacuate the island. Lubbock supported this move, but continued to urge Hébert to go on the offensive. When Galveston was soon occupied by Federal troops, Lubbock was furious and felt great relief when Hébert was replaced by Brig. Gen. John Bankhead Magruder.

Unlike Hébert, Magruder was a warrior, although he had a mixed record. Born in Virginia in 1810, and educated there, he graduated from West Point in 1830. He fought in the war with Mexico and was brevetted major for gallantry at Cerro Gordo and lieutenant colonel at Chapultepec. He resigned from the U.S. Army when Virginia seceded from the Union, and joined the forces of the Confederate States of America. He was made brigadier general as a result of his action in the Battle of Big Bethel and for a time was in command of part of the army opposing McClellan's advance during the Peninsular Campaign, but at the Battle of Malvern Hill on July 1, 1862, his regiment was late arriving on the scene of Robert E. Lee's planned assault on the Union line. Lee was furious. He stripped Magruder of his command and exiled him to Texas where he arrived in October determined to restore his reputation. Galveston presented the opportunity, and his assault on the island city commenced on January 1, 1863. The attack was successful; the occupying Federal force was overpowered and Galveston remained in Confederate hands for the duration of the war.[19]

Among other difficulties, Lubbock, in concert with other western governors, was concerned about the ability and willingness of Richmond to defend the Trans-Mississippi region. With Memphis and New Orleans in Federal hands, some speculated that the Trans-Mississippi states might be abandoned.

In fact, Governor Henry M. Rector of Arkansas went so far as to suggest that his state, along with Texas and Missouri, might consider forming their own government. Rector's proposal worried Lubbock and he wrote to President Davis to assure him that Texas was loyal to the Confederacy. Davis responded by sending Maj. Guy M. Bryan to confer with the governor. Bryan suggested that Lubbock invite the governors of Arkansas, Louisiana, and Mississippi to a conference in Marshall, Texas, to discuss defense needs.

Only Governor Claiborne Jackson of Mississippi attended the meeting, but Rector of Arkansas and Thomas O. Moore of Louisiana endorsed the outcome. The governors asked that Davis appoint a commanding general over all the states west of the Mississippi, that the Confederate treasury be empowered to issue money, and that the southwest states be provided with twenty to thirty thousand small arms to equip their soldiers. They also issued an address to their people urging support for the government and calling upon them to prepare to make further sacrifices in support of the war effort. Lubbock was pleased with the outcome of the Marshall Conference, but he was not optimistic that the government could provide the needed support.[20]

At the same time, Lubbock had other issues at home. There was growing Unionist activity in some parts of the state and increasing opposition to the conscription law passed by the Confederate Congress in April 1862. In the Red River counties, especially Cooke County, where secession had never been popular, citizens formed the Peace Party in the summer of 1862 to oppose taxation and conscription and, according to rumors, assist in a Union invasion from Kansas. Confederate supporters there rounded up many alleged members of the Peace Party, conducted mock trials, and executed forty-two people, most of them innocent. Lubbock did nothing to intervene on behalf of law and order.[21]

Simultaneously, the Union Loyal League appeared in the Hill Country. Consisting mostly of German Texans, this group sought to destabilize the Confederacy and reinstate Federal authority, by force, if necessary. In response, Lubbock sent a company of Confederate cavalry and Texas state troops to the area to suppress a possible insurrection. One group of Germans— about sixty-one people—fled this onslaught but were followed and caught near the West Texas town of Brackettville on August 10, 1862. There ensued a skirmish that came to be known as the Battle of Nueces resulting in casualties on both sides. Then, after surrendering, many of the Germans were murdered. Incidents such as these reflected the increasing tensions that were building in Texas as the war wore on, but despite these atrocities, some opposition continued.[22]

As problems concerning finances, personnel, and home defense continued to plague Lubbock and his associates, they were enraged by President Lincoln's announcement of the Emancipation Proclamation set to go into effect on January 1, 1863. In response, Lubbock called the legislature into special session in February. In his address to the lawmakers, the governor urged them to continue to support President Davis in his efforts to thwart Lincoln's "scheme" to "Africanize" the Southern Confederacy. He went on to review his own efforts. He commented on his plans to provide more troops and supplies for the military and asked the legislators for even more support. He wanted a new plan for more adequate frontier defense, more assistance for the soldiers' families, higher taxes, and finally, he called for legislation designed to limit cotton production and encourage the production of grain crops. Then, he closed by surprising the lawmakers with the announcement that he would not run for re-election.[23] It is not clear why he did this, but it was probably because he knew that, despite his obvious devotion to the cause, many believed him to be too harsh and arbitrary as an administrator.

The special session lasted for one month, from February 5 to March 6, 1863, during which time the lawmakers considered most of Lubbock's proposals. They increased the ad valorem tax and imposed additional taxes on loans, financial transactions, liquor, and certain occupations. They discussed ways to limit cotton production, but passed no bill on the issue. As for frontier defense, they created the Mounted Regiment of Texas State Troops, but appropriated only $800,000 for its support, a sum Lubbock deemed utterly inadequate. They also approved the transfer of the regiment to Confederate service, but only on condition that it remain in Texas to defend the frontier, a condition that Jefferson Davis never approved. Finally, the legislature appropriated $600,000 for the relief of soldiers' families. Lubbock was both pleased and disappointed by this measure. He was grateful for its passage, but believed the appropriation was too small.[24]

During the final months of his administration, Lubbock continued to face major problems. There had been claims of corruption and mismanagement at the state penitentiary in connection with the cloth-production program. A special legislative committee investigated, but found no indication of malfeasance, much to Lubbock's relief. Much more serious was the fall of Vicksburg to Union forces led by Ulysses S. Grant in early July. This disaster meant that Texas and the Southwest were now completely cut off from the rest of the Confederacy. To deal with this crisis, E. Kirby Smith, now in command of the Trans-Mississippi Department, called for a conference of the Southwest governors to meet in Marshall in early August.

The second Marshall Conference was well attended. In addition to Lubbock, Governor Thomas O. Moore of Louisiana and Governor Thomas C. Reynolds of Confederate Missouri were there. Also, a number of judges and senators from Texas, Louisiana, Arkansas, and Missouri attended. Lubbock was chosen to be chairman. After several days of discussion, the conferees issued a number of resolutions. They recommended the appointment of a special agent to deal with

French and Mexican authorities in Mexico, they urged Smith to assume greater power in dealing with defense issues, they gave Smith a vote of confidence, and they called on their people to support the Confederacy despite the major problems that obviously lay ahead. Lubbock was happy with the results of the conference and returned to Austin where he spent the remaining months of his term dealing with virtually never-ending pleas for money, men, supplies, and unsettling correspondence.[25]

In September and October, Lubbock received two communications that deeply angered him. The first was from Monsieur B. Therón, the French consul at Galveston, who suggested that if Texas would declare its independence, France would offer support and assistance. Outraged at such a proposal, Lubbock informed Therón that Texas had no intention of leaving the Confederacy. He then forwarded the letter to President Davis who quickly expelled the Frenchman from the country. The second troubling correspondence came from John Tyler, a son of the former president. Tyler pointed out that since Texas was once a part of the Louisiana Territory, Texans had a legal right to appeal to France for aid. Assuming that this shocking proposal was little more than an effort to split the Confederacy, Lubbock ignored it.[26]

When he left office on November 5, 1863, Francis R. Lubbock was proud of his achievements. He had secured the frontier from Indian attacks, he had improved the financial condition of the state, he had worked hard to meet troop quotas, and he had provided assistance for soldiers' families. Moreover, during his term of office, Union forces had been driven from Galveston and the invasion of Texas through Sabine Pass had been miraculously thwarted. True, the Trans-Mississippi West was cut off and there was growing war-weariness, but Lubbock was still optimistic. In fact, the Confederate victory at Chickamauga gave him real hope that the war could still be won.[27]

In December 1863, Lubbock, having been commissioned lieutenant colonel, joined the staff of Gen. John Bankhead Magruder. After a few months in that position, he was reassigned to the staff of Gen. John A. Wharton in Louisiana and then in August of 1864 he went to Richmond to serve as aide-de-camp to President Davis. Along with Davis, Lubbock fled from Richmond in April 1865, and was captured in Georgia on May 10. After serving several months in prison at Fort Delaware, Lubbock returned to Texas and resumed his business activities. His ventures were not particularly successful and after several years he re-entered politics. In 1878 he was elected state treasurer and held that post for twelve years. During the Hogg administration, he served on the State Board of Pardons after which he retired from public life in 1895. He was eighty years of age. He remained in Austin for the last ten years of his life and died there on June 22, 1905. He was buried in the state cemetery in a coffin draped with both the United States and Confederate flags.[28]

The third and last governor of Texas during the Confederate era was Pendleton Murrah. Murrah was born in South Carolina, probably illegitimate, and was raised in an orphanage. The date of his birth is unknown, but was more than likely in the late 1820s. In 1845, with the help of his benefactors, he matriculated at Brown University in Providence, Rhode Island, and graduated in 1848. He then moved to Alabama where he studied law and was admitted to the bar. Suffering from ill health, probably tuberculosis, he moved in 1850 to Texas where he hoped the dry climate would help him regain his health. Unfortunately, he settled in Marshall in East Texas where the climate was not much different from that of Alabama, so his health did not improve, but his fortunes certainly did. His law practice flourished and he married Sue Taylor, the daughter of a wealthy planter.

Murrah first entered politics in 1855 as a candidate for the state legislature, but was defeated by Lemuel Dawes of the Know-Nothing Party. Two years later he tried again and was successful and in 1858 he was chosen a member of the Democratic State Executive Committee. In 1861 he considered running for the Confederate Congress, but withdrew because of his poor health. But then, in spite of his health, he joined the Fourteenth Texas Infantry Regiment commanded by former governor Edward Clark where he served for only a short time; his health problems forcing him to resign his commission.

Apparently, over the next year or so, Murrah's health improved sufficiently for him to consider running for governor when urged to do so by some of his friends. At first, it appeared that several men would seek the office. These included Murrah; his eventual opponent, Thomas Jefferson Chambers, a wealthy Gulf Coast planter; Guy M. Bryan, a former congressman; Fletcher Stockdale, a South Texas lawyer; Milton M. Potter, a Texas legislator; and William P. Hill, Confederate judge of the Eastern District.

One by one, for various reasons, most of the candidates dropped out leaving only Murrah and Chambers to complete the race. Each man had both advantages and disadvantages. Chambers was better known than Murrah, but suffered from rumors that he was critical of Jefferson Davis's leadership. The *Tri-Weekly Gazette* in Austin supported him and attempted to quell the rumors, but Murrah had the support of most of the press because he was generally viewed as the administration's candidate. In the end, Murrah won the August 1863 election that featured a very light voter turnout.

Murrah's victory was viewed by most observers as an endorsement of the Davis administration and an indication that state officials intended to work closely with Confederate authorities. In his inaugural address, Murrah did, in fact, pledge the loyalty of the state to Richmond and stressed the need for further sacrifices by the people, but he also spoke of the need to define the borders of power and authority between the state and the Confederate government.

Shortly thereafter, in a message to the legislature, Murrah referred once again to the issues that had concerned Clark and Lubbock: the problem of frontier defense, the need for arms and ammunition, a stable economy, militia reorganization, and penitentiary reform. Implied in his remarks was the question of the mutual roles of the state and Confederate government in dealing with these vital concerns.[29]

As it turned out, Pendleton Murrah would serve as governor of Texas during the last desperate days of the Confederacy and would face problems he could never have imagined. The worst of these arose from his efforts to defend state sovereignty while at the same time cooperating with the ever-increasing demands of the Confederate military and political authorities. His problems began early in his administration in connection with his dealings with Gen. John Bankhead Magruder, still the commander of Confederate military forces in Texas. In December 1863, Magruder called upon Texas planters to provide the military with the use of their slaves to build fortifications. When Murrah objected to this proposal, Gen. E. Kirby Smith, Magruder's superior, offered a compromise by suggesting that Magruder require the use of only 25 percent of the male slaves, but again Murrah balked. In a long, detailed letter to the general he declared that he would not allow the Confederate military authorities to exercise a free hand in the matter of impressment. If the army needed slave labor, he wrote, let it be obtained by contract rather than impressment.[30]

Murrah also clashed with Magruder over the question of the enrollment of troops in the army. Since November of 1862, the state had routinely enrolled men subject to Confederate conscription in the state militia and the government, although it disapproved of this practice, had never intervened. However, in 1863 eight thousand state troops had been temporarily placed under Confederate command to defend the coast, and Magruder wanted them to remain under Confederate control for the duration of the war. In December of 1863, the legislature passed a militia act that ignored Magruder's desires and extended the policy of enrolling eligible men in the state militia. Under this law, men in the border counties would be used for frontier defense and others would be subject to the governor's call. The law caused much confusion. Men whose homes were in frontier counties but were serving elsewhere left their units and went home. Others believed the law meant that they were no longer subject to Confederate control, and still others, believing the law meant that their period of service was over, simply headed home.[31]

Meanwhile, the bickering between Magruder and Murrah continued with Magruder claiming that Confederate law trumped state law and Murrah claiming that where the Confederacy and the state had concurrent jurisdiction, the Confederacy should be willing to compromise. In February 1864, E. Kirby Smith intervened in an attempt to settle the dispute. He met with Murrah and

Magruder in Houston and proposed a compromise whereby the state would retain control of those men already under arms provided they could be called up by the Confederacy in case of emergency. Although not entirely pleased with this arrangement, Murrah agreed.[32]

Soon, the emergency occurred when in March it became clear that the Union advance up the Red River posed a major threat. Magruder called upon Murrah to transfer control of state troops to the Confederacy at once in order to reinforce those fighting in Louisiana. Murrah resisted saying that he would only turn state troops over to Magruder for service inside the state and even then he wanted them to remain under the command of their own officers and brigade organizations. Magruder agreed to the first demand but not the second and the impasse continued until early April when Murrah finally yielded to Magruder's repeated pleas for help. The governor's decision temporarily ended the controversy over the control of state militiamen, but the issue was not fully resolved before the war ended a year later.[33]

The second bitter controversy between Murrah and the Confederate authorities involved cotton, virtually the only exchange commodity of value in the state. In a desperate effort to obtain money for the purchase of arms and supplies, Kirby Smith set out to take over the cotton trade. He created the Cotton Bureau with headquarters in Shreveport and a branch office, known as the Texas Cotton Office, in Houston. Beginning operations in December 1863, the Cotton Office was empowered to buy half of a planter's crop with Confederate specie certificates. The other half would be exempt from impressment. Of course, Texas planters immediately objected to this scheme for several reasons. Most saw it as an unacceptable intrusion into their private affairs, but above all was their lack of confidence in the ability of the Confederacy to honor its financial commitments.

To counter the threat to state sovereignty by the Cotton Office, Murrah and the legislature created a "State Plan" for the purchase of cotton. Under this plan a state agency known as the Texas Loan Agency would buy cotton with 7 percent Texas bonds and transport it to the Rio Grande border. Once there, half would be returned to the owner. Since the cotton would be state property during transit, it would be safe from Confederate seizure. Most planters responded eagerly to the State Plan and by March of 1864 nearly half the baled cotton in Texas had been sold to the state. Confederate officials were angered by the State Plan and called upon Murrah to abandon it, but he refused until Kirby Smith's aide, Col. Guy M. Bryan, convinced him that speculators were taking advantage of the plan. Murrah assured Bryan that he would deal with the problem, but meanwhile, state agents continued to buy cotton.

Soon, the Confederate Congress passed new laws designed to regulate the export trade and Kirby Smith, citing these laws as his authority, issued regulations governing the overland trade between Texas and Mexico. Under these regulations, only merchants licensed by the Cotton Bureau could engage in foreign trade and, to obtain a license, merchants were required to agree to ship nothing but cotton and import nothing but machinery, agricultural tools, and ordnance. These regulations gave the military total control of the cotton trade and Murrah was furious. He deemed Smith's actions to be a violation of state sovereignty and, in fact, illegal. The general responded by simply pointing out that desperate times required desperate measures, but this did not end the controversy. In an effort to resolve their differences, Murrah and Smith met at Hempstead in July 1864. What the general told the governor there is unknown, but Murrah gave in. On July 19, he issued a message to the people, pointing out that their very survival depended on the army's ability to buy supplies and that cotton was required for exchange. He now urged planters to deliver their cotton to government agents and essentially abolished the State Plan. His action solved the dispute with Confederate authorities, but it was now far too late to save the Confederacy.[34]

To make matters worse, conditions in Texas were rapidly deteriorating. There had been little fighting there during the war, but the effect of the struggle on the state was nonetheless catastrophic. Despite the efforts of Murrah and his predecessors to meet the needs of soldiers' families, many thousands were utterly destitute by 1864, and the financial condition of the state made it impossible to help them. Even worse was the breakdown of law and order. Desertions were commonplace and many former soldiers had become outlaws. Addressing the legislature on May 11, Murrah lamented:

> In some sections society is almost disorganized; the voice of the law is hushed and its authority is seldom asserted. It is a dead letter . . . Murder, robbery, theft, outrages of every kind against property, against life, against everything sacred to civilized people are frequent and general. Whole communities are under siege in terror . . . The rule of mob, the bandit, of unbridled passions, ride[s] over the solemn ordinances of government. Foul crime is committed and the criminal steeped in guilt . . . goes unwhipped of justice.[35]

And yet Murrah carried on. As Confederate currency rapidly depreciated, the state faced the specter of insolvency and something had to be done. In May, and again in October 1864, he called the legislature into special session to deal with the worsening financial crisis. The first session accomplished little, but the second at least made an effort. Taxes were made payable in specie, and the lawmakers enacted a plan to distribute penitentiary cloth to the needy, but to no effect. The financial condition of the Confederacy and the state continued to worsen, and cloth was of little use to people living in chaos.

Murrah attempted to bolster morale. He addressed an impassioned message to the people on January 14, 1865, insisting that independence could still be won if they were willing to continue to make sacrifices in defense of liberty. His appeal had no effect, especially as news arrived of continuing losses in Virginia and the Carolinas. The situation was hopeless.[36]

As everything they had fought for collapsed around them after Lee's surrender on April 12, 1865, Murrah, Kirby Smith, and Magruder continued to urge resistance, but this proved to be impossible. In May, Smith met with the Trans-Mississippi governors in Marshall in an attempt to end the fighting without a formal surrender. Murrah was sick and did not attend the conference, but he agreed with the effort and sent Ashbel Smith and William P. Ballinger to New Orleans to meet with Federal officials in an effort to avoid military occupation by means of some sort of negotiated settlement. This attempt failed and Smith signed a formal surrender document on June 2, 1865. Meanwhile, Murrah continued to hope that Union authorities would not interfere with the civil government of the state and in late May he called for a special election to choose delegates to a convention that would meet in July to restore Texas to the Union. He also called for a special session of the legislature to meet in July, but these were naive endeavors and neither event ever took place.[37]

By the late spring of 1865, Murrah was desperately ill and emotionally drained. On June 12 he issued his last message to the people. In it he declared that he had given his all to a sacred cause that now was lost. If there was any way to continue to resist, he would seize it, but there was none. He was ill, he was bankrupt, and he feared retribution from the Federal government. He hoped for leniency, but expected none. He believed he had done no wrong and he would not wait to be tried and imprisoned. There was no alternative but to flee. He concluded by advising Texans to "accept whatever plan may be imposed by your conquerors no matter how disagreeable it may be." On that same day, Murrah turned the state over to Lieutenant Governor Fletcher Stockdale and, along with Kirby Smith and Magruder, joined Gen. Joseph D. Shelby and his cavalry unit for the long trip to Mexico. By the time they reached Monterrey, Murrah's strength was gone and on August 4, 1865, he died.[38]

Edward Clark, Francis Lubbock, and Pendleton Murrah all faced major problems involving finance, shortages, personnel, and politics, but as the war dragged on these became ever more difficult and in the final analysis were a crushing and destructive burden to Murrah. These three men, their colleagues, and most of their citizens, had cast their lot with a cause that could not succeed. Despite the dedication of its leaders at all levels and the heroics of such men as Lee, Jackson, Stuart, and others—even Magruder—the South had no chance to win, no chance to demonstrate by force that the Union was not inviolable. And yet they never gave up, never admitted that their cause was not only lost from the beginning, but was indefensible. Lubbock had declared that the war was a fight for liberty, but it was not; it was a war to defend the abomination of human slavery and the myth of states' rights.

Despite the unsavory nature of their lost cause, Clark, Lubbock, and Murrah are to be commended for their dedication to it. They were committed and determined. But it is Murrah who is to be most admired for his performance. He faced an impossible task, believing as he did in both the Confederacy and in states' rights. He was criticized by many of his contemporaries for his efforts to defend states' rights against the demands of the Confederacy, but in fact, he was willing to compromise when he saw that it was absolutely necessary. He considered himself a man of principle and honor, but he has been forgotten. Lincoln paid with his life in defense of the Union. Murrah paid with his life in defense of an impossible dream.

Notes

1   Quoted in Joe T. Timmons, "The Referendum in Texas on the Ordinances of Secession, February 23, 1861: The Vote," *East Texas Historical Journal* 11 (Fall 1973): 22.

2   Llerena B. Friend, *Sam Houston: The Great Designer* (Austin: University of Texas Press, 1954), 336–39.

3   Ibid., 339.

4   Biography of Edward Clark, Clark Papers, Center for American History, University of Texas, Austin, Texas (hereafter cited as CAHUT).

5   Clement R. Johns to Clark, March 21, 1861, Clark Papers, Texas State Archives, Austin, Texas (hereafter cited as TSA).

6   Stephen B. Oates, "Texas Under the Secessionists," *Southwestern Historical Quarterly* (hereafter cited as *SHQ*) 62 (October 1963): 174–76; Clark to John S. Ford, April 25, 1861, Clark Papers, CAHUT; John S. Ford to Clark, April 21, 1861, May 12, 1861, Leroy P. Walker to Clark, April 15, 16, 1861, Clark to the People of Texas, April 17, 1861, Clark Papers, TSA; H. E. McCulloch to Leroy P. Walker, March 30, 1861, cited in Ralph A. Wooster, "Texas," *The Confederate Governors*, W. B. Yearns, ed., (Athens: University of Georgia Press, 1985), 196.

7   A. G. Walker to Clark, May 8, 1861, Clark Papers, TSA; Clark to Ebenezer B. Nichols, May 18, 1861, Clark Papers, CAHUT; Wooster, "Texas," 197.

8   Earl Van Dorn to Clark, April 16, 1861, May 10, 12, 1861, Clark to Van Dorn, May 6, June 7, 1861, Clark to the People of Texas, April 31, 1861, Clark Papers, CAHUT; Oates, "Texas Under the Secessionists," 184–87.

9   Nancy H. Bowen, "A Political Labyrinth: Texas in the Civil War," *East Texas Historical Journal* 11 (Fall 1973): 4.

10   Clark Biography, Clark Papers, CAHUT.

11   Louis Mitchell, "Francis R. Lubbock," *New Handbook of Texas* (Austin: Texas State Historical Association, 1996), 4:319. Lubbock had three wives. After Adele's death, he married Sara E. Black Porter in 1883, and after her death he married Lou Scott in 1903.

12   Francis R. Lubbock, *Six Decades in Texas; or, Memoirs of Francis Richard Lubbock, Governor of Texas in War Time, 1861–63,* ed. C.W. Raines (Austin, Texas: Ben C. Jones, 1900), 267–94,321.

13   Ibid., 326–27.

14   Ibid., 334.

15   Ibid.,332–36. The full text of Lubbock's inaugural address appears here.

16   Wooster, "Texas," 201–2.

17   Lubbock, *Six Decades in Texas,* 360–63. Also see Charles W. Ramsdell, "The Texas State Military Board," *SHQ* 27 (April 1924): 253-75.

18   Oates, "Texas Under the Secessionists," 194–95; Lubbock, *Six Decades in Texas,* 344–46.

19   Ibid., 345, 348–51, 424–54.

20   Wooster, "Texas," 203–4; Lubbock, *Six Decades in Texas,* 388–95.

21   Oates, "Texas Under the Secessionists," 198–200.

22   Randolph B. Campbell, *Gone to Texas* (New York: Oxford University Press, 2003), 265–66.

23   Lubbock, *Six Decades in Texas,* 463–79.

24   Ibid., 480–84.

25   Ibid., 493–502.

26   Ibid., 511–14.

27   Ibid., 515–25.

28   Wooster, "Texas," 208.

29   Ralph A. Wooster, "Pendleton Murrah," *New Handbook of Texas,* 4:895–96; Bowen, "A Political Labyrinth," 5–6; Wooster, "Texas," 209; Inaugural address of Pendleton Murrah, November 5, 1863, Murrah Papers, TSA.

30   Murrah to Magruder, January 17, 1864, Murrah Papers, TSA.

31   Magruder to Murrah, November 2, 1863, Murrah Papers, TSA; Wooster, "Texas," 210.

32   General Magruder was concerned about a possible assault up the Red River as early as November 1863.) See Magruder to Murrah, November 2, 1863; Magruder to Murrah, November 4, 12, December 1, 1863, January 13, 17, February 9, 1864, Murrah to Magruder, January 12, 17, 1864, E. Kirby Smith to Murrah, January 18, 1864, Murrah Papers, TSA.

33   Magruder to Murrah, March 7, 11, 20, April 8, 23, 1864, Murrah Papers, TSA.

34   Wooster, "Texas," 211–12; Kirby Smith to Murrah, March 1, July 1, 15, 1864, Magruder to Murrah, March 28, 1864, Murrah to Kirby Smith, June 17, 21, 24, 28, 1864, Murrah to the People of Texas, July 19, 1864, Murrah Papers, TSA.

35   Quoted in Kenneth E. Hendrickson, Jr., *The Chief Executives of Texas* (College Station: Texas A&M University Press, 1995), 80.

36   Wooster, "Texas," 214; Charles W. Ramsdell, "Texas From the Fall of the Confederacy to the Beginning of Reconstruction," *SHQ* 11 (January 1908): 199–219; Murrah to the People of Texas, January 14, 1865, Murrah Papers, TSA.

37   Wooster, "Texas," 215.

38   Murrah to the People of Texas, July 12, 1865, Murrah Papers, TSA.

Chapter 14

"A Sacred Charge upon Our Hands": Assisting the Families of Confederate Soldiers in Texas, 1861–1865

by Vicki Betts

Texas has generally been considered the most fortunate Confederate state due to its geography—far from the main battle lines and the destruction that came with the presence of large armies, but close to external trade through Mexico. Indeed, Texas became a magnet to refugees from other Southern states, especially those in the Trans-Mississippi. With plenty of fertile land and minimal disruptions to life except in areas along the frontier, the coast, and the Rio Grande, Texas should have been the most desirable place for families to live during the war. However, even in Texas, physical suffering enveloped the wives and children of many absent soldiers, particularly those who had started 1861 as part of the

Illustration 16 The Influence of a Woman. *Courtesy Library of Congress.*

246

poor and yeoman classes. In order to support both the home front and the war fronts, private citizens and public officials would need to explore a range of possible solutions to the problem of relief to families on a scale previously unknown in the state.[1]

Many of the women and children of Texas greeted secession and mobilization as a festival of patriotism and bravado. Young ladies participated in processions and presented flags to hometown units.[2] Texas matrons formed "home spun societies" to support Southern-made goods, subscribed to the Confederate loan, and offered corn for the use of state or Confederate troops.[3] Girls from Rusk used an effigy of Abraham Lincoln for target practice while women across the state sewed uniforms and tents for the units forming for immediate removal to Confederate borders from Arizona to Missouri to Virginia.[4] Relatively little thought was given to the possible long-term effect of the absence of so many men from the working population of the state. However, after the initial large battles of Bull Run and Wilson's Creek, it soon became apparent that the war would not be over in six weeks, nor even six months. Husbands, sons, and fathers would not be able to return and prepare their families for winter and probably would not be allowed to take charge of spring planting. Extended families and neighbors stepped in to help, but some cases, particularly in towns, required support from the broader community. Private assistance took a variety of forms as the war progressed.

In September 1861, the *Marshall Texas Republican* appealed for food, clothing, or money to be sent to a local committee for distribution, asserting that the citizens at home were "pledged to the support and protection of the families of those who have gone forth to fight the battles of the country," and they should also assist "widows, with large families of children, who have been thrown out of employment by the times." These were "worthy people" deserving of having "their necessities . . . provided for."[5] Two months later members of the Relief Committee, through the newspaper, assured families in Harrison County that they would "take pleasure in doing all that they can to render their condition comfortable. Let none be deterred by false delicacy, from claiming assistance." The committee solicited donations of breadstuffs, meat, vegetables, dried fruit, "in fact any and everything fit to eat. Wood is very much needed at this time. Cannot some who live close to town send in a few loads?"[6]

"Certain citizens" in San Antonio, the largest city in the state, took a different approach. They created the Southern Defense Aid Society, which hired about 850 persons, including "hundreds of seamstresses" to make up uniforms for the Confederate government, "thus furnishing employment for the poor and contributing to the comfort and efficiency of our patriotic troops." Employees were paid in Southern Defense Aid Society bills, which soon circulated as change throughout San Antonio.[7] Recognizing that there would still be need among some families, a local committee formed that soon had $20,000 sub-scribed, with an additional $30,000 expected within the week.[8]

Governor Francis R. Lubbock's call for fifteen new regiments on Febru-ary 3, 1862, followed by the Confederate Conscription Act of April 16, dipped more deeply into Texas households, taking more heads of families. The *Austin State Gazette* took note of the probable impact and in its March 15 issue urged that "honor, patriotism, simple humanity, render it the imperative duty of those remaining behind to make suitable provision for the maintenance of the families of all such soldiers. . . . Associations will be absolutely necessary. Nothing we know will be done unless the ladies take the initiative." With the soldiers well clothed, "We must now look out for the hungry and half clad little ones, whose fathers, in order to fight for the hearthstones of the South, have, or will leave, a sacred charge upon our hands." Texas men would rush to fill the new regiments if they only felt assured that their families would be cared for.[9] That day a public meeting assembled in Austin, headed by J. P. Neal, in which Judge E. D. Townes urged all to "engage heart, hand, and purse" to support soldiers' families. The group set up a structure of voting beat-level committees to determine the needs and report back to the central committee, which would then allocate donated supplies.[10]

The *Bellville Countryman* took up the call, urging a similar organization but with "a commissory [*sic*] department, or depository" in every beat, available to needy soldiers' families. "Let not those who stay at home conclude that they have nothing to do but loiter about and complain of dull times, or sordelly [*sic*] seek their own gain. . . If you cannot serve your country in one way, serve it in another. . . this is no time for any to be idle."[11]

On April 14, Houston and Galveston musical amateurs offered an evening's entertainment in the form of a "parlor opera" to raise funds for the wives and children of soldiers. "The elite of our city—the most respectable and patriotic of our citizens"attended the benefit, raising $615.60.[12] The Relief Committee, filing the next month's financial report, thanked all for "the mite contributed by each" and noted that the organization had supported a total of thirty-two fami-lies, a number which was "daily increasing," and who would need continued resources.[13]

By the end of April, however, some were beginning to notice that not all gave voluntarily to the worthy cause of supporting families. As a writer to the *Houston Tri-Weekly Telegraph* noted:

Again: when individual action alone is relied upon, the patriotic citi-zen will alone bear the burden, while those who love their money more than their country, will escape. If the support of soldiers' families falls upon the neighbors, it will have the appearance of a mere act of charity, while it should be felt as a duty and as a right.[14]

This writer suggested that the county courts take charge, using county taxes paid in equivalent "articles of consumption," with justices of the peace or militia company commanders handling the distribution. Furthermore, recipient wives and mothers should help reimburse the county by weaving cloth, with the county supplying the cards, wheels, looms, and fiber if necessary. "I am aware that this apparent interference in domestic matters may be resented by some, but that is not to be regarded. We have fallen upon evil days; we are engaged in a life and death struggle, and our utmost energies will be taxed."[15]

The county level of government was already involved in relief efforts in a number of locations across the state. Ever since Texas commissioners' courts were established in 1846 they had been charged "to provide for the support of indigent persons resident in their county, who cannot support themselves,"[16] making them the logical first step of appeal in the government. As early as May 7, 1861, the Harrison County court had ordered $16,000 worth of bonds issued to buy arms and ammunition and to support soldiers' families.[17] Acknowledging the increasing drain on county treasuries, the state legislature on January 1, 1862, approved an act allowing the collection of a "special tax for war purposes," not exceeding twenty-five cents per one hundred dollars of taxable property. This tax was to be collected by the county, and the permissible uses included "the support of destitute families of persons who are now or may hereafter be regularly enlisted in the army or navy in the service of this State or of the Confederate States."[18] Not all Texas counties took advantage of this source of income immediately, nor to the full allowance. Calhoun County waited until May, but then ordered the full tax rate to go into effect, as did Travis County.[19] Fayette County commissioners decided on a tax rate of twenty cents but only on property in excess of $2,000, and that contingent upon a favorable vote in August.[20] Other counties would delay months before applying the new tax rate.

Galveston, which had already exhausted both city and county funds trying to support both soldiers' families and those left unemployed by the collapse of its blockaded economy, faced a panic when on May 17, 1862, Capt. Henry Eagle, of the blockader *Santee,* demanded the city surrender, or else it would face possible bombardment.[21] Hundreds of Galveston residents fled to Houston, overwhelming an already crowded city. The *Houston Telegraph* appealed to other towns in the interior to "open their houses and make room for the refugees."[22] Residents of Rose Hill (Harris County), Bastrop (Wharton County), Richmond (Fort Bend County), Navasota and Anderson (Grimes County), Montgomery (Montgomery County), and Vine Grove (Washington County) responded, as noted in the newspaper, offering homes to fleeing Galvestonians.[23] Houston pleasure lovers sponsored a fund-raising "Floral Festival" concert, planters and farmers sent in railcars full of corn and cornmeal, government employees took up collections, and Ladies' Aid Societies in Austin (Travis County) and Danville

(Montgomery County) sent in money and supplies.[24] By July the danger had passed, and many Galveston residents returned home.[25] The surrender of the island city on October 9 brought about another exodus, leaving a few hundred men and approximately two thousand women and children on the island for the Federals to feed. "Starvation stared them in the face."[26]

The summer months of 1862 brought no relief to San Antonio. Prices of food continued to soar, to the point that Martin Schnetz of the People's Store discontinued dealing in produce, but did announce that twice a week he would distribute fifty loaves of bread free to anyone in need.[27] The *Herald* editor, after sarcastically noting that "flour is only 20 dollars per sack; corn meal only 2½ dollars per bushel" declared that "these cheap prices afford the families of poor soldiers, who are fighting for the country, excellent facilities for sumptuous living." How would the poor widow with children feed her family on two dollars a week earned by constant sewing?[28] The *Semi-Weekly News* editor wondered "What will the laborer do who earns two dollars a day and with it feed six healthy children and a healthy wife? . . . Listen! Did'nt [sic] you hear some pale-face-weak-voiced urchin, lean and lank as a coach-whip, asking for bread, and Ma say, there is none?"[29] By September 4, he warned San Antonio that

> We hear it whispered on every street-corner that a mob is organized
> for the purpose of going to the Market and getting what they need at their
> own prices, and it is determined to have its meat and vegetables on reason-
> able terms or hang every butcher on a hook in his own stall. We tell you,
> functionaries, once for all, unless you do your duty, the people will do it
> for you, and to your sorrow. There can be a number of men raised in the
> cause in question in one hour in the morning to clean out Malitia [sic],
> Conscripts, and all the soldiers here abouts. A hungry stomack [sic] knows
> no conscience, and woe be to extortioners when this mob in its hungry
> fury breaks upon the market-stalls and takes what it wants and hangs every
> opposing voice![30]

Some community leaders tried to help. At the same time the *Semi-Weekly News* editor was warning of an impending bread riot, Gustav Schleicher, former state senator, and Sam Maverick, among others, organized the San Antonio Supply Association, the first of a number of corporations across Texas which, while not technically free markets, did attempt to procure commodities for city resident shareholders and the "families of soldiers and all others who shall need assistance" at "costs, charges, and an interest of eight per cent per annum on the money, and no more."[31] By mid-November they were providing flour at fifteen dollars per one hundred pounds, and other items, such as salt and cornmeal, at fair prices.[32]

As winter approached, commissioners' courts in more rural counties continued their work with soldiers' wives and families in destitute situations. In

November, Smith County ordered ten wives paid amounts between $25 and $100, but recognizing a larger need existed ordered a special term for the next month. At that time the court allocated $4,749.50 to 123 families or persons.[33] Henderson County appropriated $3000.00 for its "war widows," which was printed by the court as currency in fifty cent, dollar, two dollar, five dollar and twenty-five dollar bills.[34] Kaufman County sent a committee to visit homes to determine needs and authorize supplies, delivering $648.60 in "immediate assistance."[35] The committees were also told in February to ask "who will require assistance in harvesting the next season, and it be their further duty to advertise and procure hands for the same who shall be paid out of the wheat and corn."[36]

By the end of 1862, authorities in Texas were beginning to hear that the soldiers at the front were not satisfied with the attention given to their families. "Our soldiers complain that their families are not properly cared for, and from this cause others are deterred from entering the service. The subject is one of vital importance to our country."[37] A Texas soldier wrote home from Arkansas that his wife was unable to get anyone to help her chop wood. "I think it strange that where there are so many negroes no one can be found that would spare a negro to chop a load of wood for a poor soldier's wife."[38] Officers of the First Brigade, Walker's Texas Division, wrote from Arkansas on January 5 that their men entered the army trusting that their families would be protected, "that the needy should not want, nor the hungry go without food. With a spirit of hopeful confidence, they have committed these sacred trusts to the generosity and patriotism of those they have left behind. Shall that confidence be *betrayed?* Shall those trusts be violated? . . . The rumor of these things has reached the camp of your soldiers, and it has come like an evil spirit, to torture and *demoralize* them."[39] The *Marshall Texas Republican* responded, "We believe that the reports that have gone to the army are exaggerated; that many, very many of them are without foundation. But be this as it may, let there be, henceforth, no grounds for such unwelcome rumors."[40] Suffering on the home front had begun to impact both recruitment to and desertion from the battlefront.[41]

Governor Lubbock called a special session of the legislature, outlining for them in early February 1863, his concerns, which included:

the absolute necessity that exists of making further provision for the support of the families of those in the service. . . . In addition to what the counties may do, I am of opinion the State should make a most liberal appropriation for this purpose. The troops in the field are the soldiers not of a particular county, but of the entire State, and it would be but equitable that the State provide for their families.[42]

The legislature responded, and after a "hard fight," allocated $600,000 to the counties based on scholastic returns and estimates from the previous year.[43]

Lubbock considered it "a favorite measure" but conceded that "the sum should have been much larger."[44] Not all Texans agreed. Sam Maverick wrote to his wife from Austin that some lawmakers were ready to "throw away everything they can lay their hands [on] (honestly or dishonestly) in a gigantic scheme of funding the soldiers families."[45] The legislature also approved raising the ad valorem state tax from twenty-five cents to fifty cents on one hundred dollars of value, in part to fund relief, plus it allowed county-level special taxes not to exceed seventy-five cents per one hundred dollars of taxable property.[46] Lubbock considered that the increased state taxes would be "scarcely felt" due to the wide circulation of rapidly depreciating Confederate and state paper currency.[47]

During a special session of the state legislature in 1863, state leaders chartered a number of "mutual aid societies" across the state, including organizations in Houston, San Antonio, Columbus, Caldwell County, Washington County, and Goliad.[48] In later sessions, legislators added societies for Seguin, Gonzales, and Comal County.[49] Victoria, Austin, and Corpus Christi were also reported to have supported societies, but none of these appear in the Texas statutes.[50] Typically, the acts gave the groups the rights and responsibilities of a general mercantile business, providing supplies first to the incorporators, then to "families of soldiers at cost, carriage and expenses, and to others at a profit not exceeding twenty-five per cent on cost, carriage and expenses; the object of the Association being mutual aid in procuring supplies for the needy and protection against speculators and extortioners."[51] While officially incorporated on March 6, the San Antonio Mutual Aid Association had actually opened its "Aid Store" on January 5. According to the *Herald*, over ten thousand persons appeared on its lists as stockholders and beneficiaries by February 28, and "the families of soldiers and the indigent poor of this city and surrounding country are alone permitted to trade at the store."[52] Initially directors bought stock from "Mexican traders" in San Antonio, but Gen. John Magruder, commander of the District of Texas, New Mexico, and Arizona, extended his assistance to getting cotton out of the country via Mexico and getting supplies back into the city. He would later allow the association thirty conscripts and ordered officers and agents to not interfere with them but "give them the same assistance and protection it would be their duty to give were they the common carriers of the Government."[53] By limiting overhead to building rental and the hiring of clerks, the San Antonio Mutual Aid Association was able to sell flour at cost, and corn, cornmeal, sugar, shoes, and cottonade fabric at about half price.[54] Visitors to the city in February of the next year noted that "there is little or no business going on here, except what is done by the Mutual Aid Association," and within three days of the arrival of a load of supplies, it had sold $150,000 worth of goods.[55]

Another form of state direct assistance involved textiles, those produced at the state penitentiary and those produced at home. Prior to the war, most cloth had been imported either from the Northeast or from abroad. The blockade cut off most of these sources, and those fabrics coming into the state via the Rio Grande brought prices beyond the means of many soldiers' wives. The state penitentiary had initiated its textile operation in the summer of 1856, and by 1863 it was the only large factory west of the Mississippi.[56] Although the legislature incorporated several other factories during the war, most were not operational by May 1865.[57] During the war the Huntsville facility produced over seven million yards of cloth, most going to the army. As of October 1862, families of soldiers were the second priority, followed by the general public. At that point, the *Houston Tri-Weekly Telegraph* reported that "there are unfilled requisitions for the service to a larger extent, and for 500 families of soldiers; and besides these 30,000 applications of the third class are awaiting their turn. People can see that the prospect of getting anything is very small."[58] Persons requesting penitentiary cloth, consisting of osnaburgs, cotton jeans, wool kerseys, and wool plains, were required to provide an affidavit which stated that it was for personal use only and would not be sold or bartered, but John S. Besser, the facility's financial agent, noted that "some individuals with elastic consciencies [*sic*] have obtained goods under the solemnities of an oath, ostensibly for 'Soldiers' families—but [actually] to speculate on them."[59]

The Tenth Legislature, Extra Session, sought to remedy that situation by requiring the chief justice of each county to certify the accuracy of the applications from their jurisdictions.[60] Forms required that each woman swear that the goods were "for immediate use in her own family," that the cloth was "not for barter, sale, exchange or speculation," and that she was the wife of a soldier in the army of the Confederacy. She also had to give the number of whites and blacks in the household excluding soldiers and indicate whether this was her first or second application.[61] The legislative session also set the penalty for speculators misrepresenting themselves in order to obtain textiles at two to three years of hard labor, at the same prison, presumably making fabric for others.[62]

On May 30, 1863, the penitentiary raised the prices of cloth sold to the public for the first time since December 1861.[63] Osnaburgs that had cost eighteen cents per yard would now cost slaveholders eighty cents and non-slaveholders fifty cents.[64] John Osterhout of the *Bellville Countryman* was incensed. "Is not this a pretty business? The legislature passes a law appropriating money to help the soldiers' families, and as soon as they adjourn, the Governor, Gen. Besser and some others try to get the money away from the families by charging more than four times the former prices for clothing."[65] None but soldiers' families could purchase the goods.[66] However, in September a reader informed the *Countryman* of his experience with the penitentiary. He had learned that the penitentiary might exchange cotton fabrics for good, finely textured raw wool, "one yard of plain Osnaburg for one pound of wool—for the balance we will give you 80 cts., if of good quality, on delivery here."[67] He took a load of wool to Huntsville but was turned away. He was not alone.

Among the many applicants who had pilgrimaged to the factory for relief were soldiers' wives, and soldiers' mothers who had from three to five sons in the army. They had bought wool for $1,00 to $1,50 per pound, having information that the factory would exchange cloth for it. The ladies were sarcastically told to go home and attend to their spinning wheels and looms.[68]

A disabled soldier on crutches had come 150 miles with claims from needy soldiers' families, but the agent turned him away for an "insignificant" error on his form, as he did many others. "In our humble opinion there is something foul in Denmark."[69]

Gideon Lincecum traveled from Washington County to Huntsville in June, also in search of textiles. He saw the pressures that Besser was under and left without asking for anything. He sent his son and another man, also with wool, hoping to exchange it for osnaburg, twilled woolens, and weaving thread, but he wrote, "If it is not convenient for you to do so, I shall not complain, as when I was there, I saw and know that you are doing all you can."[70] They returned without the cloth, and a third try by Lincecum also failed.[71]

With the penitentiary failing to meet the complete needs of the military and Texas civilians, some had already turned to homespun. Edward Cushing of the *Houston Tri-Weekly Telegraph* had issued the call to "hog, hominy, and homespun" in August 1862, asserting that "at the present moment there are not enough imported goods in the State to clothe one-fifth of its people . . . The time must come . . . and that too very shortly, when the amount of dry goods in all the stores in Texas will not clothe one in a hundred of the population."[72] While there were women, particularly older women, who were quite capable of spinning thread and weaving cloth, the hand cards used to align the fibers, which had cost sixty cents per pair before the war, now brought $1.50 in specie in Brownsville and thirty-five to forty dollars inland in currency, if they could be located.[73] This was well beyond the reach of most poor and yeoman families. The *Marshall Texas Republican* was forced to concede, "The country is sadly in want of cotton cards. If a sufficient quantity of them could be obtained, there would be a superabundance of cloth for every one, but as it is, with all the exertions of the ladies, it will be difficult to clothe those at home, and to make clothes for our brave volunteers."[74] Cushing replied:

What ought to have been done was to have imported, during the last summer, a million pairs of cards, even if we had to buy them of old Abe himself, and pay him in good middling cotton. Government should have done this. Blockade runners should have done it. Everybody should have thought of it. Some people did think of it, but not enough. Thirty thousand pair of cotton cards will go but little way in clothing half a million of people.[75]

Actually, the state of Texas, through the Military Board, had placed an order in September, the month before Cushing's complaint, not for thirty thousand cotton cards, but for ten thousand, plus two thousand for wool. The Military Board included cards in nearly every order it placed thereafter until the end of the war.[76] By May 1, 1863, the first "large lot" of cotton cards had arrived. The Military Board allocated them to each county on the basis of the scholastic census, at the rate of ten dollars each in currency. "The needy families of those in the army are to be first supplied." It was estimated that the purchase saved recipients over $200,000.[77] The *Corpus Christi Ranchero* declared, "This is one of the good acts the Military Board, composed of the Governor, Comptroller, and Treasurer, have been guilty of, and demonstrates what good things good men can do in a good cause, without trampling upon a good Constitution or the rights of good citizens."[78] However, once divided, the cards were spread out thinly—Dallas County, for example, only received two hundred pairs.[79] The Military Board brought in another 30,000 pairs of European cotton cards in October.[80]

Even with all that private citizens, county government, state government, and even the Confederate military tried to do to help the families of soldiers, letters and petitions from Texas women continued to pour into the offices of the governor and the adjutant general.[81] Nearly all appealed for exemptions from Confederate conscription, initiated in April 1862, or the governor's call for 10,000 Texas militiamen, made in June 1863, or subsequent state troop calls.[82] "Half of the militia have been drafted for six months, and, oh, the moaning and bewailing of the feminine population," wrote Kate Stone in Tyler.[83] Mrs. Capt. J. R. Alston wrote Governor Lubbock in July, asking that her overseer be exempted. "I will be compeled [*sic*] to sell all my negroes if he is taken from me. I have 19 in number I cannot manage them myself. . . . Mr. Goodwin is a very poor man and has a wife and a house full of children to support when if he is taken from them they will be compeld [*sic*] to starve."[84] Petitions arrived often signed with both male and female or only female names, reflecting probably the first time that these women from the corners of Texas had ever directly involved themselves in any level of political appeal. From different counties and towns, the women made similar statements. They often began their petitions with a polite remark, such as, "We, the undersigned, your petitioners, citizens of the above named county and State do respectfully submit . . ."[85] or "I know that you are the father of all your people . . . ."[86] Then the women stressed that they could not survive with the loss of their last physician, shoemaker, blacksmith, spinning-wheel maker, loom maker, weaver, miller, wagon maker, coffin maker,[87] or simply a man to "aid us in preparing for a crop, direct those of us who need his advice, govern and control the negroes amongst us, and give us such aid as we, in our destitution require, and which he is ever ready to do, and is duty bound."[88] The women further emphasized that they had already sent nearly all of the men eligible for military service, and this particular man was doing more for the Confederacy at home than he ever could on the front. Notes added to the letters and petitions usually read, "I duly regret I cannot comply with her request,"[89] "and [answered] . . . as usual in such cases,"[90] or "give these parties the best explanation you can."[91] However, a few were marked "recommended."[92]

By the autumn of 1863 the citizens of Texas felt some satisfaction in the level of support they were giving the wives and children of their soldiers, although some were concerned that unless attention was maintained, contributions might diminish. "Although much has been done by the energy and liberality of our city and county authorities as also by the capital and energy of benevolent associations of the city," men attending a San Antonio war meeting established a new committee to solicit additional money, food, and fuel.[93] "Ceceola" wrote the *Houston Tri-Weekly Telegraph* reminding the "women of Texas" to "let our soldiers feel, from a noble generosity to them and their loved ones at home, that they have our sympathy and our prayers; let their families feel the comforting influence of our liberality; divide with them our last measure of meal" as a part of "a sacred obligation to those who are protecting our all from desolation."[94] The *Galveston Weekly News* reminded readers that "the comfort of the soldier's family [is] the representative duty of the home department," a responsibility that would extend beyond the end of the war, and that "its services will long be needed and appreciated."[95] However, one correspondent from Walker County wrote to the Houston paper that

> I do candidly believe that the majority of them [soldiers' families] in this portion of the State, at all events, are bountifully supplied with all the necessaries, and to a great extent, with all the luxuries of life at present obtainable in the markets of the country. Several families of soldiers, in this county, within the writer's ken, live better, are better clad, and live in greater idleness than when their "heads" were at home.[96]

Pendleton Murrah was elected to replace Lubbock as governor of Texas in November 1863, and the legislature took another look at state assistance to the needy "families, widows and dependents of such officers and soldiers of Texas as have been, may now, or hereafter may be, in the military service of the Confederate States, or in the active militia or volunteer service of the State of Texas."[97] It provided one million dollars for each of the next two years, $500,000 to be provided each six months to the county courts based on a return made by March 1 of each year. The money was to be used to purchase "necessary supplies."[98] The legislature also allowed each county to assess an "extraordinary" tax of one dollar per one hundred dollars so that soldiers' families "shall have suitable subsistence and comfort, and property in their charge shall have prudent management, to prevent loss or waste, and to promote appropriate income." The court could not "distribute money to the beneficiaries for them to use at their pleasure" but had to relieve their "actual wants."[99]

On Christmas Day 1863, the Comptroller's Office issued a circular outlining the procedure for the county courts' returns. The comptroller defined "indigent" rather broadly as "destitute of means for a comfortable support." The report was to list the name of the soldier and the number of dependents, with a total for the county. It was also to include a table of disbursements.[100] By February the county judges began sending their reports back to Austin. Some had problems. It took six weeks for the circular to reach Mason, Cooke, and Tyler counties.[101] S. B. Gray in Blanco County was not able to make a list because "the malitia was cald out and the Soldiers from this County is in so maney different comands. . . [but] I know there is a grate meny needy famileys in this County the men is all in the Service and they are nearley all poor."[102] G. W. Brown of Lamar County explained that they had families with wild livestock but no one to bring them in, William McGrew in Refugio County had families with livestock dying due to a drought, and William Gambel in Live Oak had families with means, but no breadstuffs and no transportation.[103] Brazos County set up a six-month residency requirement for eligibility for aid.[104] Harris County sent in a total of 1,603 persons, complaining that it was being inundated by wives and children moving in from other areas in order to be near their soldier husbands. Furthermore, Galveston County had done nothing to help them support its citizens who had refugeed to the mainland.[105]

On a few occasions the women of Texas took matters into their own hands to get what they needed or wanted. Up until 1864 the closest that the state had come to a "bread riot" or "seizing party" was the threat published in the *San Antonio Semi-Weekly News* in September 1862, which may have helped promote the formation of the San Antonio Supply Association. Two actual bread riots occurred in 1864, one in Grayson County and one in Galveston, although the women walked away empty-handed in each. In Grayson County, during the winter, a group of "war widows" heard that the local commissary where they drew rations had come into some coffee, tea, and sugar via the Brownsville cotton trade, but that the officers were selling it on the side. A Mrs. Savage and more than 125 others rode into Sherman with guns, axes, sledgehammers, and clubs to demand their due. Maj. [Samuel A.?] Blain, in charge of the commissary, opened the doors and showed them that he had none of those luxuries. The women decided that they must be in another building, and stormed the store of I. Heilbroner, a British subject. They broke in the doors and started helping themselves. At that moment Charles Quantrill walked in and quietly asked, "What would your husbands think of you if they could see you? They are at the front, enduring all kind of hardships, hungry, barefooted, half starved, doing their duty without any complaint. What would they think of you?" They finally became ashamed, replaced their loot, and nailed back the doors of the store as they left.[106]

On June 9, 1864, a crowd of "German women" from a neighborhood on the outskirts of Galveston marched to the house occupied by Gen. James M. Hawes and his wife and also to his office. The women, like the rest of the city residents, had been receiving rations that included cornmeal, but they demanded flour instead. Cornmeal "scrotched" their throats. Some even had a rope to hang the general if their demands were not met. All were questioned, the leaders discovered, and the next morning those women were moved off of the island.[107] Toward the end of the month they were allowed to return if they "behave[d] themselves."[108]

Accounts of seizing parties in two other locations are undated, but were probably late in the war. When a girl in Belton, Mrs. J. J. Greenwood had learned how to spin and weave, but the women in her area did not have access to the fiber they needed. They would stop the government wagons loaded with cotton, take what they needed, and send the drivers on their way. They did the same with cotton cards. "The women just went down and demanded that the cards be given to them as they had to have them and had no money to pay for them. This was done though with grumbling consent."[109]

Ann Raney Coleman, an early Texas pioneer, lived in Lavaca during the war. Divorced in 1855 and caring for her daughter and grandson while her son-in-law was in the Confederate army, Coleman often had to take matters into her own hands in order for the family to survive. When the women of Lavaca did not receive their rations regularly, they would gather, march to the men in charge, "pistol in hand," and "depend upon it, we got our rations, although previously refused." When the Baptist Church collapsed in the wind, she and her daughter got up during the night to gather boards for firewood. By dawn a dozen women were doing the same, defying a man sent to guard it. "We told him there were enough of us to whip him, so he had as well say nothing. . . . He laughed at us for spunk. We threatened to tie him hand and foot if he should resist us." When cornmeal ran out, and families in the area were hungry, a group of women approached the miller asking for some of what he was preparing for others. He refused, so while some of them guarded the miller, the rest filled their sacks, threatening to burn down the mill if they were stopped. "Be assured that it was the women that protected themselves in this war and not the men." [110]

In Southeast Texas, the Confederate military was at last forced to assist hungry families, with or without orders. H. W. Bendy, quartermaster agent at Woodville, reported to his superiors that about March 24, 1864, the women of Hardin County heard that the government corn was being hauled away at

McKinney's Ferry. They appeared with empty wagons and "expressed a determination to have the corn right or wrong." A squad of Xavier DeBray's command happened by, "crossed the wagons over the Bayou & drove them up to
the cribs & loaded them with the Government Corn then helped themselves
with what they wanted & Refused to give any receipt for the same." Within two
days, almost nineteen hundred bushels of corn had disappeared, taken by "the
women not only of Hardin County but of Jefferson" who "came up with droves
of wagons & took all that was left in the crib & it was out of any man's power
to prevent them. They declared that they were starving & would have it." News
spread, and soon many Tyler County women assembled in Woodville. They
demanded corn & said that they would not leave without it & that if I did not
sell them corn that they would burst open the doors and take what they wanted
& that there was not men enough in the County to prevent them & that if they
were gentlemen they would not prevent them as no gentleman would prevent
starving women & children from helping themselves to government corn when
they could not get it elsewhere.

Bendy decided to forestall disaster by selling small quantities to each, but
asked for official approval for his actions, at least "until the new crop is dry
enough to gather." That approval was given.[111]

Throughout 1864, paper money continued to depreciate, so that even with
cash in hand county officials were sometimes unable to purchase supplies for
their indigent soldiers' families. At the same time, the Confederate government
had been collecting a tax-in-kind to support the army. County Judge Chamberlain of Belton wrote to Governor Murrah to see if he could buy two thousand
pounds of "tithe bacon" for his poor families until he could get beef.[112] R. J.
Palmer, in Montgomery, said that his county would only be able to supply their
eight hundred indigents with meat, but the county judge thought that a tithe tax
might bring in some of the "bounteous" corn crop that could not be purchased
due to the "failure of paper money." While there were many who would "divide
to the last with the soldier's families" there were others "who are disposed to do
nothing unless under compulsion."[113] The second called session of the Tenth
Legislature took a similar position in November. It allowed each county to levy a
tax up to the amount of the state tax, but individuals could pay it in "articles of
prime necessity" needed to support soldiers' families.[114] The annual one million
dollar appropriation was cancelled and replaced with an allocation of 600,000
yards of penitentiary cloth, plus any available excess thread. The county could
use the cloth and thread "in purchase of supplies, for supporting and maintaining indigent, and in clothing them in cases of absolute necessity."[115] The state of
Texas had virtually abandoned currency in favor of tangible goods.

As news of Confederate setbacks in the Eastern Theater reached the state,
Texas newspaper editors continued to bring the plight of the suffering families

to the attention of their readers. In November 1864, Cushing of the *Houston Tri-Weekly Telegraph* scolded Texans:

There is a great cry, and little wool in these public manifestations of providing for the soldiers' families; and while our Legislature may do good, and committees appointed by public meetings may to some extent be of great benefit, yet if each citizen in the State would constitute himself a committee of one to do the utmost in his power to alleviate suffering, and take care of the indigent, how little real suffering there would be in the State of Texas. . . . Give, GIVE, GIVE as long as you have anything to give, and do not measure your gifts or liberality by the standard of any other man.[116]

He later told his readers that Houston had about three hundred families, or fifteen hundred persons, dependent on city and county charity, requiring thirty thousand pounds of beef sold at a deep discount. He called for the ladies to raise funds to seek out and assist ill indigent families.[117] The *Galveston Weekly News* published an appeal by H. B. Andrews, appointed by the county court to solicit provisions for sixteen hundred destitute residents, many only temporary. "The article of wood alone, for the poor, costs more in that county [Galveston] than the entire amount necessary to support the indigents of any county in this State." Andrews requested corn, bacon, flour, wood, and even a few bales of cotton.[118] Robert Loughery of the *Marshall Texas Republican* also appealed for firewood. He reported that E. T. Craig had hauled in twenty-five loads after he found many families out of fuel in January 1865. It was too expensive to buy, and Loughery reminded his readers that "most of these families are needy only because their husbands, sons, and brothers are in the war."[119] Efforts to relieve the needs of families continued through May, when the last large shipment of cotton cards and medicines, purchased by the state Military Board, arrived in Austin. The *Austin State Gazette* on May 10 stated that they would be distributed as soon as it could be arranged, but thought it likely that these supplies were among the "50,000 pairs of cotton cards, any quantity of quinine, satinet, domestics, etc." that was plundered from the government in mid-June. At that point, the cards, once carefully conducted into Texas around the blockade and costing fifty dollars a pair and up in Confederate currency, were worth from one to three bits.[120]

Texas's first experiment with state-level public welfare ended with the collapse of the Confederacy. As historian Paul D. Escott has pointed out, the traditional Southern (and Texas) emphasis on limited government fell before the needs of hungry Confederate families. "Relief, not political principles, was paramount in the minds of many suffering southerners, and they wanted all levels of government to use their powers to respond to people's needs." The Confederate states, including Texas, "established during the war the most extensive system of welfare which the South had ever had."[121] It would be years before Texas would attempt anything approaching the same level of direct assistance, and again it would be focused on its (former) Confederate soldiers and their families.[122]

Notes

1   The most comprehensive look at assistance to the Confederate poor, including the families of soldiers, is found in Paul D. Escott, "'The Cry of the Sufferers': The Problem of Welfare in the Confederacy," *Civil War History* 23 (September 1977): 228–40. While very useful as an overview, this article never mentions Texas. Another fine study is Jennifer Lynn Gross, "'And for the Widow and Orphan': Confederate Widows, Poverty, and Public Assistance" in Lesley J. Gordon and John C. Inscoe, ed. *Inside the Confederate Nation* (Baton Rouge: Louisiana State University Press, 2005), 209–29, which looks at assistance both during and after the war. It also does not mention Texas. Two local studies from the eastern Confederacy are Elna C. Green, *This Business of Relief: Confronting Poverty in a Southern City, 1740–1940* (Athens: University of Georgia Press, 2003), 68–82, for Richmond, Virginia, and Lee Ann Whites, *The Civil War as a Crisis in Gender: Augusta, Georgia, 1860–1890* (Athens: University of Georgia Press, 1995), 64–95. Two studies associate the hardships faced by the women at home with ultimate Confederate defeat: George C. Rable, *Civil Wars: Women and the Crisis of Southern Nationalism* (Urbana: University of Illinois Press, 1989), and Drew Gilpin Faust, "Altars of Sacrifice: Confederate Women and the Narratives of War," *Journal of American History* 76 (March, 1990): 1200–28. Anne Sarah Rubin, in *A Shattered Nation: The Rise and Fall of the Confederacy, 1861–1868* (Chapel Hill: University of North Carolina Press, 2005), maintains that despite the hardships, Confederate women maintained their loyalty. Older studies on the impact of shortages on the homefront include Charles W. Ramsdell, *Behind the Lines in the Southern Confederacy* (Baton Rouge: Louisiana State University Press, 1944), and Mary Elizabeth Massey, *Ersatz in the Confederacy: Shortages and Substitutes on the Southern Homefront* (Columbia: University of South Carolina, 1952), 33–53.

2   Vicki Betts, *The Public Voices of Texas Women*, http://www.uttyler.edu/vbetts/texas_women_public_voices.html; Robert Maberry, Jr. *Texas Flags* (College Station: Texas A & M University Press in association with the Museum of Fine Arts, Houston, 2001), 58–67.

3   "Woman at Work," *Dallas Herald*, February 27, 1861, p. 4, C1; *Austin State Gazette*, April 27, 1861, p. 3, C4; Martha J. Blassingame to Governor Clark, 1861, Governor's Papers, Ed Clark, Box 301–36, Folder 19, Texas State Library and Archives), Austin, Texas (hereafter referred to as TSLA).

4   *Dallas Herald*, May 22, 1861, p. 2, c. 5; *Dallas Herald*, May 8, 1861, p. 4, c. 1; "Letter from Dallas," *Marshall Texas Republican*, May 18, 1861, p. 2, c. 3; "Patriotism," *Austin State Gazette*, May 18, 1861, p. 2, c. 6; *Austin State Gazette*, June 15, 1861, p. 3, c. 1; *Marshall Texas Republican*, June 22, 1861, p. 2, c. 3; *Austin State Gazette*, June 22, 1861, p. 3, c. 1; "Assembly of Notables," *Clarksville Standard*,

June 22, 1861, p. 2, c. 4; *Austin State Gazette*, July 6, 1861, p. 2, c. 2. Home production of clothing for Texas soldiers would continue throughout the war.

5   "To the Benevolent," *Marshall Texas Republican*, September 28, 1861, p. 2, c. 2.

6   *Marshall Texas Republican*, November 2, 1861, p. 2, c. 2.

7   "Southern Defense Aid Society," *San Antonio Herald*, March 15, 1862, p. 2, c. 2.

8   *Austin State Gazette*, March 29, 1862, p. 3, c. 2. Samuel Maverick served as treasurer of the group. Paula Mitchell Marks, *Turn Your Eyes Toward Texas: Pioneers Sam and Mary Maverick* (College Station: Texas A&M University Press, 1989), 226.

9   *Austin State Gazette*, March 15, 1862, p. 2, c. 2.

10   "Public Meeting," *Austin State Gazette*, March 22, 1862, p. 2, c. 4.

11   *Bellville Countryman*, March 29, 1862, p. 1, c. 3.

12   *Houston Tri-Weekly Telegraph*, April 4, 1862, p. 2, c. 1; April 7, 1862, p. 2, c. 2; *Galveston Weekly News*, April l8, 1862, p. 1, c. 1; April 15, 1862, p. 1, c. 2.

13   *Houston Tri-Weekly Telegraph*, April 16, 1862, p. 1, c. 2.

14   *Houston Tri-Weekly Telegraph*, April 25, 1862, p. 4, c. 4.

15   Ibid. Gideon Lincecum, in Washington County, made a similar comment on selective patriotism and the need for county taxes in a letter to his county judge dated April 24. Having recently been turned down for penitentiary cloth and soon to embark on home textile production himself, this letter may well have come from his rather prolific pen. He would contribute a number of letters to the *Telegraph* by the end of the war signed "Thine Gid." Jerry Bryan Lincecum, Edward Hake Phillips, and Peggy A. Redshaw, eds., *Gideon Lincecum's Sword: Civil War Letters from the Texas Home Front* (Denton: University of North Texas Press, 2001), 190–91.

16   "An Act Organizing County Courts," *Laws Passed by the First Legislature of the State of Texas*, 333–38, reprinted in H. P. N. Gammel, comp., *The Laws of Texas 1882–1897* (Austin: Gammel, 1898), 2:1639–44.

17   Randolph B. Campbell, *A Southern Community in Crisis: Harrison County, Texas, 1850–1880* (Austin: Texas State Historical Association, 1983), 202; *Marshall Texas Republican*, May 17, 1862, p. 2, c. 3.

18   Gammel, *Laws of Texas*, 5:467–69; William Frank Zornow, "Texas State Aid for Indigent Soldiers, 1861–1865," *Mid-America: An Historical Review* 37, no. 3 (1955): 172.

19   Brownston Malsch, *Indianola: The Mother of Western Texas* (Austin: State House Press, 1988), 165; *Austin State Gazette*, May 24, 1862, p. 1, c. 1.

20   *Inventory of the County Archives of Texas, No. 75, Fayette County (La Grange)* (San Antonio: Texas Historical Records Survey, 1940), 20, http://texashistory.unt.edu/data/UNT/County_Inventory/meta-pth-25251.tkl.

21   *Galveston Weekly News*, May 6, 1862, p. 2, c. 1; Edward T. Cotham, Jr., *Battle on the Bay: The Civil War Struggle for Galveston* (Austin: University of Texas Press, 1998), 52–53.

22   "Duty of the People," *Austin State Gazette*, May 31, 1862, p. 1, c. 2.

23   "Relief for the Poor," *Houston Tri-Weekly Telegraph*, May 28, 1862, p. 2, c. 4; "Offers of Aid," *Houston Tri-Weekly Telegraph*, June 2, 1862, p. 3, c. 1; June 4,

1862, p. 1, c. 5; p. 4, c. 5; June 6, 1862, p. 2, c. 5; *Austin State Gazette*, June 7, 1862, p. 1, c. 5.

24   *Houston Tri-Weekly Telegraph*, May 17, 1862, p. 2, c. 3; "The Concert," May 19, 1862, p. 2, c. 1; May 28, 1862, p. 4, c. 2; "Donations to the Galveston Poor," May 30, 1862, p. 2, c. 3; "Acknowledgements," May 30, 1862, p. 2, c. 4; "Acknowledgements," *Houston Tri-Weekly Telegraph*, June 4, 1862, p. 2, c. 3; "Acknowledgements," June 6, 1862, p. 2, c. 5.

25   *Houston Tri-Weekly Telegraph*, July 4, 1862, p. 2, c. 3; "Letter from Galveston," *Houston Tri-Weekly Telegraph*, July 28, 1862, p. 2, c. 4; "Galveston," *Houston Tri-Weekly Telegraph*, October 6, 1862, p. 1, c. 4.

26   *Galveston Weekly News*, October 22, 1862, p. 1, c. 1; Cotham, *Battle on the Bay*, 69; "Later from Galveston," *Austin State Gazette*, December 31, 1862, p. 1, c. 2.

27   *San Antonio Semi-Weekly News*, July 21, 1862, p. 2, c. 1.

28   *San Antonio Herald*, August 2, 1862, p. 2, c. 2.

29   *San Antonio Semi-Weekly News*, August 25, 1862, p. 2, c. 1.

30   *San Antonio Semi-Weekly News*, September 4, 1862, p. 2, c. 1. For bread riots east of the Mississippi, see E. Susan Barber, "'The Quiet Battles of the Home Front War': Civil War Bread Riots and the Development of a Confederate Welfare System" (master's thesis, University of Maryland, 1986). Bread or commodity riots also appear in almost every study of the Confederate home front, although none mention Texas.

31   Thomas A. Jennings, "San Antonio in the Confederacy" (master's thesis, Trinity University, 1957), 60; "Supply Association," *Galveston Weekly News*, September 10, 1862, p. 2, c. 1; *Handbook of Texas Online*, s.v. ""Schleicher, Gustav," http://www.tsha.utexas.edu/handbook/online/articles/SS/fsc9.html; Marks, *Turn Your Eyes Toward Texas*, 226.

32   Jennings, "San Antonio in the Confederacy," 61.

33   Smith County Commissioners Court Minutes, County Clerk's Office, Smith County Courthouse, Tyler, Texas, C:272–85.

34   J. J. Faulk, *History of Henderson County Texas* (Athens, Texas: Athens Review Printing Co., 1929; n.p.: Walsworth, 1975), 131.

35   Jack Stoltz, "Kaufman County in the Civil War," *East Texas Historical Journal* 28, no. 1 (1990): 41.

36   Ibid.

37   *Marshall Texas Republican*, December 20, 1862, p. 2, c. 1.

38   *Little Rock Weekly Arkansas Gazette*, December 20, 1862, p. 1, c. 2.

39   "To the People of Texas," *Marshall Texas Republican*, January 15, 1863, p. 1, c. 5.

40   "Keep It Before the People," *Marshall Texas Republican*, January 29, 1863, p. 2, c. 3.

41   Mark A. Weitz, *More Damning Than Slaughter: Desertion in the Confederate Army* (Lincoln: University of Nebraska Press, 2005), 74–77, 122–23.

42   Francis R. Lubbock, *Six Decades in Texas: The Memoirs of Francis R. Lubbock, Confederate Governor of Texas*, ed. C. W. Raines (Austin: Pemberton Press, 1968), 467.

43   Gammel, *Laws of Texas*, 5:601; Zornow, "Texas State Aid for Indigent Soldiers, 1861–1865," 172.

44 Lubbock, 477.

45 Marks, *Turn Your Eyes Toward Texas*, 232.

46 Lubbock, 478, Gammel, *Laws of Texas*, 5:617–18.

47 Lubbock, 478.

48 Gammel, *Laws of Texas*, 5:642–43, 645–47. See also Clayton E. Jewett, *Texas in the Confederacy: An Experiment in Nation Building* (Columbia: University of Missouri Press, 2002), 218–19, 230–31, 276–78, 283–85.

49 Gammel, *Laws of Texas*, 5:731, 794–95.

50 *Galveston Weekly News*, March 4, 1863, p. 1, c. 2; "Mutual Aid Association in Corpus Christi," *Galveston Weekly News*, October 28, 1863, p. 1, c. 3.

51 Gammel, *Laws of Texas*, 5:646.

52 "The San Antonio Mutual Aid Association," *San Antonio Herald*, February 28, 1863, p. 2, c. 3.

53 "The San Antonio Mutual Aid Association," *San Antonio Semi-Weekly News*, May 28, 1863, p. 2, c. 5.

54 "The San Antonio Mutual Aid Association," *San Antonio Herald*, February 28, 1863, p. 2, c. 3; *Galveston Weekly News*, February 10, 1864, p. 1, c. 7. The Houston Mutual Aid Association offered flour at half price in December, 1863, but at that time had not expanded enough to supply other needs. (*Galveston Weekly News*, December 30, 1863, p. 1, c. 1).

55 *Galveston Weekly News*, February 16, 1864, p. 2, c. 3.

56 Michael Rugeley Moore, "The Texas Penitentiary and Textile Production in the Civil War Era" (honors paper, University of Texas at Austin, 1984), 30, 128. See also Jewett, *Texas in the Confederacy*, 149–65.

57 Harold S. Wilson, *Confederate Industry: Manufacturers and Quartermasters in the Civil War* (Jackson: University Press of Mississippi, 2002), 147–50.

58 *Houston Tri-Weekly Telegraph*, October 3, 1862, p. 2, c. 3.

59 Moore, "The Texas Penitentiary and Textile Production in the Civil War Era," 109–11.

60 Gammel, *Laws of Texas*, 5:608.

61 *Houston Tri-Weekly News*, May 8, 1863, p. 2, c. 3.

62 Gammel, *Laws of Texas*, 5:610.

63 Moore, "The Texas Penitentiary and Textile Production in the Civil War Era," 112.

64 *Bellville Countryman*, July 25, 1863, p. 1, c. 4; August 22, 1863, p. 1, c. 2.

65 Ibid., June 20, 1863, p. 1, c. 4.

66 Ibid., August 22, 1863, p. 1, c. 2.

67 "A Huntsville Item," *Bellville Countryman*, September 26, 1863, p. 1, c. 3.

68 Ibid.

69 Ibid.

70 Lincecum, *Lincecum's Sword*, 193.

71 Ibid.

72 *Houston Tri-Weekly Telegraph*, August 27, 1862, p. 2, c. 1. On the production of homespun in Texas during the Civil War, see Paula Mitchell Marks, *Hands to the*

Spindle: Texas Women and Home Textile Production, 1822–1880 (College Station: Texas A&M University Press, 1996), 74–91.

73 *Little Rock Arkansas True Democrat*, January 16, 1862, p. 3, c. 2; *Houston Tri-Weekly Telegraph*, December 24, 1862, p. 3, c. 1; *Dallas Herald*, February 18, 1863, p. 2, c. 4.

74 "Home Manufactures," *Marshall Texas Republican*, September 6, 1862, p. 2, c. 2.

75 "Clothing for the Soldiers," *Houston Tri-Weekly Telegraph*, October 31, 1862, p. 2, c. 1.

76 Charles W. Ramsdell, "The Texas State Military Board, 1862–1865," *Southwestern Historical Quarterly* 27, no. 4 (1924): 266–67.

77 *Houston Tri-Weekly Telegraph*, May 1, 1863, p. 2, c. 2; *Galveston Weekly News*, May 6, 1863, p. 2, c. 4, May 13, 1863, p. 1, c. 1; *San Antonio Semi-Weekly News*, May 7, 1863, p. 2, c. 1; *Dallas Herald*, May 13, 1863, p. 2, c. 2; *Bellville Countryman*, May 16, 1863, p. 1, c. 5; *Marshall Texas Republican*, May 16, 1863, p. 2, c. 1.

78 "Cotton Cards," *Corpus Christi Ranchero*, May 21, 1863, p. 2, c. 3.

79 "200 Pairs Cotton Cards," *Dallas Herald*, May 20, 1863, p. 2, c. 2.

80 "Cotton Cards for the Counties," *Austin State Gazette*, October 28, 1863, p. 2, c. 1.

81 Mark Weitz in *More Damning Than Slaughter* highlights petitions sent to the Texas Adjutant General. For a survey of petitions sent to the Confederate Secretary of War, see Escott, "'The Cry of the Sufferers,'" and Amy E. Murrell, "'Of Necessity and Public Benefit': Southern Families and Their Appeals for Protection," in *Southern Families at War*, ed. Catherine Clinton (New York: Oxford University Press, 2000), 77–99. While no petitions from Texas are mentioned in either of the two articles, they do point out a potential source for further research. However, correspondence from Texas to Richmond during the latter part of the war, when the need was greatest, was probably hindered by the loss of control of the Mississippi River.

82 Lubbock, *Six Decades in Texas*, 487.

83 Sarah Katherine Stone Holmes, *Brokenburn: The Journal of Kate Stone, 1861–1868*, ed. John Q. Anderson (Baton Rouge: Louisiana State University Press, 1972), 229.

84 Mrs. Capt. John R. Alston to Gov. Lubbock, July 28, 1863, Governors' Papers, Francis R. Lubbock, Box 301-41, Folder 48, TSLA.

85 Petition from Williamson County to His Excellency P. Murrah, January 22, 1864, Governors' Papers, Pendleton Murrah, Box 301-44, Folder 14, TSLA.

86 Sarah Hughes to Governor Murray [*sic*], August 5, 1864, Governors' Papers, Pendleton Murrah, Box 301-45, Folder 39, TSLA.

87 Governors' Papers, Francis R. Lubbock, Boxes 301-41 and 301-42 and Pendleton Murrah, Boxes 301-44, 301-45, and 301-46, TSLA.

88 "Ladies residing in Beat No 11, in the said County of Upshur" to P. Murrah, 1864, Governors' Papers, Pendleton Murrah, Box 301-44, Folder 14, TSLA.

89 Alston, Governors' Papers.

90 Mrs. E. E. Lott to F. R. Lubbock, 1863 Aug 2, Governors' Papers, Francis R. Lubbock, Box 301-41, Folder 49, TSLA.

91   Petition of the Ladies of Bryants Station, Texas to F. R. Lubbock, 1863, Governors' Papers, Francis R. Lubbock, Box 301-42, Folder 51, TSLA.

92   Mary Cravy and others to F. R. Lubbock, September 16, 1863, Governors' Papers, Francis R. Lubbock, Box 301-42, Folder 51, TSLA.

93   "War Meeting," *Austin State Gazette*, October 7, 1863, p. 1, c. 2.

94   "To the Women of Texas," *Houston Tri-Weekly Telegraph*, October 17, 1863, p. 2, c. 3.

95   "Soldiers' Families," *Galveston Weekly News*, October 21, 1863, p. 2, c. 3.

96   *Houston Tri-Weekly Telegraph*, November 10, 1863, p. 2, c. 1.

97   Gammel, *Laws of Texas*, 5:675–76.

98   Ibid.

99   Ibid., 5:682–83; Zornow, "Texas State Aid for Indigent Soldiers, 1861–1865," 173.

100 Texas Comptroller's Office, *Circular to the Chief Justices of the Several Counties* (Austin, 1864), 7–8. These lists appear in Linda Mearse, *Confederate Indigent Families Lists of Texas, 1863–1865* (San Marcos, Texas: L. Mearse, 1995) and online from the Texas State Library and Archives Commission at *Confederate Indigent Families Lists (1863-1865),* http://www.tsl.state.tx.us/arc/cif/index.html.

101 Mearse, *Confederate Indigent Families Lists (1863–1865),* 296, 298, 386.

102 Ibid., 48.

103 Ibid., 232, 341, 286.

104 Ibid., 159.

105 Ibid., 191.

106 Mattie Davis Lucas and Mita Holsapple Hall, *A History of Grayson County, Texas* (Sherman, Texas: Scruggs Printing, 1936), 118–21.

107 *Galveston Weekly News*, June 15, 1864, p. 2, c. 3; Maria Jane Southgate Hawes, *Reminiscences of Maria Jane Southgate Hawes: Written in 1882* (n.p.: Mary Hawes Wood, 1986), 28; Cotham, *Battle on the Bay*, 164.

108 *Austin State Gazette*, June 29, 1864, p. 1, c. 1.

109 Mrs. A. D. Gentry, "Reminiscences of Mrs. J. J. Greenwood," *Frontier Times* 2, no. 3 (1924): 12.

110 Ann Raney Coleman, *Victorian Lady on the Texas Frontier: The Journal of Ann Raney Coleman*, ed. C. Richard King (Norman: University of Oklahoma Press, 1971), 153–55.

111 H. W. Bendy to W. D. Douglas, April 20, 1864, Confederate Papers Relating to Citizens or Business Firms, War Department Collection of Confederate Records, Record Group 109.

112 Chamberlain to Murrah, April 16, 1864, Governors' Papers, Pendleton Murrah, Box 301-45, Folder 29, TSLA.

113 R. J. Palmer to Pendleton Murrah, September 28, 1864, Governors' Papers, Pendleton Murrah, Box 301-46, Folder 42, TSLA.

114 Gammel, *Laws of Texas*, 5:817.

115 Ibid., 5:816.

116 "'Go Thou and Do Likewise,'" *Houston Tri-Weekly Telegraph*, November 16, 1864, p. 2, c. 1-2.

117 "To the Amateurs of Houston & Galveston," *Houston Tri-Weekly Telegraph*,
December 14, 1864, p. 4, c. 3. Houston had a population of 3,779 in 1860. Paul
A. Levengood, "In the Absence of Scarcity: The Civil War Prosperity of Houston,
Texas," *Southwestern Historical Quarterly* 101, no. 4 (1998): 402. Levengood
acknowledges Houston faced shortages of some goods, but asserts that relative to
other Confederate cities, Houston fared very well.

118 "To the Patriotic and Charitable," *Galveston Weekly News*, December 28, 1864,
p. 1, c. 7. In 1860, Galveston County had a population of 8,229. Alwyn Barr,
"The 'Queen City of the Gulf' Held Hostage: The Impact of War on Confederate
Galveston," *Military History of the West* 27 (Fall 1997): 120.

119 *Marshall Texas Republican*, February 3, 1865, p. 2, c. 2.

120 *Austin State Gazette*, May 10, 1865, p. 2, c. 1; *Dallas Herald*, June 15, 1865, p. 1,
c. 5.

121 Escott, "'The Cry of the Sufferers,'" 231.

122 Thomas L. Miller, "Texas Land Grants to Confederate Veterans and Widows,"
Southwestern Historical Quarterly 69 (July 1965): 59–65; Mary L. Wilson, "The
Confederate Pension Systems in Texas, Georgia, and Virginia: The Programs and
the People" (Ph.D. diss., University of North Texas, 2004).

Chapter 15

On the Edge of First Freedoms: Black Texans and the Civil War

by Ronald E. Goodwin and Bruce A. Glasrud

In many, perhaps most, respects, Texas is a Southern state. Historians examining the Texas antebellum and Civil War eras traditionally turned their attention to how the war and the end of slavery affected white Texans. Few authors discussed the war's impact on the thousands of African American slaves residing within Texas. This chapter attempts to remedy this oversight by showing the direct impact of the Civil War on the institution of slavery in Texas by looking at the war from the slaves' perspective. One reason that scholars avoided studying this topic in depth was the limited number of primary resources available that recounted the African Americans' perspective. Their point of view, however, can be obtained from a close reading of the Works Progress Administration's (WPA) *Slave Narratives*, interviews with ex-slaves taken during the 1930s. These documents not only capture the former slaves' general recollections of slavery, but also reveal much about slavery during the Civil War. In particular, the interviews with Texas's former slaves illustrate the master-slave relationship, the nature of slavery during 1861–1865, and, lastly, the slaves' reactions to their first freedoms.[1]

The study of African Americans in Texas during the Civil War has been analyzed from additional perspectives. Three thought-provoking analyses of the overall status of black Texans during the Civil War have been produced. James Marten, in "Slaves and Rebels: The Peculiar Institution in Texas, 1861–1865," notes that two conflicting pre-war situations—"the general faithfulness of most slaves counter-pointed to the constant threat that they posed to the institution"—continued in Texas during the war. In his path-breaking study of African American slavery in the Lone Star State, Randolph B. Campbell concludes his book, *An Empire for Slavery*, with a chapter entitled "The Civil War and 'Juneteenth,' 1861–1865." Campbell points out that during the Civil War "the Peculiar Institution remained less disturbed in Texas than in any other Confederate state." More recently, the dean of black Texas historians, Alwyn Barr, depicts the situation of black slaves in an article entitled "Black Texans during the Civil War." Barr argues that black slaves survived the war years by receiving support from families, religion, music, and, when possible, escape or resistance. As he summarizes, black Texans "participated in a period of danger, hope, and change."[2]

Other historians also discuss the state of black Texans during the Civil War. Both Carl H. Moneyhon, in "Texas in 1865," and Elizabeth Silverthorne, in "The End," touch on the demise of slavery and the status of black slaves and white owners in the declining moments of the Confederacy in their respective works. James M. Smallwood, in a chapter entitled "First Freedom" from his book, *Time of Hope, Time of Despair*, describes the period during 1865 from a slightly different perspective as the beginning of Reconstruction. Scholars Drew Gilpin Faust ("'Trying to do a Man's Business': Gender Violence and Slave Management in Civil War Texas"), Nancy Cohen-Lack ("A Struggle for Sovereignty: National Consolidation, Emancipation, and Free Labor in Texas, 1865"), and Anne J. Bailey ("A Texas Cavalry Raid: Reaction to Black Soldiers and Contrabands") aid our understanding of Texas black history by publishing more specialized studies that consider Afro-Texan experiences during the Civil War. Additional information from the slave narratives can also be located in two chapters from the compendium of Texas slave narratives, "The Freedom War" and "Free at Last" by Ronnie C. Tyler and Lawrence R. Murphy.[3]

By the end of the Civil War, there were considerably more slaves (as many as 50,000) in Texas than at the beginning. This situation leads to two considerations. First, what factors facilitated the great increase in the slave population? And second, why did not more slaves resist, revolt, or run away during the disturbances of the war? The increase in the slave population during the war occurred when large numbers of black slaves were brought as refugees by their masters from areas of the Confederacy that were undergoing pitched battles or Union military occupation, especially from nearby states such as Louisiana and Arkansas, but also from Missouri, Tennessee, and Mississippi. Some slaves marched all the way from Virginia. The population also increased because of a strong birth rate and the fact that few slaves escaped successfully; certainly only slightly higher numbers escaped or ran away during the Civil War than during the antebellum period. As former Prairie View professor of history George R. Woolfolk determines in *The Cotton Regency*, the black population of Texas continued to increase even after the war's end when freedmen from the East headed for the Southwest, and, hopefully, better opportunities.[4]

For those Afro-Texans who sought escape from the pernicious institution of slavery, Texas's proximity to Mexico offered a unique opportunity. Estimates place at least 4,000 black runaways in Mexico prior to the Civil War, a process that continued during the war. As former slave Jacob Branch remarked, "After the war started, lots of slaves ran off to get to the Yankees. All them in this part [near Galveston] headed for the Rio Grande River. The Mexicans rigged up flatboats out in the middle of the river, tied to stakes with rope. When the colored people got to the rope they could pull themselves across the rest of the way on those boats." Felix Haywood declared that "in Mexico you could be free. They didn't care what color you was, black, white, yellow, or blue." Although slave owners who worried about losing runaways disliked the situation, officials of the Confederacy impressed or hired slaves to transport cotton to Matamoros. As a result, according to Sallie Wroe, when her father hauled a load of cotton to the Rio Grande on the Mexican border, he and other drivers then paddled a bale of cotton to Mexico where he remained until the war ended.[5] The majority of Texas slaves, however, waited and hoped for freedom.

Ex-slaves also evinced considerable loyalty to white families who had their own misfortunes during the war. Texas did not experience the ravages of war to the same devastating degree as other Southern states, even as strict discipline and order became difficult to enforce because of the absence of the male slave owners. However, Texas's slaves did fear the increasing brutality of Texas's white soldiers who reportedly massacred black soldiers in battles, either heading toward or leaving a battle area, and randomly killed or mutilated slaves found in the locale. What would happen, Texas slaves might suppose, if they tried to rebel or escape? The racist ferocity of white Texas soldiers in their treatment of African Americans can be found in the writings of Anne J. Bailey, including her "A Texas Cavalry Raid: Reaction to Black Soldiers and Contrabands" as well as her "Was There a Massacre at Poison Spring?"[6]

Until the publication of Randolph B. Campbell's *An Empire for Slavery*, very little scholarly attention was devoted to slavery in Texas despite the fact that slavery had been a part of Texas since the first expeditions of the Spanish conquistadors.[7] Most of the white immigrants to Texas during the antebellum era arrived from Southern states and brought their propensity for slavery and the supposed proper relationship between the races with them. Essentially, as Campbell argues, slavery in Texas was no different from that found in other slaveholding states throughout the South.[8] Slaves were denied the right to own individual property, buy or sell goods, or carry a firearm; they were forbidden to testify against a white man in court. The most important aspect of the slave's life was his or her obedience to the will of the white master.[9] The need to maintain this obedience led the plantation elite to develop a culture that kept blacks in a specific sociological and political place in Southern culture. This subordinate place continued as blacks became the underclass of Texas society during the late nineteenth and twentieth centuries.

After Mexico gained its independence from Spain, Stephen F. Austin led the initial colonization of Texas with 297 families (known in Texas lore as the "Old Three Hundred"). As did the previous Spanish government, the Mexican government believed slavery was immoral, and in fact, as Paul D. Lack depicts so well, slavery was *a*, if not *the*, principal cause of the Texas Revolution.[10] By 1836, there were 5,000 slaves in Texas, located mostly along the Brazos, Colorado, and Trinity rivers in the southeastern part of the state. Texas independence removed the last remaining obstacles to slavery realizing its full potential. Texans, as did Southerners, believed slave labor would produce economic profits if supported by favorable governmental policies. Consequently, slavery increased in the new republic as Texas became economically dependent on cotton and slave labor.[11]

By the 1850s slavery and cotton production were interlaced; the slave population increased by nearly 125,000 while cotton production increased from just over 58,000 bales per year in 1850 to nearly 183,000 bales per year in 1860. Texas slave owners recognized the positive relationship between the number of slaves and the ability to increase cotton production.[12] As a result, regardless of the number of slaves on any plantation or farm, the living conditions of slaves often were brutal. Slave beatings were common and severe; their general living conditions were just good enough to keep them sufficiently healthy to work the land. When interviewed in the 1930s, former slaves commented on such topics as their former masters, overseers, slave drivers, the food they ate, the clothes they wore, and the houses in which they lived.

Even with the brutality associated with slavery, some slave owners believed their role in the master-slave dynamic was purely paternalistic. In *Roll, Jordan, Roll*, historian Eugene Genovese describes this tenuous relationship: "Cruel, unjust, exploitative, oppressive slavery bound two peoples together in bitter antagonism while creating an organic relationship so complex and ambivalent that neither could express the simplest human feelings without reference to the other."[13] Numerous ex-slaves remembered with fondness the master-slave relationships in Texas. They recalled how many slaves earned the respect of their owners so that they and their families could enjoy special privileges. Others remembered the brutality of the master, especially when production quotas were not met.[14]

While there was no consensus on the legacy of the slave master, almost all of Texas's former slaves recalled the overseer with disgust and hatred. Former slave Mary Reynolds remembered that overseers seldom hesitated when it came to the punishment of slaves. Reynolds recalled not her owner, Dr. Kilpatrick, but an overseer, whom she referred to as Solomon, who would beat slaves so severely that he "could cut the flesh 'most to the bone." Reynolds detested Solomon; she later commented that "I know that Solomon is burnin' in hell today and it pleasures me to know it. An' though they was good white folks that I heard tell of, I think they is plenty mo' of them in hell too."[15]

Even in such perilous conditions, slaves might reach positions of authority. On large plantations it was not uncommon for a select few trusted black slaves to rise to the position of driver, allowing them to manage other field slaves. Even

Illustration 17 Sarah Ford. *Courtesy Library of Congress.*

when the professional overseer was present, several drivers may have been present depending upon the division of labor on the plantation. On smaller plantations, when the slave owners were unable to hire a professional overseer, they "promoted" trusted field hands who assisted in local production management.[16]

Even though the family members of drivers enjoyed special privileges, black drivers occasionally treated fellow slaves with more contempt than did white overseers.[17] For example, former slave Sarah Ford recalled the vicious driver on the Kit Patton plantation near West Columbia. Known as Uncle Big Jake, the driver was as black as any slave on the plantation, according to Ford. But she said he was as mean and cruel as any white overseer. Ford said, "He so mean I 'spect de devil done make him an overseer down below a long time ago." Ford blamed Patton for allowing Uncle Big Jake to punish the slaves so severely that many often ran away.[18]

Since conditions during the war in Texas did not change to the extent of other Southern states, aspects of slave life remained similar to those that existed before the war. The basic slave diet consisted of cornmeal and salt pork or bacon. Typically, the slave owner spent less than $30 annually per slave.[19] While the nourishment of slaves was an important investment for most slave owners, even with their weekly rations and the ability to grow their own food, many slaves indicated that they still did not have enough food to eat. Hunger and discontent combined with the lack of variety in the diets led many slaves to steal food from their masters whenever they could.[20] For instance, former Texas slaves Betty Powers and Jenny Proctor remembered stealing food. Powers recalled:

> All de rations measure out Sunday mornin' and it have to do for de week. It am not 'nough for heavy eaters and we has to be real careful or we goes hungry. We has meat and cornmeal and 'lasses and 'taters and peas and beans and milk. Dem short rations causes plenty trouble, 'cause de niggers has to steal food and it am de whippin' if dey gits cotched. Dey am in a fix if dey can't work for bein' hungry, 'cause it am de whippin' den, sho' so dey has to steal, and most of 'em did and takes de whippin'. Dey has de full stomach anyway.[21]

Most studies of slave clothing usually found slave attire to be as inadequate as their diets. Typically slave females were responsible for making the clothes, and in some cases shoes, for their families. On those plantations where the owner provided clothing, slaves generally received one set of winter and one set of summer clothing. Male slaves usually received two suits (shirt and pants) per year and a single pair of shoes. Women, especially those working in or near the main house, might receive castoffs from their mistresses. Children, regardless of gender, usually wore a shirt with no pants or shoes until they were about ten to twelve years of age.[22]

While slaves often reported that food and clothing were inadequate, there was no consensus on the quality of slave housing, which must have varied significantly. Some considered the homes they lived in to be satisfactory, while others said their housing resembled "stalls like pens they use for cattle."[23] Most slaves lived in cabins or large multifamily barracks that were typically twenty-foot-square single-room structures with a single window and sometimes a fireplace for heating and cooking. The cabins were most often built from material that provided basic shelter from the elements, but that was hardly sturdy enough to last several seasons. The floors usually were dirt-covered; wooden floors were considered a luxury.[24] In his classic study, *Before the Mayflower*, historian Lerone Bennett quotes a former slave who remarked, "Everything happened in that one room—birth, sickness, death—everything."[25]

Black Texas slaves were also affected by events on the national and regional scale. Though President Lincoln argued that "it would be a war to restore national unity, a war in which slaves would be, at best, interested spectators whose status and circumstances would remain unchanged," secession and war quickly involved slaves in the state.[26] Texas joined the secessionist movement over the objections of the famed Sam Houston who considered secession "unjustifiable, unconstitutional, and revolutionary."[27] Texas experienced few military conflicts and generally escaped the ravages the war brought to other states throughout the Confederacy. Nonetheless, the impact of the Civil War remained significant. Texas was on the western frontier of the Confederacy and vulnerable to attack from the north, west, and south. Indian raids were commonplace as state leaders never successfully protected frontier settlements. Additionally, despite the Union army's defeat in the Battle of Galveston, the Texas coastline remained vulnerable to further attacks. Furthermore, Texans feared Federal invasions of East Texas through Louisiana and the Indian Territory.[28]

Despite the bravado, not all white Texans were eager for battle. When interviewed in the 1930s, many of Texas's former slaves recalled how whites in Texas responded to the call to arms. They described how some took leadership positions in training local volunteers for service in the militia, others collected food and supplies, while some actively participated in combat.[29] There were some white males in Texas who tried to avoid active military service altogether. As former slave Susan Ross said, "Lots of 'em didn't want to go, but dey has to."[30] Ellen Payne of Marshall, Texas, reported that she knew of many young white males who tried to get out of military service, and said, "I 'member the white southern men folks run off to the bottoms to git 'way from war." [31] Other Texas men must have regretted their initial choice of service. Harrison Beckett, interviewed in Beaumont, Texas, told a secondhand story of a slave owner's son who deserted his Confederate unit in Arkansas: "When dat first cannon busts at Li'l Rock, he starts runnin' and never stops till he gits back home, I don't see how he could do det, 'cause Li'l Rock am way far off, but dat what dey say. Den de men comes to git 'serters and dey gits Li'l Ide and takes him back."[32]

Eventually the war became synonymous with freedom as blacks throughout the country, free and slave, came to see it as a war that would end slavery, allowing them to live free of intimidation, free from physical and emotional restraints, and free to receive a reasonable wage for their labor, or better, obtain title to their own land. At the beginning of the war there were nearly two hundred thousand slaves in Texas; by the end the total reached as many as two hundred and fifty thousand. The presence of Union armies in the state had little impact on slavery, but almost everyone, slave and slave owner, knew changes in the state's social, economic, and political institutions were forthcoming.[33]

Among the changes to come was the master-slave dynamic. Texas plantation records of the period often indicated that the master-slave relationship was benign, supporting the claim of Southern apologists of the paternalistic nature of slavery. According to Abigail Scott Curlee, in "The History of a Texas Slave Plantation," the records of the Peach Point plantation imply that slaves were treated with "consideration" and were generally "comfortable and happy."[34] Scholars such as Randolph Campbell arrive at a variant interpretation. If slave owners believed their slaves were comfortable and happy, why did so many worry about

Illustration 18 Martin Jackson. *Courtesy Library of Congress.*

the loyalties of their slaves once the inevitability of the war became apparent? The master-slave dynamic changed dramatically during the Civil War in Texas because of the awareness that the war might bring about the end of slavery. Many slave owners intimidated their slaves into a verbal acknowledgment of their loyalty to them and the Confederacy. Even though the slaves readily raised their hands in acknowledged support of their continued bondage, nearly seventy years later many slaves indicated that they dared not disagree with their owners. Former slave William Adams remembered a white preacher telling slaves that they should pray for the Confederacy to win or else they would be homeless, hungry, and live like "de wil' animals." Adams said, "We all raised our hands 'cause we were skeered not to, but we sho' dodn' wan' de South to win."[35]

As did Adams, former slave Martin Jackson was not only aware of the implications of the war—that the slaves might be freed with a Union victory— but also recalled wanting the Confederacy to lose. Jackson said he followed his "young master" to war and eventually ended up with the First Texas Cavalry. He remembered feeling that the North would win, but curiously said he did not want the First Texas Cavalry defeated in the process. He said, "I knew the Yanks were going to win, from the beginning. I wanted them to win and lick us

Southerners, but I hoped they was going to do it without wiping out our company." Jackson also remembered that his father cautioned him that regardless of the outcome of the war, they were going to have to get along with whites after the war.[36]

These interviews, and many others, illuminated aspects of the master-slave relationship that are too often absent from surviving plantation records. First, even though numerous Southerners claimed the war was not about slavery, the fear that their slaves would be freed was evident from the beginning. Second, not only were white Texans aware of this possibility, slaves were as well. Finally, slaves were cognizant enough of the war and its implications that they knowingly misled their owners as to their loyalty to them and the sanctity of slavery. The *Slave Narratives* indicate clearly that slaves were intelligent, rational beings, not the unintelligent, childlike brutes most white antebellum Texans asserted them to be.[37]

Despite the war, the farms and plantations of Texas still operated, and massive amounts of labor–slave labor–were needed to keep them profitable. Just as the master-slave dynamic changed during the war, the nature of slavery also changed. For many slaves, this change was for the worse. As brutal as slavery in Texas was before 1861, it is difficult to conceive that it could descend further into an abyss of hopelessness. It did. With the Confederate conscription act in place, nearly all of the able-bodied white males, and many of their slaves, joined the fighting. Former slave Willie Forward reported that many slaves served the Confederate cause as cooks in the field, bodyguards, or nurses to their masters and other Confederate soldiers. He also believed every slave owner took a slave to war with him.[38]

As a result, many slave owners hired new overseers to ensure proper order and continued production while they were away. These overseers often were cruel taskmasters; many of the former slaves indicated that their lives changed for the worse during the war. Slave Andy Anderson remembered their food rations were reduced, but the new overseer demanded even more production. Anderson said, "De hell start to pop," and further stated, "He half starve us niggers and he want mo' work and he start de whippin's."[39]

Overseers were not the only ones responsible for increased levels of cruelty. Many slave owners avoided service in the Confederate armies and reportedly felt the need to intensify the viciousness of slavery because of the fear that slaves might escape. "We wore chains all the time," remembered former slave Ben Simpson in discussing slavery during the war. He continued, "When we work, we drug them chains with us. At night he lock us to a tree to keep us from runnin' off. He didn't have to do that. We were 'fraid to run. We knew he'd kill us."[40]

There was one other type of slave owner directly affected by the war—white women. On the many smaller plantations in the Lone Star State, neither overseer nor male owners were present, and white women endeavored to run the plantations. They had difficult times trying to establish their credibility. A sophisticated account of one white Texas woman's situation can be found in Drew Gilpin Faust, "'Trying to Do a Man's Business': Gender, Violence, and Slave Management in Civil War Texas." White women, Faust remarks, felt compelled "in slave-owning households to become the reluctant agents of power they could not embrace as rightfully their own."[41]

The pressures of the war caused intense hardship and distress for many white Texans and their slaves. Former slave Annie Row recalled how her former master reacted when news reached the farm that one of his sons had been killed. In his anguish he struck Row's mother about the head with a poker and sent her falling to the dirt floor. He followed this by grabbing his gun and Row recalled how he stormed out the door toward the slaves' quarters. She then said, "My sister and I sees that and we'uns starts runnin' and screamin', 'cause we'uns has brothers and sisters in de field. But de good Lawd took a hand in that mess and de marster ain't gone far in de field when him drops all of a sudden. De death sets on de marster and de niggers comes runnin' to him. Him can't talk or move and dey tote him in de house." The next day he was dead. When the other son returned from the war, he informed the slaves that they were free, and could stay or go. Row remembered, "Mos' of 'em left as soon's dey could." As a result, Row stated that the surviving son later killed himself by cutting his own throat with a razor. A note found next to his body said he didn't want to live, "'cause de nigger free and dey's all broke up."[42]

While antebellum slavery in Texas often resembled that of other Southern states, the slaves' narratives imply that the vile practice changed and intensified during the war. The fear of retaliation from the slaves for prior acts of brutality combined with the need to maintain order and discourage escape attempts led many overseers and slave owners to intensify the use of the whip. In "Dave: A Rebellious Slave," Paul D. Lack summarizes well the overall status of black slaves during the Civil War; as he notes, Dave's life "demonstrates the disruptive nature of the Civil War for both master and slave. The wartime experience presented increased possibility for a slave to grasp his liberty, but it brought too a greater amount of displacement and physical suffering." Moreover, the change in the master-slave relationship together with the increased brutality of slavery set the tone for the end of the war and the inevitability for first freedoms.[43]

Initially, first freedoms were merely concepts with little tangibility for the thousands of Texas blacks suddenly freed. Most, if not all, of Texas's former slaves remembered the first rush of excitement when they learned of the defeat of the Confederacy and their resultant freedom. Former slave Andy Anderson said he left the plantation as soon as he found out they were free.[44] Likewise, former slave Susan Ross of Jasper recalled her brother's reaction after being told he was free. She said he "whoop, run and jump a high fence and told mammy goodbye. Den he grab me up and hug and kiss me and say, 'brother gone, don't 'spect you ever see me no more.' I don't know where he go, but I never did see him 'gain." Felix Haywood recalled that "everyone was singing. We was all walking on golden clouds. Hallelujah!"[45]

However, many also recalled a feeling of intense fear; they were now responsible for their own welfare, something they had never known before.[46] For example, former slave Elsie Reece said:

> You should seed dem cullud folks. Dey jus' plumb shock. Dere faces long as dere arm, and so pester dey don't know what to say or do. Masas never say 'nother word and walks away. De cullud folks say "Where we'uns gwine live? What we'uns gwine do?" Later they agree to stay and work for wages. Well, sar, dere a bunch of happy cullud folks after dey larnt dey could stay and work, and my folks stays nearly two years after 'mancipation.[47]

Confused and without direction for the first time in their lives, many blacks were overwhelmed by first freedoms. Former slave Jack Bess of San Angelo commented that he was definitely glad when freedom came, but recalled facing an uncertain future. He said, "We didn' know nothin' to do but jes stay on dere, and we did 'bout three years and de boss pays us a little by de month for our work."[48] However, Will Adams recalled the slaves shedding tears of joy *and* fear. He said, "They's lots of cryin' and weepin' when they sot us free. Lots of them didn't want to be free, 'cause they knowed nothin' and had nowhere to go."[49]

The former slaves also noted that they were not the only ones experiencing feelings of fear and uncertainty. Many white Texans never accepted the defeat of the Confederacy, believing instead that they merely quit for the benefit of the country. Now they were facing their own uncertainties because of the rapid social and economic changes they were experiencing.[50] News of Lee's surrender was difficult enough to comprehend for many of Texas's slave owners, but it was the presence of the Union army as an occupation force that caused a tremendous amount of hostility and resentment.

Much of this hostility was a result of the Union army forcing reluctant slave owners to release their slaves, or pay them for their labor. Many owners refused to do either. Those who did immediately free their slaves did so under duress. Former slave Cato Carter said his owner was in tears as he announced to his slaves that slavery was over and they were free. He recalled, "You are free to do as you like, 'cause the damned Yankees done 'creed you are. They ain't a nigger on my place what was born here or ever lived here who can't stay here and work and eat to the end of his days, as long as this old place will raise peas and goobers. Go if you wants, and stay if you wants."[51]

Illustration 19 Will Adams. *Courtesy Library of Congress.*

Former slaves William Mathews, Susan Merrit, and William Thomas also remembered that their former slave owners responded with hostility and resentment when told they had to release their slaves. Mathews said they were forced to keep working well after freedom in 1865 because their owner, "old Buck Adams," would not let them go. It was not until "de freedom man come and read de paper, and tell us not to work no more 'less us gits pay for it," did Adams release them.[52] Interviewed in Marshall, Texas, Merrit informed her interviewer that they were not told of their freedom for three months. She and the other slaves were kept ignorant of the outcome of the war until a "Union man" came to the plantation and read the order stating they were free. Nonetheless, Merrit further commented that they were still not given the option to go or stay. She said, "massa make us work sev'ral months after that. He say we git 20 acres land and a mule but we didn't git it."[53] Like Mathews and Merrit, William Thomas also stated that he and his fellow slaves were unaware of emancipation until Union soldiers came through the area and forced slave owners to comply.[54]

There were numerous occasions when the former slave owners verbally and physically expressed their animosity towards their former chattel and the Union soldiers. One slave recalled the following song as an example of the animosity felt by white Texans at the end of the war:

> O, I'm a good old rebel, and dat's jus' what I am,
> And for dis land of freedom, I do not give a damn;
> I'm glad we fought again 'em, and only wish we'd won,
> And I ain't asked no pardon for anything I've done.
> I won't be reconstructed, I'm better dan dey am,
> And for a carpetbagger I do not give a damn.
> So I'm off to de frontier, soon as I can go—
> I'll fix me up a wagon and start for Mexico!
> I can't get my musket and fight dem now no more,
> But I'm not goin' to love dem, dat an certain sho' —
> I don't want no pardon for what I was or am,
> I won't be reconstructed, and I don't give a damn.[55]

Historians Leon Litwack and Frank Tannenbaum point out that it mattered little if the former slaves left their former masters immediately after emancipation or stayed. This decision was still their first exercise of freedom as they began making decisions for their lives and those of their families and community. However, in time many began slowly moving away from the plantation and the memories of slavery.[56]

This was certainly the case in Texas. During her 1930s interview, former slave "Aunt" Pinkie Kelly admitted to not knowing much about the war; her owner did not immediately tell his slaves they were free. While news of their sudden freedom seemed a dream come true, Kelly and her fellow slaves soon realized they had nowhere to go. "Law, we sho' shout, young folks and old folks too. But we stay there, no place to go, so we jes stay, but we gits a little pay."[57] Similarly, former slave Betty Powers remembered her owner advising the former slaves to remain with him on the plantation until they were able to take care of themselves and make their own decisions for their lives. She said, "He 'vises dem to stay till dey git de foothold and larn how to do. Lots stayed and lots go. My folks stays 'bout four years and works on shares." Her father eventually saved enough money and purchased his own farm near the plantation.[58]

The decision on whether to stay or leave ought to have been easier. The freed men and women desired, expected, and needed land. However, in the contest among Northern whites, emancipated black Texans, Texas planters, and non-planter whites, the needs and goals of the freed men and women were overlooked and dismissed. As Nancy Cohen-Lack summarizes, black Texans "perceived that if they arose from bondage without the material resources to defend themselves against the new form of dominion enthroned by free labor, they would lose the opportunity to wrest freedom, independence, and equal citizen-

Illustration 20   Betty Powers. *Courtesy Library of Congress.Congress.*

ship as they understood them from the Union's grant of legal equality and free contract."[59] Black Texans understood well the consequence; no land ultimately meant white Texans' denial of black rights.

The workings of the institution of slavery in Texas were fundamentally similar to those in other slave states throughout the South during the antebellum years. During the Civil War many changes did occur that were not readily noticeable from an examination solely of plantation records. The strain of the master-slave relationship, already tenuous before the war, increased after 1861 as the possibility that their property might be freed caused slave owners to intensify their hatred both of the North and of their slaves. Understanding this, many slaves indicated that they feigned ignorance of the events occurring around them, all the while privately hoping that the war would somehow fulfill their dreams of freedom.

The very nature of slavery in Texas changed as more overseers were needed, as many Southern white males joined the fighting, leaving mostly women and children to maintain crop production and order. Texas's slaves recalled these overseers, and the slave owners that stayed behind, as exceedingly brutal. Such treatment made the reactions to first freedoms even more complex. Many slaves certainly wanted to be free to live their lives on their own terms, but they recalled the absolute fear inherent in being slaves one morning and a freed people that evening. As a result, many of Texas's former slaves initially remained near their former owners, but eventually ventured away from the plantation, their former owners, and slavery.

Notes

1   President Franklin D. Roosevelt created the Works Progress Administration in May 1935 as the new cornerstone of his New Deal Depression-era initiatives. The WPA employed millions of Americans and signified Roosevelt's ideological shift from dole distribution to work relief as remedies to the rampant poverty and hopelessness caused by the Great Depression. The *Slave Narratives* project was a component of the WPA where unemployed white-collar professionals interviewed former slaves. While there were other independent efforts to document the life experiences of former slaves, this was the first sponsored by the federal government using common questions regarding such topics as food, housing, work, and clothing. There were admittedly limitations in the oral interview process. Many of the interviewers were inexperienced and some of the former slaves either did not recall events from their childhood or were hesitant to discuss them. Nonetheless, the WPA *Slave Narratives* have become an accepted primary source in examining slavery from the perspective of the enslaved.

2   James A. Marten, "Slaves and Rebels: The Peculiar Institution in Texas, 1861–1865," *East Texas Historical Journal* 28 (Spring 1990): 29–36, quote 35; Randolph B. Campbell, "The Civil War and 'Juneteenth,' 1861–1865" in *An Empire for Slavery: The Peculiar Institution in Texas, 1821–1865* (Baton Rouge: Louisiana State University Press, 1989), 231–51, quote 231; Alwyn Barr, "Black Texans during the Civil War," in *Invisible Texans: Women and Minorities in Texas History*, ed. Donald Willett and Stephen Curley (Boston: McGraw Hill, 2005), 86–93, quote 92. For a list of additional works on this topic, see Bruce A. Glasrud and Laurie Champion, "Civil War and Reconstruction, 1861–1874," *Exploring the Afro-Texas Experience: A Bibliography of Secondary Sources about Black Texans*, ed. Bruce A. Glasrud and Laurie Champion (Alpine, Texas: SRSU Center for Big Bend Studies, 2000), 31–40.

3   Carl H. Moneyhon, "Texas in 1865, " *Texas after the Civil War: The Struggle of Reconstruction* (College Station: Texas A&M University Press, 2004), 6–20, 207–8; Elizabeth Silverthorne, "The End," *Plantation Life in Texas* (College Station: Texas A&M University Press, 1986), 191–212; James M. Smallwood, "First Freedom," in *Time of Hope, Time of Despair: Black Texans during Reconstruction* (Port Washington, New York: Kennikat Press, 1981), 25–42; Drew Gilpin Faust, "'Trying to Do a Man's Business': Gender Violence and Slave Management in Civil War Texas," in *Southern Stories: Slaveholders in Peace and War*, ed. Drew Gilpin Faust (Columbia: University of Missouri Press, 1992), 174–92; Nancy Cohen-Lack, "A Struggle for Sovereignty: National Consolidation, Emancipation, and Free Labor in Texas, 1865," *Journal of Southern History* 58 (February 1992): 57–98; Anne J. Bailey,

"A Texas Cavalry Raid: Reaction to Black Soldiers and Contrabands," *Civil War History* 35 (June 1989): 138–52; Ronnie C. Tyler and Lawrence R. Murphy, eds., "The Freedom War," in *The Slave Narratives of Texas* (Austin: Encino Press, 1974), 96–112; "Free at Last," in *Slave Narratives of Texas*, 113–27.

4   Marten, "Slaves and Rebels," 29–36; Campbell, "The Civil War and 'Juneteenth,'" in *Empire for Slavery*, 231–51; Barr, "Black Texans during the Civil War," 86–93; George Ruble Woolfolk, *The Cotton Regency: The Northern Merchants and Reconstruction, 1865–1880* (1958; repr., New York: Octagon Books, 1979), 94–97.

5   Barr, "Black Texans during the Civil War," 91; Marten, "Slaves and Rebels," 29–36; Tyler, *Slave Narratives of Texas*, quotes 101, 69; Campbell, *An Empire for Slavery*, 248.

6   Bailey, "A Texas Cavalry Raid," 138–52; Anne J. Bailey, "Was There a Massacre at Poison Spring?" *Military History of the Southwest* 20 (Fall 1990): 157–68.

7   Campbell, *An Empire for Slavery*, 10–12; Rupert N. Richardson, Adrian Anderson, Cary D. Wintz, and Ernest Wallace, *Texas: The Lone Star State* (Upper Saddle River, New Jersey: Pearson / Prentice Hall, 2005), 49–50, 56–72.

8   Robert A. Calvert and Arnoldo De León, *The History of Texas*, 2nd. ed. (Wheeling, Illinois: Harlan Davidson, 1996), 66; Campbell, *An Empire for Slavery*, 257–58; Steven Mintz, *African American Voices*, 3rd. ed. (St. James, New York: Brandywine Press, 2004), 101.

9   Calvert, *The History of Texas*, 65–66; Ioannis Miliatos, "Some Aspects of Slavery and Slave Care in Texas" (MA Thesis, Texas Southern University, 1972), 1; Eugene Genovese, *Roll, Jordan, Roll: The World the Slaves Made* (New York: Pantheon, 1974), 12; William Williams, *Slavery and Freedom in Delaware, 1639–1865* (Wilmington, Delaware: Scholarly Resources, 1996), 88. Like Genovese, Miliatos believes it was the overseer, when there was one, and not the master, who exercised strict control over the slaves. Genovese states: "The blame for much of the cruelty to slaves, as well as for much of the inefficiency in southern agriculture, nevertheless fell on the overseers." Williams argues that threats of familial separation were an effective tool in slave control. In Delaware, and throughout the Upper South, Williams notes that masters often threatened to sell their rebellious slaves to owners who would most likely treat them harshly. In the eighteenth century, the most feared states were Georgia and the Carolinas. In the nineteenth century, Alabama, Mississippi, Louisiana, Texas, and Arkansas also became known for their brutal treatment of slaves.

10   Paul D. Lack, "Slavery and the Texas Revolution," *Southwestern Historical Quarterly* 89 (1985), 181–202; Paul D. Lack, *The Texas Revolutionary Experience: A Political and Social History, 1835–1836* (College Station: Texas A&M University Press, 1992).

11   Calvert, *The History of Texas*, 65–66; Federal Writers' Program "The Negro in Texas," Box 4H350, Center for American History, University of Texas at Austin (hereafter cited as CAHUT-Austin).

12   Federal Writers' Program, *Blacks in Texas*, WPA Fact Book, Box 4H350, CAHUT-Austin.

13   Genovese, *Roll, Jordan, Roll*, 3.

14   Eli Coleman and Will Adams, *Slave Narratives*, CAHUT-Austin.

15   Mary Reynolds, *Slave Narratives*, CAHUT-Austin.

16   Harrison Trexler, *Slavery in Missouri, 1804–1865* (Baltimore: Johns Hopkins Press, 1914), 209; John Boles, *Black Southerners, 1619–1869* (Lexington: University of Kentucky Press, 1983), 83, 112; Alton V. Moody, "Slavery on Louisiana Sugar Plantations" (Ph.D. diss., University of Michigan, 1923), 22; Timothy Dwight Weld, *American Slavery As It Is: Testimony of a Thousand Witnesses* (New York: Arno Press and New York Times, 1968), 69.

17   Campbell, *An Empire for Slavery*, 127; Larry Hudson, *To Have and to Hold: Slave Work and Family Life in Antebellum South Carolina* (Athens: University of Georgia Press, 1997), 127; Mintz, *African American Voices*, 111.

18   Sarah Ford, *Slave Narratives*, CAHUT-Austin. Also see the slave narratives of Cato Carter, Green Cumby, Campbell Davis, and Josephine Howard.

19   Using the Federal Reserve Bank Consumer Price Index, $30 in 1860 represents approximately $680 in 2006.

20   Joe Gray Taylor, *Negro Slavery in Louisiana* (Lafayette: Louisiana Historical Association, 1963), 109; Peter Kolchin, *American Slavery, 1619–1877* (New York: Hill & Wang, 1993), 113; Weld, *American Slavery As It Is*, 34; Sylviane Diouf, *Growing up in Slavery* (Brookfield, Connecticut: Millbrook Press, 2001), 36–38; Genovese, *Roll, Jordan, Roll*, 603–5.

21   Betty Powers, *Slave Narratives*, CAHUT-Austin. Also see the narrative of Jenny Proctor.

22   Richardson, et al., *Texas: The Lone Star State*, 186; Randolph Campbell, *Gone to Texas* (New York: Oxford University Press, 2003), 223; John Winston Coleman, *Slavery Times in Kentucky* (Chapel Hill: University of North Carolina Press, 1940), 63–64; Charles Joyner, "The World of the Plantation Slaves," *Before Freedom Came: African American Life in the Antebellum South*, ed. Edward D. C. Campbell, Jr. (Charlottesville: University Press of Virginia, 1991), 55–56; Kenneth Stampp, *The Peculiar Institution* (New York: Knopf, 1956, 1972), 290–91; Lerone Bennett, Jr., *Before the Mayflower: A History of Black America*, 6th ed. (New York: Penguin Books, 1988), 89–90; F. N. Boney, *Slave Life in Georgia* (Savannah, Georgia: Beehive Press, 1991), 8. Also see the narratives of Tom Holland, Mary Reynolds, William Matthews, Mary Johnson, Toby Jones, Jenny Proctor, and Ben Kinchlow.

23   Mintz, *African American Voices*, 107.

24   Campbell, *Gone to Texas*, 223; Mintz, *African American Voices*, 103–4.

25   Bennett, Jr., *Before the Mayflower*, 90.

26   Ira Berlin, Barbara Fields, et al., eds., *Free at Last: A Documentary History of Slavery, Freedom, and the Civil War* (New York: New Press, 1992), 3. Also see William Freehling, *The Reintegration of American History: Slavery and the Civil War* (New York: Oxford University Press, 1994), 114, 139–40; Kenneth M. Stampp, *The Era of Reconstruction, 1865–1877* (New York: Knopf, 1965), 32–33, 44–45. Freehling argues that Lincoln's support of a constitutional amendment prohibiting Federal intervention in the issue of slavery indicates that slavery could not have been the

principal cause of the Civil War and that the sixteenth president was ambivalent toward equality for blacks. Stampp finds that during the 1850s Lincoln openly confessed that blacks should never be considered equal to whites. Stampp asserts that even in the months preceding the Emancipation Proclamation, Lincoln continued having doubts about sudden freedom and favored instead gradual emancipation of Southern blacks.

27   Lewis Newton, et al., *A Social and Political History of Texas* (Dallas: Southwest Press, 1932), 289.

28   Ibid., 297–98; T. Lindsay Baker and Julie Baker, *Till Freedom Cried Out: Memories of Texas Slave Life* (College Station: Texas A&M University Press, 1997), xxi; Richardson, et al., *Texas: The Lone Star State,* 209, 216.

29   See the narratives of Thomas Johns, Harrison Boyd, Lizzie Jones, Elsie Reece, and James Hayes, *Slave Narratives*, CAHUT-Austin. Jones said her master came home early from military service because of an illness, while Reece, interviewed in Fort Worth, said her slave owner's son came back after having his leg "shot off," and died shortly thereafter because of his injuries. Hayes said his master's body was shipped home and recalled, "All de old folks, cullud and white, was cryin'. Missy Elline she fainted. When de body comes home, dere's a powerful big funeral and after dat, dere's powerful weepin's and sadness on dat place."

30   Susan Ross, *Slave Narratives*, CAHUT-Austin.

31   Ellen Payne, *Slave Narratives*, CAHUT-Austin.

32   Harrison Beckett, *Slave Narratives*, CAHUT-Austin. Also see the narratives of Mary Kindred and Abram Sells.

33   Robin D. G. Kelley and Earl Lewis, *To Make Our Own World Anew: A History of African Americans* (New York: Oxford University Press, 2000), 236; Campbell, *An Empire for Slavery*, 231, 233.

34   Abigail Scott Curlee [Holbrook], "The History of a Texas Slave Plantation, 1831–63," *Southwestern Historical Quarterly* 26 (October 1922), 79–127, quote 114.

35   William Adams, *Slave Narratives*, CAHUT-Austin.

36   Martin Jackson, Ibid. Also see the narrative of Allen Price, whose father, like Jackson's, cautioned him that the end of the war and slavery may not necessarily mean improved black-white relationships.

37   Also see the narratives of Jack Bess, Abram Sells, and Henry Lewis, *Slave Narratives*, CAHUT-Austin.

38   Willie Forward, *Slave Narratives*, CAHUT-Austin. Also see Charley Mitchell, Allen Price, and Harriet Barrett.

39   Andy Anderson, *Slave Narratives*, CAHUT-Austin.

40   Ben Simpson, *Slave Narratives*, CAHUT-Austin.

41   Faust, "'Trying to Do a Man's Business'," 174–92, quote 191.

42   Ben Simpson, *Slave Narratives*, CAHUT-Austin. Also see Lu Perkins. Perkins recalled how her former owner was devastated "on account of losing his darkeys" and told his slaves, "You is free on account of the war. You don't have to stay no place where you don't want to stay, but if you want to stay here you can." Even though he was unsure of his own future, Perkins's former owner gave her father

200 acres of land. However, Perkins commented to her interviewer that her former owner's sons prevented her father from assuming possession of the land.

43 Not only did slave owners attempt to prevent blacks from escaping from slavery by running away, former slave John Ogee commented that many slaves left the farms and plantations and joined the Union armies as they passed nearby. Paul D. Lack, "Dave: A Rebellious Slave," in *Black Leaders: Texans for Their Times,* ed. Alwyn Barr and Robert A. Calvert (Austin: Texas State Historical Association, 1981): 1–18, quote 14.

44 Andy Anderson, *Slave Narratives,* CAHUT-Austin.

45 Susan Ross, *Slave Narratives,* CAHUT-Austin; Tyler and Murphy, *Slave Narratives of Texas,* 113.

46 See the narratives of William Adams, Armstead Barrett, and Martin Ruffin, *Slave Narratives,* CAHUT-Austin. These individuals described the intense feelings of happiness upon hearing of their freedom.

47 Elsie Reece, *Slave Narratives,* CAHUT-Austin.

48 Jack Bess, *Slave Narratives,* CAHUT-Austin. Also see the narratives of Liza Jones, Emma Watson, and William Paxton.

49 Will Adams, *Slave Narratives,* CAHUT-Austin.

50 Barry A. Crouch, *The Freedmen's Bureau and Black Texas* (Austin: University of Texas Press, 1992), 12; Smallwood, *Time of Hope, Time of Despair,* 25–26.

51 Cato Carter, *Slave Narratives,* CAHUT-Austin.

52 William Mathews, *Slave Narratives,* CAHUT-Austin.

53 Susan Merrit, *Slave Narratives,* CAHUT-Austin.

54 William Thomas, *Slave Narratives,* CAHUT-Austin. Also see the narratives of Walter Rimm and Julia Malone.

55 Alan Price, *Slave Narratives,* CAHUT-Austin.

56 Frank Tannenbaum, *Slave and Citizen: The Negro in the Americas* (New York: Knopf, 1947), 110–11; Leon Litwack, *Been in the Storm So Long* (New York: Knopf, 1979), 297, 331.

57 Aunt Pinkie Kelly, *Slave Narratives,* CAHUT-Austin.

58 Betty Powers, *Slave Narratives,* CAHUT-Austin. 59 Cohen-Lack, "A Struggle for Sovereignty," 98.

Chapter 16

Feed the Troops or Fight the Drought: The Dilemma Texas Beef Contractors Faced in 1861–1865

by Carol Taylor

At the beginning of the twentieth century, Confederate veteran A. T. Ball expressed a feeling held by all former Confederate soldiers when he wrote, "If we could have gotten a little something to eat, why, I would be fighting for our beloved South today." Other Confederate veterans remembered having little or nothing to eat, subsisting on mule meat in the days before the surrender of Vicksburg and Port Hudson, feasting on turnips and green persimmons or parching the corn found on the ground after horses were fed. Without a doubt, the recurring theme of most memoirs and regimental histories of the Southern

Illustration 21 Branding cattle on the prairies of Texas. *Courtesy Library of Congress.*

armies is the lack of food and near starvation of the troops. The deprivation of food was extremely severe east of the Mississippi River where population ratios were higher and arable lands were more likely to be used for the production of cotton than those found west of the Mississippi. Yet, west of the Mississippi River, soldiers complained of a shortage of provisions. Lt. Julius Glesecke of Company G, Fourth Texas Cavalry, Sibley's Brigade, a predominantly German unit, noted the shortage of provisions as early as the second of November 1861, less than two weeks into the march to Santa Fe.[1]

Historians have dismissed Texas as a source of beef for the Confederacy for two reasons: the difficulty of crossing the Mississippi River after the fall of Vicksburg in the summer of 1863 and the lack of manpower in the grazing areas of the state to initiate a large, or even medium sized, cattle drive. While it was futile to attempt a crossing of the Mississippi after the spring of 1863, there were men in the ranching areas of Texas to be hired as drovers prior to the fall of Vicksburg and Port Hudson, albeit to the chagrin of the Confederate government and military. Far more serious factors were the climatic conditions that prevailed in the Lone Star State from the summer of 1857 through the fall of 1864. The weather and lack of adequate transportation were the major factors in the decision regarding the amount of beef moved eastwards during the war. The beef contractors were forced to sell off their more mature steers and to hold their breed stock in reserve in order to survive the devastating drought that racked the South and Southwest from Alabama westward to California, including Texas. Lack of rains and extremely high temperatures have always had the combined capacity to wipe out stock raisers in any period and were, therefore, especially fatal to the Texas cattle industry in its infancy and in wartime.

While there were no weather records kept in the mid-nineteenth century, incidental reports indicate that the drought conditions began as early as 1857, resulting in the withering of grazing lands and consequently leading to the starvation of many Texas cattle, especially in the northern part of the state. The cattle industry remained in a weakened state throughout 1858 and many ranchers suffered even greater losses due to the infamous blizzard of 1859. Conditions temporarily improved with increased rainfall in late in 1859, but by that time, an economic recession had emerged throughout the Southern states.[2]

The drought reached its peak during the summer of 1864 when the entire wheat crop in North Texas was lost, causing near starvation of the civilian population. The regular session of the Texas House of Representatives in February 1863 implied that the situation was dire in the grain-producing areas of North Texas, when the members discussed the need for cotton plantations to "set aside acreage in the fertile river bottoms for the production of corn because in other areas of the state where white labor [had been drained by the war effort] could no longer be relied upon to produce enough grain without the threat of famine." Col. James G. Bourland of Bourland's Border Regiment furloughed one-third of his troops to go home in the late spring to replant wheat in hopes of a better crop. Though many Confederate leaders questioned the loyalty of North Texas troops, Brig. Gen. Henry McCulloch granted Bourland's request for the furloughs. The following March, Bourland again received permission from McCullough to furlough a portion of his men to replant wheat for a second time. The men were sent home on February 18, 1865, with instructions to return to camp by the end of March.[3]

The heat in North Texas reached triple digits by July 2, 1860, when a thermometer in Marshall, Texas, broke at 115 degrees. Dallas, Denton, and Pilot Point also recorded such extreme heat. In Pilot Point, the temperature caused newly invested and highly volatile phosphorous matches to burst into flames on the shelves of a mercantile store, causing the tinder-dry wooden frame of the building to catch fire.[4] During the winter of 1863 through 1864, drought conditions once again crippled the cattle industry in Texas. In North and South Texas, the drought contributed to a loss of perhaps 50 to 90 percent of the cattle in those regions.[5]

During World War II, Frank E. Vandiver compared contemporary food supplies in the North African campaign with those in the Confederate army. Vandiver concluded that Rebel soldiers lived on a meat-and-potato diet with their meats being primarily beef and pork that they imported from Midwestern states prior to the war. Vandiver found that the Confederacy's most pressing question became how to continue to provide adequate food supplies in an area with inadequate transportation and no stable economy; few roads, a shortage of wagons and teams; few or no railroads, especially west of the Mississippi River; virtually no water transportation; and a rapidly devalued currency. In an early study, Charles W. Ramsdell attributed the problems facing the Confederacy to antebellum conditions when the South preferred to raise cash crops such as cotton, tobacco, indigo, and rice, while purchasing subsistence food crops from their northern neighbors. Thus, an inadequate transportation system and lack of locally grown food crops created a disastrous situation that the Confederate government was ill-prepared to prevent. As the war continued, farmlands of northern Virginia and the Valley of the Mississippi were destroyed. Food supplies were so limited in Virginia that the War Department and Commissary-General of Subsistence Lucius B. Northrup suggested that Confederate troops should commandeer food from the civilian population and use the cavalry troops for foraging expeditions if they were to be properly fed. Such suggestions left Gen. Robert E. Lee distraught, fearing a loss of support among poor Southerners.[6]

Not only did General Lee confront an ongoing battle with the commissary-general of subsistence, but Gen. P. G. T. Beauregard and Gen. Joesph E. Johnston routinely fired salvos at Northrup and his department. Northrup responded by decreasing rations for the fighting men. By the end of April 1862, rations were down to ten ounces of pork or bacon and one pound of salt or fresh beef per day. Pork and bacon were limited to two days per week while fresh and salt beef were served five days in seven. As the war continued, the rations continued to fall. Northrup, who was a practicing vegetarian, strongly believed that protein from animal sources was unnecessary for physical health. Yet, he prescribed an additional eight ounces of lard as often as practicable. The constant bickering between Northrup and the Confederate military command added nothing to the relief of the common soldier.[7]

Missing from the dialogue was the question of Texas cattle. In January of 1862, Northrup reported that "beeves must be provided for the coming spring." Texas cattle were desperately needed east of the Mississippi River before the spring rains began. As such, the Confederate government entered into contracts with Texas cattlemen for orders totaling nearly 200,000 head of cattle. The ranchers were to herd their livestock across the Mississippi River to various points in the Eastern Theater. By the end of 1862, Texas cattle were making their way to the Mississippi and beyond. In Richmond, Virginia, one newspaper editor reported that herders had driven 20,000 head of Texas cattle across the Mississippi River near Natchez where the water was at its lowest level and trailed them from there to Virginia for Lee's army. In Raymond, Mississippi, the newspaper noted that herds of 400 to 600 head of cattle continued to pass through the town regularly during the early spring of 1862.

During the summer and fall of 1862, the traffic in Texas cattle peaked. The following fall and winter, Alabama and Mississippi experienced a severe drought, leaving the pasture lands of these Southern states desolate. As a result, the drovers found very little pasturage and adequate water as they moved eastward through the South. The terrain, as well as the condition of land previously the site of large battles and still used for cotton production, was not conducive to grazing large herds of cattle. Rail lines were destroyed as the Union army moved south from Shiloh. Ranchers found it extremely difficult, if not impossible, to herd their cattle to the Eastern Theater of the war.[8]

Away from the centers of war, cattle were abundant on the frontier areas of Texas where stockmen had trailed cattle to California during the Gold Rush and into Utah as late as 1861. Finding available markets for Texas beef had been the major problem of the antebellum cattle industry in Texas. Some stockmen such as Dan T. Waggoner and John S. Chisum of North Texas were anxious to find marketing outlets for the abundant cattle on Texas ranges. They had driven herds to the railhead at Sedalia, Missouri, along the Texas Trail through the eastern part of Indian Territory during the late 1850s. But most stockmen in the state thought that a long drive was not profitable. The trail must have excellent pasturage to a considerable depth on both sides of the route, available water, an occasional salt lick and five or six drovers per one thousand head of cattle. Since Texas cattle were grass-fed, the herd would need an ample supply of grass or the leading edge of the herd would exhaust the food supply and those in the rear would become hungry and unable to maintain the pace. A strung-out herd was a drover's nightmare. Crossing rain-swollen rivers created another potential crisis, especially if two different herds crossed the river at the same time. It sometimes took days to sort the cattle on the other side of the river. Additionally, any loud noise, be it thunder or the sound of battle, would startle the herd and spark a stampede. At the beginning of the drive, the cattle were usually restless. For the first three or four days, the herd generally traveled twenty-five to thirty miles per day; then the rate dropped to fifteen miles a day as the herd adjusted to the new experience. The faster the herd moved the more weight the steers lost. A slow, fairly leisurely pace kept the steers quiet and helped minimize weight loss in the animals.[9]

At the time of the Civil War, the cattle frontier in Texas had reached the one hundredth meridian. The advanced grazing line extended from Grayson County on the Red River through Wise, Stephens, Shackelford, Brown, San Saba, and Bandera counties to Kenedy County on the Gulf Coast. For nearly a decade, the Blackland Prairie and the Grand Prairie near Fort Worth had been used almost exclusively for stock raising. The tax rolls for 1860 showed 3,786,443 head of cattle in the Lone Star State, a figure that was probably low. When Fort Sumter fell to the Confederates in April 1861, Col. Richard King's Santa Gertrudis Ranch in South Texas had 84,100 acres of grazing land with 65,000 head of cattle, 10,000 horses, and approximately 8,000 goats. This large amount of livestock was worked by three hundred Mexican *vaqueros* mounted on one thousand saddle horses. At the same time the O'Connor Ranch on the San Antonio River had 40,000 head of cattle. Every year during the Civil War, they branded 12,000 calves. Yet King and O'Connor chose to hold their herds for future use, rather than risk the dangers of driving a herd of semi-wild longhorn cattle into dangerous territory. King preferred to engage in blockade-running and trading Southern cotton across the Mexican border with British and French merchants. His Texas herds grew fat and proliferated in the meantime.[10]

Driving cattle during peacetime was dangerous, but the drives that occurred during wartime were especially hazardous. Prior to the war, South Texas stockmen sent their four-year-old steers to markets in New Orleans and Mobile. Cattle steamers, referred to as "coasters" or "sea lions," regularly sailed out of the Texas ports of Indianola, Galveston, and Sabine Pass. The steamers were owned by the Morgan Line that had created a monopoly before the war by charging enormous rates for freight to anyone outside the company. Once the war began, these steamers were too bulky and slow to run the Federal blockade. Stockmen then resorted to the age-old method of walking cattle to market. In South Texas, the financial burden of shipping overland and the lack of reliable manpower caused ranchers to rethink the cattle industry and begin to assist the Confederacy in shipping cotton overland to ports located in Mexico.[11]

Col. John "Rip" Ford, commander of the Second Texas Cavalry in far South Texas, managed to purchase meat and flour from local merchants in 1861, but not enough to feed his 800 cavalrymen. The Thirty-Second Texas Cavalry took an even stronger stand to obtain food along the Rio Grande. They roped and butchered beeves from nomadic herds, paying the owners with vouchers. The warm, dry weather in Texas allowed those troops to preserve the meat by the traditional Native American method of jerking. Long, thin strips of beef were strung up by ropes to dry in the sun with no need for salt as a preservative. This preserved meat became the staple diet for cavalry troops throughout South Texas. In areas of higher humidity this method simply could not be used without the technology to dry the beef strips and that technology was not available to military troops.[12]

One of the few and very earliest firsthand accounts of cattle drives out of Texas during the Civil War is that of Joseph Morse Bickford, whose diary also doubled as a logbook for expenses incurred during the trail drive. The entries begin on Friday, March 15, 1861, when Bickford was a schoolteacher in Saluria on the eastern end of Matagorda Island in the southern part of Calhoun County. The area around Saluria was a thriving ranching center by the 1850s. Cattle were left to roam the salt grass dunes of the island and rounded up only once a year to be branded and castrated. On Thursday, April 25, 1861, U.S. troops that had fled to Saluria surrendered to Col. Earl Van Dorn. The next day, Bickford closed his school, and on the following Monday, he enlisted along with two other men in the Confederate army. However, they were not immediately mustered into service. Therefore, Bickford decided to aid the Confederate cause by joining a cattle drive to New Orleans. During the first full week in May, Bickford settled his affairs, and purchased saddlebags, boots, and other items he considered necessary for the trail. The following week, he said goodbye to friends and joined the cattle drive. Bickford does not mention who owned the cattle, or who was the trail boss, but it is clear throughout the diary that he is at least the top assistant, probably the tally master or bookkeeper. More than likely a man named L. DuBois was the trail boss. Before the drive began, the cattle were rounded up, counted, and branded. On Tuesday, May 21, 1861, Bickford purchased the final round of supplies and headed the cattle out. They crossed over to the mainland to circle the town of Lavaca, now Port Lavaca. From there they paralleled the Texas coastline, remaining about fifty miles inland. Their route roughly followed the Opelousas Trail, a thoroughfare used for hundreds of years by Native American tribes before the Spanish explorers and soldiers made use of it. During the Mexican regime, the trail was used by early Texans to herd large droves of cattle, mules, and horses to market in New Orleans. By 1836 the trail was the post route and the scene of the "Runaway Scrape" when frightened Texans fled Mexican troops toward the Sabine River and safety in the United States.[13]

Bickford recorded crossing at least two dozen rivers on the drive to New Orleans. The herd consisted of 500 to 600 head of cattle driven by five men in addition to Bickford and DuBois. The trip lasted from late May to early July, moving up to twenty-five miles per day at the beginning of the drive when the cattle were restless. This speed lasted about three or four days until the cattle settled into a routine where they traveled five to ten miles daily. The Colorado River crossing was the only place where the water level was high enough to pose a real danger. There they allowed the herd to graze until the water level went down. Cattle tend to mingle and it was here that the Bickford herd mixed with two other herds causing problems and delays in sorting the cattle. Several horses were lost in the high water but no steers. While waiting for the river to recede, DuBois attempted to profit from his unplanned delay by purchasing another herd to sell in New Orleans. Whether he actually profited from the transaction is not known because no records are extant to show the cost or size of the second herd or the financial arrangements made. Crossing the Brazos River at the town of Richmond, two steers were lost, one dying while stuck in the mud. At Cyprus City between Buffalo Bayou and the San Jacinto River, Bickford and DuBois realized they were on the wrong trail and had to make adjustments, losing time and putting additional stress on the herd. Bickford wrote about the "famous Trinity [River]" that they crossed at Liberty. No reason was given for the definitive term, though. The herd crossed the Neches River at either Tevis's or Collier's Ferry to avoid the streets of Beaumont, where citizens awoke daily during the Civil War to the bellowing of cattle being driven east to feed Confederate troops. After crossing into Louisiana at the Sabine River, the drovers began to experience chills and fevers associated with the low-lying swamps riddled with mosquitoes and other disease-bearing insects. Rain set in and Bickford reported heavy rainfalls every day. None of the men died on the trail but two were ill enough to be left at the homes of strangers along the way. When recovered, they rejoined the herd.[14]

As the tally man, Bickford kept accurate records of the expenses involved in the cattle drive. While the steers swam the rivers, the supply wagon and extra horses crossed on a ferry. The toll for ferries increased as the herd moved eastward. The cheapest was near Lavaca on the Navidad River where they paid ninety-five cents total. The most expensive ferry cost $20.25 at the Sabine River. Extra hands were hired to help cross the Brazos and Sabine rivers. Pasturage in Texas cost between four and five dollars per night, but because of denser populations and lack of open range in Louisiana the price rose to fifteen dollars. When the herd got into a field of corn and ate the ripening crop, Bickford was forced to settle with the farmer for thirty dollars. On June 29, nearing New Orleans, the men met their first Confederate soldiers. By July 9, 1861, the herd was close enough to New Orleans to separate the steers by weight. Most of the drovers left for home soon after, but Bickford and DuBois remained when they loaded the herd onto a steamboat bound for New Orleans. An intelligent single man, Bickford rode into the Crescent City with the herd and spent several days seeing the sights of the city. He did not record the buyers of the herd, who may have been butchers in the city or Confederate commissary agents. At this early date, Southerners were still optimistic of winning the war quickly. Some historians quote the beef prices in New Orleans in 1861 as high as thirty to fifty dollars a head. Scores of herds out of Texas were driven to New Orleans, Natchez, Memphis, and Shreveport. The drovers, like Bickford and DuBois, were buying Texas stock on speculation for resale in Louisiana where they were paid double the prices of the antebellum period. It is entirely possible that Bickford and DuBois intended to capitalize on the higher prices before entering the Confederate army. Bickford remained in Louisiana with DuBois until the fifteenth of October of that year. DuBois had relatives in the area whom he visited and from whom Bickford learned the French language. Fourteen days after leaving the New Orleans area, Bickford returned to Matagorda Island. The trip was successful, little stock was lost, and no men died.[15]

Between 1861 and 1863 more than 30,000 steers were delivered to the Confederate government at the military stockyards at New Iberia for slaughter at the packing plant in nearby Alexandria, Louisiana. By December of 1861 the Confederate army in Department Number One had heavily armed the areas of pasturage near New Orleans and expected to create a citadel around the city. At Calcasieu Bay, two 24-pound cannons were installed to prevent Union foraging parties from reaching cattle-grazing pastures around the head of the lake. Atchafalaya River was even more fortified with one 32-pounder rifled gun and four 24-pounders. The main channel of the Atchafalaya was filled with trees, leaving space wide enough for blockade runners to enter and leave. Major-General M. Lovell of the Confederate army expressed optimism about the defense of New Orleans. In a report of December 5, 1861, he stated that "beef cattle from Texas . . . would enable us to stand a siege of two or three months, if it should be necessary." Reliance upon Texas cattle seemed to be one of the key issues.[16]

Beef for the Confederacy also came from the North Texas area. From the very beginning of the Civil War, North Texas had been a thorn in the side of the Confederacy. The counties bordering the Red River had voted against secession, and though many of the men in the region eventually joined the Confederate army, there were pockets of Union sympathizers who firmly opposed the Confederacy. Very few cotton plantations were found in the area and the number of slaves was limited to fewer than a dozen on farms owned by yeomen farm-ers who migrated to the region from states in the Midwest and Upper South. Most families were subsistence farmers who lived on the frontier. Fear of Indian attacks and the security of the Federal forts along the frontier line were reasons for many to vote to remain in the Union.

As the war dragged on, the area became a haven for deserters and draft-dodgers from both armies. These men were attracted to the thickets found inter-mittently throughout the region. These dense woods were so immensely thick as to be nearly impenetrable and once inside the thicket, one could easily get lost and wander for days until either dying or stumbling upon an egress. Yet, the North Texas area also served as an excellent range land for cattle. In good years when water was plentiful, native grasses were extremely nutritious. And it was here that some of the earliest Texas cattlemen began to search for markets in eastern and northern cities and in the newly established packing plants like the one in Jefferson, Texas. Here cattle were less likely to be predominantly the Spanish longhorns, but a mixed breed of Durhams, Herefords, Devons and Gal-loways brought by the earliest Red River settlers from homes on the eastern side of the Appalachian Mountains in North and South Carolina. These mixed-breed cattle differed considerably from the Spanish cattle of South and East Texas in that they were stockier with shorter legs making it more difficult to trail over long distances. They were much less inured to the hardships of drought than the wild longhorns. This difference in stamina may have influenced the high death rates of livestock during the 1857–1864 drought.[17]

John S. Chisum and Dan Waggoner were Confederate beef contractors. Both men began their cattle-ranching operations before the Civil War and nei-ther had a great interest in Texas secession. Like fellow North Texans James W. Throckmorton of Collin County and Ben Epperson of Red River County, both men saw no reason to leave the Union. However, unlike Throckmorton and Epperson, Chisum and Waggoner did not join the Confederate army once the state seceded. Waggoner did volunteer later in the war in the Brush Battalion, ostensibly to defend the frontier, and Chisum is reported to have served in the frontier militia.[18]

John Simpson Chisum was born in Hardeman or Madison County in west-ern Tennessee in 1824. By 1837 the family had moved to Red River County, Texas, where young John Chisum began a career as a building contractor. When the family moved west to Lamar County, Chisum built the new courthouse there and served as county clerk from 1852–1854. While in Lamar County, he became involved in the cattle business. With New Orleans investor Stephen K. Fowler, Chisum filed on land in northwestern Denton County near the pres-ent-day town of Bolivar. Later, Chisum bought out his partner and began a large-scale cattle operation in North Texas. He bought up small herds and drove them to the packing house in Jefferson, Texas. By 1860 he owned 5,000 head of cattle and showed a net worth of $46,000 on the 1860 census. Of that fortune, $10,000 was invested in real estate. At the beginning of the war, Chisum was exempted from service in order to oversee at least six other herds of cattle in his district. It is known that he drove a herd of cattle along the Red River into Arkansas, crossed the Mississippi River south of Memphis at what was then known as the Bluffs. From there he and his men trailed the herd into Vicksburg in the fall of 1862.[19]

Another prominent North Texas rancher, Dan T. Waggoner, was born in Lincoln County, Tennessee, in 1828. By 1853 he established a cattle ranch in Wise County, Texas, where he, too, began buying up small herds and trailing them to eastern markets, including the packing plant in Jefferson. Waggoner was a single-minded individual who was intent on maintaining his cattle business. He did not become involved in any form of political activities or even attend any of the political rallies held prior to the election of 1860. He virtually removed himself from the issues in his efforts to build a cattle empire in Texas, some six years before others began to show interest in the industry during the postbellum years. After the war began, Waggoner took three hundred of his oldest steers to Shreveport with a three-man outfit, including his wife's two younger brothers, ages ten and twelve, and himself. They rolled up blankets for bedrolls, gathered some rations, loaded them on two mules, and drove the herd eastward for three weeks before reaching Shreveport. There Waggoner sold the steers to the Confederate commissary agent for ten Confederate dollars per head. Waggoner took the $3,000 home and reinvested his profit to enlarge his herd, buying cattle from his neighbors, usually women and old men, for three or four dollars per head. He paid his two drovers with a heifer each from his own herd. Both boys continued to work for Waggoner throughout the war while increasing the size of their own herds.[20]

In 1862 Waggoner cut five hundred of his biggest steers out of the herd and made another drive. This time he took his cattle all the way to Vicksburg, Mississippi, where the Confederate commissary agent paid twenty Confederate dollars per head. Once again he reinvested in his herd when he bought 2,500 head of cattle with the profits. By the fall of 1862 Waggoner found a new source of labor in northern Texas. He made profitable use of the deserters from both the Confederate and Union armies as well as draft-dodgers from both armies who were holed up in the thickets throughout the area. Most of the men were experienced with horses and cattle so Waggoner put them to work with no questions asked. In the spring of 1863 Waggoner rounded up five thousand head of his cattle that he branded and worked. He again took 1,500 steers to Vicksburg with a crew of eight, including five men from the thickets as well as the Halsell boys. More than likely, he chose men from the thickets whose homes were at a great distance so that they would not be recognized when they neared Union and Confedérate forces. At Shreveport, Waggoner learned that General Grant and his forces controlled the Mississippi River with Union gunboats. Waggoner found a Confederate commissary agent to purchase his herd in Louisiana for 50,000 Confederate dollars rather than sell at a more lucrative price in Union gold. The Confederate dollars he received were worth roughly 10 percent or $5,000 in United States gold.[21]

In April of 1863 Maj. George L. Gillespie, commissary of subsistence for the Second Military District in Vicksburg, wrote to Maj. W. H. Dameron, the commissary of subsistence at Jackson, Mississippi, that the fate of Vicksburg depended on two big *ifs*. The first unknown was whether the South could continue to hold off Union gunboats and the second was whether the Confederates could protect the river crossings in order for Texas cattle to arrive. By May of that year, cattle were wandering through the city. Captain W. O. Dodd, CSA, later wrote down his recollections of the siege. Dodd and his men were in the trenches facing the Union army. The only grazing area was right in front of Dodd's trenches. Early every morning Union sharpshooters would pick off one or two steers. If the men in the trenches attempted to dress the carcasses, they too became a moving target for the Yankees. If they stayed in the trenches, the carcasses soon rotted in the heat of the Vicksburg summer, the stench became unbearable and the agony of having meat so close and yet so completely out of reach made the hunger more intolerable. On July 18, 1863, some two weeks after the surrender of Vicksburg, Gen. U. S. Grant wrote to Maj. Gen. H. W. Halleck of the U.S. Army that five thousand head of Texas cattle had been captured at Natchez; two thousand were sent to General Banks in the field and the remainder were brought to feed the soldiers and civilians in Vicksburg.[22]

After the fall of Vicksburg and Port Hudson, the western states of the Confederacy were all but isolated from Richmond. Much has been written about the trials the Trans-Mississippi region faced, but the cattle industry has been ignored. The Texas House and Senate in regular and special sessions argued about aspects that did little to aid the drought-ridden cattlemen. One of the earliest legislations enacted was the Act Regulating the Fees for Swimming Cattle at Ferries. Once the need for cattle in the Trans-Mississippi region was recognized, ferrymen saw the opportunity for additional revenue. Whereas cattle had been allowed to freely cross rivers and streams at low-water sites, the ferrymen began to charge per head for crossing. Instead of abolishing the extra expense, the Texas Legislature decided to regulate the fee in 1862. In his opening address to the regular session of the Tenth Legislature in November 1863, Gov. Francis R. Lubbock lambasted the "swarms of men engaged in profitable business on their own account" who were exempted from military duty. He would place the "thousands" who were driving cattle in the army and turn the work over to slaves, the elderly, the very young, and the infirm.[23]

In the summer of 1863 John Chisum and three other men petitioned Texas Governor Lubbock through Brig. Gen. William Hudson of the Twenty-first Brigade, Texas State Troops, for permission to move their cattle out of Denton County to better pastures near the Concho River in West Texas. Chisum noted in his petition that he and the other men had served in the frontier militia. More importantly, he had provided 15,000 head of cattle to the Confederate cause and had never failed to provide beef when requested. Now he wanted to be exempt from all military service to tend to his cattle business. Chisum was careful to point out the effects of the current drought conditions on livestock and the need to move the cattle before winter set in. He believed that the Indian depredations to the west of Denton County had caused an influx of settlers from the frontier. Bringing their livestock into an already drought-stricken area, these settlers had worsened the situation. Chisum planned to move his cattle in small herds to better pastures along the Concho River near present-day San Angelo. There his herds would have less competition from other livestock. Both Col. James Bourland and Brig. Gen. Henry C. McCullough believed that Chisum was planning to move his herd to California to trade with the Union army. Both Confederates were exemplifying the standard attitude that it was necessary to throw as many poor whites into the foray to prolong the agonies of war. Neither man nor his government was interested in the fact that the army and civilians were starving to death as a result of the drought and the poor system of transporting the few available supplies to the front.[24]

Throughout the war, lack of transportation hindered the entire Confederate army in its military endeavors. With no railroads of any significance in Texas, moving beef cattle from the state to the Trans-Mississippi was virtually impossible. The few attempts to trail beef to Lee and his army in Virginia ended in dismal failure for the Rebels and on occasion provided fresh beef for the Union army. But the question, Did the heat, drought and abnormally cold weather affect the South's food supply? begs to be answered. With no official weather records available, historians have suggested that from 50 to 90 percent of Texas cattle perished before the drought broke with the winter and spring rains of 1865. The industry would have been hurt by a loss of even half of the cattle. With the number of cattle driven out of state for the military, and the loss of cows and calves due to weather-related problems, the future of the industry appeared bleak. With the closure of the Mississippi River by Union gunboats, Texas cattle were needed only in the Trans-Mississippi region. This break allowed stockmen like John S. Chisum to move their herds further into the frontier where grass and water were prevalent. That, along with the decision made early in the war by

South Texas cattlemen to hold their beef cattle and concentrate on the shipment of cotton to Mexico, allowed Texas herds to survive the devastating drought as it worsened in 1864. Early in 1865, the drought broke with torrential rains throughout the entire state. As the Civil War came to an end, ironically, so did one of the worst droughts in the history of Texas.

Notes

1   Mamie Yeary, comp., *Reminiscences of the Boys in Gray 1861–1856* (Self-published, 1912), 33–34, 55, 59, 63; Julius Glesecke, "The Diary of Julius Glesecke, 1861–1862," trans. Oscar Hans, *Military History of Texas and the Southwest*18, no. 3 (1988): 61 .

2   William Curry Holden, *A Ranching Saga: The Lives of William Electious Halsell and Ewing Halsell* (San Antonio: Trinity University Press, 1976), 32–34; Don E Reynolds, *Editors Make War: Southern Newspapers in the Secession Crisis* (Nashville: Vanderbilt University Press, 1970), 7.

3   Charles Kenner, review of *Southwestern Agriculture: Pre-Columbian to Modern*, by Henry C. Dethloff and Irvin M. May, Jr., *Journal of Southern History* 49 (August 1983): 438; Patricia Adkins-Rochette, *Bourland in North Texas and Indian Territory During the Civil War: Fort Cobb, Fort Arbuckle and the Wichita Mountains* (Self published, 2006), A-21; Texas State Legislature. *House Journal of the 9th Texas Legislature regular session, November 1861–January 1862*, 23.

4   Reynolds, *Editors Make War*, 108.

5   Love, Clara M., "History of the Cattle Industry in the Southwest," *Southwestern Historical Quarterly Online* 19 (April 1916): 370–99.

6   Frank Vandiver, "Texas and the Confederate Army's Meat Problem," *Southwestern Historical Quarterly* 47 (January 1944): 137; Charles W. Ramsdell, "Some Problems Involved in Writing the History of the Confederacy," *Journal of Southern History* 2 (May 1936): 140–44; R. E. Lee to James A. Seddon, March 27, 1863, *The War of the Rebellion: A Compilation of the Official Records of the Union and Confederate Armies* (hereafter noted as *OR*), comp, Robert N. Scott (Washington, D. C. : U.S. Government Printing Office, 1880–1901) 1, 25, 2:686–88; R. E. Lee to James A. Seddon, February 8, 1865, *OR*, 1, 46, 1:381–82; R. E. Lee to James A. Seddon, January 16, 1865, *OR*, 1, 46, 2:1075.

7   G. T. Beauregard to S. Cooper, May 1, 1862, *OR*, 1, 10, 2:478, G. T. Beauregard General Order 30(?), *OR*, 1, 10, 2:531–32, L. B. Northrop to George W. Randolph, May 31, 1863, *OR*, 1, 10, 2:571–72,

8   Vandiver, "Texas and the Confederate Army's Meat Problem," 136; Merton E. Coulter, *The Confederate States of America 1861–1865* (Baton Rouge: Louisiana State University Press, 1950), 246; B. Byron Price, "Don't Fence Me In: The Range Cattle Industry in the Confederate Southwest, 1861–1865," *Southwestern Agriculture: Pre-Columbian to Modern*, ed. Henry C. Dethloff (College Station: Texas A&M University Press, 1982), 60.

9   Love, "History of the Cattle Industry in the Southwest," 377.

10   William Curry Holden. *Alkali Trails or Social and Economic Movements of the Texas Frontier, 1846–1900* (Dallas: Southwest Press, 1930), 23, 31; "Interview with C. O. Edwards by Sheldon F. Gauthier," Rangelore, WPA (http://memory. loc.gov/cgi-bin/query/r?ammem/wpa:@field(DOCID+@lit(wpa335020208) accessed 26 April 2007; Love, 370–99.

11   Paul Horgan. *Great River: The Rio Grande in North American History: Mexico and the United States,* Vol. 2. (New York: Rinehart & Co., 1954), 872; Love, "History of the Cattle Industry in the Southwest," 389.

12   Horgan,. 883; Oates, Stephen, "Supply for Confederate Cavalry in the Trans-Mississippi, Military Affairs," *Civil War* 25 (Summer, 1961): 94–95.

13   "Joseph Morse Bickford Diary 1861," Sidney R. Weisiger Collection, Victoria Regional History Center, Victoria College/UH-Victoria Library; s.v., "Saluria, Texas," *The New Handbook of Texas* (Austin: Texas State Historical Association, 1996); W.T. Block, "A History of Jefferson County, Texas: Early Livestock Industry," www.wtblock.com/wtblockjr/History, accessed 18 June 2007.

14   "Joseph Morse Bickford Diary 1861"; Block, "A History of Jefferson County, Texas: Early Livestock Industry."

15   "Joseph Morse Bickford Diary 1861"; Price, "Don't Fence Me In," 60–61.

16   M. Lovell to J. P. Benjamin, December 5, 1861, *OR,* 1, 6, 774–76; Price, "Don't Fence Me In," 61.

17   Holden, *A Ranching Saga,* 6.

18   Patricia Adkins-Rochette, *Bourland in North Texas,* A-337, A-330; Ralph A. Wooster, *Texas and Texans in the Civil War* (Austin: Eakin Press, 1995), 108.

19   Harwood P. Hinton, s.v., "John Simpson Chisum," *Handbook of Texas.*

20   Holden, *A Ranching Saga,* 7–8.

21   Holden, *A Ranching Saga,* 37–39.

22   W. O. Dodd, "Recollections of Vicksburg During the Siege," *The Bivouac* 1, no. 1 (September 1882); George L. Gillespie to C. L. Stevenson, March 3, 1863, *OR,* 1, 24, 3:651–52.

23   Texas State Legislature, *Senate Journal of the Tenth Legislature Regular Session of the State of Texas, November 3, 1863–December 16, 1863,* 9.

24   Adkin-Rochette, *Bourland in North Texas,* A-268.

Chapter 17

Distress, Discontent, and Dissent: Colorado County, Texas, during the Civil War

by Bill Stein

At the end of April 1861, little more than two weeks after hostilities between the newly established Confederate States of America and the United States of America erupted at Fort Sumter, Hermann Nagel, an educated and articulate physician living on the northeastern edge of Colorado County, Texas, laid out his personal conflict. He was a Union loyalist who regarded secession as "neither justified nor advantageous, but merely as the most unprompted rebellion there ever was." However, he felt a sense of duty to defend his new country against invasion from the North. As he put it, "it may come down to it that I myself go off to fight against the so-called invasion of the so-called abolitionists." He summed up his dilemma with the entirely correct prediction: "It looks like we are in for hard times." Deprivation, hardship, distress, and grief, generated by that pervasive and comprehensive calamity known as the American Civil War, would soon be more pronounced for Nagel and virtually all of his neighbors. And he, and many others, would be forced to decide whether to serve their new country in a war against their old country, a war they disagreed with, but one which, nonetheless, threatened to bring an invading army to their homeland.[1]

Colorado County, with its seat of government at Columbus, was an original county of the Republic of Texas. It was a part of Stephen F. Austin's first colony in Texas, and had been settled by people who had roots in the United States of America since the early 1820s. Some of these people owned slaves. In 1860, there were not quite 8,000 people in the county. About 45 percent of them were slaves. Of the remaining 4,000 or so people, about 1,000 were born in foreign countries. By and large, these foreign-born residents lived in ethnic communities that were located in the northern and northeastern parts of the county, near the areas known as Frelsburg and New Mainz. They did not speak English. Mostly, they spoke German, though there were also some who spoke Czech. The 3,000 or so English-speaking people in the county lived in the southern and western parts of the county, in and around the towns of Columbus, Alleyton, and Eagle Lake. They owned nearly all the slaves in the county, and were suspicious that their non-English-speaking neighbors were abolitionists. Those suspicions were raised by the results of the February 23, 1861, referendum on secession. More than 85 percent of those who voted in the county's predominantly German precincts voted against secession. Elsewhere in the county, 85 percent of the people voted for it.[2]

When the war broke out, enthusiastic men from all over the county rallied to the cause of the Confederacy, including men from areas that voted strongly against secession. At least five companies for service in the national military of the Confederate States of America were raised primarily in Colorado County. Many other men from the county joined other companies that were raised nearby. The rates at which citizens of the county enrolled in the Confederate military varied by nationality. Nearly half of the American-born males of eligible age enrolled, compared to only one in four of the German speakers and one in six of the other foreigners. The companies raised in the county served in various theaters of the war, and were generally absent from home for the duration. One became Company A of the Fifth Texas Cavalry and, under General Henry Hopkins Sibley, participated in the failed invasion of New Mexico. Bad news about the considerable number of casualties they suffered reached the county early. Their original captain, a Columbus attorney named John S. Shropshire, was killed at the Battle of Glorieta. Another local company was admitted into the Confederate army as Company B of the Fifth Texas Infantry, a part of General John Bell Hood's Texas Brigade, which was a part of Robert E. Lee's Army of Northern Virginia. Bad news about the many casualties they suffered came in throughout the conflict. Their original captain, a farmer named John C. Upton, was killed at Second Manassas. When the war ended, the company had only ten remaining men. During the war, twenty-nine members of the company had sustained fatal wounds in action; fifteen others had died of disease or other causes; twenty-seven had been discharged for various reasons; eleven had been transferred; and eleven others had deserted. In addition, when the war ended, nine of the company's members were listed as absent without leave, eleven were in federal POW camps, and two were in hospitals. In all, of the slightly more than 500 men who were in the county in 1860 and who served in the Confederate military, sixty-five were either killed in action or died of disease or other causes. Many others were wounded.[3]

The departure of so many men and the circumstances of the war caused great changes within the county. Perhaps most visibly, with the owners and their employees in the military, the county's only newspaper, the *Colorado Citizen,* went out of business. Even before their enlistments, however, the effects of the war could be seen on the newspaper. Because it was unable to acquire paper, it nearly suspended publication in June 1861. It continued only after Caleb Claiborne Herbert, a state senator who lived in the county, secured a small supply of paper from friends in Galveston. Two months later, still lacking paper, the editors cut the size of their newspaper in half. Merchants, too, must have had a hard time staying afloat. Many, if not most, local stores had for years stocked their shelves with merchandise purchased in New York. Naturally, after the war broke out, such commerce stopped. Local merchants may have enjoyed a brief surge in profits, as they apparently refused to pay for goods that had only recently been obtained from their New York suppliers. But soon, the awful economic pressures of the war began taking their toll. Even before the end of the first year of the war, Nagel noted that there was "a shortage of everything beyond what we need to stay alive and to defend ourselves." He noted that clothing and shoes, plus coffee, rice, salt, drugs, nails, and tools were virtually unavailable.[4]

Money itself was in short supply, and many of the men who had departed to fight in the war had left behind wives and children who were scarcely able to support themselves. On March 17, 1862, the county government addressed both problems. First, the commissioners court adopted a special property tax of six cents per $100 valuation to pay expenses generated by the war. Then, it voted to print and immediately issue its own currency, and to use the scrip to support the families of men absent in the service of the Confederate government. They named several men to committees for each of seven precincts in the county. By May, the scrip had been printed. For the next few months, it presumably was issued via the various precinct committees. But in November 1862, the county took over at least one of the administrative details. The commissioners voted to employ someone to take a census of the wives, children, and mothers of absent soldiers, and to have it completed by January 1.[5]

The census was presented at the January 5, 1863, meeting of the court. It listed sixty families. The court allocated each family either $10, $20, $30, or $40, evidently depending on its size, to last until March 1. On February 17, the court laid out the second payments, these to last until May 1. The second census contained sixty-four names. Families were again paid between $10 and $40, but the court also ordered that one woman be provided with a rented house. They also specified that the families of anyone who was working in the service of the government as a teamster were not eligible for support, and imposed a significant tax increase (25 cents per $100) to help pay for the war. The third list of dependent families, filed in April, contained seventy names. Some families were to receive as much as $100. The number of dependent families kept rising, from 89 in August, to 96 in November, to 119 in February 1864, to a high of 220 in February 1865. The final list, filed with the court on April 3, 1865, contained 156 families. In 1860, there had been only 773 households in the county. If that number remained static, then at the end of the war, one in every five families received some kind of relief from the county.[6]

As the rolls of dependent families swelled, taxes continued to rise. On May 18, 1863, the county imposed an additional tax of 5.25 cents per $100 valuation to be used specifically to support soldiers' dependents. For the same reason, on January 3, 1865, the court ordered certain merchants and professionals to pay annual fees and, for some, a sales tax. Wholesale merchants were required to pay $150 and retail merchants, $50. Both also had to pay one-half of one percent of annual gross sales. Retail liquor dealers were required to pay a $100 fee plus 2.5 percent of gross sales. Druggists, auctioneers, peddlers, cotton compressors, warehousers, and ferry operators had to pay a flat fee of $50 per year. For slave traders, and pool hall and bowling alley operators, the fee was $100. Lawyers and doctors were assessed annual fees of $10, plus 1 percent of annual gross receipts. Hotel and livery stable keepers had to pay $25; restaurateurs half that much. Butchers had to pay only $5, but every employee of a railroad, from the president on down, had to pay $10, and the railroad itself, one-fourth of one percent of gross receipts. Stagecoach lines were taxed at 50 cents per mile of route inside the county.[7]

In an effort to use the money more efficiently, in February 1865, the county began buying certain necessities at a fixed rate and distributing them to the dependent families. Despite the county's attempt to save money via more efficient purchasing and the directly visible use to which the increased taxes were being put, several merchants balked at them. Only now, scant weeks before the end of the conflict, did the citizens of the county raise any serious objections to higher taxes. In March 1865, a number of merchants presented a petition to the commissioners stipulating that the new taxes levied against them were too high and ought to be reduced. The court refused.[8]

Though resistance to higher taxes came only late in the war, resistance to any kind of military service by the men who remained in the county began early and continued throughout the war. These men, the least willing and the least able-bodied, were organized into the local units of the state militia, formally known as Texas State Troops. The militia existed to help repel incursions onto Texas soil by United States troops. Generally, they were not expected to leave Texas. They did not remain in the field. Usually, they slept in their own beds at night, and were only called out for training and, once in a while, for special military assignments. For instance, in October 1861, a local militia unit known as the Columbus Greys was sent to the mouth of the Brazos River to help guard against invasion. Two years later, elements of the Colorado County militia were stationed at Sabine Pass where their commander, the plantation owner Charles W. Tait, found himself dealing with a near mutiny. When Colonel Augustus Buchel ordered them to a post across the Sabine River in Louisiana, Tait's men, grumbling about the rations that both they and their horses received and convinced that they were of little value to the war effort, refused to leave the state. Efforts to persuade them succeeded only in dividing the unit into two factions, who bitterly debated each other's respective cowardice and foolishness. Angered

Illustration 22 Dr. Charles W. Tait plantation house, 1847. *Courtesy Library of Congress.*

by the incident, Buchel requested that he be sent no more state militia units and
Tait offered to resign his commission. Tait's resignation was refused. Instead,
he won a promotion, from major to lieutenant colonel. His militia companies
apparently never left Texas.[9]

Tait and his men were acting under the provisions of a law that had been
passed by the state legislature on December 25, 1861. That law reorganized
the militia, and made, with few exceptions, "every able bodied free white male
inhabitant" between the ages of eighteen and fifty subject to service in it. Section 34 of the act gave the governor the authority to send the militia into the
field. To do so, he was first required to ask for a sufficient number of volunteers from among the local militia units. If, however, fewer volunteers than he
deemed necessary responded to the call, he was authorized to conscript other
members of the units. The conscription process was quite simple. The local officers were to write the names of the members of their company on individual
slips of paper and draw enough names from a hat to fill the governor's quota.
The revised militia system found its way to Colorado County in March 1862.
In that month, twelve companies were organized in the county. Those companies were designated a regiment, and, on April 24, 1862, they elected William
S. Delany, a thirty-six-year-old attorney from Columbus, as their commanding
officer. He was accorded the rank of colonel. Significantly, the men elected to

Illustration 23 Dr. Charles W. Tait plantation house, 1863. *Courtesy Library of Congress.*

be his junior officers, Lt. Col. John Zwiegel and majors Mathias Malsch and Frederick Becker, were all native German-speakers. The Colorado County regiment, together with units from three other counties along the Colorado River, (Matagorda, Wharton, and Fayette), comprised the Twenty-Second Brigade, Texas State Troops, under the overall command of Brig. Gen. William G. Webb. Webb, who lived in the Fayette County seat, La Grange, expected his men to come together periodically in rendezvous, and to conduct drills near their homes once a week. They were not diligent about either.[10]

For Hermann Nagel and the other German settlers in northern Colorado County and the surrounding settlements in Austin and Fayette counties, the new militia system, and indeed the war itself, was a most unwelcome intrusion into their lives. In 1861, they had voted heavily against secession, and the fact that they were in the minority statewide did nothing to change their minds about the morality of their arguments. On November 28, 1862, A. J. Bell, the Confederate army's enrolling officer in Austin County, notified his superior, Major J. P. Flewellen, that a number of local people, most of whom were German, were balking at being conscripted into a state militia unit. He went on to state that the rebels had held a number of very well-attended meetings, many of which were secret, at which they resolved to resist the draft. According to his information, at the last meeting, they had decided to petition the governor, stating that they would not submit to the draft law until and unless they were armed and clothed and their families provided for. Bell requested that a force be sent to compel the rebels to enroll on government terms.[11]

On December 4, Flewellen sent the report to Gen.John Bankhead Magruder, the Confederacy's recently installed commander of the District of Texas, New Mexico, and Arizona, and volunteered to lead a force to ensure compliance. Two days later, Magruder, evidently believing the reports to be alarmist, ordered Flewellen to conscript first, those who were most resistant, and to have them shipped to regiments in other departments, but to do so in a manner that would not stir up a rebellion. Whatever measures Flewellen took were ineffective, for, after a draft was held just before Christmas, the spirit of rebellion increased. Many of the drafted men refused to be sworn in, and on one occasion, a group of them assaulted the officer in charge of administering the oath, driving him from the area. Another man, a friend of the enrolling officer, was mobbed and beaten as well. On Christmas Day, a small regiment of cavalry under the command of Lt. Col. Peter Hardeman, who had been ordered to Columbus some two weeks earlier, arrived in town.[12] Hardeman's arrival did little to restore order in the county. In fact, anti-conscription meetings increased in frequency.

On December 30, 1862, a number of armed men were seen traveling through Frelsburg, on their way to Fayette County for a meeting the next day. About 600 people, including delegates from Colorado, Austin, Lavaca, Fayette, and Washington counties, reportedly attended the meeting, and resolved to resist the draft by force of arms if necessary. The following day, a group of German draft resisters met at the home of a man who had been drafted and organized themselves into a military unit with the express purpose of resisting conscription. In early January, more reports of the draft resisters began reaching the high command. One stated that the Germans were openly rebellious. Another claimed that more than 1,000 Germans were gathering at Frelsburg, planning to resist the draft and, of course, to free the slaves.[13]

On January 4, 1863, in a meeting at Biegel Settlement, calmer elements among the resisters adopted a long declaration. On January 8, they presented it to General Webb at La Grange. It outlined their concerns for the support of their families, pointing out that if they served in the militia for the three-month period being demanded, they would miss planting season. They also expressed anger that while they and their families found it nearly impossible to obtain cloth, slaveholders seemed to have little difficulty in doing so; noted that they were philosophically opposed to the war; and declared that though they were willing to serve as state troops, they were not willing to take an oath of allegiance to the Confederate States of America. They concluded with an appeal to Webb to use his influence to postpone their impressments until after planting season. Webb, who had been ordered to raise a militia unit and get it to Houston as rapidly as possible, was not in the least responsive to their arguments. He claimed that the document itself provided enough evidence of sedition to send the ringleaders to prison for more than two years. On the day that Webb received the declaration, martial law was authorized in Colorado, Fayette, and Austin counties, and Texas Governor Francis R. Lubbock arrived in La Grange to assess and deal with the revolt. He remained for two days, receiving the ringleaders and listening to their complaints.[14]

Meanwhile, Magruder ordered Hardeman and other elements of the army to move against the resisters. On January 11, Hardeman's adjutant reported that twenty-five men under Maj. George T. Madison had been sent to La Grange and twenty-five under Lt. R. H. Stone to Bellville (the county seat of Austin County), and that Hardeman himself had taken fifty men north from Columbus to arrest the ringleaders and disarm the disloyal citizens. Within a week, the insurrection was over. Those who previously had refused now agreed to serve, and by the middle of January were on their way to Houston. Comically, in light of the extreme effort that had been expended to get them there, shortly after they reached Houston, they were sent home. Meanwhile, local and military authorities in Colorado County were attempting to deal with the complaints by several Germans of rough treatment and theft by the Confederate troops. As the reports came in, Magruder ordered Hardeman to severely restrict the ability of his men to leave camp. By January 21, Magruder's adjutant, Lt. Col. Henry L. Webb, was in Colorado County, investigating the situation. On February 10, he reported that discipline among Hardeman's troops was sadly lacking; that Hardeman was ill and Madison in effective command; and that indeed "the arrests [of draft resisters] were made with much cruelty and violence to women and children and to the prisoners arrested." He had turned the prisoners over to the civil authorities in their home counties, and promised to punish any soldier or officer who had committed any depredation against any civilian.[15]

Shortly after this, Webb discovered that the abuses had not been committed by any of Hardeman's soldiers, but rather by civilian guides he had hired. Two of the guides, slave-owners who lived near Frelsburg and who had been reviled or shunned by their neighbors for years, had taken the opportunity to exact a measure of revenge. They and the other civilian guides rather rudely ensured that the women and children of the households did not interfere as the men were being arrested. One woman in particular, in the confusion and anxiety of the moment, received slight wounds from both a bayonet and from the butt of an army rifle. No charges were ever brought against anyone for any injury inflicted during the arrests. To the chagrin of the military, the local authorities, with only the mildest of admonitions, quickly released the men who were arrested for leading the draft revolt.[16]

As the investigation into the draft revolt reached its conclusion, dissent became more common among Confederate soldiers, erupting within Hardeman's command. On January 19, 1863, nine men attempted to leave the unit. All were arrested and charged with desertion. They were placed in the Columbus jail on January 21. Their court-martial began three days later, but had reached no conclusion by February 8, when their captain ordered the prisoners released. Two months later, Hardeman's men marched off to Victoria. Late in August 1863, another Confederate unit, the Thirty-Seventh Texas Cavalry Regiment commanded by Col. Alexander Watkins Terrell, established a camp near Columbus. Shortly afterward, Colonel Terrell went to Houston on business, leaving Lt. Col. John C. Robertson in charge. On September 10, a group of soldiers went to Alleyton on a shopping spree. They wanted to buy boots, but when they offered to pay for them in Confederate specie, the store owner refused to accept it. Determined to have the boots, but unable to pay in any other currency, they took them by force. The store owner complained to Robertson, and he passed the matter on to the company captain, Caldean G. Murray. Murray apparently took no action on the matter, for other, more serious matters soon occupied his mind.[17]

On September 11, Robertson received orders from General Magruder to temporarily dismount his troops and take them to Galveston to aid in that city's defense. It was the second such order the regiment had received. On August 15, while camped in Richmond, the regiment had sent such a detachment to Galveston. This time, however, the troops balked. The orders asked the troops to leave their horses in the Colorado County camp, and a number of the men, championed by Captain Murray, refused to do so. They were suspicious that once they had been transformed into infantry, they would never be remounted. Murray, who had apparently been subjected to just such treatment earlier in his military career, confronted Robertson and stated that he had promised his men that they would not be dismounted. As Murray spoke, the men cheered, and Robertson grew fearful that an armed rebellion was about to break out. He turned to the troops and made a speech denouncing Murray and assuring the troops that their conversion to infantry was only temporary. But, as Robertson stated in his report on the incident six days later, he "found that insubordination had been increased and excited by Captain Murray to such an extent that the troops were beyond [his] control." He dismissed the men hoping that a night's sleep would calm them down.[18]

The next morning, however, Robertson found "a large number of horses saddled up and the troops preparing to leave." He again assembled the men and addressed them, this time claiming that he intended to call for volunteers only to go with him to defend Galveston. As he stated in his report, he had no intention of living up to the promise, but was only stalling until the troops could be subdued. He returned to his quarters thinking that the rebellion had been stopped. A short time later, Murray, Lt. Jesse G. Chancellor, and about 100 men rode out of camp. Apparently, they took several of the horses that had belonged to the men previously sent as infantry to Galveston. They also took the men's saddles, which had been stored under guard in Alleyton. Robertson took most of the remaining men to Galveston where he filed his report on the mutiny. Murray and Chancellor were charged with desertion.[19]

On September 30, a number of Murray's fellow company captains wrote headquarters attempting to explain the desertions and imploring that their unit be "remounted at once and permitted to pursue our original purpose," that is, permitted to engage the enemy as an active cavalry unit. The captains claimed that the men who had deserted had only done so because they wanted a more direct role in the war, and that since they left, they had attempted to join other units. The deserters were not pursued for a month. On October 17, Robertson and twenty-five men, who had returned from the coast, set out from their camp near Columbus to find Captain Murray. On the road they met Lt. Russell J. Starr, who was returning to the camp with a few of the deserters. Starr informed Robertson that Murray could probably be found near his home in Wood County. Robertson learned from other sources that Murray and about sixty men were camped near Springville, in Wood County, and that they were armed and prepared to resist arrest. Robertson selected four men and directed them to pose as deserters, join Murray's party, and return with reports on his strength and intentions. He then proceeded to Henderson County where he captured Lieutenant Chancellor near his home. He rendezvoused with his spies near Tyler on October 28 and started the next morning for Wood County. He arrested three of Murray's men on the twenty-ninth, learned from them where Murray had gone, and arrested him without incident. In November 1863, Confederate authorities allowed Murray to resign his commission and promoted Lieutenant Starr to take his place.[20]

In addition to commanding the area's militia, Gen. William G. Webb also played a role in raising new units for the national Confederate army, asking for volunteers and, if necessary, organizing drafts. There were never enough volunteers, and the response to conscription calls was meager. He fielded constant requests for exemptions. When, shortly after a draft in early July 1863, it became known that men who served the Confederacy as teamsters were exempt from military service, he complained that his office was "literally besieged by an anxious, eager hard-to-satisfy crowd of drafted men, all eager to get a detail to haul [freight] ... like a hungry set of vultures." Such service shortly became a very popular way of avoiding military duty. [21]

Despite the aggressive suppression of the draft revolt, many Germans would continue to surreptitiously resist serving the Confederate government.

Even those who faced no harsher duties than those of the state troops continued to evade service. When Webb called a rendezvous of his state troops at
Harvey's Creek in western Colorado County for the second week in July 1863,
only about one-fourth of his men attended. Later that year, when Webb submitted a list of draft evaders from his district to his superiors, most of the forty-
four people from Colorado County on the list were German. In October 1863,
Webb sent a detachment of about twenty-five men to the German settlements
in northern Colorado County to look for those who had failed to respond to
the draft, men he characterized as deserters. By then, most of them had secure
hiding places. All, it seems, had systems in place to feed them, and to warn them
of the approach of Webb's conscription gangs, whom they derisively referred
to as "Heel Flies." After searching for four days, the Heel Flies arrested only
one man, Valentin Hans. As they approached his home, the Heel Flies believed
that they saw Hans. But when they arrived, he was nowhere to be found, and
his wife declared that he was gone. In a back room, they found a trunk large
enough for a man to hide in, but it was locked and, the wife reported, the key
had been lost. However, when Webb's men threatened to force the lock open,
perhaps by shooting it open, the wife suddenly found the key and delivered her
husband to the military. He was court-martialed for desertion, found guilty,
and sentenced to one week of double duty in camp. Even such light sentences,
and later offers of complete amnesty, failed to induce any of the other draft
resisters to come out of hiding. Reportedly, in October 1863, some twenty-
five to thirty of them had armed themselves and were camped in a thicket in
northern Colorado County, determined to shoot it out with the authorities.
The same month, Webb's men found two small stone fortifications in northern
Fayette County, one with eighteen "port holes" and the other with six. Inside
the forts, Webb's men found part of a German-language newspaper and signs
that a number of horses had been present. Whoever had occupied the forts had
fled before Webb's men arrived.[22]

In the last year of the war, Aaron T. Sutton, a Union soldier imprisoned in
Texas, was aided by Germans, both when he escaped his captors and when he
was in custody. Hermann Nagel, the physician who lived near Cat Spring, clung
to his Unionist sympathies and anti-slavery beliefs despite apparent danger to
his life. Some people referred to him as the devil, both "because of his opinions
and his long beard," according to his son. He seems to have been involved in
underground activities, evidently paying regular visits to draft evaders in hiding and at least once conspiring with a friend to keep him out of military service. Nagel's friend wanted to fake his own death, going so far as to be buried
and then rescued from the grave before his air ran out. Nagel thought this too
risky, and suggested to his friend, who was tall and already rather slender, that
instead, he should lose so much weight that no doctor would pass him into the

army. The friend starved himself, and continued to do so even after his physical examination was postponed. When the day finally came, the man was too weak to walk, and he was loaded into the back of a wagon. Fearing for the man's life, Nagel went along. He carried him up the stairs to the second floor of the courthouse in Bellville and laid him on the floor. There, the man was declared unfit for military service, but fit enough to herd cattle for the army. In November 1863, concerned about his continued well being and the possibility that his unusually tall fourteen-year-old son, Charles, might soon be conscripted, Nagel conveyed his herd of cattle to his wife, after which he, Charles, and a group of other men secretly fled to Mexico.[23]

Mexico was, naturally, the most popular destination for the area's German draft evaders. Another such, Frank A. Laake had been in America for only a few years and in Colorado County for just a few months when the question of secession came up for a vote. A Unionist and, by trade, a freighter, he avoided the draft, as did many others, by signing on to haul cotton from the railhead at Alleyton to Mexico. But eventually Laake's service as a freighter was not enough for the Confederacy and he was conscripted in Columbus. Given leave to take his wagon and team home, he did so, then fled into Mexico. He, however, was averse only to serving in the Confederate army, for he left Mexico shortly afterward for New Orleans, where he enlisted in a U.S. infantry unit. He served until June 1, 1866, after which he returned to his home in Texas. Another German, Henry Dedrich, who in the early stages of the war was accused of harboring a runaway slave, actually served in the Confederate army for a time, before returning home, evidently without authorization from his commanders. He was apparently sheltered by another German, Joseph Dungen, who was indicted for doing so. Neither the case against Dedrich for harboring the slave nor that against Dungen for harboring Dedrich came to trial until after the war, at which time, on November 2, 1865, both were dismissed. Friedrich Meyer found the simplest way around military service. On June 18, 1862, he formally declared that he was a subject of Germany, that he had never applied for citizenship of either the United States or the Confederate States of America, and that he was not a permanent resident of the country.[24]

Life for the slaves in Colorado County was little different during the war than it had been before. However, with so many of the county's white men away at war, anxiety in the white community about the potential for a slave rebellion grew more pronounced. In 1856, such anxiety had led the county's authorities to severely punish several slaves. When one slave told his owner that a general rebellion had been planned, dozens of slaves were taken into custody. Though they were not tried, three were hanged and many were flogged. During the war, three slaves were convicted of crimes. The punishments, lashings administered by the county sheriff in the most public place in the county, on the courthouse lawn, were certainly meant to induce dread. The first such spectacle occurred in 1863. At the spring term of district court, a slave named John was convicted of aggravated assault and battery for attacking a white man with a knife some three years earlier. He was sentenced to 1,000 lashes, to be inflicted in ten weekly sessions of 100 lashes each, beginning at four o'clock on Saturday, May 9, 1863. The lash was described as "a Strop of leather sixteen inches long and two wide with handle twenty inches long." The following spring, a slave named Allen was found guilty of manslaughter for killing another slave on December 29, 1863. He too was sentenced to 100 lashes on his bare back on ten consecutive Saturdays on the courthouse square. The third case was decided at the fall term in 1864. Four slaves were indicted for breaking into and burglarizing a home, stealing a pistol, some cloth, and a coat. One of the four, a man named Low, was convicted and, like the others, sentenced to 1,000 lashes on his bare back to be administered in ten sessions beginning on Saturday, November 5, 1864. But Low was not given a week to recover from the beatings. His sessions on the square were scheduled for every other day. These were the only public floggings in the county's history, and certainly reflected the growing apprehension in the white community, as the war came nearer to what for them was an unfavorable conclusion, that their lives would never return to antebellum standards.[25]

Notes

1   Letter of Hermann Nagel, April 28, 1861, printed in Walter D. Kamphoefner and Wolfgang Helbich, eds., *Germans in the Civil War: The Letters They Wrote Home* (Chapel Hill: University of North Carolina Press, 2006), 395.

2   Eighth Census of the United States (1860), Colorado County, Texas, Schedules 1, 2; Colorado County Election Records, [Book 1] 1854–1866.

3   The number of soldiers from the county who were either killed or died of disease is derived from a study that hoped to identify every man who appeared on the 1860 federal census of Colorado County who served in the Confederate military. The study was published as an appendix to Bill Stein, "Consider the Lily: The Ungilded History of Colorado County, Texas," Part 6, *Nesbitt Memorial Library Journal* 7 (May 1997): 111–42. See also Muster Rolls, Company B, 5th Texas Infantry, Microfilm edition in Archives of the Nesbitt Memorial Library, Columbus.

4   *Colorado Citizen*, August 15, 1857; March 5, 1859; June 15, 1861; June 29, 1861; August 10, 1861; Colorado County District Court Records, Civil Cause File No. 1650: *Walter Tufts and Charles A. Colley v. D. J. Hollister, H. C. Drew, and A. F. Smith;* Civil Cause File No. 1695: *Lathrop & Wilkinson v. Henry M. Johnson;* Kamphoefner and Helbich, eds., *Germans in the Civil War,* 196 (Nagel quote). The last known edition of the *Colorado Citizen* until after the war was issued on November 2, 1861. The Confederate government actually passed a law, on May

21, 1861, that made it a crime for Confederate citizens to pay debts to individuals or corporations anywhere in the United States except Delaware, Maryland, Kentucky, Missouri, or Washington, D.C. The law suggested that the debts be paid into the Confederate treasury, which would then issue a certificate that would be redeemable after the war. See James M. Matthews, ed., *The Statutes at Large of the Provisional Government of the Confederate States of America* (Richmond: R. M. Smith, 1864), 151.

5   Colorado County Police [Commissioners] Court Minutes, Book 2, pp. 419–20, 422–23, Book 1862–1876, 3.

6   Colorado County Police [Commissioners] Court Minutes, Book 1862–1876, pp. 5–6, 10–13, 18, 21; Colorado County Marriage Records, Book C, 67–75.

7   Colorado County Police [Commissioners] Court Minutes, Book 1862–1876, 15, 33.

8   Colorado County Police [Commissioners] Court Minutes, Book 1862–1876, 35, 36.

9   *Colorado Citizen*, October 29, 1861; Augustus Buchel to Edmund P. Turner, October 24, 1863, *The War of the Rebellion: A Compilation of the Official Records of the Union and Confederate Armies* (hereinafter cited as *OR*), comp. Robert N. Scott (Washington, D. C.: U. S. Government Printing Office, 1880–1901), 26, 2:351; Letter of Richard V. Cook, November 11, 1863, printed in Ernest Mae Seaholm and Bill Stein, comp., "Richard V. Cook and the Battle of Sabine Pass," *Nesbitt Memorial Library Journal* 1 (February 1991): 256–57.

10   Hans Peter Nielsen Gammel, comp., *The Laws of Texas 1822–1897* (Austin: Gammel Book Company, 1898), vol. 5, 455–64; Texas State Militia Muster Rolls; Election Results, April 29, 1862, Adjutant General Records, Texas State Troops, 22nd Brigade Correspondence, Archives and Information Services Division, Texas State Library and Archives Commission. Those who did not have to serve in the militia included postmasters and mail carriers, ferrymen on public roads, railroad engineers and conductors, steamboat officers and crews, district judges and district clerks, and county clerks, chief justices, and sheriffs.

11   A. J. Bell to J. P. Flewellen, November 28, 1862, *OR*, 1, 15:887.

12   J. P. Flewellen to Edmund P. Turner, December 4, 1862, *OR*, 1, 15:886, E. P. Turner to J. P. Flewellen, December 6, 1862, *OR*, 1, 15:890, A. J. Bell to J. P. Flewellen, January 3, 1863, *OR*, 1, 15:925, "Diary of James Pitman Saunders," in John Bennett Boddie, comp., *Historical Southern Families* 7 (Ann Arbor, Michigan: 1963), 175–76.

13   J. B. McCown to [Thomas Green], [January 1863], *OR*, 1, 15:921, A. J. Bell to J. P. Flewellen, January 3, 1863, *OR*, 1, 15:925.

14   J. B. McCown to [Thomas Green], [January 1863], *OR*, 1, 15:921, A. J. Bell to J. P. Flewellen, January 3, 1863, *OR*, 1, 15:926, William G. Webb to Henry L. Webb, January 12, 1863, *OR*, 1, 15:945, John Bankhead Magruder to Francis R. Lubbock, February 11, 1863, *OR*, 1, 15:974.

15   Special Orders, No. 35, January 5, 1863, *OR*, 1, 15:931, Special Orders, No. 37, January 8, 1863, *OR*, 1, 15:936, Henry L. Webb to Benjamin Bloomfield, January

11, 1863, *OR*, 1, 15:942, William G. Webb to Henry L. Webb, January 12, 1863, *OR*, 1, 15:946; Henry L. Webb to Edmund P. Turner, January 21, 1863, *OR*, 1, 15:955–56, Special Order, Issued at Columbus, Colorado County, Texas, January 21, 1863, *OR*, 1, 15:956, John Bankhead Magruder to Francis R. Lubbock, February 11, 1863, *OR*, 1, 15:974, Henry L. Webb to Edmund P. Turner, January 19, 1863, *OR*, 1, 53:844, Henry L. Webb to John Bankhead Magruder, February 10, 1863, *OR*, 2, 5:831; *[La Grange] True Issue*, February 5, 1863 and February 12, 1863.

16 Henry L. Webb to Edmund P. Turner, February 11, 1863, *OR*, 1, 15:978–79, Henry L. Webb to Edmund P. Turner, February 18, 1863, *OR*, 1, 15:981–82, Report of Lieut. William J. Wheeler concerning certain charges preferred against Lieut. R. H. Stone by certain German citizens of New Ulm and its vicinity, *OR*, 1, 15:989–90. The civilian guides were identified as the Muckleroys and the Hendersons. The Muckleroys had operated a slave plantation in the Frelsburg area for a few years. The woman who was injured by the bayonet is identified as "Mrs. Rouge." Her name may have been Runge. Lt. William J. Wheeler, who investigated the incident, filed his report on February 23, 1863. The report states "Mrs. Rouge, the lady who is reported to have been so badly misused, states that she received no injury at the hands of Lieutenant Stone, and she does not think from any of the men under his command; that Lieutenant Stone did not come into her house, and that she was injured, but to the best of her knowledge the injury she received was at the hands of men who were not under Lieutenant Stone's command, but were citizens, neighbors, living in that vicinity, and not from any of Lieutenant Stone's command; that she was knocked down, not by any of Lieutenant Stone's command, and that she received one or two scratches from a bayonet, whether it was thrust at her or whether in the confusion of the moment, which she thinks most likely, she ran against it, she cannot tell; that she received the butt of a gun, but says the blow was not aimed at her; that being excited and alarmed for her husband's safety she accidentally ran against it; and that she is confident, from the general conduct and demeanor of the lieutenant and the men of his command, that they intended no injury or insult to her whatever."

17 "Diary of James Pitman Saunders," 177–84; A. W. Terrell to John Brashear, September 18, 1863, *OR*, 1, 26, 2:237–38; John C. Robertson to A. W. Terrell, September 17, 1863, *OR*, 1, 26, 2:238–39.

18 A. W. Terrell to John Brashear, September 18, 1863, *OR*, 1, 26, 2:237–38; John C. Robertson to A. W. Terrell, September 17, 1863, *OR*, 1, 26, 2:238–39.

19 A. W. Terrell to John Brashear, September 18, 1863, *OR*, 1, 26, 2:237–38; John C. Robertson to A. W. Terrell, September 17, 1863, *OR*, 1, 26, 2:238–39; *Compiled Service Records of Confederate Soldiers who Served in Organizations from the State of Texas*, National Archives Microfilm Publication No. 323, Rolls 177, 179.

20 S. H. B. Cundiff et al. to Edmund P. Turner, September 30, 1863, *OR*, 1, 26, 2:278–80, N. C. Gould to Henry E. McCulloch, October 12, 1863, *OR*, 1, 26, 2:330, John C. Robertson to Edmund P. Turner, December 2, 1863, *OR*, 1, 26, 2:469–71.

21   William G. Webb to Jeremiah Y. Dashiell, July 7, 1863, Adjutant General Records, Texas State Troops, 22nd Brigade Correspondence, Archives and Information Services Division, Texas State Library and Archives Commission.

22   William G. Webb to Jeremiah Y. Dashiell, July 15, 1863, October 16, 1863, October 19, 1863, October 30, 1863, Proceedings of the Court Martial on the Trial of V. Hans, October 14, 1863, Adjutant General Records, Texas State Troops, 22nd Brigade Correspondence, Archives and Information Services Division, Texas State Library and Archives Commission. Heel flies are a common pest of cattle.

23   Aaron T. Sutton, *Prisoner of the Rebels in Texas* (Decatur, Indiana: Americana Books, 1978), 97–101, 116–19; Charles Nagel, *A Boy's Civil War Story* (St. Louis: Eden Publishing House, 1935), 207–16, 227–54.

24   Frank W. Johnson, *A History of Texas and Texans*, ed. Eugene Campbell Barker and Ernest William Winkler (Chicago: American Historical Society, 1914), vol. 3, 1538; Colorado County District Court Records, Criminal Cause File No. 482: *State of Texas v. Henry Dedrich*, Criminal Cause File No. 501: *State of Texas v. Joseph Dungen,* Minute Book C2, 423, 425; Colorado County Bond and Mortgage Records, Book E, 662, 669. Though the cotton freighters avoided the perils of life in the military, their occupation was not without its dangers. According to family tradition, on one of Laake's trips, his caravan was attacked by bandits. One of his companions was killed and he himself was hit in the head with a metal object. The wound left a scar that remained bald for the rest of his life. See Ernest W. Laake, *The History and Living Descendants of the Frank Albert Laake Family* (n. p., n. d.).
On July 25, 1887, twenty-five years after he declared that he was a temporary resident, Meyer, long past the age at which he could be drafted into military service, applied for United States citizenship. He received it on September 30, 1891. He died November 7, 1903, and was buried at Trinity Lutheran Church in Frelsburg, where, undoubtedly, he will remain permanently. See Colorado County Naturalization Records, District Clerk Record Book 1, 127, County Clerk Declaration of Intention Book 1, 82; Tombstone of Friedrich Meyer, Trinity Lutheran Cemetery.

25   Kamphoefner and Helbich, *Germans in the Civil War,* 196–97; Colorado County District Court Records, Criminal Cause File No. 364: *State of Texas v. John, a slave,* Criminal Cause File No. 499: *State of Texas v. Allen, a slave,* Criminal Cause File No. 511: *State of Texas v. Low, a slave,* Minute Book C 2, 350. For a fuller discussion of the supposed 1856 Colorado County slave rebellion, see Bill Stein, "Consider the Lily: The Ungilded History of Colorado County, Texas," Part 5, *Nesbitt Memorial Library Journal* 7 (January 1997): 5–6.

ABOUT THE CONTRIBUTORS

Alwyn Barr

Alwyn Barr is Emeritus Professor of History at Texas Tech University. His publications include *Polignac's Texas Brigade* (1964; 2nd ed. Texas A&M University Press, 1998); *Reconstruction to Reform: Texas Politics, 1876–1906* (1971; 2nd ed. Southern Methodist University Press, 2000); *Black Texans: A History of African Americans in Texas, 1528–1995* (1973; 2nd ed. University of Oklahoma Press, 1996); *Texans in Revolt: The Battle for San Antonio, 1835* (University of Texas Press, 1990); *The African Texans* (Texas A&M University Press, 2004); three edited books and introductions or forewords to four volumes; forty-five book chapters or articles in journals, including *Civil War History, Journal of Negro History, Social Science Quarterly, Military Affairs*; fifty-three articles in thirteen encyclopedias; about 100 book reviews in twenty-five journals, including: *American Historical Review, Journal of American History, Journal of Southern History*. He has won numerous awards for his publications and his service in the classroom including the Coral Tullis Award for the best book in Texas history, Texas State Historical Association, 1971; President's Excellence in Teaching Award, Texas Tech University, 1986–87; President's Academic Achievement Award, Texas Tech University, 1991–92; Matthews Award for best article in *Military History of the West*, 1997; Outstanding Researcher, Arts & Sciences, Texas Tech University, 2001; Faculty Distinguished Leadership Award, Texas Tech University, 2005.

Vicki Betts

Vicki Betts, a native of Tyler, Texas, has been a librarian at the University of Texas at Tyler since 1977. She earned a B.A. in history from East Texas State University in 1976, with an honors thesis entitled "Smith County, Texas, during the Civil War," and an M.L.S. from North Texas State University in 1977. She is a member of the Smith County Historical Society and Texas State Historical Association, and has spoken before the local Sons of the Confederacy, United Daughters of the Confederacy, the Smith County Historical Society, and the

Texas State Historical Association. She has also presented programs nationally on mid-nineteenth-century Southern homespun dresses. Publications include: *Smith County, Texas, during the Civil War*, "'Private and Amateur Hangings': The Lynching of W. W. Montgomery, March 15, 1863," *Southwestern Historical Quarterly* 88 (October 1984): 145–66; "'Dear Husband': The Civil War Letters of Sophronia Joiner Chipman, Kankakee County, Illinois, 1863–1865," *Military History of the West* 29 (Fall 1999): 147–98; "Civilian Reaction to the Red River Campaign, 1864, Natchitoches to Mansfield, Louisiana," *Military History of the West* 34 (2004): 29–50; and numerous articles in *Chronicles of Smith County, Texas*. She maintains a website largely devoted to transcribed Southern newspaper articles related to the Civil War home front, and to Smith County local history.

Edward T. Cotham, Jr.

Edward T. Cotham, Jr., was born in Dallas, Texas. He is president of the Terry Foundation in Houston, Texas. The Terry Foundation is the largest private source of scholarships at Texas universities with more than 600 Terry Scholars on full scholarship. Ed holds an undergraduate degree in economics from the University of Houston and a master's degree in economics from the University of Chicago. A native Texan, Ed returned to Texas to obtain a law degree from the University of Texas in 1979. Ed is a former president of the Houston Civil War Roundtable and is active in the Civil War preservation movement. He is a life member of the Civil War Preservation Trust. He is also a member of the Company of Military Historians and the Author's Guild. In September 2005, Ed was awarded the Jefferson Davis Historical Gold Medal by the United Daughters of the Confederacy. In May 2006, Ed was awarded the Frank C. Vandiver Award of Merit by the Houston Civil War Round Table. His published works include *Battle on the Bay: the Civil War Struggle for Galveston*, which was published in 1998 by the University of Texas Press. His second book, *Sabine Pass: the Confederacy's Thermopylae*, was published in August 2004. The Sabine Pass book was the winner of the Dan and Marilyn Laney Prize for Civil War Battlefield Preservation. That award is given annually by the Austin Civil War Round Table to the author of the book that best promotes the heritage and preservation of endangered battlefields of the Civil War. His third book, *The Southern Journey of a Civil War Marine: The Illustrated Note-Book of Henry O. Gusley*, was published by the University of Texas Press in January 2006. The unique nature of this book has made it a best-seller and led to an interview on National Public Radio that brought Ed and his book to the attention of Civil War enthusiasts across the country.

Bruce A. Glasrud

Bruce Glasrud is the retired Dean of the School of Arts and Sciences and Professor of History at Sul Ross State University, Alpine, Texas. Before joining Sul Ross, Glasrud worked for more than a quarter century at California State University, Hayward. While at CSUH, Glasrud served as Department Chair, as Associate Vice President for Research and Faculty Affairs, as Academic Senate Chair, as California Faculty Association President, as CSU Statewide Academic Senator, and for numerous other committees, boards, and positions. He received his B.A. degree at Luther College, his M.A. at Eastern New Mexico University, and his Ph.D. in history at Texas Tech University. His dissertation topic at Texas Tech was "Black Texans, 1900–1930: A History." A specialist in United States ethnic and regional history, Glasrud taught courses in Black History, Southern History, Blacks in the West, Asians in the South, and Mexican Americans in the Southwest as well as standard introductory courses in United States History. Glasrud is the author or co-author of seven books, (with three more under contract), including his recent publication with Laurie Champion entitled *The African American West: A Century of Short Stories* (2000) and with Arnoldo De León, entitled *Bibliophiling Tejano History* (2003). Glasrud also is general editor and consultant for two special education sets: the *American Biographies Series* (30 vols.) and *United States History* (3 vols.). Additionally, Glasrud has published more than fifty articles, twenty-five book reviews, and fifty abstracts.

Ronald E. Goodwin

Ron Goodwin is an Assistant Professor of History at Prairie View A&M University. He completed the M.S. degree in urban planning and an M.A. in history from Texas Southern University. Goodwin completed his undergraduate degree at Texas Lutheran while on active duty in the U.S. Air Force.

John W. Gorman

John W. Gorman has been a professor of history at Blinn College in Bryan, Texas, for the last thirteen years. He received his B.A. in history and political science in 1990 and his M.A. in history in 1993 from Stephen F. Austin State University. At present he is working on his Ph.D. in history at Texas A&M University. Mr. Gorman specializes in late nineteenth and twentieth-century United States history with a focus on Civil War enlistment patterns, WWI, and Civil Rights.

Charles D. Grear

Charles D. Grear is an Assistant Professor of History at Prairie View A&M University. He has numerous publications on the Civil War, including *The Fate of Texas: The Civil War and the Lone Star State* (University of Arkansas Press, 2008); "For Land and Family: Local Attachments and the Grapevine Volunteers," Military History of the West 33 (2003): 1–12; "Texans to the Home Front: Why Lone Star Soldiers Returned to Texas during the War," *East Texas Historical Journal* (Fall 2007); and a forthcoming article "Why Texans Fought in the Far West: The Effects of Local Attachments on Texans Fighting in New Mexico," *New Mexico Historical Review*. He is currently working on several book projects, including *In Defense of My Native State: Why Texans Fought in the Civil War* (under advance contract and review with Texas A&M University Press), *Fighting Alongside Confederate Indians: A History of Gano's Brigade in the Civil War* (McWhiney Foundation Press), and co-authoring with Alexander Mendoza, *Causes Lost But Not Forgotten: George Littlefield and the Confederacy Legacy at the University of Texas at Austin*. He currently serves as book review editor of H-CivWar and was the recipient of the Lawrence T. Jones III Research Fellowship in Civil War Texas History from the Texas State Historical Association (2005).

Kenneth E. Hendrickson, Jr.

At Midwestern State University, Hendrickson served as chair of the History Department for 36 years (1970–2006). Today he holds the rank of Regents' Professor and Hardin Distinguished Professor of American History, Emeritus. He has published ten books, *Bolivia I: A Report on Peace Corps at the University of Oklahoma*, (co-author, 1962), *The Public Career of Richard F. Pettigrew of South Dakota* (1968), *Essays and Commentaries in American History*, 2 Vols. (1981), *Hard Times in Oklahoma: The Depression Years* (ed., co-author, (1983), *The Water of the Brazos: A History of the Brazos River Authority* (1981), *The Chief Executives of Texas* (1995), *Profiles in Power: Twentieth Century Texans in Washington* (ed. with Michael L. Collins, 1993, revised ed, 2004), *The Spanish-American War* (2003), *The Life and Presidency of Franklin Delano Roosevelt: An Annotated Bibliography*, 3 Vols. (2005), *Primary Source Accounts of the Spanish-American War* (2006), and contributed to a dozen more. He is the author of over one hundred articles, essays, and reviews. Hendrickson is past president of Phi Alpha Theta, the East Texas Historical Association, and the Texas Oral History Association. Also, he is a Fellow of the Texas State Historical Association and the East Texas Historical Association.

Linda Sybert Hudson

Dr. Hudson received her Ph.D. from the University of North Texas. She is an Assistant Professor at East Texas Baptist University. Hudson has also taught at Panola College, Texas Christian University, Tarrant County College, the University of North Texas, North Central Texas College, Kilgore College, Tyler Junior College, and Stephen F. Austin State University. Her current publications include "Slave Cases in the Texas Supreme Court, 1841–1907" (manuscript in preparation); "Women and the Texas Revolution," International Conference on Education, Natural Science, Humanities and Social Science, Lanzhou University of Technology, Lanzhou, Gansu Province, China, July 24–26, 2005; "This Business of Louisiana; Winning the Great Game," *Texas Journal of Genealogy and History* 3 (2004): 6–10; "Texas Women: A Pioneer Spirit," in *Texas Heritage*. 4th ed., edited by Archie McDonald and Ben Procter (Wheeling, Illinois: Harlan-Davidson, 2003); *Mistress of Manifest Destiny: A Biography of Jane McManus Storm Cazneau, 1807–1878* (Austin: Texas State Historical Association, 2001), winner of Fehrenbach Award, Best Book in Texas History in 2001; Honorable Mention, Best Book in History, Texas Institute of Letters, 2001; "Jane McManus Storm Cazneau and the Galveston Bay and Texas Land Company," *East Texas Historical Journal* 39 (Spring 2001).

Gary D. Joiner

Gary D. Joiner earned his Bachelor of Arts with a double major in history and geography (1973) and Master of Arts in history (1975) degrees from Louisiana Tech University. He earned his doctorate in history at Lancaster University in England (2004). He also has conducted postgraduate work in classical, military, and regional archaeology. He is a professional cartographer specializing in geographic information systems. He taught Louisiana history and western civilization at Bossier Parish Community College (1991–1995) and served as adjunct instructor at Louisiana State University in Shreveport (1995–1997), instructor at Louisiana State University in Shreveport (1997–2004), and is currently an assistant professor in the Department of History and Social Sciences. He is the director of the Red River Regional Studies Center on the LSU-S campus. Dr. Joiner teaches Louisiana history, Civil War in Louisiana, Colonial and Revolutionary War, modern Middle East, Louisiana geography, maps and mapping, demographics of aging, and independent studies in history and geography. Dr. Joiner's research interests include the exploration, study, and preservation of Civil War battlefields, nineteenth century steamboats, Civil War map interpretation, regional history, and the preservation of historic sites. He is the chief consulting cartographer for the Civil War Preservation Trust. His recent research projects include the mapping of the Vicksburg National Military Park for the National Park Service; mapping the battlefields of Mansfield, Pleasant Hill, Monett's Ferry, Mansura, and Yellow Bayou in Louisiana for the Civil War Preservation Trust; mapping the battlefields of Poison Springs, Jenkin's Ferry, Elkin's Ferry, and Prairie d'Ane in Arkansas for the Civil War Preservation Trust; and mapping the Petersburg Campaign in Virginia for the Civil War Preservation Trust. He has also conducted historical surveys for the National Park Service, the U.S. Department of Agriculture, the Louisiana Division of Archaeology, and the City of Shreveport, among others. Dr. Joiner's publications include "The Union Naval Expedition on the Red River Campaign," *Civil War Regiments* 4, no. 2, 1994 (co-author), "Photographs and Drawings," *The American Civil War: Handbook of Literature and Research*, Greenwood Press, 1996; *Red River Steamboats*, Arcadia Publishing, 1999 (co-author); *Shreveport-Bossier History*, Historical Publishing, 2000 (co-author); *The Red River Campaign: Studies in Union and Confederate Leadership in Louisiana*, Parabellum Press, 2002 (editor); *One Damn Blunder from Beginning to End: The Red River Campaign in 1864*, Scholarly Resources, 2003; *No Pardons to Ask Nor Apologies to Make: The Journal of William Henry King, Gray's 28th Louisiana Infantry*, University of Tennessee Press, 2006 (editor); *Through the Howling Wilderness: The Red River Campaign of 1864 and Union Defeat in the West*, University of Tennessee Press, 2006; and numerous chapters and articles.

Archie P. McDonald

Archie McDonald is a Professor of History at Stephen F. Austin University. He is a well-known author of Texas history. He has authored fifteen books, edited nineteen books, and has written more than nine monographs. His edited volume, *Make Me a Map of the Valley: The Journal of Jedediah Hotchkiss, 1862–1865*, was listed in *Civil War Illustrated* in 1980 as one of the One Hundred Best Books on the Civil War, in Richard Harwell, *In Tall Cotton: The 200 Most Important Confederate Books for the Reader, Researcher, and Collector* (Austin, 1978), and again in *Civil War: The Magazine of the Civil War Society* (January 1995) as one of the 100 Best Books on the Civil War. It is in its fourth printing. McDonald's *Hurrah for Texas! The Diary of Adolphus Sterne* was listed in John H. Jenkins' *Basic Texas Books* (Austin, 1983), as one of the 269 essential works for a research library in Texas history. The late novelist and writer James A. Michener listed Dr. McDonald's monograph, *The Trail to San Jacinto*, as one of the ten most helpful books that he used in preparation of his novel, *Texas* (New York, 1985).

Mary Jo O'Rear

Recipient of a Bachelor of Arts degree in History and English from Centenary College of Louisiana in 1966, Ms. O'Rear earned a Master of Interdisciplinary Arts (history and English) from Texas A&M University-Corpus Christi in 1977 and a Master of Arts in history and political science from Texas A&M University-Kingsville in 2001. During the interim, she taught American and world history, world geography, economics, and English in the Corpus Christi Independent School System. Since her retirement from secondary school teaching, she has taught United States history as an adjunct instructor for Texas A&M University-Kingsville, University of Incarnate Word ADCaP Del Mar Center, and Del Mar College. Her articles include "Silver-Lined Storm: The Impact of the 1919 Hurricane on the Port of Corpus Christi," *Southwestern Historical Quarterly* (January 2005); and "Review of *The Man from the Rio Grande: A Biography of Henry Love,*" in the *East Texas Historical Journal*. It was for "Silver-Lined Storm: The Impact of the 1919 Hurricane on the Port of Corpus Christi" that Ms. O'Rear received the H. Bailey Carroll Award for Best Article in *Southwestern Historical Quarterly* (2005) as well as the Keith Guthrie Memorial Award for best article on Nueces County history. Officer in two local and regional historical societies, Ms. O'Rear has spoken at the Texas State Historical Association, the Borderlands in Transition Conference, the Gulf Coast Historical Association, and the East Texas Historical Association, as well as to numerous local organizations. Her manuscript, *Risk-Takers and Dream-Makers: The People of Corpus Christi and their Port,* is currently being considered for publication by a state university press.

James M. Smallwood

James Smallwood is Emeritus Professor of History at Oklahoma State University. He has also taught at Texas A&M at Commerce, Southeastern Oklahoma State University, Texas Tech University, the University of Texas at Tyler, Seton Hall University in New Jersey, and the University of Kyoto, Japan. He is the author of sixteen books. His *Time of Hope, Time of Despair: Black Texans during Reconstruction* won the Texas State Historical Association's Coral Tullis Award in 1982 for the best book of the year on Texas history. His most recent book, *The Indian Texans*, won the Texas Library Association's 2005 Texas Reference Source Award. Smallwood has also edited fourteen books, including ten on the writings of Will Rogers, Oklahoma's Favorite Son. He is a fellow of both the Texas State Historical Association and the East Texas Historical Association.

Charles D. Spurlin

Charles Spurlin is a retired history professor, former chair of the Social Sciences Department at Victoria College, and author of many professional articles and book reviews. His book publications include *West of the Mississippi with Waller's 13th Texas Cavalry Battalion, CSA: The Civil War Diary of Charles A. Leuschner,* and *Texas Volunteers in the Mexican War.* He has served as president of the South Texas Historical Association and the South Texas Social Studies Association. He has also served on the Executive Council of the Texas State Historical Association. Spurlin's honors include being listed in *Who's Who of the South and Southwest,* the Daughters of the American Revolution Medal of Honor, Jefferson Davis Medal for Historical Achievement, Texas House of Representatives Certificate of Citation, Texas Historical Commission Citation for Distinguished Service, 1996 Piper Professor, and Fellow of the Texas State Historical Association.

Bill Stein

Bill Stein is a native of Columbus, Texas. While working in a corporation in Houston, he became keenly interested in the history of his hometown and county. After reading published material, he was appalled to discover, upon checking original sources, just how much misinformation local histories contained. In 1987, as a complete amateur, he was hired to be the first archivist at the Nesbitt Memorial Library in Columbus. He has since published dozens of articles on Colorado County, including a chronological history of the county from its origins until 1883. He established a journal of local history which was published from 1989 until 2000. In the ensuing years, he designed and developed a website which presents thousands of pages of resource material on Colorado County history. More recently, he had an article published in the *Southwestern Historical Quarterly,* and a piece (the only one he's ever done that had nothing to do with Colorado County) in the new book *Texas Women on the Cattle Trail.*

Carol Taylor

Carol Taylor is the Librarian for Genealogy and Local History at the W. Walworth Harrison Public Library in Greenville, Texas. She is finishing a master's program in history at Texas A&M University Commerce where her thesis covers the Mercers Colony of Texas. Mrs. Taylor has both bachelor's and master's degrees from Midwestern State University in Wichita Falls. She is a frequent presenter of papers relating to Texas and the Civil War. In addition to her thesis, Mrs. Taylor, with James M. Smallwood and Kenneth W. Howell, is a coauthor of *Ben Bickerstaff, Northeast Texans, and the War of Reconstruction* (2007).

Donald Willett

Don Willett, a past president of the East Texas Historical Association, is an associate professor of history at Texas A&M University at Galveston. He is a member of the Board of Directors for the Gulf South Historical Association and is an active member of the Galveston Historical Foundation. He researches and publishes in Texas and United States maritime history. He (with Stephen Curley) recently published *Invisible Texans: Women and Minorities in Texas History* (2004). He is currently working on a book titled *"Dear General": Letters from Texas to Albert Sidney Johnston Concerning Politics, 1836–1861* and an anthology of Galveston history.

INDEX